Mappings

Mappings

FEMINISM AND THE

CULTURAL GEOGRAPHIES

OF ENCOUNTER

• *SUSAN STANFORD FRIEDMAN* •

PRINCETON UNIVERSITY PRESS

PRINCETON, NEW JERSEY

Library of Congress Cataloging-in-Publication Data

Friedman, Susan Stanford
Mappings : Feminsm and the cultural geographies of
encounter / Susan Stanford Friedman.
p.   cm.
Includes bibliographical references and index.
ISBN 0-691-05803-2 (cl : alk. paper) — ISBN 0-691-05804-0 (alk. paper)
1. Feminist Theory. 2. Multiculturalism. 3. Feminist geography.
4. Feminist criticism. 5. Gender studies. I. Title
HQ1190.F77   1998
305.42′01—DC21   98-11525

This book has been composed in Times Roman

Princeton University Press books are printed on acid-free paper and meet the guidelines for
permanence and durability of the Committee on Production Guidelines for Book
Longevity of the Council on Library Resources

http://pup.princeton.edu

Printed in the United States of America

1   3   5   7   9   10   8   6   4   2

1   3   5   7   9   10   8   6   4   2
(Pbk.)

For Ruth and Joanna

i command you to be
good runners
to go with grace
go well in the dark and
make for high ground
my dearest girls
my girls
my more than me

—Lucille Clifton

• C O N T E N T S •

• I L L U S T R A T I O N S •

• A C K N O W L E D G M E N T S •

MAPPINGS originated in a sequence of conference papers, campus presentations, and articles that I felt compelled to write as a feminist keenly alive to the urgent debates and conflicts taking place within the academy about the future of academic feminism in a climate of renewed attack as the Culture Wars of the 1980s and 1990s ignited anew. Like the identities and cultures I examine in *Mappings*, books are products of syncretist interaction and stimulation. Full and proper acknowledgment to all the individuals, groups, and institutions that made *Mappings* possible would involve a complete cartography of my overlapping professional and personal landscapes, an autobiographical excursion that I will not make at this time.

I must, however, express my deep gratitude to many for their inspiration, ideas, challenges, criticisms, and encouragement. Edward Friedman has been my most important teacher over the years, showing me by example how to question the orthodoxies of all perspectives. I have benefited immeasurably from his prescient originality and brilliance, intellectual courage and integrity, knowledge of Asia and social theory, and the constancy of his respect, love, and companionship. My great appreciation also goes to Rachel Blau DuPlessis, for her intellectual éclat, friendship, and the suggestion that I do this book; my editor, Deborah Malmud, for her intelligent judgment in helping me to shape this book; Joseph Boone and R. Radhakrishnan, for their astute readings of the manuscript that provided vitally useful criticism and broader contexts; Linda Gordon, Judith Walzer Leavitt, and Nellie Y. McKay, for their companionship, the example of their feminist work, and our long walks and talks in shared lives; the many graduate students in my feminist theory seminar, especially Dawn Keetley (whose dissertation on space and subjectivity in antebellum America sparked my interest in spatialization), Thomas Foster (whose dissertation on theory and women's writing first introduced me to feminist "border talk"), and Raffaella Baccolini (whose dissertation on fluidity and subjectivity in H.D. sharpened my adaptations of poststructuralism and whose generous efforts brought me in contact with many European feminists); the women's studies undergraduate students I have taught at the University of Wisconsin–Madison since 1975, especially those in my seminar for majors, for their irreverence and passion for rigorous learning; James Phelan, for his leadership in broadening narrative studies and bringing me into the Society for the Study of Narrative Literature; Simon Gikandi and R. Radhakrishnan, for their work and conversations that first led me more deeply into postcolonial studies; Neil L. Whitehead, for his work on hybridity and his guidance in my developing interest in ethnographic theory; my tireless research assistants, especially Heather Hewett and Deidre Egan; the lively audiences who responded to portions of the book at the University of Bologna, City University of New York–Graduate Center, Duquesne University, University of Maryland at College Park, Michigan State University, the Institute for Research on Women at Rutgers University, the

State University of New York at Buffalo, University of Utah, Lawrence University, Network of Interdisciplinary Women's Studies in Europe (N♀ISE) at Utrecht University, the Modern Language Association conventions, Narrative Conferences, the Institute for Research in the Humanities at UW–Madison, the UW International Gender Studies Circle, UW Cultural Pluralism Seminar, UW Border Studies Group, and the UW English Department and Draft Group. For time to write, I am particularly endebted to grants from the American Council of Learned Societies, the UW Graduate School, and the UW Institute for Research in the Humanities, where the interdisciplinary exchange across the humanities has been particularly important for my thinking.

Grateful acknowledgment is made for permission to reprint in full or in revised form the following articles and book chapters:

"'Beyond' Gynocriticism and Gynesis: The New Geographics of Identity and the Future of Feminist Criticism." *Tulsa Studies in Women's Literature* 15.1 (June 1996): 13–40. © 1996, the University of Tulsa. Reprinted by permission of the publisher.

"Beyond White and Other: Relationality and Narratives of Race in Feminist Discourse." *Signs* 21 (Autumn 1995): 1–49. © 1995 by The University of Chicago Press. All rights reserved.

"Uncommon Readings: Seeking the Geopolitical Virginia Woolf." *South Carolina Review* 29.1 (Fall 1996): 24–44. © 1996 Clemson University.

"Post/Poststructuralist Feminist Criticism: The Politics of Recuperation and Negotiation." *New Literary History* 22 (Spring 1991): 465–90. © by *New Literary History*, the University of Virginia, Charlottesville, Virginia.

"Making History: Reflections on Feminism, Narrative, and Desire." *Feminism Beside Itself.* Ed. Diane Elam and Robyn Wiegman. London: Routledge, 1995. 11–53. © 1995 by Routledge.

Craving Stories: Narrative and Lyric in Contemporary Theory and Women's Long Poems." *Feminist Measures: Soundings in Poetry and Theory.* Ed. Lynn Keller and Cristanne Miller. Ann Arbor: University of Michigan Press, 1994. 15–42. © by the University of Michigan, 1994.

Acknowledgment is also gratefully made to the following for illustrations:
Chip Kidd, for the cover design for *Mona in the Promised Land*, by Gish Jen. New York: Alfred A. Knopf, 1966. © by Gish Jen.

Mappings

Locational Feminism

What you chart is already where you've been. But
where we are going, there is no chart yet.
—*Audre Lorde,* Interview

Yet the struggle of identities continues, the struggle of
our borders is our reality still.
—*Gloria Anzaldúa*, Borderlands / La Frontera

BORDER talk is everywhere—literal and figural, material and symbolic. The "cartographies of silence" pioneered by feminists like Adrienne Rich in the 1970s have morphed into the spatial practices of third wave feminism as national boundaries and personal borders become ever more permeable in the face of rapidly changing cultural terrains and global landscapes. Borders have a way of insisting on separation at the same time as they acknowledge connection. Like bridges. Bridges signify the possibility of passing over. They also mark the fact of separation and the distance that has to be crossed. Borders between individuals, genders, groups, and nations erect categorical and material walls between identities. Identity is in fact unthinkable without some sort of imagined or literal boundary. But borders also specify the liminal space in between, the interstitial site of interaction, interconnection, and exchange. Borders enforce silence, miscommunication, misrecognition. They also invite transgression, dissolution, reconciliation, and mixing. Borders protect, but they also confine. As Néstor García Canclini writes: "At every border there are rigid wires and fallen wires" (*Hybrid Cultures* 260–61). He speaks not only of the electrified fences and walls between countries like the United States and Mexico but also of the psychological and symbolic "wires" that separate imagined communities of people everywhere. What gets formed as rigid also falls, then re-forms, then falls again. In an increasingly globalized and transnational context, feminism has become ever more acutely attuned to the meanings of borders as markers of positionality and situatedness. From an earlier emphasis on silence and invisibility, feminism has moved to a concern with location—the geopolitics of identity within differing communal spaces of being and becoming.[1]

The main project of this book is to propose future lines of development for feminism by examining its encounters with other progressive movements as they are staged in the realms of cultural theory and the practices of scholarship and teaching in the institutions of knowledge. The book maps the engagements of feminist theory with multiculturalism, postcolonial studies, cultural studies, and poststructuralism as debates have evolved over the past twenty years. It probes the accomplishments and the limitations of intersecting cultural theories and argues strongly for new ways of thinking that negotiate beyond the conventional boundaries between us and them, white and other, First World and Third World, men and women, oppressor and oppressed, fixity and fluidity. Crossing borders between disciplines, the book addresses the politically explosive and urgent issue of identity, raising in particular the meanings of gender, race, ethnicity, class, sexuality, religion, and national origin as these axes of difference constitute multiplex identities and challenge binarist ways of thinking. The book insists on going "beyond" both fundamentalist identity politics and absolutist poststructuralist theories as they pose essentialist notions of identity on the one hand and refuse all cultural traffic with identity on the other. It argues for a dialogic position in the borderlands in between notions of pure difference and the deconstructive free play of signifiers. It argues as well that the passion for difference evident in some forms of nationalist, chauvinist theory on the one hand and poststructuralist theory on the other renders invisible the symbiotic, syncretist, interactive formations in the borderlands in between difference. The future of feminism and other progressive movements lies, I suggest, in a turning outward, an embrace of contradiction, dislocation, and change.

In its advocacy of dialogic negotiation, *Mappings* polemically suggests that the time has come to reverse the past pluralization of feminisms based on difference, not to return to a false notion of a universal feminism that obliterates difference but rather to reinvent a singular feminism that incorporates myriad and often conflicting cultural and political formations in a global context. The move from *feminism* to *feminisms*, heralded in the United States by the publication in 1980 of Elaine Marks and Isabelle de Courtivron's classic anthology, *New French Feminisms*, insisted upon the acknowledgment of different feminist theories and movements both between and within national boundaries.[2] The plural form of the noun *feminism* forced a recognition of difference as a way of refusing the hegemony of one kind of feminism over another. Emerging out of the volatile and deep divisions within national and international kinds of feminism by the late 1970s, the politics of pluralization forcibly interrupted the tendency of some (especially white, heterosexual, western feminists) to attempt to speak for all, as if patriarchy were a monolithic cultural formation, as if women were the same everywhere, as if the female subject of feminism were homogeneous. This pluralization has contributed profoundly to the expansion and diversification of feminism; it has been vitally necessary, I strongly believe, for the development of a multicultural, international, and transnational feminism. Its very success, however, has spawned the need for a new singularization of feminism that assumes difference without reifying or fetishizing it. The borders between sites of feminism surely exist, but just as surely they are and must be transgressed. They are not fixed in stone, but shift with changing cultural formations, conditions, and alliances. Upon this fluidity, the survival and spread of feminism depends.

The feminism in the singular that I advocate assumes a locational epistemology based not upon static or abstract definition but rather upon the assumption of changing historical and geographical specificities that produce different feminist theories, agendas, and political practices.[3] A locational approach to feminism incorporates diverse formations because its positional analysis requires a kind of geopolitical literacy built out of a recognition of how different times and places produce different and changing gender systems as these intersect with other different and changing societal stratifications and movements for social justice. Locational feminism thus encourages the study of difference in all its manifestations without being limited to it, without establishing impermeable borders that inhibit the production and visibility of ongoing intercultural exchange and hybridity.

Locational feminism also acknowledges the travels and travails of feminism as it migrates across multiple borders, adapting itself to new conditions. Borrowing from Edward Said's account of "traveling theory," we need to acknowledge that feminism seldom arises in purely indigenous forms, but, like culture itself, develops syncretistically out of a transcultural interaction with others. Feminism's migrancy is "never unimpeded," to echo Said. "It necessarily involves processes of representation and institutionalization different from those at the point of origin. This complicates any account of the transplantation, transference, circulation, and commerce of theories and ideas" ("Traveling" 226). Locational feminism pays attention to the specificities of time and place, but unlike fundamentalist identity politics, it is not parochially limited to a single feminist formation and takes as its founding principle the multiplicity of heterogeneous feminist movements and the conditions that produce them. *Mappings* is itself a case in point for what it means to break out of a specifically American localism, for the influence of work (whether feminist or not) produced on or by people whose heritage is rooted in other parts of the world is pervasive—particularly South and Southeast Asia, the Caribbean, Africa, and Latin America.

Locational feminism requires a geopolitical literacy that acknowledges the interlocking dimension of global cultures, the way in which the local is always informed by the global and the global by the local. This is in part what Inderpal Grewal and Caren Kaplan advocate in their definition of a "transnational feminism" (*Scattered Hegemonies* 1–36) and what Gayatri Chakravorty Spivak calls for in her concept of "transnational literacy" (*Outside* 255–84). *Mappings* assumes that feminism needs to be understood in a global context, both historicized and geopoliticized to take into account its different formations and their interrelationships everywhere. As such, *Mappings* resists certain overly reductionist metanarratives of globalization. One such narrative is the notion that women suffer the same gender oppression in all societies, an approach to internationalizing feminism that bases affiliation solely on gender victimization, thus muting women's agency, ignoring cultural contextualizations, and suppressing understanding of gender's interaction with other constituents of identity. The commitment to universal human rights for women (which I share) should not be founded on a script of a uniform gender oppression that decontextualizes the condition of women in various locations.

Another such inadequate metanarrative bases its globalization on binaries of First World/Third World or the West/the Rest, telling the story of a unidirectional hegemony in which white/western people (always already) dominate people of color/nonwestern people. Whether it tells the history of the world through the lens of western modernity (colonialism) or western postmodernity (late-capitalist global markets), this narrative remains mired in the eurocentrism and ethnocentrism it deplores. It obscures how conquest and colonialism have been and still are worldwide phenomena, generated not only in the West but also in many other powerful societies. It ignores the rise of dominant cultures and civilizations in Asia, Africa, South America, the Caribbean, and Pacific Asia at various points in history, including the current ascendency of Asia in a phenomenon sometimes termed "the Asianization of the world" (Edward Friedman, "Rise of China"). It renders largely invisible the existence of stratification in nearly all (if not all) societies, inequities that highly complicate their interactions with western nations. Moreover, it does not take into account the historical agency of all individuals and groups, the role of intercultural exchange and symbiosis in all cultural formations, and the heterogeneity of both "the West" and "the Rest."

In resisting simplistically universalist and binarist narratives, *Mappings* undertakes a difficult negotiation between insistence on multidirectional flows of power in global context and continued vigilence about specifically western forms of domination. Given my own location in the United States (with its particular history and configuration of racism) and positionality as a white woman, I have found particularly challenging the need to acknowledge the material effects of racial privilege at the same time that I argue for broadening the American dialogue about race beyond its dominant templates of white/black, white/people of color, oppressor/oppressed. I remain convinced that a broadly comparative, global/locational feminism can change our analysis of "home" as well as "elsewhere," helping to break repetitive logjams of thought by casting the conditions of home in a new light and by illuminating the structures interlocking home and elsewhere.

The global contextualization that I advocate for feminism in *Mappings* is consistent with Spivak's various critiques of First World/Third World binaries as the route to internationalizing feminism. "I think we should also look at the West as differentiated," she says in an interview. "I'm not really that moved by arguments for homogenisation on both sides" (*Post-Colonial Critic* 39). She insists that "transnational feminism is neither revolutionary tourism, nor mere celebration of testimony" (*Teaching Machine* 39). She worries that if we take "the astonishing construction of a multicultural and multiracial identity for the United States" as the "founding principle for a study of globality, then we are off base" (279).[4] Instead, she suggests, "the point is to negotiate between the national, the global, and the historical as well as the contemporary diasporic. We must both anthropologize the West, and study the various cultural systems of Africa, Asia, Asia-

Pacific, and the Americas as if peopled by historical agents" (278). A geopolitical, locational feminism travels globally in its thinking, avoiding the imposition of one set of cultural conditions on another, assuming the production of local agencies and conceptualization, and remaining attentive to the way these differences are continually in the process of modification through interactions within a global system of diverse, multidirectional exchanges.

Mappings maintains throughout an unapologetic focus on feminism in the academy. It rests upon the premise that intellectual work within the institutional setting of higher education matters. The production and dissemination of knowledge through research, publication, and teaching are not reflections upon the world from some neutral position outside the objects of study but are rather productions of and for that world. The academy produces, preserves, collects, organizes, passes on, and constantly re-forms old and new knowledge—for consumption by its own members, the students it educates, and the larger society. The academy does function in certain ways as a space apart: where the institution of tenure (when it exists) protects to some degree the intellectual freedom of those who have it, where the campus (when it exists) expands to some degree the horizons and opportunities of its students before they "return" to the "real world" of work.[5] But the academy is no ivory tower. Its focus on knowledge in no way exempts it from the diverse populations and conflicting attitudes, ideologies, power relations, and stratifications that operate in any large societal institution. Moreover, as a primary institution for the reproduction of new generations, the academy's power to influence society should never be underestimated. However much the general public thinks of the academy as irrelevant to the "real world" (its knowledges arcane, even laughable, most often useless); its professors absentminded, altruistic, underworked, and overprivileged; its values either too elitist or too revolutionary; its students party animals), higher education is a major societal player. The borders between the academy and the "outside" world have always been permeable and are increasingly so at the dawning of cyberspatial transformations.

The Culture Wars of the 1980s and 1990s attest to the importance of the cultural work performed in and by the academy. The heat is on because the stakes are high. Very high. And ever more so as the accelerating Knowledge Revolution ushers in the Information Age, in which who and what control knowledge and its discontents are likely to be ever more critical to the structures and operations of power. However clichéd it has become to invoke the new millennium and the passing of the Industrial Age, I maintain their significance. In both global and national contexts, human societies are moving rapidly through thresholds of change at least as profound as those instituted by the dissemination of movable type and advances in navigation, emergent globally some five hundred or more years ago as dominant forces in the sharply increased travel of ideas, goods, and people in economies of intercivilizational contact.[6] "There is no chart yet," to echo Audre Lorde, for the virtual, material, and symbolic landscapes of knowing to be ushered in by the computer. With H.D., we might say, *"we are voyagers, discovers / of the not-known, // the unrecorded; / we have no map"* (*Trilogy* 59).

Mapless in the face of paradigmatic shifts in how knowledge will increasingly be produced, organized, and disseminated, we can nonetheless be sure that intellectual workers of all kinds, including those in higher education, will be ever more critical.

To focus on academic feminism as I do in *Mappings* is therefore to ask what role feminism plays in the deconstruction and reconstruction of the symbolic order and its material effects. Developing as an oppositional discourse within higher education, academic feminism has assumed the significance of the academy's regulatory power to shape how people and culture think about women and gender systems. On the other hand, academic feminism has equally assumed the academy to be a potential site for the development of knowledge that resists ideological formations. Knowledge and its dissemination are therefore the grounds upon which academic feminists center their activism, their commitment to social change. Like Homi Bhabha, I resist entirely the binary of theory/activism, which in relation to feminism has often distinguished between the "abstract" work of feminist educators and the activism of those who work "in the community," in organizations like rape crisis centers, shelters for battered women, women's health and abortion clinics, and other advocacy groups. Bhabha argues in "The Commitment to Theory" for a "politics of address," based in "*negotiation* rather than *negation*," a "*negotiation* of contradictory and antagonistic instances that open up hybrid sites and objectives of struggle, and destroy those negative polarities between knowledge and its objects, and between theory and practical-political reason" (*Location* 25). As "hybrid sites" of knowledge, education, and activism, rape crisis centers (and the like) produce and disseminate knowledge; feminist scholarship and classrooms engage in political activity that has material effects in the deformation and reformation of the symbolic and social orders. As different locations for feminism, however, community organizations and academic institutions require different modes of operation. To be successful, intellectual work must remain particularly open to change and challenge, especially resistant to orthodoxies of any kind, including those of feminism and other progressive practices. It is in part for this reason that I stress the contradictions and debates in academic feminism as the fertile location for future development.

Narrative as a multiplicitous form of meaning-making thought remains a central concern throughout the book's cartographies of feminist debate. At a meta-level, these debates take the form of story, playing out agonistic plots of opposition and reconciliation, performing as well negotiations that move back and forth, weaving dialogic and heterogeneous narrative lines of inquiry. At another level, identity is literally unthinkable without narrative. People know who they are through the stories they tell about themselves and others. As ever-changing phenomena, identities are themselves narratives of formation, sequences moving through space and time as they undergo development, evolution, and revolution. Thirdly, narrative texts—whether verbal or visual, oral or written, fictional or referential, imaginary or historical—constitute primary documents of cultural expressivity. Narrative is a window into, mirror, constructor, and symptom of culture. Cultural narratives encode and encrypt in story form the norms, values, and ideologies of the social order, what Fredric Jameson calls "the political uncon-scious" embedded in "narrative as a socially symbolic act" and what Rachel Blau DuPlessis identifies in *Writing beyond the Ending* as the "cultural scripts" around which institutions of gender, race, class, and sexuality are organized. Cultural narratives also tell the strategic plots of interaction and resistance as groups and individuals negotiate with and against hegemonic scripts and histories. The postmodern turn widespread in the academy has sensitized many fields to the significance of language (especially linguistic textuality) for cultural studies. I argue that narrative is equally important. *Mappings* intends to enhance narrative literacy among academics in many fields, including women's studies. Narrative poetics—the study of the form and function of story in their broadest dimen-sions—provides not only strategies for reading narratives but also a theoretical framework for interpreting the significance of narrative itself in all cultural formations.[7]

Organized around narratives of encounter, *Mappings* is a collection of distinct but conceptually linked chapters with a common project and overarching, inter-locking themes. However, each chapter was written to stand alone, making its own particular contribution to feminist theory as a self-contained entity and ges-turing to some degree toward the setting and time of its production at some point between 1989 and 1997.[8] The trope of encounter substitutes for chronology as the organizing principle of the chapters. *Mappings* intentionally stages a transgres-sion of borders between and hybridic mixing of discourses along three axes of analysis: feminism/multiculturalism, feminism/globalism, and feminism/post-structuralism. I do this in the spirit of what Bhabha means by *negotiation*, what Spivak refers to as productive *interruption* and *crisis*, and what James Clifford, Ruth Frankenberg, Lata Mani, Norma Alarcón, and Kamala Visweswaran vari-ously associate with *conjuncturalism*.[9] I do *not* mean to suggest that feminism (in theory and practice) is completely distinct from multiculturalism, geopolitics, or poststructuralism. I do not envision an encounter between pure difference. The slash between each pair (/) indicates connection as well as distinctness. (It is no Lacanian "bar," cutting off the one from the other irretrievably as Lacan main-tains the separation between the signifier and the signified.) Indeed, I assume that multiculturalism, globalism, and poststructuralism either have been or must be an integral part of academic feminism, not as token addition but built into its founda-tional assumptions. I also insist, however, that feminism is not simply cotermi-nous with the other three. Each of the four discourses has its distinct history, emphases, debates, internal divisions, problematizations, knowledge bases, meth-odologies, and cultural effects; even the terms I have used to constellate each discourse (*feminism, multiculturalism, globalism*, and *poststructuralism*) are hotly contested. Although overlapping in part, the intellectual/political project of each is separate enough to "interrupt" each other, as Spivak would say. In adopt-ing a conjuncturalist approach, I mean to juxtapose feminism with other progres-sive discourses, thereby echoing what Clifford means by "a modern 'ethnogra-phy' of conjunctures," which he defines as a constant "moving *between* cultures, . . . both regionally focused and broadly comparative" (*Predicament* 9). By examining the conjuncture of feminism with multiculturalism, globalism, and poststructuralism, I intend to map the encounters necessary to the creative growth of a locational feminism in the singular that encompasses situational differences in a global context.

Part I, focusing on the encounter between feminism and multiculturalism, examines the ways in which academic discourses based in gender and those based in race, ethnicity, and/or sexuality throw each other into creative crisis. All three chapters are written around the observation of feminist impasse and the attempt to intervene by theorizing a movement "beyond" repetitive and often nonproductive patterns of thought. Mary Louise Fellows and Sherene Razack have named the issue "the difference impasse" ("Seeking Relations" 1051), reflecting the way in which the differences among women by reasons of class, race, ethnicity, class, religion, sexuality, national origin, and so forth make coalition and affiliation around the category "woman" or "women" very difficult, if not impossible or undesirable. "'Beyond' Gender" (chapter 1) argues that the need to avoid gender as an exclusive category for analysis has involved a significant shift from developmental to geographical ways of thinking about identity. I map six distinct but overlapping positional paradigms for identity that have evolved in the past two decades, theorize a locational feminism, and suggest the continuing need for feminism as a distinct theory and practice (written in 1994–95, 1997). "'Beyond' White and Other" (chapter 2) identifies three repetitive and binarist scripts dominating feminist narratives of race and gender (scripts of denial, accusation, and confession) and promotes the further development of relationality as a discourse sufficiently flexible to deal with the multidirectional power relations structuring different women's lives (written 1992–95). "'Beyond' Difference" (chapter 3) argues that the hegemony of "difference talk" in American feminism suppresses the real effects of and utopian desires based in intercultural exchange and syncretist mixing. It maps the various models of and debates about hybridity in cultural, postcolonial, and global studies, and offers an in-depth reading of Anzaldúa's *Borderlands/La Frontera* as a mythopoetic narrative encompassing the full terrain of diverse views (written 1997).

In Part I, I use the term *beyond* in a special sense, not to insist that categories like gender and difference should be abandoned but rather to suggest that they need to be supplemented. Impasses in feminist theory result from their hegemony, not their existence. I argue for the continued political importance of academic feminism's distinct foregrounding of gender and for the ongoing need for consideration of difference. But I also argue that feminists need a terrain "beyond" these categories in which to take account of the contradictory, fluid, and multiplex nature of identity. As Bhabha writes about the trope of "beyond" in cultural studies in general, "The 'beyond' is neither a new horizon, nor a leaving behind of the past. . . . [There is] a sense of disorientation, a disturbance of direction, in the 'beyond': an exploratory, restless movement caught so well in the French rendition of the words *au-delà*—here and there, on all sides, *fort/da*, hither and thither, back and forth" (*Location* 1).[10]

Part II takes up the more recent encounter between feminism and globalism as a result of the growing influence of postcolonial studies, global, and transnational studies. The section explores what it means to think geopolitically, not only about others "elsewhere" but also about how the global context affects our thinking about "home." The emphasis on group affiliations based on race, ethnicity, and nation, I argue, has obscured the way in which geographical location and spatial migrancy are distinct constituents of identity, often closely related to but not coextensive with these imagined communities. "Geopolitical Literacy" broadens the conventional notion of geopolitics to theorize a spatial thinking that complements historical analysis privileging the temporal; by way of example it performs uncommon readings of familiar passages from Virginia Woolf to show how internationalizing feminism involves defamiliarizing what we think we know about the local and the domestic (written 1996, 1997). "Telling Contacts" operates in the interstices between literary studies and anthropology to examine how intercultural interaction in a global context serves as fuel driving the engine of story; it advocates locational/spatial thinking to go beyond theorizing narrative energy largely in terms of oedipal and pre-oedipal triangulations based in plots of family romance. " 'Routes/Roots'" adapts James Clifford's opposition cited in the title to argue that narratives about identity and the identity of narrative itself involve an underlying dialogic negotiation between assertion of difference (roots) and acceptance of hybridity produced through travel in time and space (routes); it pairs Julie Dash's film *Daughters of the Dust* about the black diaspora with Gish Jen's novel *Mona in the Promised Land* about immigration to examine the narrative alternations of "roots" and "routes" in the formation and performance of identity (written 1997).

Part III revisits the encounter between feminism and poststructuralism that dominated the scene of academic feminism in the humanities in the 1980s and explores the meanings of history writing for feminism. As a whole, its three essays constitute an instance of geopolitical interaction, as critical theory flowed across the Atlantic from France and took root in highly divergent forms in the United States. As precursor to the theoretical impact of postcolonial, transnational, and global studies on feminism, it serves nonetheless as an example of transculturation and transplantation. In charting the hybridic blending and clashing of French poststructuralism and American feminism, this section also discloses the story of my own hybridic embrace of and resistance to poststructuralism, a narrative that underlies the prior chapters, as well as the work I have done in modernist studies.[11] Avoiding discipleship, I have nonetheless adapted many aspects of poststructuralist theory in what I believe is a fruitful mix of discourses that reflects my location as an academic feminist in the United States open to rethinking the local in the light of ideas from elsewhere.

First drafted in December of 1989, "Negotiating the Transatlantic Divide" (chapter 7) tracks an earlier moment of transition in the academy, the period when the hegemony of critical theory began to give way to a cultural studies informed by that theory but significantly distinct from it because of an insistent return to history and material effects. At that time, I sensed a sea change, but could not fully anticipate the dazzling swiftness with which cultural studies (originally a transplant from Britain) would supplant poststructuralist theory in the North American academy. Examining the return of history and the "Real" to theory, "Negotiating the Transatlantic Divide" argues for a historicized theory and a theorized history that blends the insights of poststructuralist and materialist feminisms with the reintroduction of such concepts as identity. "Making History" (chapter 8) uses the various feminist histories of the introduction of French poststructuralism into American feminist discourse as an instance of the double epistemology of women's studies: the objectivist search for suppressed truths about women and gender and the constructivist perspective that all truths are relative to the subjectivities that produce and use them. Arguing for a negotiation between the two, "Making History" resists the tendency of history writing to privilege the winners and affirms the need for narratives to produce feminist histories "in the plural" (written 1994–95). "Craving Stories" (chapter 9) questions the prevalent poststructuralist distrust of narrative and privileging of the lyric as revolutionary discourse by setting up an encounter between these views initially forged in France and the actual poetic practice in American women's late-twentieth-century long poems. Using Irena Klepfisz's *Keeper of Accounts* as exemplary text, "Craving Stories" argues that instead of a hostile relationship between narrative and lyric, women's long poems exhibit a collaborative negotiation between these modes that claims women's agency to write both history and myth.

The multilayered border crossings of the encounters engendered in Parts I–III include disciplinary as well as theoretical and geopolitical ones. Even as academic feminism needs to retain its distinct identity as a heterogeneous social theory and movement, it must also develop interdisciplinary strategies for the hybridic mixing, blending, and weaving of other theoretical discourses and academic disciplines. *Mappings* reflects my grounding in the humanities, most specifically in literary studies, with its hermeneutic emphasis on representation, textuality, narrative poetics, and the practices of writing and reading. Reflecting the growing interdisciplinarity of the academy, the book draws heavily upon other disciplines, especially anthropology, geography, cinema and mass media studies, history, and psychoanalysis. Additionally, its arguments and methodologies are thoroughly informed by work produced in various arenas of interdisciplinary cultural studies—particularly women's studies, African American studies, ethnic studies, postcolonial studies, social theory, poststructuralism, gay and lesbian studies, queer theory, and global studies. In looking elsewhere for insight into the issues debated by feminists, I have not limited myself to feminist work in disciplines outside literary studies; instead, I have found that theoretical configurations outside feminist scholarship facilitate breaking the logjams within academic feminism.

The greatest source of theoretical illumination, however, has been narrative texts—visual, verbal, reportorial, historical, mythopoetic. They constitute my laboratory where I discover new avenues of thought and test out certain propositions developed in theory. *Mappings* depends upon a text-centered approach, deliberately drawing on and juxtaposing different sorts of largely narrative material while taking into account sufficient contextualization—high modernist novels, best-selling fiction, popular and avant-garde films, video and theater, newspaper clippings, theory, poetry, essays, and polemic. Complemented by a host of more briefly mentioned texts, those singled out for extended discussion and illustrative purposes include James Joyce's *Ulysses* (chapter 1); June Jordan's "Report from the Bahamas," Mira Nair's *Mississippi Masala*, and Neil Jordan's *The Crying Game* (chapter 2); María Lugones's essays, Anna Deveare Smith's *Fires in the Mirror* and *Twilight*, and Gloria Anzaldúa's *Borderlands/La Frontera* (chapter 3); Virginia Woolf's *To the Lighthouse* and *A Room of One's Own* and Zora Neale Hurston's *Their Eyes Were Watching God* (chapter 4); Nella Larsen's *Quicksand*, Jean Rhys's *Wide Sargasso Sea*, and E. M. Forster's *A Passage to India* (chapter 5); Julie Dash's *Daughters of the Dust* and Gish Jen's *Mona in the Promised Land* (chapter 6); work by Christina Hoff Sommers, Linda Gordon, Joan Scott, Elaine Showalter, Gayatri Chakravorty Spivak, and Toril Moi (chapter 8); and Irena Klepfisz's *Keeper of Accounts* (chapter 9). While attempting to respect their rich complexity and unresolved contradictions, I have turned to these texts with a frankly instrumentalist intent—for what they have to teach academic feminism, for their potential interventions in the great debates of the day, and for their collective wisdom and pleasure. The stories they tell matter. So do the stories we tell about them.

• PART I •

Feminism/Multiculturalism

"Beyond" Gender:
The New Geography of Identity and the
Future of Feminist Criticism

I BEGIN this book of feminist mappings with a metacritical excursion, a series of reflections on gender and identity, on where we have been and where we are going, especially as we head past the millennial divide into the twentieth-first century. By "we," I am speaking most directly of and to the collectivity of academic feminists who make up the divergent and polyvocal feminisms of higher education. But I also mean to include by implication the larger collectivity of the progressively minded whose intellectual projects and political commitments parallel and intermingle with those of academic feminists. I am also much aware that the collectivity of differences gathered in such a "we" contains a sometimes difficult mix of different intellectual generations—from those who came of age in the 1960s and 1970s (like myself), on through those who emerged in the 1980s and early 1990s, to those who are graduate students today, necessarily building upon the evolving work of their elders, but eager to move on and beyond prior questions, frameworks, and paradigms. "We" includes the graduate students and new assistant professors who are expected to know all the transformations in literary and cultural studies of the past thirty years at the same time that they hone the newest cutting edges of knowledge. It also includes the older generations who, having experienced and contributed greatly to these transformations, must try to make themselves anew, to keep up with the ever-changing terrains. Some days, there seems to be no rest for the weary—the anxious graduate student, the burned-out professor. But other days, the new geographies of literary studies provide ever-expanding horizons for travel and growth.

It is in this spirit of a multidimensional "we" that I make the argument that the future of academic feminism involves moving *beyond* gender, involves, to be more precise, recognizing and intensifying shifts that have already begun taking place in part because of what I am calling the new geographics of identity. Such movement "beyond" gender is unsettling, if not dangerous. After all, it has been the pioneering breakthrough of academic feminism to establish gender as a legitimate framework for intellectual inquiry. This achievement did not come easily, and more to the point, the existence of this new field is under constant threat of erasure or marginalization in an academy beset by institutional downsizing and attacks from without. Nonetheless, the shift beyond the strongly privileged focus on gender is well underway, producing major theoretical and pedagogical breakthroughs of its own. New positional, locational, spatial—that is, geographical—concepts of identity have fostered this evolution in academic feminism. In charting and reinforcing this change, I will focus particularly on the case of feminist criticism, suggesting by implication that other fields within academic feminism are experiencing parallel transformations.

In feminist literary studies, the preeminence of gender as the organizing category for analysis has taken two major forms: the theory and practice of gynocriticism and gynesis. I invoke here Elaine Showalter's 1984 identification of two highly influential and broadly defined feminist critical practices for the 1980s: first, gynocriticism, that is, the historical study of women writers as a distinct literary tradition; and second, gynesis, a term she borrowed from Alice Jardine to suggest theoretical readings of the feminine as a discursive effect that disrupts the master narratives of western culture.[1] During the 1980s, gynocriticism and gynesis sometimes clashed, each of its proponents often dismissive of the other. With the spread of poststructuralism in the American academy, however, gynocriticism and gynesis have increasingly functioned collaboratively.[2] Whether distinct or intermingling, gynocriticism and gynesis have shared an emphasis on sexual difference and a privileging of gender as constituent of identity. For gynocriticism, the existence of patriarchy, however changing and historically inflected, serves as the founding justification for treating women writers of different times and places as part of a common tradition based on gender. For gynesis, the linguistic inscriptions of masculine/feminine—indeed, language's very dependence on gendered binaries—underlie various feminist unravelings of master narratives and discourses.

Like the privileging of gender across the subfields of academic feminism, the insights of gynocriticism and gynesis have had far-reaching political consequences in the academy. But their foregrounding of gender has also produced certain blindnesses[3] that have left them seriously out of step with advances in theories of identity and subjectivity concurrently developing in many different fields, including feminism itself, multiculturalism, postcolonial studies, poststructuralism, gay and lesbian studies, queer theory, cultural studies, anthropology, political theory, sociology, and geography. My aim in this chapter is to chart these advances, articulate the challenges they pose for gynocritical and gynetic feminist criticism, identify emergent forms of feminist criticism currently developing in tandem with these advances, and caution against the potentially dangerous loss of feminism's distinctive political project and energy. I want ultimately to suggest that moving *beyond* gender does not mean forgetting it, but rather returning to it in a newly spatialized way that I call a *locational feminism*.

GEOGRAPHICS

I attempt with the term *geographics* to crystallize momentarily a new, rapidly moving, magnetic field of identity studies. Interdisciplinary in scope, this new field represents a terrain of common concerns and rhetoric that crisscross boundaries between the humanities and social sciences, between so-called essentialists and constructivists, between identity politics and coalitional politics. I am struck by the centrality of space—the rhetoric of spatiality—to the locations of identity within the mappings and remappings of ever-changing cultural formations.[4]

This new geography involves a move from the allegorization of the self in terms of organicism, stable centers, cores, and wholeness to a discourse of spatialized identities constantly on the move. Rhetorically speaking, geographics involves a shift from the discourses of romanticism to those of postmodernity, with a stop in between for the metaphorics of early-twentieth-century modernism, whose emphasis on split selves and fragmentation looks back to the discourse of organic wholeness and forward to the discourse of spatialized flux.[5] Instead of the individualistic telos of developmental models, the new geographics figures identity as a historically embedded site, a positionality, a location, a standpoint, a terrain, an intersection, a network, a crossroads of multiply situated knowledges. It articulates not the organic unfolding of identity but rather the mapping of territories and boundaries, the dialectical terrains of inside/outside or center/margin, the axial intersections of different positionalities, and the spaces of dynamic encounter—the "contact zone," the "middle ground," the borderlands, *la frontera*. Moreover, this geographic discourse often emphasizes not the ordered movement of linear growth but the lack of solid ground, the ceaseless change of fluidity, the nomadic wandering of transnational diaspora, the interactive syncretisms of the "global ethnoscape," or the interminable circuitry of cyberspace. Its mobile figurations adapt the landscapes of accelerating change, the technologies of information highways, and the globalization of migratory cultures.[6]

Not a static space—or field—this new geography performs a kind of dialectic that reflects opposing movements in the world today revolving around the issue of identity. There is, on the one hand, the erection of boundaries between people ever more intent on difference, on distinctions between selves and others, whether based on history or biology or both, as a form of dominance or resistance. There is, on the other hand, the search both material and utopian for fertile borderlands, for the liminal spaces in between, the sites of constant movement and change, the locus of syncretist intermingling and hybrid interfusions of self and other. This dialectic between difference and sameness is embedded in the double meaning of the word *identity* itself. *Identity* is constructed relationally through difference from the other; identification with a group based on gender, race, or sexuality, for example, depends mostly on binary systems of "us" versus "them," where difference from the other defines the group to which one belongs. Conversely, *identity* also suggests sameness, as in the word *identical*; an identity affirms some form of commonality, some shared ground.[7] Difference versus sameness; stasis versus travel; certainty versus interrogation; purity versus mixing: the geographics of identity moves between boundaries of difference and borderlands of liminality.

Mirroring these directional movements, the new geography of identity is polyvocal and often contradictory. Its metaphorics, now sweeping many different fields within and outside of literary studies, has been influenced especially by postcolonial studies, for which the issues of travel, nomadism, diaspora, and the cultural hybridity produced by movement through space have a material reality and political urgency as well as figurative cogency.[8] But the intellectual genealogy of this geographical figuration centers in the different discourses of identity and subjectivity that have developed over the last three decades as effects of late-twentieth-century political and cultural change. Pioneered frequently by people of color and by people from nonwestern countries, these developments have often been the center of conflict in the North American academy, even among those most committed to progressive change. Those whose daily survival most depends on understanding identity as the product of complex intersections and locations have provided the most leadership as they reflect upon their often double or triple marginalization within the institutions of higher education and knowledge. More generally, the blending and clashing of overlapping or parallel discourses of feminism, multiculturalism, poststructuralism, and postcolonial studies in the academy within disciplines as diverse as literary studies and geography have produced new ways of configuring identity that have moved well beyond the achievements of gynocriticism and gynesis.

My purpose here is not to provide a full genealogy or a "thick description" of the historical production of this new geography of identity.[9] Nor can I unravel all its theoretical complexities and implications. Rather, I will delineate six related but distinct discourses of identity within this new geography of positionality, all of which have seriously undermined or complicated the projects of gynocriticism and gynesis as they were originally formulated. These are the discourses of multiple oppression; multiple subject positions; contradictory subject positions; relationality; situationality; and hybridity. As cultural formations, these discourses developed to some extent sequentially in response to the changing political landscapes of the academy and progressive social movements. But they do not represent stages of feminist discourse. Rather, they often overlap, appearing multiply and simultaneously in spite of their different histories and intellectual influences. I propose them in the form of provisional schematization not as a taxonomy but as a useful outline that can pinpoint the theoretical impasse into which the gynocritical and gynetic strategies of the 1970s and 1980s have fallen by the mid-1990s.

The first of these discourses to develop was the feminist figuration of identity in terms of "multiple oppression" or "double jeopardy" during the 1970s and 1980s.[10] This approach stresses the differences *among* women. It focuses on oppression as the main constituent of identity and leads to the additive naming of kinds of victimization on the basis of race, class, religion, sexuality, national origin, ableness, and the by-now formulaic "et cetera" and "so forth." At times, this discourse expresses a kind of interminable negativity evident in the pileup of oppressions, with its implicit hierarchization of suffering. But this discourse has also developed a dialectical analysis whereby the multiplication of oppression creates its antithesis, a multiple richness and power centered in difference, as Audre Lorde theorizes in "Age, Race, Class, and Sex: Women Redefining Difference" (1980). In *Zami: A New Spelling of My Name*, for a more extended example, Lorde charts the barriers and exclusions she experiences as a developing woman, lesbian, African American of West Indian descent, and child of the working class who moves up to a precarious middle-class existence through education.

Each of these liabilities within the system of multiple oppression she reclaims as a creative source of strength. Hence, her subtitle, *Biomythography*, by which she acknowledges that multiple oppression initiates an oppositional autobiographical self-creation that transforms multiple jeopardies into multiple strengths.[11] In sum, the discourse of multiple oppression forcefully insists that to define identity solely in terms of gender reinscribes other forms of oppression by rendering them invisible.

The second discourse of positionality emerged gradually out of the discourse of multiple oppression, beginning in the mid- to late-1980s and reflecting the development of a geographic rhetoric. I refer to the notion of identity as the site of multiple subject positions, as the intersection of different and often competing cultural formations of race, ethnicity, class, sexuality, religion, and national origin, et cetera, and so forth.[12] Within this paradigm, the self is not singular; it is multiple. The location it occupies contains many positions within it, each of which may well depend on its interaction with the others for its particular inflection. Like the concept of multiple oppressions, the constituents of identity emerge from a succession of categories. But unlike notions of multiple jeopardy, the definitional focus is not so exclusively on oppression and victimization but rather on various combinations of difference that may or may not be tied to oppression. Categories such as "woman of color," "white woman," "Chinese American woman," "black lesbian," "middle-class woman," or "Third World woman" are not, by themselves, sufficient parameters of a more complicated, multifaceted identity. Virginia Woolf, for example, was a white woman and a subject of the British crown born at the height of Victorian imperial power. She was not only upper-middle class, but also a married woman with strong lesbian desires and relationships. She was a writer, not a mother, and as a child and young woman she was sexually abused by her half-brothers. Her identity sits at the crossroads of many different formations of power and powerlessness. In sum, the discourse of multiple positionality fosters an interactional analysis of identity as the product of interdependent systems of alterity.

The third discourse of identity further develops the concept of multiple subject positions into the theorization of contradictory subject positions, a discourse that appeared sporadically in the 1980s and has become more common in the 1990s.[13] This discourse focuses on contradiction as fundamental to the structure of subjectivity and the phenomenological experience of identity. Thus a woman might be simultaneously oppressed by gender and privileged by race or class or religion or sexuality or national origin. Conversely, a man might be privileged by gender, but oppressed by sexuality or race or class or religion. In Nella Larsen's *Quicksand* (1928), for example, the central figure, Helga Crane, is biracial, the orphaned daughter of a Danish American mother and an African American father. Money (though no contact) from her mother's family in the United States cushions her life, providing her with an education and a bourgeois identity that alienates her from the black underclass in Chicago and Harlem. Whether hostile or friendly, white society regards Helga as black. She is alternately banished by her American white relatives and exoticized by her adoring Danish family in Copenhagen.

Acceptance among the black bourgeoisie comes, however, only with Helga's denial of her white mother and suppression of her lack of "family." The contradictions of her identity within conflicting systems of race, class, gender, national origin, and sexuality induce a kind of pathological hysteria, which leads ultimately to her suffocation within the conventional role of mother and minister's wife in the Deep South. This kaleidoscope of contradictions emphasizes the interplay of power and powerlessness along different axes of alterity and suggests that the global distributions of power do not fall into two fixed categories of power and powerlessness.[14]

The fourth discourse of positionality, that of relationality, emphasizes the epistemological standpoint for identity. That is, it asserts that subjectivity is not only multiple and contradictory, but also relational.[15] One axis of identity, such as gender, must be understood in relation to other axes, such as sexuality and race. Adapting psychoanalytic and poststructuralist notions of relationality, this relatively new discourse of the late 1980s and early 1990s posits identity as a fluid site rather than a stable and fixed essence. Identity depends upon a point of reference; as that point moves nomadically, so do the contours of identity, particularly as they relate to the structures of power. Anthropologist Ruth Behar illustrates the principle of relationality as she reflects upon the shifting flows of power and privilege in her family background as it overdetermines and informs her research in Spain and Cuba.[16] She is a Jewish Latina born in Cuba and raised in Brooklyn, New York, after her family emigrated to the United States in the aftermath of the Cuban Revolution when she was five years old. Refugees from anti-Semitism, the families of her Ashkenazi mother (from Poland) and Sephardic father (from Turkey) had emigrated to Cuba, unable to gain admittance to the North American promised land after the Immigration and Exclusion Act of 1924 severely limited the immigration of Jews, East Europeans, and other nonwhite peoples. During this period, Cuba eagerly welcomed Jews and any other "white" immigrants in their efforts to "lighten" the racial mix in Cuba as a way of maintaining their own system of racial stratification within which Afro-Cubans remained on the bottom. To Europeans and North Americans, Behar explains, the Jewish emigrants were not "white"; but in Cuba, they were welcomed for their "whiteness" in relation to black and mixed-race Cubans. Kept out of the United States as Jews, the family was finally embraced as anticommunist during the Cold War, achieving through geopolitical mediation the "whiteness" they had formerly lacked.

Complicating this racial fluidity were the ethnic, cultural, and class divisions among the Jews: the conflict between the "lighter," better-off, more educated and "European" Ashkenazi side and the "darker," Middle Eastern, less educated and privileged Sephardic side of Behar's family. Threaded through this power difference was the memory deeply embedded in her Turkish family's history of the expulsion of their ancestors from Spain in 1492, with bittersweet ties to Hispanic culture kept alive down through the centuries in speaking Ladino (the Hebrew/Spanish creole spoken by Turkish Jews) and singing old Spanish songs. Discriminated against in Poland and Turkey, Behar's maternal and paternal families were able to work their way out of poverty in Cuba, the more "European" branch changing considerably more successfully than the Middle Eastern side in spite of the cultural Spanish ties. Although her father felt inadequate in the face of his Ashkenazi in-laws, he went to night school, became an accountant, and had enough money to employ an Afro-Cuban domestic worker who cooked and cared for the children.

Within this web of shifting power relations, Behar conducts her research. One project takes her back to a village in Spain where she first did her anthropological fieldwork, but this time she goes to study the reaction of the farmers to the government's policy of Christian/Jewish reconciliation on the five-hundredth anniversary of the expulsion of the Jews. Recalling the shame she had felt years before in keeping her Jewish identity secret in the village, she cannot bring herself to tell anyone that she is a descendant of the expelled Jews. Another project takes her back to Havana, to tell the story of her family's Afro-Cuban maid. It is an "unspeakable" story, Behar observes, for the white North American anthropologist to write about her family's black maid, the one she, as a Latina, associates with her motherland and motherculture, but the one left behind as her family became "white" and made it after all to the promised land. As the stories of Jewish and African diaspora intersect, Behar's self-reflexive ethnographic gaze ultimately calls into question the fixity of power relations, social categories, and group affiliations. Class, race, ethnicity, religion, national origin, and gender—all function relationally as sites of privilege and exclusion. In sum, the relational discourse of positionality stresses the constantly shifting nature of identity as it is constituted through different points of reference and material conditions of history.

The fifth discourse of positionality is situational and represents another recent development as literary studies has become increasingly engaged with issues of postcoloniality, travel, and ethnography. Like relational discourses, situational approaches assume that identity resists fixity, but they particularly stress how it shifts fluidly from setting to setting.[17] Geographic allegorization, in other words, is not merely a figure of speech, but a central constituent of identity. Each situation presumes a certain setting as site for the interplay of different axes of power and powerlessness. One situation might make a person's gender most significant; another, the person's race; another, sexuality or religion or class. So while the person's identity is the product of multiple subject positions, these axes of identity are not equally foregrounded in every situation. Change the scene, and the most relevant constituents of identity come into play. The other axes of identity do not disappear; they are just not as salient in this particular scene. A white, middle-class, Christian woman who is battered by her husband occupies a multiple subject position made up of race, class, religion, and gender. At the moment of battery, gender is highlighted, while the other constituents of her identity remain in the structural background. Melissa Steel quotes a biracial student who implicitly understands such situational shifts in remarking: "If my mom yelled at me in Spanish this morning, I feel Hispanic; if I went out last night and listened to rap, I feel black" ("New Colors" 47).

The significance of space as a situational marker of identity underlies the narrative structure of Larsen's *Quicksand*, as Helga moves from the southern black college, to Chicago, then Harlem, then Copenhagen, then back to Harlem, and finally ends in the return "home" to the South, a *nostos* that kills. Each of these sites foregrounds a different aspect of her identity, empowering or limiting her in ways that shift according to her location. Moreover, in many of these geographical locations, different scenes foreground different elements of identity. In Harlem, for example, she experiences a class vulnerability in her dependence on wealthy blacks, evident especially at their lavish parties, and in her own bourgeois foundation, evident in her attraction to and revulsion from the surging crowds of lower-class blacks on the streets and in the jazz clubs. In sum, situational identity focuses on the way different aspects of subjectivity move fluidly from the foreground to the background in different locations.

The sixth discourse of positional identity, that of hybridity, has emerged most directly out of ethnic, postcolonial, and diasporic studies. Its rhetoric emphasizes not the hybridity born of scientific interventions in organic processes but rather the cultural grafting that is the production of geographical migration. In turn, this theorization of identity has often drawn heavily on narratives by writers like Maxine Hong Kingston, Salman Rushdie, and Gloria Anzaldúa, all of whom explore the conditions of hybridity produced by immigration, exile, or existence in the borderlands, in what Anzaldúa calls the "juncture of culture" (*Borderlands* ix). As a discourse of identity, hybridity often depends materially, as well as figuratively, on movement through space, from one part of the globe to another. This migration through space materializes a movement through different cultures that effectively constitutes identity as the product of cultural grafting. Alternatively, hybridity sometimes configures identity as the superposition of different cultures in a single space often imagined as a borderland, as a site of blending and clashing. "To survive the Borderlands," Anzaldúa writes, "you must live *sin fronteras* [without borders]/ be a crossroads" (195). In either case, identity is not "pure," "authentic," but always already a heterogeneous mixture produced in the borderlands or interstices between difference. Such grafting often takes the form of painful splitting, divided loyalties, or disorienting displacements. Sometimes it leads to or manifests as regenerative growth and creativity. Moreover, this discourse frequently moves dialectically between a language of diasporic loss of origin or authenticity and a language of embrace for syncretic heterogeneity and cultural translation.[18] As I discuss in greater detail in chapter 3, the potentially violent, contradictory, absurd, even humorous dimensions of such oscillations are evident in Anzaldúa's partially ironic lines about postmodernity in the United States:

> To live in the Borderlands means to
>   put *chile* in the borscht,
>   eat whole wheat *tortillas*,
>   speak Tex-Mex with a Brooklyn accent;
>   be stopped by *la migra* at the border checkpoints;

                                                                                (194)

In *The Woman Warrior*, to recall a particularly influential text about hybridity, Maxine Hong Kingston represents herself as a young Chinese American girl growing up in the interface between Chinese and American forms of patriarchy, between Chinese and American forms of familial and communal tyranny. At first, the experience of hybridity silences Kingston's emergent identity. As an elementary-school child, she beats another Chinese American girl to make her speak and then takes to her bed for two years in response to her punishment of her silent double. Gradually, however, she emerges out of this silence into speech through the act of negotiating pathways of connection between Chinese and American stories, through translating the heroics of Fa Mu Lan (the legendary swordswoman who avenged her people with the crimes against them etched in words on her back) into an American destiny as a Chinese American writer, and through her identification with Ts'ai, the Chinese poet who transformed her captivity among the barbarians into the source of a syncretist poetry. It is a hard-won syncretism, however, one that depends upon the processes and memories of painful splitting, doubling, and grafting of different identities, histories, and locations.[19]

FEMINIST CRITICAL PRACTICE

All six of these discourses of identity—multiple oppression, multiple subject positions, contradictory subject positions, relational subjectivity, situational subjectivity, and hybridity—have undermined conventional forms of gynocriticism and gynesis, with their privileging of one difference—sexual and/or gender—above all others. Unsettling the sufficiency of gender as the determinant of identity, they have problematized the project of gynocriticism, which by definition uses gender as the first principle of selection in the discussion of writers. To some extent, gynocriticism met this challenge in the 1980s through pluralization into multiple gynocriticisms: the production, for example, of African American, Asian American, Chicana, lesbian, Euro-American traditions of women's writing.[20] These new gynocriticisms typically combine gender with one other constituent of identity for the purposes of selection and literary history, thus altering gynocriticism's original sole emphasis on gender, but nonetheless not providing a sufficiently flexible discourse to accommodate more complex subjectivities. Gynocriticism, however revitalized, retains gender as the assumed foundation of feminist critical practice and thus remains out of step with locational discourses of identity and subjectivity.

The new geography of identity has been even more troubling for gynesis. It has made increasingly suspect the kind of synchronic, transhistorical assertions about subjectivity characteristic of gynesis, particularly psychoanalytic and deconstructive forms of it. This accounts in part, I suspect, for the way in which concepts of performativity and masquerade in the field of queer theory have in some sense supplanted the energy that gynesis used to crystallize.[21] The allegorization of subjectivity as performance is often able to accommodate the notion of shifting constituents of identity, particularly because of its constructivist emphasis. One "performance" might play with gender, another with class, still another with sexuality as forms of masquerade. Or, performative identities might activate an interplay of multiple roles. If gynesis in some ways mutated into queer theory, however, it nonetheless remains true that the exclusive focus on gender characteristic of gynesis no longer exhibits the kind of explanatory power it had in the 1980s. Moveover, the figurative force of the rhetoric of performativity—with its suggestion of intentionality—undermines the insistence on historical and material embeddedness that permeates the geographical rhetoric of positionality.[22]

In spite of their adaptations on the changing terrain of literary studies, the new geography of identity remains a serious challenge to gynocriticism and gynesis. Too often even pluralized gynocriticisms and a more eclectic or performative gynesis require a unitary foil of male writing, of western humanism, "dead white men" or the Law of the Father against which to read women's diverse voices. Sexual difference remains an assumed categorical foundation even though gender may no longer be privileged as the single lens for reading. This continued emphasis is not flexible enough for the new geography of identity in which other constituents of identity are equally important, in which interactional analysis of codependent systems of alterity replaces the focus on binary difference, in which relational and situational subjectivities move liminally from site to site, in which the always already heterogeneous belies the fixity of imagined authenticity, in which syncretist interminglings in the contact zone, middle ground, or global ethnoscape mute clear demarcations of difference.

So what kind of feminist critical practice does the new geography of identity foster? First, let it be said that feminist criticism has not been and should not be limited to discussions of identity and subjectivity. But since these issues have been so foundational for much feminist criticism, it is important for us to think through the implication of the new geographics for work that continues to explore the production and reception of women's writing and the textuality of gender. Second, feminist critical practice focused on questions of identity and subjectivity has already begun to change significantly as a result of the new geographics. What I want to do here is metacritically highlight this shift as a way of clarifying what has been happening and encouraging future developments along these lines for feminist criticism. For illustrative purposes, I will outline how three different focuses in narrative studies—the writers, the characters, and embedded cultural narratives—are being and can even more self-consciously be reconfigured in relation to the new geography of identity.[23]

First, the writers. Gynocriticism, even in its pluralized form, focuses on women writers. Whether self-reflexively addressed or not, the decision to write only on women necessarily privileges gender as the principle of selection. Gynesis, emerging out of a poststructuralist critique of the author as source or origin of expressivity, has been more concerned with the textual effects of gender than with gendered writers. But particularly for feminist critics who have blended gynocriticism and gynesis, the goal has often been, in Nancy K. Miller's words, "to discover the embodiment in writing of a gendered subjectivity; to recover within representation the emblems of its construction" (*Subject* 80). Such gynocritical and gynetic emphasis on the writer's gender has the effect of subsuming, repressing, or marginalizing other aspects of the writer's identity. The new geography of identity insists that we think about women writers in relation to a fluid matrix instead of a fixed binary of male/female or masculine/feminine. In so doing, the justification for focusing on women loses its cogency. Instead, the interactional, relational, and situational constituents of identity for both male and female writers should be read together. The multiple and contradictory subject positions of writers need to be accounted for, and the very presence of hybridity undermines the gynocritical predisposition to single out gender.

In focusing attention on the multiplex identity of writers, I do not mean to reinstitute the hegemony of deterministic biography and authorial intentionality in the reading of narrative texts. The writer's epistemological standpoint cannot be read as the absolute and unmediated predictor determining the locational subjectivities of the text. Nonetheless, writer and text are connected as inescapably as spider to web, to invoke Miller's arachnological trope (*Subject* 77–101). Moreover, consideration of the writer's positionality forms an important element in interpreting the processes and problematics of narrative authority. Consequently, reading the subjectivities within a text involves tracing the mediated link between the multiply situated, historically specific producer and product, writer and text, scriptor and narrative voice.

To be more concrete, let me consider the changing critical terrain for the discussion of four British modernists: James Joyce, Virginia Woolf, D. H. Lawrence, and Jean Rhys.[24] (I select writers of current canonical status associated with a movement often privileged in twentieth-century literary studies to dispel any notion that the new geographics of identity is suited only to noncanonical writers and movements.) Gynocriticism would most typically emphasize the difference between Joyce and Lawrence as men on the one hand and Woolf and Rhys as women on the other, thus fostering broad generalizations about male versus female modernism in British literature. Gynesis would focus on the feminine as it operates discursively in their texts, thus encouraging analysis of how the text's feminine Other exists as disruptive trace, gap, or aporia that tears open the master narratives of the symbolic order represented in or constructed by the text. In contrast, the new geography of identity brings into focus a fluid matrix rendered invisible by the discourses of gender difference. In relation to Woolf and Rhys, Joyce is a man whose texts assert a kind of patriarchal privilege from which both felt excluded because of gender. But unlike the Englishwoman Woolf, Rhys grew up as a colonial subject in Dominica as the daughter of a Welsh father and a Creole mother; she writes as an expatriate living at the fringes of British and European culture. More like Rhys than Woolf in this regard, Joyce is also an Irish colonial subject who writes within and at the margins of the English language and literary tradition—a master discourse celebrated by Woolf's father, Leslie Stephen, the epitome of the Victorian man of letters. As an expatriate in Paris and Zurich, Joyce's location as a colonial subject differs significantly from that of Rhys, who lived much of her writing life in the homeland of imperial power. Joyce's expatriatism differs as well from that of his family or of his fellow Irish subjects engaged in a struggle against their colonial status. Born into the privileged heart of the British Empire, both Woolf and Lawrence "voyage out" (to echo the title of Woolf's first novel) of its "civilized" center—Lawrence, by engaging in appropriative and objectifying forms of masculinist primitivism;

Woolf, by using gender as the basis for affirming home as the Society of Outsiders.

To complicate matters further, Woolf's position as a member of Britain's upper-middle-class intelligentsia gives her writer's voice a class-inflected authority and wit that is distinctly different from that of Joyce, who grew up within the context of rapidly decaying genteel poverty, or of Rhys, whose survival in England and on the Continent variously depended on her marginal employment as an actress, on the vulnerable class positions of her husbands, or on the largesse of lovers. In relation to gender, Woolf writes as a woman who fears to speak female desire precisely because of the censoring effects of the phallocentric desire that Lawrence at times advocates in his novels and essays. But in relation to class, Lawrence, the son of a miner and a lower-middle-class woman who married "down," inscribed in his writings his fascination for and exclusion from the class from which Woolf came, as well as his suppressed erotic attraction to working-class men. In terms of sexuality, Joyce aligns himself with the heterosexual position of privilege (however titillated by identifications with the feminine, homosexual, or bisexual), while Rhys experiences and writes about heterosexual desire from the location of the victimized Other. The differences between Joyce and Rhys, however, begin to coalesce when we read their sites of heterosexuality in relation to Woolf and Lawrence, who exist in different places along the periphery of veiled bisexual, homoerotic, and lesbian desire.

I have purposely attempted to sketch the weblike matrix out of which multi-faceted subjectivities emerge to highlight the inadequacy of binaries like male/female or masculine/feminine to characterize the full play of difference and identity. In some ways, these writers share common locations; in other ways, their positions are different. The location of each writer continually shifts in relation to the others and to their different and often contradictory positions within systems of privilege and alterity. The relational notion of identity that emerges from such fluid epistemological standpoints discourages the construction of grand narratives about female modernism versus male modernism to which gynocriticism tends. It discourages as well metanarratives about masculine/feminine binaries upon which gynesis depends.

Second, the characters. Like writers, the characters who move through narrative space and time occupy multiple and shifting positions in relation to each other and to different systems of power relations. Unlike gynocriticism and gynesis, the new geography of identity encourages interactional analysis of different constituents of identity, no one privileged over the other. Take, for example, Antoinette in Rhys's *Wide Sargasso Sea*, her rewriting of the story of Bertha Mason in Charlotte Brontë's *Jane Eyre*. The novel is set first on the island of Jamaica, then in the "honeymoon house" on a nearby tropical island, and finally at Thornfield Hall in England. Within the intersecting caste systems based on race, gender, class, and colonialism, Antoinette occupies a contradictory subject position in which power and powerlessness are constantly shifting and must be defined relationally and situationally. Her Creole planter family exploits the labor of the newly emancipated slaves, who rise up to terrorize the isolated family in retaliation for their continued economic and political enslavement. Landed but penniless, the family is ostracized by neighboring gentry and scorned by the still landless blacks, whose disenfranchisement in the public sphere intensifies their psychological power to induce white paranoia. Antoinette's mother remarries, which ultimately makes the young Antoinette an heiress who can attract a husband from England who has gentry status, but as the younger son, no money or land (until his older brother dies). Rochester's entrapment of Antoinette originates in his relative powerlessness as the younger son who must do his father's bidding to enhance his class position. It begins as well in Antoinette's refusal to marry the man she loves, her biracial cousin Sandi.

In relation to Antoinette, the racially mixed and black characters all suffer from the racial system that privileges the white Creole. But in relation to Rochester, Antoinette is the exoticized Other who draws power from the tropical landscape and syncretist Caribbean culture, power that must be contained by removal to England, where she is reduced to madness and imprisonment. Within either a gynocritical or a gynetic framework, Antoinette's gender remains the central constituent of identity, but the new geography of identity emphasizes the fluid interaction of race, class, sexuality, and national origin along with gender.

Third, cultural narratives. Like writers and characters, the cultural narratives embedded in a texts are also rich sites for the multivocal and often contradictory geographics of identity to be set in play. In spatial terms, these cultural narratives originating in the text's larger historical contexts exist consciously or unconsciously as a vertical dimension within the horizontal narrative space and time the characters inhabit.[25] Where gynocriticism and gynesis focus mainly on the cultural narratives of gender, the new geography of identity looks for traces of all the circulating discourses of subjectivity and alterity. The task of the critic involves decoding and contextualizing these discourses within the larger terrain of cultural and political history. Secondarily and perhaps more importantly, it involves interpreting how such cultural narratives are negotiated within the text and what kind of cultural work they perform as they are read and reread in the public domain of letters. Are, for example, these cultural narratives textual sites of contradiction, clashing against each other, or do they intensify each other in collaboration? Which ones are privileged and which ones are marginalized by the writer or the text as a whole? Do they function progressively or regressively? Do different readers bring different readings to these cultural narratives depending on their own epistemological locations?

Consider, for example, Bloom's confrontation with the citizen in the "Cyclops" episode of *Ulysses*. In the horizontal space and time of the text—about 4:30 in the afternoon of June 16, 1904—Bloom faces a group of Irish patriots at Kiernan's pub at the very time he knows that his wife Molly and Blazes Boylan are having sex. The patriots defensively proclaim the superiority of ancient Irish culture over the imperial culture of Britain. Their nationalist loyalties inspire Bloom to a double assertion, that he too is Irish and that he, like Jews everywhere, is persecuted as much as the Irish. On the one hand, he resists their essentialist equation of nation with race. At a historical moment when national and racial identities were often assumed to be synonymous, he radically insists that "A nation is the same people living in the same place" and answers the citizen's mocking request for his nation by insisting that even as a Jew, his nation is Ireland—"I was born here. Ireland" (12:1422–23).[26] On the other hand, as the citizen spits out an oyster in laughing contempt, Bloom defiantly announces his oppression as a Jew: "And I belong to a race too, says Bloom, that is hated and persecuted. Also now. This very moment. This very instant. . . . Robbed, says he. Plundered. Insulted. Persecution. Taking what belongs to us by right. At this very moment, says he, putting up his fist, sold by auction in Morocco like slaves or cattle" (12:1467–68).

Facing intensified mockery, Bloom swerves away from all essentialized nationalisms—whether Irish or Jewish—to advocate the end of injustice and life based on love: "love, says Bloom. I mean the opposite of hatred" (12:1485). Although Bloom has a few defenders, his temporary absence leads to anti-Semitic grousing by some of the patriots, who mistakenly believe that Bloom just won some money at the races and was too stingy to stand a round of drinks. Upon his return, the citizen drunkenly hurls more anti-Semitic insults, embarrassing even his fellow patriots. Bloom leaves the pub in (mock)heroic triumph, asserting both the humanity and divinity of Jews: "Mendelssohn was a jew and Karl Marx and Mercadante and Spinoza. And the Saviour was a jew and his father was a jew. Your God" (12:1804–6).

In the vertical axis of the text, cultural narratives of western anti-Semitism, British anti-Irish stereotyping, sexism, heterosexism, and orientalism co-mingle as interdependent discourses in the scene. Bloom's assertion of his Irishness elicits a paean of praise to a masculinist Celtic imaginary that reduces the power and agency of the feminine within that tradition to a deified or demonized Other. Drinking, spitting, and swearing raucously, the citizen embodies in satiric form this contemporary reconstruction of ancient glory. (The citizen is Joyce's fictional portrait of Irish patriot Michael Cusack, well known for his attempt to reinstate ancient Celtic sports in Ireland.) Condensing multiple cultural narratives, one of the patriots puts Bloom into the stereotypic position of the feminized, homosexualized, and orientalized Jew: "Old lardyface standing up to the business end of a gun. Gob, he'd adorn a sweepingbrush, so he would, if he only had a nurse's apron on him . . . as limp as a wet rag" (12:1476–80). As a man who regularly uses orientalizing discourses for the women subjected to his masculinized gaze, Bloom is himself orientalized and objectified by the patriots, a process that anticipates the transformation of Bloom into a sodomized, bestial Other in Nighttown in thrall to Bella/o of the "Circe" episode.

Bloom's confrontation with the citizen in the "Cyclops" episode sets in play a series of cultural narratives that are both radically critiqued and ultimately, I would argue, reinscribed in the novel: the vulgar, drunken Irishman; the feminized, homosexual, and usurious Jew; the impotent fag; humiliation figured as housewife and nurse. The critique the text makes possible of interlocking essentialisms depends upon evoking the very stereotypes that the text seems to undermine. Irigarayan parody, however disruptive, does not displace the hegemonies it cracks open because the text's mimicry requires the (re)activation of the cultural narratives it would expose. Which of these narratives does the rest of the text discredit? Which does it privilege? From what epistemological standpoint do readers interpret these narratives? Are preexisting anti-Semitic, anti-Irish, homophobic, or patriarchal attitudes in various readers erased or reinforced by the text's parodic mimicry? What cultural work does the text perform as it takes on new life in different times and places?

Whatever the answers to these questions, one thing is certain: gynocriticism and gynesis do not have sufficient flexibility to explore the negotiation of multiple and interlocking cultural narratives in *Ulysses*. The new geographics of identity calls into question readings of gender in isolation from other cultural narratives based in anti-Semitism, heterosexism, and the colonization of the Irish; instead, they foster interactive readings that demonstrative how these cultural narratives function as symbiotic and interdependent systems.

FEMINISM AND LOCATIONAL CRITICISM

Gynocriticism and gynesis, I have argued, are too focused on gender and binary difference in isolation to get at the kind of readings of writers, characters, and cultural narratives that I have just sketched and that feminists have been developing in narrative and modernist studies. However, having suggested that we must move beyond gynocritical and gynetic strategies of reading, I want to conclude with a problematization of the word *beyond* in my title and the implications for future feminist critical practice.[27] As Yung-Hsing Wu argues, the word *beyond* in feminist theory often suggests a linear model of change that involves leaving behind prior formations or positions as no longer functional or progressive.[28] I advocate instead a palimpsestic view of changing critical practices, a spatialized metaphoric of history in which what has gone before synchronically remains, continuing to influence the new, however much it is itself subject to change. There are still compelling reasons—both epistemological and political—to do a kind of feminist critical work rooted in gynocriticism and gynesis and modified by the new geography of identity.

First, the production of any knowledge necessarily involves the foregrounding of certain categories and the muting of others. To echo Paul de Man's well-known phrasing with which I began the movement *beyond* gynocriticism and gynesis, insight necessitates a corollary blindness. Bringing one set of phenomena into focus depends upon allowing others to go out of focus. Highlighting one kind of context backgrounds other potentially illuminating ones. Given that such categories of literary study as historical period (e.g., Renaissance, Victorian), geographical/national entity (American, Chinese, West African), genre (novel, play), movement or convention (realism, modernism), or historically produced group identity (lesbian, African American, Jewish) currently exist as recognized and widespread focuses for analysis and pedagogy, so should gender still be affirmed a legitimate and necessary category. A gynocritical reading of women writers in the context of a female literary tradition makes visible such patterns as mother-daughter relations, resistance to the marriage plot, and the double jeopardy of identities formed in between race and gender—patterns that did not come into focus by reading these women in the context of categories like the Victorian novel, modernism, or the Harlem Renaissance. A gynetic probing of the linguistic processes and effects of gender as distinct from other constituents of subjectivity can bring to the fore the binaries of body and desire as they shape and are shaped by language—issues that went unexamined in poetics that ignored a consideration of gender.

Second, we should remember that epistemology always has a politics; knowledge is always situated, produced out of and addressing specific locations and constituencies. The insistence on a linear move *beyond* gynocriticism and gynesis runs the risk of an overly stagist and politically dangerous notion of social change in the production and dissemination of knowledge. The binary difference upon which gynocriticism and gynesis are founded—male/female and masculine/feminine—have had and continue to have a powerful ideological force in the various cultural formations of sexism and patriarchy, which I do not take to be fixed or essential conditions of oppression, but which, however varied and historically specific, nonetheless exist in material forms. Those critics, feminist or otherwise, who have never had much interest in women writers can all too easily appropriate the linear tendencies of *beyond* to justify their continuing indifference to women's textual agency. The word *beyond* flirts dangerously with a regressive discourse of postfeminism, suggesting that the political advocacy implicit in categories such as *woman, women,* or *feminine* is no longer necessary, that such terms reflect a naive historical stage through which we have already passed en route to ever-greater sophistication. And the word *beyond* encourages the displacement of gender as old-fashioned in favor of the newest "in" categories on the ever-changing horizons of critical theory and practice. We must resist such displacements—whether they reflect the charisma of the new, whether they come from retrogressive or progressive directions, whether they appeal to the urgency of other important categories like race or national original or queerness.[29]

Precisely because patriarchal formations have continued material reality, because the historical conditions that led to the rise of gynocriticism and gynesis still exist, these pedagogical and scholarly projects have continued legitimacy and urgency. Literary histories and theory still regularly appear in which women writers as producers of culture remain invisible, in which the feminine exists under constant threat of erasure or appropriation. It is politically imperative that the discourses of gynocriticism and gynesis continue as long as women writers and the issue of the feminine are marginalized or trivialized. The attention to gender that has been central to women's studies in general and feminist criticism in particular remains a necessity to ensure the continued existence of feminism as a distinct cultural and political set of loosely related and often diverse projects. Politically speaking, it is premature to advocate the seamless integration of feminism with all other forms of progressivism. Such a move could easily dilute the effect of feminist analysis, all too quickly setting in motion the processes by which the specificities of women's lives are once again pushed aside and forgotten. As I have learned through participation in a women's studies program, feminists are most likely to have a transformative effect on their traditional disciplines when they also have a separate power base outside those disciplines to legitimate their activities within. Integration, in other words, often requires a concurrent separation. In relation to feminist criticism, this means that the continued vitality and growth of gynocriticism and gynesis may well be a precondition to the continued development of an integrative analysis of the multifaceted constituents of identity.

Third, as the new geography of identity sweeps the landscape of literary studies, we must ask, as Mary Helen Washington argues, "Who benefits from these changes?"[30] Does the rhetoric of multiple positionality foster the greater participation of marginalized and oppressed peoples, precisely those who have had the most difficulty in having their voices heard, in producing visible and transmittable cultural formations, both inside and outside the academy? Does the emphasis on the fluidity of interminably shifting identities facilitate or inhibit the energy and vision necessary for activism, coalitional politics, and alliance building? And as Sangeeta Ray observes in her critique of Homi Bhabha's celebration of hybridity as "always already empowering," does the discourse of multiple *locations* tend to displace the materiality of "multiple *dislocations* vis à vis one's gender, sexuality, race, ethnicity, postcoloniality, and migrancy" ("Rethinking Migrancy," 11, 13, my emphasis)? Ray argues forcefully against the tendency of postcolonial studies to ignore gender in its analysis of nationalism, using a reading of a woman's text to support her contention that nationalism is always a gendered discourse ("Gender").

"What—if anything—belongs to feminism?" Nancy K. Miller wonders. "Doesn't it all become cultural studies, if we don't 'privilege gender'??"[31] If feminist critics abandon the "privileging" of women and gender transformations in favor of a diffused progressivism, then who can be trusted to resist the historic forces producing gender backsliding and backlash? Precisely because feminists have the most at stake to win or lose on behalf of women, it is most likely feminists who will serve as the intellectual and activist guardians against the return of women and gender to categorical invisibility and trivialization. If feminist critics don't defend highlighted use of the category gender, who will?

In spite of these epistemological and political imperatives for the continued foregrounding of gender, I strongly believe that the new ways of theorizing identity and subjectivity—preeminently the new geography of identity—reflect substantial changes in our increasingly postmodern, migratory, syncretist, and cyberspatial global world. These historical changes in turn have compelled and continue to necessitate substantial adaptations in gynocriticism and gynesis as they were first practiced in the 1970s and 1980s. In developing with the times, they need more fluid and flexible critical practices that do not regard sexual or gender difference as a priori, fixed, primal, or primary assumption to be grasped in pristine isolation. Feminists should guard against using male writers or masculinity as fixed foils, as categorical Others whose static nature allows for the iden-

tification of female diversity and difference. Instead, future gynocritical and gynetic projects should interrogate such assumptions and vigilantly take into
account how gender interacts with other constituents of identity. Within the rapidly changing terrain of the new geography of identity, there is a vital need for a
modified gynocriticism and gynesis to travel.

In calling for a gynocriticism and gynesis adapted to the geographics of interdisciplinary identity studies, I am in essence asking for a more self-consciously
locational feminist criticism, a form of critical practice that applies the lessons of
the new fluid, relational, and situational geography of identity to the act of doing
feminist criticism itself.[32] Instead of fixed forms of gynocritical or gynetic analysis, a locational feminist criticism involves fluid movement among methods in
accord with the sites of production and dissemination. We might ask, who is the
audience of our work, and what is the politics of our speaking or writing at a given
moment in space as well as in time? What is our responsibility to the kind of
cultural work our criticism performs? If we address an audience either hostile to
or bored with the category of gender, we might privilege gender as a necessary,
compensatory move. Conversely, if we speak or write to those who already understand the importance of or who focus exclusively on gender, we might stress
that the identity or subjectivity of women can never be understood solely in relation to gender construction. In this location, analysis of the geographical interplay
of gender with multiple constituents of identity has epistemological and political
urgency.

Locational feminist criticism might involve not only attention to the sites of
critical production but also sensitivity to the way in which gender as a constituent
of identity might itself be strategically foregrounded or muted in different situations. "Bodies matter," as Judith Butler puns. Narratives about and inscriptions of
the body might well feature gender difference and thus require major scrutiny of
gender in relative isolation from other facets of identity—textual moments such
as Woolf's account in "A Sketch of the Past" of how her brother's fingers would
not stop exploring her private parts; or the semiotic discourse of pregnancy that
H.D. experiments with to capture the associational movements of Hermione's
thoughts as they counter the march of soldier's feet in her World War I novel,
Asphodel.[33] However, even such provisional privileging of gender must guard
against inadequate attention to how gender interacts with other systems of
stratification. The particular form that molestation took in Woolf's life (e.g., its
kind of secrecy and "gentility") is ultimately not separable from the function of
gender within the Victorian class system at the height of the British Empire. In
Toni Morrison's *Beloved*, to cite another example, the gender marking of Sethe's
lactating body is inseparable from its racial marking as Schoolteacher's men rape
and "milk" her in front of the despairing eyes of her slave husband (esp. 68–73).
Even at textual moments of great violence against the female body, where gender
surely takes on heightened significance, locational feminist criticism needs to be
attuned to the intersection of gender with other constituents of identity.

In sum, the task of a locational feminist criticism is often contradictory, involving a ceaseless negotiation between attention to sexual and gender difference

upon which gynocriticism and gynesis depend and scrutiny of the multifaceted matrices in which gender is only one among many axes of identity. It must on the one hand ensure the survival of feminist criticism as a powerful and distinctive set of voices within literary studies. It must on the other hand continue its leadership role in the formation of new, more complex geographies of identity and subjectivity that are being produced in the mobile terrains of the coming millennium.

"Beyond" White and Other:
Narratives of Race in Feminist Discourse

THE BEATING of Rodney King by four police officers and the violent aftermath of their acquittal in Los Angeles in April of 1992 underlines the explosive status of race and ethnicity in the United States in the 1990s. The videotape of the beating—played and replayed on television screens for months—captures the "black and white" of the beating in a double sense. It images metonymically the whiteness of the police and the blackness of Rodney King, the brutality of power and the powerlessness of victimization, and the binary of white/black as it has materialized in the history of European American racism toward African Americans in the United States. But the violent upheaval after the trial—also imprinted repeatedly on the national consciousness by the media—tells other stories, ones that supplement rather than replace the story of white and black in America.

These narratives pit not just black against white but African Americans, Latinos, and Asian Americans (especially Korean Americans) against each other. Reginald Denny was not the only man to be pulled from his truck. Guatemalan immigrant Fidel Lopez, for instance, was seized, beaten, doused with gasoline, and nearly torched by an angry mob that included the same African American men accused of attacking Denny—Damian Williams and Henry Watson. Like Denny, Lopez was saved by courageous African Americans (Gross, "Body"). In spite of the media's tendency to emphasize African American violence, the rage and looting were not restricted to a single cultural group. Unlike during the Watts uprising of 1965, Asian American, African American, Latino, and Euro-American shopkeepers faced rainbow mobs of people joined in anger, resentment, and desire overdetermined by the politics of race, ethnicity, class, gender, and immigration. Blacks and Latinos in particular attacked Korean American shopowners and targeted Koreatown, scapegoating the group that the media has made into "the model minority," the new American Dream story, whose very "success" covertly blames those who remain poor for their "failure" to succeed. Moreover, fault lines erupted between members of related racial or ethnic groups, often exacerbated by differences of class and immigration status—particularly Mexican Americans versus Central Americans and Korean Americans versus other Asian Americans. What essayist and PBS commentator Richard Rodriguez calls the dualistic "black and white checkerboard" of race that has long dominated the American consciousness of racism has been reconfigured in multiracial, multicultural terms by the aftermath of the white police officers' acquittal for beating Rodney King ("Changing Faces" 14).[1]

These narratives of multiethnic, multiracial, and multicultural conflict do not, of course, render irrelevant the systemic forms of white racism against people of color in the United States. As both Elaine Kim ("Home") and David Polumbo-Liu ("Los Angeles") demonstrate in their analyses of media representations of Korean Americans during the Los Angeles events, the institutional and attitudinal manifestations of white racism played a significant role in the media portrayal of besieged Korean Americans both as near-white, model Americans defending their property against barbaric African Americans and Latinos and as ruthless shopkeepers at blame for the economic deprivations of other Americans. The media focus on the interracial, interethnic, and intraethnic dimensions of the uprising performs in part the cultural work of suppressing awareness of the way the structures of white racism intensify conflict between racial and ethnic others. The worsening socioeconomic profile for inner cities all across the United States in which white racism plays a large part functions as a crucial context in which immigrant groups are set up to scramble with impoverished African Americans for less and less in an increasingly polarized and transnational economy.

At the same time, however, these events urgently testify to another reading that exists as a supplement to, not a displacement of, the effects of white racism. This reading of multiethnic, multiracial, and multicultural conflict and connection focuses on the significance of the changing demographics in the United States as we move into the twenty-first century in an increasingly globalized, mobile, and cyberspatial world. (I do not mean *multiethnic, multiracial,* and *multicultural* to refer only to people of color, a usage that reinforces the racist notion that whiteness or Euro-Americanness is a "natural" identity, not a social construct.)[2] For many, Los Angeles represents the avant-garde of the "browning of America," a phrase that ambiguously invokes the rise of nonblack racial minorities, the enormous influx of nonwhite immigrants into the United States, the proportional decrease of Euro-Americans, the widespread phenomenon of racial and ethnic mixing, the growing heterogeneity or syncretism of all cultural groups (and individuals within those groups), and even the dissolution of fixed boundaries in the "conventional black and white dialectic" (Rodriguez, "Changing Faces" 14). As parable, the events in Los Angeles suggest that binary categories of race should be supplemented with a more complicated discourse, one that acknowledges the ongoing impact of white racism but also goes beyond an analysis of white strategies that divide and conquer people of color. We need a language beyond fixed categories of good and evil, of victims and victimizers, a discourse beyond the binary of black and white, a language that could explain the statement by Lopez's daughter, who said she did not hate her father's attackers because "I understood why they were so mad" (Gross, "Body").[3]

Feminists have much to learn from the demographic landscape and tumult of Los Angeles as race and ethnicity become ever more central concerns in our classrooms, organizations, conferences, and writing.[4] Since the 1970s, feminism in the United States has increasingly had to come to grips with issues of racism: with race as a central constituent of identity and as the basis of both domination

and resistance. The feminist analysis of gender and race (along with other components of identity) as interactive systems of stratification has developed exten-
sively, alongside the rapid expansion of knowledge about the varied specificities
of women's cultural histories. American feminists have had more difficulty confronting the issue of racism and engaging in meaningful cross-racial interaction,
however. The shattering of binary thinking represented in the Los Angeles events
holds out creative possibilities for feminists to think about, talk about, and act
upon this difficult dimension of race in a more fruitful way.

   "The very act of writing or speaking about race," Dominick LaCapra writes in
his introduction to *The Bounds of Race*, "is fraught with difficulty even when one
attempts to go about it in a critical and self-critical manner," especially for "those
who are not 'people of color'" (2). As a Euro-American woman who inevitably
benefits from the system of racial stratification in the United States, I am particularly aware of how difficult it is for me to address these questions, affected as the
process is by my own and my readers' different positions within a society in
which "racism is the clearest way Americans have of understanding social division" (Rodriguez, "Changing Faces" 14). This problem is all the more pressing in
the context of the academy's current "race for race," especially for white academics to teach and write about race.[5] As Ann duCille points out in reference to black
women, this desire on the part of white academics to write about black women
(for example) all too often includes a failure to include real black women in the
discussion or to understand black women as cultural producers rather than simply
as objects of the racial gaze. Nonetheless, I cannot accept the notion that the racial
privilege of my whiteness should enforce my silence about race and ethnicity,
issues of vital ethical and political importance not only in the United States but
also in a global context. The landmines are everywhere—my own ignorances
based on racial privilege and the rush of others to dismiss, censor, not hear, condemn, withdraw. Yet I ask that you hear me out. I offer these reflections in the
spirit of dialogue, of what duCille calls "complementary theorizing" among people of different perspectives and racial identities ("Occult of Black Womanhood"
624)—a precondition, I believe, for growth and change in the academy and feminist movement.

   In my view, feminist discourses about race and ethnicity are too often caught
up in repetitive cultural narratives structured around the white/other binary: victims and victimizers, colonized and colonizers, slaves and masters, dominated
and dominators, "us and them," the "good guys against the bad guys." As a result,
discussions about race and racism often collapse in frustration, anger, hurt, yell-
ing, silence, withdrawal, and profound belief that different "sides" are unable to
listen and learn from the other. This all-too-familiar dead end, what Mary Louise
Fellows and Sherene Razack have called "the difference impasse" ("Seeking Relations" 1051), often occurs in spite of the best intentions and efforts of many
feminists to move beyond such repetitive patterns. Overdetermined by the different locations feminists occupy in racial hierarchies, these discussions often recapitulate instead of moving through and beyond the ignorance, anger, guilt, and

silences about race and racism that are the products of power relations in the larger society.[6]

More hopefully, attempts by women of color to build bridges across their own differences with other women of color have usefully initiated the dissolution of the white/other and white/black binaries by looking at relations between two or more marginalized groups and by insisting that racial issues in the United States need to be more broadly understood than as the power relations between European Americans and African Americans. But because these coalitions are based on a shared difference from white women, they often end up reconfiguring binary thinking in the form of white women/women of color or First World/Third World polarities. Vast differences in culture and history among nonwhite women of different racial and ethnic backgrounds and even among women of the same racial or ethnic backgrounds have made alliances difficult, often conflict-ridden and ephemeral.[7]

Such tentative progress around issues of race among different groups of feminists is still matched by the anger, failures of dialogue, and withdrawal that can suddenly explode or slowly sour the dynamics of feminist classrooms, conferences, and organizations. The existence of racism within the larger society has surely undermined many efforts of feminists to move the dialogue forward. But the cultural narratives in which we think about race and ethnicity not only reflect but also shape the material realities of racism. The binary structures of thought that generally serve to shape these narratives may well develop out of what Jean-François Lyotard regards as the very nature of language and narrative, which he views as agonistic, or based in conflicting oppositions revolving around a struggle.[8] Historically produced discursive formations about race often take narrative forms that circulate overtly and covertly throughout both ideological and oppositional values, texts, and cultural artifacts of all kinds. These cultural narratives about race thus both reflect and shape racial politics. Like David Theo Goldberg, editor of *Anatomy of Racism*, I do not see racial thinking as fixed, "singular and monolithic, simply the same attitude complex manifested in varying circumstances" (xii). Rather, I see it as an unfixed set of figural and narrative formations that emerge from, respond to, and help construct changing historical conditions. Consequently, a great deal is at stake in understanding the narratives that underlie our racial discourse. To move forward, the feminist agenda against racism requires not only an examination of power and privilege; it also requires interrogation of the cultural narratives about race that affect what we see, say, write, and do. As Masao Miyoshi writes, "Discourse and practice are interdependent. Practice follows discourse, while discourse is generated by practice" ("Borderless" 726). Just as the material effects of racism affect patterns of thought about race, so the language of race matters, has material consequences.

Binary modes of thinking about race often have explanatory power, especially for identifying certain systems of domination. Witness the "black and white" of Rodney King's beating or of Harriet Jacobs's *Incidents in the Life of a Slave Girl* (1861); the "brown and white" of Gloria Anzaldúa's *Borderlands/La Frontera*

(1987); the "red and white" of Leslie Marmon Silko's *Storyteller* (1981); the "yellow and white" of Joy Kogawa's *Obasan* (1981). I want neither to deconstruct nor to displace this binary thinking. But I do believe that by themselves such binaries create dead ends. They must be supplemented by what I call relational narratives in which the agonistic struggle between victim and victimizer is significantly complicated, as it is in the Los Angeles events. The legitimate insight of binary narratives is blind to many other stories that cannot be fully contained within them. Most especially, binary narratives are too blunt an instrument to capture the liminality of contradictory subject positions or the fluid, nomadic, and migratory subjectivities of what I have elsewhere called the "new geography of identity."[9] A feminist analysis of identity as it is constituted at the crossroads of different systems of stratification requires acknowledging how privilege and oppression are often not absolute categories but rather shift in relation to different axes of power and powerlessness.

To explore ways in which feminist discourse might move beyond binary thinking, I will identify four cultural narratives about race and ethnicity that have circulated since the late 1960s in the often highly charged and overdetermined arenas of North American feminist conferences, classrooms, manifestos, collectives, coalitions, rallies, marches, meetings, essays, collections, and books. The first three scripts—which I call narratives of denial, accusation, and confession—have operated within the agonistic white/other binary. While they have all contributed important narratives to the formation of a multicultural feminism, they also represent stories that are caught in a cul-de-sac, in a round of repetition. By themselves, they cannot lead beyond the boundaries and into the fertile borderlands. The fourth script—the narrative of relational positionality—moves beyond binary thinking. It has begun to emerge more recently, initially muted considerably in the 1980s by the first three scripts, but gaining visibility and frequency in the 1990s.

What I intend to do here is to call greater attention to the script of relational positionality as a supplement to, not a replacement for, the scripts of denial, accusation, and confession. I do so in an effort to jump-start a stalled dialogue about racism and racial interaction. To encourage self-reflection and conversation across racial boundaries, I suggest that feminists can also look outside the academy for cultural narratives about race and ethnicity that forge a discourse beyond the white/other binary—not only in the multilayered parable of the Los Angeles upheavals but also in representations of race and ethnicity in the news media and in popular cultural texts like film. Cultural praxis sometimes outpaces feminist theory, as I will attempt to show with a discussion of globalized accounts of race and ethnicity in the news media and in the fictionalized explorations of relational identities in two contemporary films, Mira Nair's *Mississippi Masala* and Neil Jordan's *The Crying Game*. In spite of the mediated nature of news and film as commodified and ideological institutions of mass culture, both at times break out of the white/other binary; both perform important cultural work around issues of race from which feminists can learn a great deal.

CULTURAL NARRATIVES OF DENIAL, ACCUSATION, AND CONFESSION

These three feminist scripts about race—denial, accusation, and confession—are, on the one hand, diachronic cultural formations that reflect the epistemological positionalities of the feminists who produced them and the historical conditions out of which they arose. They are, in other words, what Donna Haraway calls "situated knowledges," located at the intersection of different systems of alterity.[10] On the other hand, they can also function synchronically as theoretical formulations about race that stake out different political stances. A "thick description" of these scripts (to echo Clifford Geertz, *Interpretation*) would detail their deployment in space and time as reflections of different locations on the terrain of racial stratification. My purpose here, however, is to evoke these narratives in starkly structural terms. I use them not as a fixed taxonomy but rather as a strategic schematization designed to address the theoretical gridlock that characterizes much current feminist discourse about race, racism, and ethnicity.

Scripts of denial, produced largely by white women for whom race has not been a source of oppression, cover a range of stories affirming female and feminist sisterhood that, in their exclusive focus on gender, covertly refuse the significance of race. Such texts as *Sisterhood Is Powerful* (1970) and *Woman in Sexist Society* (1971) represented an exhilarating assertion of the category *woman* as a central prism through which to perceive human experience. Women's lives, these scripts held, had been ignored, trivialized, or distorted in the structures and repositories of human knowledge—in what has come to be called the symbolic order. Feminism would create, so the story went, an alliance of women everywhere based in the commonality of women and in opposition to the patriarchal societies within which women live. This insight—and I stress the importance of its initial and continuing contribution as a foundational premise of women's studies—represents a blindness to categories of race and ethnicity as coordinates of identity. In defining the otherness of woman, it denies the structural process of "othering" by a host of other factors such as race, ethnicity, class, sexuality, religion, national origin, and age.

Scripts of denial implicit in such a framework reflect an epistemological standpoint of racial privilege from which they are largely spoken. They take many forms, but some of the underlying narrative fragments can be provisionally reconstituted as follows: "I'm not a racist." "I'm a feminist, so how could I be a racist?" "I'm oppressed, so how could I be an oppressor?" "My experience is just like your experience." "We are all sisters." "Tell me all about yourself; I'm sure I can understand." "Are you a woman or are you black (Jewish, Chicana, etc.)?" "Which have you suffered from more, being a woman or being a minority?" "We are all oppressed as women," with its unsaid corollary, that other oppressions are not relevant to feminism.[11] And so forth.

Scripts of accusation, produced largely by feminist (or womanist, as some prefer to be called) women of color who were marginalized by racism both in and beyond the feminist movement, sprung up dialectically in response to the scripts of denial in the 1970s and 1980s. Denying the universality of *woman*, these scripts accused white feminists of ignoring, trivializing, or distorting the lives of women who were "different" through other forms of othering. As an advance in feminist theory pioneered especially by women of color, lesbian women, and Jewish women, these accusations led to important reconceptualizations of feminist theory in relation to other systems of oppression. In structural terms, they paralleled those that all feminists had been making against men—but with a difference. Many feminists who engaged in scripts of accusation felt themselves to be in a liminal position—linked to the men of their cultural group by race and ethnicity but separated from them by gender and, conversely, linked to other feminists by reason of gender but separated by reasons of race and ethnicity. In academic feminism specifically, essays like Alice Walker's "In Search of Our Mothers' Gardens" (1974) and "One Child of One's Own" (1979), Barbara Smith's "Toward a Black Feminist Criticism" (1977), and Audre Lorde's essays from the 1970s and early 1980s collected in *Sister Outsider* (1984) led to a groundswell of (still) necessary attack on white feminists for suppressing the differences among women, to the formation of distinct feminisms based on racial and ethnic identities, and to the creation of coalitions among women of color and Third World feminists. Scripts of accusation resulted in the important formation of the categories women of color and Third World women, and of discourses that have fostered analysis of the common ground shared by nonwhite women of different racial and ethnic groups.

Scripts of accusation, reflecting the material and psychological effects of racism, often contain core messages that can be synopsized as follows: "You are a racist." "I am not like you." "You haven't confronted your racial privilege." "I am both a woman and black (Jewish, Chicana, Native American, etc.), and I can't sort out the oppressions of race and gender." "Gender can't be separated from race and class." "You can never understand my experience or perspective." "You are oppressing me and you don't even know it." "You have left out women of color and assumed that your own experience is like all other women's." "You shouldn't write (teach, talk, etc.) about women of color because we women of color must speak for ourselves." "You must include women of color in your classes, books, articles." "You have to take the responsibility for learning about us on your own; we should not have to take the responsibility, time, energy (etc.) to educate you." "I don't want to waste my time trying to talk with you; I'm going to devote all my energy to my sisters of color." And so forth.

Scripts of confession, produced overwhelmingly by white women for whom their own racial privilege had recently become visible or denaturalized, mushroomed in response to scripts of accusation in the 1980s and 1990s. Agreeing with the attacks, many white feminists rushed to turn the accusations upon themselves—as individuals and collectively as white, ethnocentric feminists.[12] Not all accusation was met with confession; some women responded by reconstituting scripts of denial. But white feminist stories of guilt proliferated from the late 1970s on, taking a number of forms, some more constructive than others. At its best, this confessional script led to significant reformulations of feminism that acknowledged some women's complicity in other systems of oppression and called for social change that addressed all forms of alterity.[13] But at times, this gaze at the Medusa of white feminist racism has led to paralysis, frozen guilt, perpetual mea culpas, chest beating, hand wringing, race to confession—in short, to a performance of guilt whose very display tends to displace and thereby reconstitute the other as other. At still other times, this guilt has resulted in an embrace of "other" women—which in academic feminism has meant a rush to include, focus entirely on, or even become the other, as Biddy Martin and Chandra Talpade Mohanty point out ("Feminist Politics" 207). At its most extreme, this embrace tends toward a fetishization of women of color that once again reconstitutes them as other caught in the gaze of white feminist desire.[14] Called into being by scripts of accusation, scripts of confession nonetheless have contributed importantly to feminist theory by making white women in particular turn the lens of critique upon themselves, upon the web of racial and ethnic privilege that had remained invisible to them.

Scripts of confession, reflecting the racial privilege of those who attempt (with questionable success) to disavow that historically given power, circulate among such familiar lines as these: "I am a racist." "I am guilty." "I'm so guilty that I can't do anything but think about how guilty I am." "Feminism is a white, middle-class movement." "Western culture is totally oppressive." "There must be something bad in being white." "I want to help women of color." "I must listen to women of color and not answer back."[15] "White women (always) leave out women of color." "I am not going to leave out women of color anymore." "I want women of color to like me, approve of me, be my friend." "Women of color are more authentic than me, more oppressed than me, better than me, and always right." And so forth.

These three cultural narratives of denial, accusation, and confession—emerging as they do from different locations in the societal distribution of power along racial lines—can be interpreted provisionally as parts of a single story about race and ethnicity in the feminist movement, a metanarrative that can be reconstructed in its simplest structural form as follows. "I'm not a racist, we are all women," says a white feminist. "You are a racist, you are different from me," says a woman-of-color feminist. "You are right, I am a racist," says a white woman. I do not propose this metanarrative as a fixed structure that drives all feminist discourses on race. To do so would be reductionistic, blind to the nuanced heterogeneity of many manifestations of these cultural narratives. Moreover, each script has made and continues to make important contributions to feminist discourse. But what this strategically constituted metanarrative discloses is the underlying binary of white/other that operates within a victim paradigm of race relations. This is, I want to suggest, a story we have heard repeatedly. By itself, it represents a dead end. It is hindering the development of a more broadly defined multicultural feminism whose agenda centrally includes the eradication of racism and the globalization of feminist theory and praxis.

Both the metanarrative and the dead end are starkly present in Gloria Anzaldúa's description of a course on U.S. women of color that she taught at the

University of California, Santa Cruz. I quote at length to give full play to the "soundings" of denial, accusation, and confession that reverberate throughout her account:[16]

> At first, what erupted in class was anger—anger from *mujeres*-of-color, anger and guilt from whites, anger, frustration and mixed feelings by Jewish women who were caught in the middle . . . , and anger and frustration on my part from having to mediate between all these groups [note the scripts of denial and accusation]. Soon my body became a vessel for all the tensions and anger, and I dreaded going to class. Some of my students dreaded going to class. But gradually the *mujeres*-of-color became more assertive in confronting and holding whites accountable for their unaware, "blocked" and chronically oppressive ways [accusation]. . . . When whitewomen or Jewishwomen attempted to subvert the focus from women-of-color's feelings to their own feelings of confusion, helplessness, anger, guilt, fear of change and other insecurities [confession], the women-of-color again and again redirected the focus back to *mujeres-de-color* [accusation]. When several whitewomen stood up in class and either asked politely, pleaded or passionately demanded (one had tears streaming down her face) that women-of-color teach them, when whitewomen wanted to engage women-of-color in time-consuming dialogues [confession], *las mujeres-de-color* expressed their hundred years weariness of trying to teach whites about Racism. They were eloquent in expressing their skepticism about making alliances with whites when most whitewomen . . . needed reassurance, acceptance and validation from *mujeres-de-color* [accusation]. . . . The problem was that whitewomen and white Jewishwomen, while seeming to listen, were not really "hearing" women-of-color and could not get it into their heads that this was a space and class on and about women-of-color [denial and accusation]. As one student-of-color wrote: "I think the hardest thing for me was having to understand that the white students in class... [could not] understand the experiences we have lived" [accusation]. Though there were important lessons learned, the inability to listen and hear, along with the confusion, anger and doubts about ever being able to work together almost tore our class apart [dead end]. (*Making Face* xx)

Anzaldúa is to be commended for her honesty in exposing the difficult racial dynamics in her class. The pedagogical processes of frustration, anger, guilt, and miscommunication produced by these interwoven scripts of denial, accusation, and confession no doubt raised consciousness about racial and ethnic chasms. But I think that, as educational and inevitable as these scripts are because of the different racial and ethnic positionalities represented in the class, they contribute greatly to the "difference impasse," the blocked movement, and the dead-endedness of many feminist discussions about race and racism—for several reasons.

First, these cultural narratives foster the continued production of scripts in which white remains the center, the defining core, in opposition to the other, which remains at the margins. As a result these cultural narratives end up reinscribing the very pattern they set out to replace. Second, they require the construction of white (or western) as a monolithic, unchanging category that even in racial and ethnic terms erases vast differences of culture and history punctuated by violence—witness the conflict between the English and Irish; the Germans and the French; the Bosnians, Serbs, and Croats; the Europeans and the Jews or the Gypsies, both of whom in the European context have been treated as scapegoat races (not ethnicities). Along with the Holocaust and decades of twentieth-century ethnic violence in Europe (both of which have been fueled by racial concepts of national identity), World Wars I and II ought to be sufficient in themselves in calling into question the concept of white and western as unitary categories.[17]

Third, the binary of white/other embedded in these scripts is itself ethnocentric, not sufficiently global in perspective. It does not acknowledge how the processes of racial and ethnic othering are a worldwide phenomenon, not the exclusive product of Caucasians or the West in dealings with people of color. (More on this later.) Fourth, these scripts inhibit the development of scripts about the relation of one kind of other to (an)other—an African American to an Asian American woman, a Korean to a Japanese woman, a Cuban American to an African American woman, a Hindu to a Muslim woman in India, a Hutu to a Tutsi woman in Rwanda, for example. Not all boundaries between nonwhite or nonwestern women can be explained in terms of white or western racism. Too often, the word *racism* implies the assumed modifier *white*. This construction of *racism* as always already *white* reflects the hegemony of white racism in the United States. But it also rests on biologism and operates to make invisible the existence of other racisms (whether in the United States or elsewhere in the world).

Fifth, these cultural narratives are often founded on a misleading notion of racial and ethnic purity that denies the worldwide phenomenon of constantly produced biological and cultural syncretism. People and cultures are not so easily put into fixed categories based on race and ethnicity; claims for such purity are often based on the binary opposition of pure/impure in which mixing constitutes a form of pollution. As Anzaldúa writes in "En rapport," "Racial purity, like language purity, is a fallacy" (146). She attacks specifically the Chicana/o "denial of our sisters who for one reason or another cannot 'pass' as 100% ethnic—as if such a thing exists" (146). It is a cornerstone of racist thinking that people and cultures do and must be made to occupy spaces of racial or ethnic purity. In her visionary call for "the new *mestiza* consciousness," Anzaldúa configures the liminal space she occupies as a frightening, disorienting, but ultimately fertile borderland beyond the stagnations of purist identity politics (*Borderlands* esp. 77–98).[18]

Sixth, these cultural narratives that proscribe the white/other binary implicitly privilege race and ethnicity as the primary category of oppression to which all other systems of alterity must be subsumed, thus reproducing, with all its limitations, the categorical hegemony attempted by certain Marxists with class and radical feminists with gender. Consequently, for all their explanatory power in some contexts, these three scripts actually hinder the analysis of how different systems of stratification intersect in the construction of identity and the experience of oppression. In particular, they suppress an understanding of contradictory subject positions.[19] Nor can they explain the interplay of privilege and alterity in a woman who is part of both a dominant culture and a marginalized one—such as a relatively dark-skinned Brahman woman who moves back and forth between London and Calcutta. As a Brahman she is privileged by caste; as a woman, she is oppressed. As a frequent traveler, she is well off in class terms, but called black by the British and subject to the disorientations of a bicontinental postcolonial identity. As a dark-skinned woman, she is differently disadvantaged within the Indian context of colorism and the British context of racism. The categories "woman of color" and "Third World woman" are insufficient to explain her position at the crossroads of different formations of power relations.

Finally, these binary scripts dim to near invisibility any common ground that might exist between women who occupy the opposing sites of "white" and "color." At times, exclusive emphasis on the differences among women threatens the category of feminism itself, eliminating not only the concept of worldwide efforts to better women's status but also the very possibility of multiple feminisms. Even in the plural, feminism depends upon the premise that gender, in combination with other categories, is a constituent element of hierarchical social organization. I am not for a moment suggesting an abandonment of the recognition and celebration of differences as a necessity and source of strength in feminism. But the identification of differences among women needs to be complemented by a search for common ground, however differently that commonality is materially manifested. For example, a white woman raped by a black man and a black woman raped by a white man in the United States share the experience of rape and have much to learn from each other about its psychological, sexual, familial, and legal consequences. But the different histories of interracial rape between whites and blacks with the legacy of slavery color what these women share, inflecting their commonality with difference. Understanding this difference depends upon first identifying rape as a shared issue based on gender.[20]

"The shared ground [between Us and Them]," writes S. P. Mohanty in his critique of cultural relativism, "helps us situate and specify difference, understand where its deepest resonances might originate" (21). In his view, "a simple recognition of *differences* across cultures" leads only "to a sentimental charity, for there is nothing in its logic that necessitates our attention to the other" (23). The primary shared ground between Us and Them, he argues, begins with the assumption of the other's agency, which he defines as "the capacity that all human 'persons' and 'cultures' in principle possess to understand their actions and evaluate them in terms of their (social and historical) significance for them" (23). The white/other binary discourages the location of such shared ground and tends to deny the agency and subjectivity of the other.

"Women all over the world have a lot of things in common," said Wang Jiaxiang, a women's studies activist and teacher from Beijing and an exhilarated delegate at the United Nations Conference on Population and Development in Cairo (Crossette, "Women's Advocates"). Given the multiple systems of domination that separate women, the search for common ground often seems utopian. This longing for alliance represents a desire for pleasure in and connection across difference, not a pleasure that oppresses but one that flourishes in the intimate spaces that confound the pathologies of otherness.[21] Such desire underlies the kind of agency that exists as a form of healing in Anzaldúa's *Borderlands/La Frontera*: "But it is not enough to stand on the opposite bank, shouting questions, challenging patriarchal, white conventions. A counterstance locks one into a duel of oppressor and oppressed; locked in mortal combat, like the cop and the criminal, both are reduced to a common denominator of violence. The counterstance . . . is a step toward liberation from cultural domination. But it's not a way of life. At some point, on our way to a new consciousness, we will have to leave the opposite bank, the split between the two mortal combatants somehow healed so that we are on both shores at once" (78).[22]

CULTURAL NARRATIVES OF RELATIONAL POSITIONALITY

What I call (for want of a better term) scripts of relational positionality began to emerge during the 1980s in feminist theoretical discourse out of the accusatory and confessional stories about race, ethnicity, and racism. Produced by women and men of different racial and ethnic standpoints, these scripts regard identity as situationally constructed and defined and at the crossroads of different systems of alterity and stratification. They rest upon significant advances in feminist discourse initiated by narratives of accusation and confession: namely, the analysis of multiple oppressions and interlocking systems of oppression that has been pioneered especially by women of color and the new discourses of location, positionality, and standpoint. It is also rooted in feminist object relations theory, which in its feminist revision of psychoanalysis has emphasized how the formation of identity, particularly women's identity, unfolds in relation to desire for and separation from others. Moreover, it shows the influence of poststructuralist and postcolonial critiques of identity and formulations of subjectivity, which stress the nonunitary, indeterminate, nomadic, and hybrid nature of a linguistically constructed identity.[23]

But cultural narratives of relational positionality go beyond these foundations by resisting and dissolving the fixities of the white/other binary. They deconstruct what Homi Bhabha describes as "an important feature of colonial discourse": "its dependence on the concept of 'fixity' in the ideological construction of otherness" ("Other Question" 18). Within a relational framework, identities shift with a changing context, dependent always upon the point of reference. Not essences or absolutes, identities are fluid sites that can be understood differently depending on the vantage point of their formation and function. For example, in relation to white people, Leslie Marmon Silko and Paula Gunn Allen are women of color, Native American, and partially white. In relation to women of color, they are Native American. In relation to Native Americans, they are members of the Laguna Pueblo. In relation to each other, they are individual women who characterize the Laguna Pueblo culture in startlingly different ways. Scripts of relational positionality construct a multiplicity of fluid identities defined and acting situationally. They also go beyond feminist discourses of static positionality, which are often (re)appropriated for scripts of accusation and confession.

The fluidity of situational identity suggests as well a concept of permeable boundaries, a notion that adapts object relations theory to the theorization of cultural syncretism. Such mixtures of cultural strands are especially (but not exclusively) evident in the United States, a nation that has drawn immigrants from all over the world. Hyphenation, however denied, is built into American identity formation, even for members of American Indian nations. Moreover, different hyphenated Americans continually affect other hyphenated Americans. Scripts of relational positionality are more suited to dealing with the permeable boundaries between races and ethnicities. Such scripts also move beyond the essentialism of fundamentalist identity politics without denying the material realities of identity, as poststructuralist deconstructions and performance theory tend to do.[24] Stressing that individuals are constituted through many group identities and cannot be reduced to any one collectivity, they are able to be flexible in dealing with global variation in forms of otherness and contradictory subject positions.

The concept of relational positionality should not be confused with pluralism, which always runs the risk, as Chandra Talpade Mohanty points out, of suppressing the analysis of structural power relations and systems of domination. American celebrations of diversity, she rightly argues, all too often domesticate difference and descend into an empty "discourse of civility" by presenting it in individualistic, personal terms ("On Race and Voice" 203). I do not mean to suggest that all positions are unique and "equal" within a menu of differences. Scripts of relational positionality foster neither pluralism nor identity politics based on a single collectivity. Rather, they acknowledge that the flow of power in multiple systems of domination is not always unidirectional. Victims can also be victimizers; agents of change can also be complicitous, depending on the particular axis of power one considers. This complicates analysis of power relations by insisting on identification of what R. Radhakrishnan calls a "totality" of the different constituent elements of identity (*Diasporic Mediations* 189). It complicates as well organizational strategies: around which collectivities can one organize political entities if everyone belongs to multiple groups? Nonetheless, scripts of relational positionality still open the door for dialogue, affiliations, alliances, and coalitions across racial and ethnic boundaries.

June Jordan's autobiographical essay "Report from the Bahamas" (1982) lends concreteness to my attempts to theorize scripts of relational positionality. As a deliberately self-reflexive and pedagogical narrative, the essay takes us through Jordan's discovery of how to read the complexities of relational identity in which no single system of domination determines the totality of experience. Jordan tells the story of how she, an African American of West Indian descent, harried by the demands of teaching at a New York public university, settles wearily into the Sheraton British Colonial Hotel in the Bahamas for a relaxing vacation. Denying her the pleasure of escape, the hotel greets her with markers of colonial, racial, and class history within which she—as black, West Indian, college professor, single mother, tourist—occupies contradictory subject positions. What does she share and not share with Olive, the maid who cleans her room, she wonders? In relation to race, they are connected; in relation to class, they are disconnected. She reflects: "even though both 'Olive' and 'I' live inside a conflict neither one of us created, and even though both of us therefore hurt inside that conflict, I may be one of the monsters she needs to eliminate from her universe and, in a sense, she may be one of the monsters in mine" (47).

Both the bond and the gulf between Jordan and Olive trigger reflections about fluid identities based in race, class, and gender. She recollects the bond she shared with a Jewish student who brought her Anzia Yezierska's *The Bread Givers*, a novel about a Jewish woman's immigration that resonated with her own experience. His love of Yiddish matched her own love of West Indian language. But the racial gulf opened suddenly when he said he did not care about the cutbacks in aid to college students, a policy that directly affected her son and many other African Americans. Jordan's experience of her own otherness in the white student's indifference interweaves with the otherness of Olive from whom she is separated by geography and class in spite of their shared race and ethnicity.

Such shifting positionalities form the basis, Jordan reflects, for life-saving connections made out of need and partial commonalities. She recalls such a connection she helped make between a white Irish American woman (Cathy), who had had an alcoholic, abusive father, and a black South African woman (Sokutu), whose alcoholic husband, Jordan's friend in the antiapartheid movement, was beating her to death. Power and powerlessness, privilege and oppression, move fluidly through the axes of race, ethnicity, gender, class, and national origin. In relation to race, Jordan and Sokutu were connected not only because of Jordan's activism in the antiapartheid movement but also because she "grew up terrorized by Irish kids who introduced me to the word 'nigga'" (48). But in relation to gender, the Irish and South African women had more in common than either had with Jordan because of their shared experience with battery. Shy because of their racial difference, Cathy reaches out to Sokutu to provide the help that Jordan cannot give her. "I walked behind them," Jordan remembers during her trip home from the Bahamas, "the young Irish woman and the young South African, and I saw them walking as sisters walk, hugging each other, and whispering and sure of each other and I felt how it was not who they were but what they both know and what they were both preparing to do about what they know that was going to make them both free at last" (49).

Like feminists before her, Jordan in "Report from the Bahamas" insists that we understand race, class, and gender as multiple and interlocking systems of oppression. But she writes against the grain of fundamentalist identity politics as she questions the use of race, class, and gender "as automatic concepts of connection" (46). "The ultimate connection" between people, she writes, "cannot be the enemy. . . . It is not only who you are, in other words, but what we can do for each other that will determine the connection" (47). She breaks through to a new story—a new multicultural feminist discourse—in proposing fluid identities that shift in focus depending upon situation and reference point and in mapping connections forged by different peoples struggling against complex oppressions. Her approach suggests the possibility of opening up the kind of impasse that tore apart Anzaldúa's class and that stymies so many feminist attempts to cross racial and ethnic boundaries.

Jordan is not alone in contemporary feminist discourse in promoting and performing relational thinking about identity. Others, here and there, speak in similar terms. Scripts of relational positionality are variously present in the work of such people as Gayatri Chakravorty Spivak, Sara Suleri, William Boelhower, Radhakrishnan, Meena Alexander, Papusa Molina, Jenny Bourne, Mary Louise Fellows, Sherene Razack, Arjun Appadurai, Ruth Behar, Eve Kosofsky Sedgwick, Aída Hurtado, Carole Boyce Davies, Minnie Bruce Pratt, Patricia Williams, Biddy Martin, and Chandra Talpade Mohanty—to name a sampling. Martin and Mohanty's "Feminist Politics: What's Home Got to Do with It?" (1986), for example, uses Pratt's autobiographical reflections in "Identity: Skin Blood Heart" (1984) to theorize "the fundamentally relational nature of identity" (196). As a white, lesbian southerner whose father and grandfather were town patriarchs, Pratt lives in a predominantly black community in Washington, D.C., where she realizes that every exchange with her African American neighbors is overdetermined by the politics of racial location. But her status as a lesbian— ever an outsider in her father's world—holds out some hope for the remapping of "community." Concerned that "white" or "western" feminism tends to "leave the terms of West/East, white/nonwhite polarities intact," Martin and Mohanty find in Pratt's essay resistance to "the feigned homogeneity of the West and what seems to be a discursive and political stability of the hierarchical West/East divide" (193). Although not theorized as such, some feminist theorists and teachers have begun to posit relational positionalities in which power circulates in multifaceted ways instead of flowing unidirectionally according to a white/other binary.

BEYOND WHITE/OTHER IN CONTEMPORARY NEWS MEDIA

In spite of the scattered existence of relational narratives in contemporary feminist discourse, the scripts of denial, accusation, and confession tend to dominate feminist classrooms, conferences, organizations, and research. This state of affairs is due partly, I believe, to the rise of racial polarization and nationalist/ separatist sentiment in the United States, developments that reflect the worsening socioeconomic health of inner cities and the growing racially inflected backlash against immigrants, the poor, and affirmative action—all symptomatically evident in the overwhelming, multiracial support for California's Proposition 187, aimed at eliminating aid for illegal immigrants, in the 1994 election.[25]

But I also believe that the repetitive round of denial, accusation, and confession among feminists is also partly the result of a degree of hermeticism in feminist theory itself, especially in the academy. I refer to the tendency of academic feminism to feed off itself, in spite of our interdisciplinarity—an insularity that is endemic to the development of intellectual fields of discourse. This aspect of the culture of the academy accounts for much of its insight, but also for some of its blindness to cultural praxis. In the United States, demographic and societal changes have converged to produce in the mass media an increasing number of relational scripts—far more than occur within feminist discourse. The mass media bombard us daily with varied cultural narratives about race, ethnicity, and racism—some structured by the white/other binary, but many constituted outside it. I suggest that we feminists, whatever our racial and ethnic standpoints, step outside our academic frameworks for a moment to see what surrounds us, to seek what might release us from the broken record of so many of our exchanges about race, ethnicity, and racism. In some ways a powerful avant-garde, we are in other ways behind the times.

Television, newspapers, magazines, and movies abound in narratives about racial/ethnic conflict and bridge building that exist outside the white/other binary. This is not to say that the white/other binary and narratives of denial, accusation, and confession do not exist pervasively in popular culture. They certainly do. (The campaign advertisements using Willie Horton in 1988 and promoting Proposition 187 in 1994 testify to that.) Even the celebrations of "diversity" encased in the metaphors of American pluralism—American culture as a gorgeous mosaic, tossed salad, stir-fry, stew, orchestra, patchwork quilt, symphony, or rainbow, for instance—contribute to the essentialism toward which some forms of identity politics tend. Such metaphors depend heavily on the senses—above all sight—which figure prominently in racialism in all its forms. Like a mosaic itself, they tend to fix everyone's difference in stone, safely bordered within impenetrable boundaries. Even the widely used term *multicultural* in its most common meanings operates as a code signifying nonwhite races and ethnicities, thus covertly reinstating the white/other binary.[26]

Nonetheless, the mass media also produce, reflect, and report narratives that refuse fixity, exhibit relational thinking, and operate beyond the white/other binary—narratives to which we academic feminists would do well to pay attention. I urge this immersion in mass and popular culture with some trepidation. First, feminist theorists seldom look to such sources for theoretical insight; rather, such cultural formations are more often a site for critique. Second, these cultural texts are highly mediated, subject to the demands of an increasingly globalized market, and prone to package "facts" and stories as commodities aimed at gaining the greatest possible market share. As is evident in the accounts of the Los Angeles upheavals, the news media often sensationalize stories, playing the "race card" for all it is (financially) worth. As Jimmie Reeves and Richard Campbell write in *Cracked Coverage*, the news media do not objectively report facts, but function "as a vital social force in the construction of reality, . . . the enforcement of norms, and the production of deviancy" (7). And in the Hollywood entertainment industry, the wider the audience, the more likely white perspectives define issues of race and ethnicity and the less likely people of color (especially women of color) shape the production of their own social realities.[27] Such mediations, particularly the economically driven ones, appear to make mass culture a poor source for theoretical insight.

Some cultural studies approaches to mass culture, however, refuse a reductionistic equation of media with ideology as a hegemonic force allied with power.[28] Instead, many critics insist that mass media texts can be read as sites of contested meaning in which producers, consumers, and various constituencies interpret events and stories in accord with different agendas and political standpoints. In writing of television representations of race, for example, television critic Herman Gray delineates "possible strategies of counter hegemonic readings, locations, and interruptions of television's domesticating power" ("Endless Slide" 194) and asserts that the meanings of such representations as *The Cosby Show* "are not given; rather, viewers define and use the representations differently and for different reasons" ("Television" 376). Although I acknowledge mass and popular culture as mediated articulations, I treat them as locations for wresting meanings about race and ethnicity beyond the white/other binary, meanings that feminists can use for progressive political and theoretical purposes.

Take, for example, newspaper accounts of events about race and ethnicity (sometimes inseparable from religion) for which the white/other binary offers only partial or no explanatory power. A brief catalog of stories (however mediated) that I have clipped from national and local newspapers since the events in Los Angeles forcefully suggests that we should broaden our understanding of racial and ethnic division.[29] These stories can potentially internationalize our understanding of othering as a global phenomenon that includes but cannot be reduced to white racism against nonwhite people. Some events reflect binary thinking in which neither side is "white"; others reflect racial or ethnic othering with more than two groups. All demonstrate how conflict over resources and power tends to be racially or ethnically inflected, whether racism/ethnocentrism is the cause or the effect of such conflict. I list these reports provisionally, not to argue for a transhistorical and universal racism, but in full recognition that each instance is historically specific, multilayered, and overdetermined. I do so strategically, in catalog form, to let the sheer weight of global events force us out of an exclusive focus on white/other in the context of the United States.

- The forty-eight ethnic wars being fought in Europe, Asia, Africa, South America, and the Middle East during 1993 (Binder).
- The Serbian use of systematic rape, concentration camps, and merciless shelling of besieged civilians as part of its "ethnic cleansing" of the Bosnian Muslims—this, in the context of a three-way ethnic/religious war rooted in centuries of conflict, evident not so long ago in the Croat and Bosnian Muslim genocidal extermination of hundreds of thousands of Serbs during World War II.
- Clan warfare in Somalia that led to millions of deaths by starvation.
- The long-standing conflict between the majority Hutus and minority (but traditionally dominant) Tutsis in Rwanda that flared up into the killing of some half million people in April and May of 1994, this on top of the murder of some 100,000 Tutsis and Hutus in Burundi in 1993.
- Fundamentalist Hindu destruction of a sixteenth-century mosque at Ayodhya (supposedly the site of a Hindu temple destroyed with the Muslim conquest of India)

that led to thousands of deaths, especially in pogroms against Muslims in Bombay.

- The Israeli-Palestinian conflict in which the victims of anti-Semitism become victimizers of cousin Semites, in which each victim group lashes out against the other for who they are, in which attempts at peace are regularly subverted by violence on both sides.
- The racial/ethnic/political cauldron in South Africa among Zulu, Hxosa, South Asian, "coloreds," Afrikaaners, Jews, and other whites of British or European descent.
- The seventy-six areas of ethnic strife emerging after the breakup of the Soviet Union, including the Armenian and Azerbaijani hostilities.
- The Protestant/Catholic violence in Northern Ireland, rooted in a centuries-old English racial and ethnic prejudice against the Irish.
- Kuwaiti abuse of Asian women who enter the country as domestic workers.
- Conflict between the Buddhist Tamils and Hindu Sinhalese in Sri Lanka.
- Long-standing racism of the Japanese against the Koreans, evident most vividly in the recent exposure of the Japanese use of Korean women as "comfort women" held captive in camps for sexual exploitation by Japanese soldiers during World War II.
- Resurgence of anti-Gypsy, anti-Jewish, and anti-"foreign" feelings in Germany and Eastern Europe.
- Ethnic strife between the Katangans and the Kasai in Zaire.
- Clan conflict in China, as well as Chinese racism against its African students and the Chinese policy of wiping out Tibetan culture in its occupation of Tibet.
- Divisions between the Spanish-Indian Mestizos and the British-Indian-African Creoles of Belize.
- The uprising in Chiapas, Mexico, heavily inflected with conflict between indigenous Indians and the dominant *mestizos*, of mixed Spanish and Indian descent.
- The complicated multiethnic, decades-old war in Myanmar (formerly Burma) among the ethnic Burmese, Kachin, Wa, Kikang, Palaung, Shan, and other groups.
- Three-way divisions threatening national unity among the First Nation peoples, the Euro-Canadians of British descent, and the Quebecois in Canada, increasingly complicated by extensive immigration from East Asia, South Asia, and the Caribbean.
- Conflicts between African Americans and Korean Americans in Los Angeles and Brooklyn, between African Americans and Latinos in Los Angeles, between Latinos and Asian Americans in Los Angeles, between African Americans and Cuban Americans in Miami, and between African Americans and Jewish Americans in Crown Heights. This, in the context not only of the structural foundations of white racism in the United States, but also of a 1994 survey showing that "minorities held more negative views of other minorities than do whites." (Holmes)[30]

The point of this catalog is not to fetishize racial and ethnic conflict. The news media tend to report, even sensationalize, racial and ethnic violence and to ignore efforts at building bridges across cultural divides. Douglas Martin's *New York Times* story of the Korean-American Grocers Association of New York, which now sponsors scholarships for African American students, is a rare exception to the focus on violence. So also are such examples as the plea for "rooting out the unfortunate link between ethnicity and the bogeymen" by Sri Lankan poet Indran Amirthanayagam in the *New York Times*; a PBS documentary on Malaysia, which includes a segment on not only the 1969 race riots but also a joint business school effort by a few Chinese and Malays to move beyond the racial hatred and distrust that divides their society; and a CNN feature on the village in Northern Ireland, home of an IRA terrorist whose bomb killed a little boy, that produced a Christmas play in the boy's home town as a peace offering. The U.S. news media's focus on ethnic violence around the world may well function as a commodified displacement of violence at home, mostly perpetrated by the institutions of white racism. The covert effect of such mediated reporting might feed white paranoia about racial others and ease white guilt about racism in the United States.

But as sites of contested meaning, these news reports can also be read as forceful disruptions of the white/other binary. Thick descriptions of some of the events behind these reports reveal some continuing effects of white and western racism. As colonial rulers, for example, the Belgians issued ethnic identity cards in the 1930s to the majority Hutus and minority Tutsis, groups between whom the physical differences were so insignificant that "ownership of cattle became the basis for ethnic classification—an owner of 10 or more cattle became a Tutsi," whom the Belgians made their middlemen (Bonner, "Once Peaceful Village"). But the slaughter in Rwanda cannot be explained solely in terms of Belgian colonialism since the notion of biological difference between Hutus and Tutsis has explanatory power for many Rwandans today, indeed enough cogency to justify murder. As one woman told a reporter, "They said, 'You are Tutsi, therefore we have to kill you'" (Bonner). When power is at stake, as it is in Rwanda, people often resort to ethnic and racial othering to explain and justify conflict. Whether as cause or effect of conflict, racial and ethnic division is a global phenomenon where people compete for resources. Such global instances of othering shatter the fixity of the white/other binary as exclusive explanation for all racial and ethnic conflict.

Some theorists and critics regard race and ethnicity as constructions of western culture, particularly post-Renaissance conquest and post-Enlightenment imperialism. I share their constructivist view of racial and ethnic classifications as products of culture, not absolutes of nature. I acknowledge as well that western science, especially in the nineteenth century, systematized racial and ethnic classifications to an extraordinary, indeed obsessive, degree, a development that provided ideological rationales for imperialism, slavery, various legal apartheids, anti-immigration laws, and other forms of racial and ethnic stratification. But the notion that the West invented racial and ethnic classifications and their institutionalization or has been the only culture to engage in such otherings is highly ethnocentric, itself an embodiment of the white/other binary.[31] To cite some counterexamples, the Chinese, according to Frank Dikötter, had a fully developed concept of racial difference and hierarchy before contact with the West. Many people believe that the caste system in India originated in hierarchical divisions based on or significantly accompanied by color variations produced in the wake of the Aryan invasion of the Dravidian people on the Indian subcontinent, a view supported by the Hindu word for caste, *varna*, which also means "color."[32] A Somali saying reported in relation to clan conflict applies more generally to the shifting collectivities of human society: "My clan against the enemy, my family against the clan, my brother and I against my family, me against my brother" (Ozanne, "Old Clan Rivalries").

I am not proposing a homogenized, universal, static, transhistorical, primal, or biologically deterministic view of conflict based in ethnocentrism. Each form of "centrism" clearly takes on historically specific forms and can be understood only through a synchronic and diachronic thick description of any given society. But the capacity of human societies to engage in a kind of us-against-them thinking is global—not, in my view, because of some genetic feature of the human species, but because of the competition for resources, power, and position as a central ingredient in the production of racial and ethnic othering.[33] The white/other binary has a powerful explanatory power in some contexts, but it does not encompass countless narratives about race and ethnicity worldwide that appear daily in our newspapers and on our television screens. Internationalizing our thinking on these issues can contribute to breaking the logjam in our discourses about race and ethnicity in the United States.

RELATIONALITY IN POPULAR CINEMA

Contemporary popular film, like newspapers, is an arena of representation in which the white/other binary of race relations is often shattered. Like many other mass culture artifacts, films package, commodify, market, and disseminate "race" and "ethnicity" as social constructs. As a site of contradiction (like fictional narrative), film potentially subverts and reinscribes racism—simultaneously working through and containing widespread anxieties about difference. It both allows and co-opts expression of taboo anger. It both imagines utopian desire for connection and underlines its impossibilities. Rather than seek a single meaning—particularly the meaning—of a given film, I see a film text as a site for negotiating meanings that might well function both regressively and progressively, depending on who is doing the reading and for what purpose. I want to discuss two such films, both of which show limited insight about gender (feminist theory is certainly more advanced in this regard) but provide fascinating explorations of relational identity from which feminists can learn a great deal. Mira Nair's realist romance *Mississippi Masala* (1991) and Neil Jordan's postmodern *The Crying Game* (1992) were produced outside the mainstream Hollywood film industry but nevertheless "caught on" to achieve popularity and success far beyond initial expectations.[34] This success—like that of such other recent films as *The Wedding Banquet, Fried Green Tomatoes, Secrets and Lies*, and *Farewell, My Concubine*—may reflect the way that race and ethnicity titillate and "sell" in today's market. But it may also reflect how the relational narratives and utopian desire for cross-racial connection in both films tap into a longing for new ways to think about race beyond the white/other binary.

In providing relational readings of the films' transgressive bordercrossings, it is not my intent to present here a full analysis of the richly layered cultural narratives in these films, to produce a cultural studies analysis of the production and consumption of these representations, to offer a feminist reading of their gender politics, nor to hold each film up as a perfect example of relational thinking. I offer instead a reading that intends to make more visible to feminists the potentialities of relational thinking about race and ethnicity, with full awareness that the gender and racial politics of both films are nonetheless open to critique.[35]

Mississippi Masala centers around a love story between an Indian American woman and an African American man living in Greenwood, Mississippi, in 1990—a new take, with a happy ending, on the old plot of *Romeo and Juliet* and its more recent avatar in *West Side Story*. Mina, an obedient young woman of twenty-four, lives and works in a motel with her parents, is pressured by her mother to marry and by her father to go to college; Demetrius passed up college after his mother's death, runs his small carpet-cleaning business out of a truck, and takes care of his father, Willie Ben, and his brother, Dexter. Living in the United States, both Mina and Demetrius are figures of diaspora: she has never been to India and he has never been to Africa.

The film cuts back and forth between the sharply etched worlds of Mina and Demetrius, reproducing for a popular audience the ethnographic, documentary style of Nair's earlier films.[36] Mina belongs to the tight-knit community of Indian refugees who were forced to flee from Uganda when Idi Amin's black nationalist dictatorship outlawed the Indian immigrant class, which was as a whole much better off economically than were most black Ugandans. Trying to hold on to their religious and cultural traditions, experiencing the intergenerational conflict common to many American immigrants, they pursue the American dream of material success by living frugally and helping each other get started in businesses such as motels and liquor stores. Demetrius's world is the family-centered southern black community, where each of the African American characters images the considerable generational, gendered, and individual variation in black response to centuries of racism. In his community, the white/other binary is fully in play. The racist paternalism of the white restaurant owner and banker constitutes a backdrop of threat and humiliation countered by the strength of the black family, the hard work of people like Demetrius and Willie Ben, and the richness of black culture, clearly rooted in but distinct from African traditions.

The film undermines the white/other binary by exploding the unitary nature of the category of other while leaving the white power structure monolithically in place. The racism of white America is assumed, evoked with the occasional presence of synecdochal figures who function as reminders of a fixed, hostile, and racist power structure built on economic and political dominance over all people of color. But this power structure is not the narrative center of the film, which focuses on the racism, distrust, and longing for love that can exist between two different racial/ethnic groups. As lovers, Mina and Demetrius constitute a Mississippi masala—a mixture of spices—that is violently ruptured by the anger of the Indian community for whom intermarriage in America (as in Africa), constitutes a disgrace to family honor. Both the Indian and black communities come down hard against the lovers—the Indians against Mina for shaming her family by having sex with a black man, the African Americans against Demetrius for a variety of reasons, including what they see as his rejection of black women, as his desire for a light-skinned woman like Lisa Bonet (the actress who played Denise on *The Cosby Show*), as his foolishness for getting involved with a foreigner, or as his ambition in owning his own business. The Indian community, which has more collective economic power than the black community, retaliates by canceling all its orders for Demetrius to clean motel rugs; this in turn leads the banker to cancel his loan, to which Demetrius responds by filing a suit against one of the Indian motel owners.

The unity of "people of color" against white racism that another Indian had touted to Demetrius earlier in the film disintegrates into a bitter confrontation between Asian Americans and African Americans. "United we stand, divided we fall," sarcastically snorts Demetrius's friend Tyrone, who leaves in disgust for Los Angeles. The film's relational approach to race and ethnicity exposes the racism endemic in Indian culture, prejudice directed not only at African Americans but also at the darker-skinned people like Mina within their own cultural group. This conflict between two groups constituted as other by white society reveals the process of othering with which each of these groups regards the other. This represents a partial displacement of the white/other binary: the category of other explodes into its heterogeneous parts, while the category of whiteness remains fixed and monolithic.

The film's relational approach complicates the story of Indian racism, however. The film opens in Uganda with the terror and pain caused by Amin's decision in 1972 to "cleanse" the country of its Asian Ugandans. Mina's grandfather had immigrated to Uganda to work on the railroad; her father was born there and achieves considerable affluence as a lawyer—living out an African version of the American dream held by many immigrants, progress that leaves many black Ugandans disadvantaged (just as the success of immigrants from other groups to the United States has often been instrumental in keeping African Americans as a group from substantial advancement). What hurts the most is the loss of her father's closest friend, his black "brother" Okelo, who tells Jay that he must leave, that "Africa is for Africans, black Africans." Mina and her mother weep at the parting from Okelo while Jay refuses to say good-bye, hurt far more by Okelo's rejection and the loss of his homeland than the theft of his material goods and position.

As the love story unfolds, both Mina and her father are haunted by images of Uganda, flashbacks that underline how what happened in 1972 shapes the events in 1990. Mina's attraction to Demetrius begins at the Leopard Lounge, a black dance club whose sights and sounds echo—with a difference—some of the film's Ugandan scenes. Mina's love for Demetrius triggers memories of Okelo. As they make love on her birthday in Biloxi, Ugandan music plays on the soundtrack, and Mina remembers an earlier birthday in Uganda when her father's preoccupation with Ugandan politics makes him forget to sing "Happy Birthday." As

Demetrius sings "Happy Birthday," her longing for her father, Okelo, and Uganda merge, only to be brought up short by her nightmarish memory of finding the dead body of a black Ugandan covered by flies. Demetrius comforts her, but she cannot tell him about Uganda, just as she remained silent when his family asked why she left. She can only explain herself to him as "mixed masala": born in Africa of Indian descent, refugee in London for fifteen years, resident of Greenwood for three.

Mina's father is similarly unable to explain to Demetrius what he means by saying that he has forbid the relationship to "spare her the struggle." Unaware of the family's experiences in Africa, where Jay had been known for his criticism of Indian racism and his advocacy on behalf of black Ugandans, Demetrius accuses him of trying to act white. Ignorant of the long-standing racialism in Indian culture that pre-dates (and had been intensified by) British colonialism, Demetrius does not understand that in blocking the relationship, Jay is "acting Indian," that is, aligning himself with racist elements within his own tradition. But speaking out of his own racial location in the United States (a positionality that Jay likewise does not understand), Demetrius reflects the anger of African Americans who have been embittered by the Americanization of successive immigrant groups, a process that Toni Morrison describes as learning to say "nigger"—learning, in other words, to raise their own status by seeing African Americans at the bottom of a system of racial stratification.[37] Demetrius taunts Jay with the color of his own skin, only a shade lighter than his own, and angrily denounces the Indian community's destruction of everything for which he has worked so hard. Within an American context, as a member of a preferred minority (even "model minority"), Jay has the license to "act white." Like Mina before him, Jay cannot speak to Demetrius about the events in Uganda that at least partially govern his actions. Instead, memories of Uganda flood the silent Jay, especially Okelo's rejection, repeated in expanded form for the second time in the film: "'Go to London, Bombay.' 'Uganda is my home.' 'Not any more. African is for Africans, black Africans.'"

Jay tries to explain to Mina what he could not say to Demetrius: "After thirty-four years, what it came down to was the color of my skin. People stick to their own kind. I am only trying to spare you this pain." Mina responds by reminding him that Okelo risked his life to get Jay out of jail after he rashly spoke against Amin on the BBC. This act of love across racial barriers in Uganda validates her attempt to do likewise with Demetrius and foreshadows her decision to leave her family to be with him. Jay's subsequent return to Uganda to get back his home from a new regime sustains Mina's interpretation of Okelo's brotherhood. Jay learns that Okelo's help of his Indian "brother" cost him his life in 1972. The film ends with Jay holding a black Ugandan child who has reached out to touch his face as they watch a woman joyously dancing for a circle of admiring Ugandans. This utopic moment of racial and cultural communion fades out to the film's credits, which are twice interrupted by the brilliantly lit embrace of Mina and Demetrius—she in sparkling Indian dress, he in an African hat and shirt, both in a seemingly timeless space beyond racial division. Like all utopic moments, it leaves us with a lingering question about how long it can last in the "real" world of racial separateness, stratification, miscommunication, and silence. The very power of the film's depiction of conflict based in cultural and historical difference calls into question the happy ending of the lovers' future.

In *Mississippi Masala* cultural identity, privilege, and oppression remain fluidly open to redefinition in changing contexts. Although power based in white hegemony remains fixed, other power structures do not flow unidirectionally but rather circulate among the two racially other groups. In relation to most black Ugandans, the Indian Ugandans are both economically advantaged and politically vulnerable. In Uganda, the Indians refuse intermarriage, a point Nair emphasizes by having Amin's television diatribe against the racism of the Asians drone on in the background of Mina's birthday party. And as Jay himself points out moments before his arrest, the Ugandan Asians have focused entirely on acquiring wealth for their "own kind." "Amin is a monster of our own making," he tells his Asian friends. Yet expelled from their homeland, they too are victims of racism, as the black Ugandan soldier's brutal treatment of Mina's mother demonstrates. As immigrants in the United States, they are recipients of racist and culturally insensitive remarks, from black as well as white communities. But like other immigrant groups, their economic situation in relation to African Americans improves more rapidly. The Indian community uses its economic power to destroy Demetrius's business, but Demetrius's ignorance about the history of South Asians in Uganda leads him to misread the complexities of Jay's opposition to his relationship with Mina.

Calling into question the whole concept of race, the film probes the irony that Jay is more African than Demetrius, although Demetrius is the same "race" as the black Ugandans who expelled Jay from Africa. Conversely, the film through its structural parallels between Uganda and Greenwood highlights how Jay repeats with Demetrius the racism of which he himself was a victim in Uganda. And as a woman, Mina exists in a racially liminal position: as darker than her parents, Mina requires a higher dowry to get a good husband in the Indian community; in the black community, her lighter skin and long, straight hair make her ambivalently desirable, akin to light-skinned women with straight hair like Lisa Bonet. In relation to white society, both the Indian and African American communities experience racism as "people of color." But in relation to each other, the conditions of their privilege and alterity continually shift, dependent upon ever-changing reference points for judgment.

The Crying Game goes even further than *Mississippi Masala* to explode the fixity of the white/other binary. Where *Mississippi Masala* focuses on the (dis)connections between two groups that exist as other in relation to a fixed white society, *The Crying Game* calls into question the unitary concept of white (and its corollaries, European and western), as the film proliferates a dizzying array of shifting alterities. Gender and sexuality supplement race, ethnicity, and nationality as components of fluid identities. Set first in Northern Ireland and then London, the film narrates the Irish Republican Army's kidnap of a black British soldier (Jody), the relationship he forms with one of his IRA captors (Fergus), and the aftermath of Jody's death. Seduced into capture by a white woman (Jude) in the IRA, Jody weans Fergus from his fixed notions of good and evil through a human fellowship that Fergus cannot resist. Their friendship across racial, cultural, and political boundaries begins when Fergus has to remove the tied-up soldier's penis from his pants to help him urinate. The bond is cemented when Jody gives Fergus a picture of himself in cricket clothes with his beautiful lover, Dil, and extracts a promise that Fergus will find Dil if he dies. It culminates in Fergus's inability to shoot Jody at his commander's order. Jody dies in an attempted escape under the wheels of the British convoy—in part saved, in part killed by Fergus.

In fulfilling his promise, Fergus increasingly comes to occupy the position of the black soldier in London. His attempt to protect Dil becomes love, in part a displaced love for the man he could not protect or love openly. This love mutates first into revulsion when he discovers that Dil is a transvestite who is gendered female, bodied male, and then into an ambivalent continuation of desire and protectiveness. In the place of Jody, he plays "the gentleman" to Dil and eventually goes to jail in Dil's place for the murder of Jude, who tries to kill Fergus for failing to perform an IRA execution. The film concludes with Fergus telling Dil during jail visiting hours the symbolically important story about a frog and a scorpion that Jody had told him. The colonial subject becomes the captor, then the captured; the woman becomes a man, then a woman again. The heterosexual turns into the homosexual, then back into (at least the appearance of) the heterosexual. No identity is a fixed essence; no hierarchy is unchanging; every positionality is open to change in the processes of historical deconstruction and becoming.

The film's radical relationality shows how the position of otherness shifts according to one's comparative reference point. On the issues of race, ethnicity, and nationality, for example, Jody and Fergus are each—but differently—"(ambiguously) non-hegemonic," to echo Rachel Blau DuPlessis's resonant refrain for contradictory subject positions ("For the Etruscans"). Fergus is a colonial subject but also a white man; Jody is a black man but also a member of an imperial army. As a member of the Catholic minority in Northern Ireland, Fergus belongs to the group economically and politically dominated by the Protestant majority that Jody defends. But Jody tells Fergus that "he has been sent to the only place in the world where they call you nigger to your face" and tell you to "go back to your banana tree, nigger" (191).[38] From the point of view of the IRA, Jody is a member of an occupying army, but from Jody's perspective he is a victim of Irish racism and the IRA. Jody signed up for the army because he needed a job in racist England, yet Fergus gets a job immediately in London as a construction worker on an all-white crew. In relational terms, each occupies the position of racial/ethnic victim and victimizer in terms of the other.

Jody's association with cricket encapsulates these contradictions. Photos and surreal images of Jody in cricket whites flash repetitively on the screen, clashing his very dark skin against the very white uniform. As tropes, these cricket images juxtapose the aristocratic sport of the colonialists with the colonized's embrace of that sport as their own. Jody's love of cricket comes from his father, who taught him the game in Antigua, where "cricket's the black man's game" (191). But in

Tottenham, to which the family came from Antigua, the game is played by whites. Preferring the Irish game of furling, Fergus associates cricket with the colonizers, a point visually made as he watches English schoolboys play cricket from the scaffolding at his construction job.[39] Similarly, Fergus's gun functions as a trope that emphasizes the relational duality of his position. As colonial subject and IRA soldier, Fergus is relatively powerless to remove the British from Northern Ireland. But his gun brings him enormous power of life and death over individuals selected for leverage and execution. It is this power that his relationships with Jody and Dil convince him to renounce; and it is this power for which he atones when he accepts responsibility for Dil's crime of murdering Jude with the very gun he had used to terrorize Jody.

Gender and sexuality complicate the shifting power relations of race, ethnicity, and nationality in *The Crying Game*. Fergus thinks of himself as a heterosexual. Misled by Jody's clear references to Dil as a woman and deaf to his coded allusion to her ambiguous status, Fergus is repulsed by homosexuality, bisexuality, and transvestism. Occupying the position of heterosexual privilege, he wants fixed and clearly delineated categories: male/female, heterosexual/homosexual. But just as his essentialist notions of Irish victim and British oppressor break down in his relation with Jody, so he must face, in the form of Dil, the displacement of gender, sex, and sexuality binaries.

As a liminal figure of racial and sexual ambiguity, Dil exists between fixed categories of white and black, male and female, and functions in the film as a disruption of all rigid definitions. As such, she functions much like the figure of the modern "tragic mulatta" that, as Hortense Spillers notes, carries the potential for "neither/nor" ("Notes"). Gendered feminine, Dil is Jody's "girl" and then Fergus's. The revelation of Dil's male body shocks Fergus, not only because of his homophobia but also because of his belief in absolute sexual difference. Try as he might, he cannot quite stop loving Dil-as-woman and must forcibly remind himself that "she" is also "he." His demand that Dil cut her long hair, remove her makeup, and dress in the soldier's cricket whites is a ruse designed to protect Dil from the IRA, but it also represents his attempt to force Dil out of a feminine identification, as if the clothes and appearance could construct a masculine gender to go along with Dil's male body. This violation of Dil's gender, however motivated by protectiveness, recapitulates Fergus's earlier violence against Jody, whose clothes Dil now wears. At a covert level, dressing Dil in Jody's clothes may also act out what Fergus has been unable to admit: his own homoerotic attraction to Jody.[40] The film's final scene cuts sharply from the murder of Jude, performed by Dil in bobbed hair and Jody's cricket suit, to the jail's visiting room, where wives visit their incarcerated husbands. Dil's reasserted feminine gender as she occupies the position of wife in relation to Fergus gives the appearance of heterosexuality to their relationship. Dil's third transformation calls into question once again binary notions of fixed identities of gender, sex, and sexuality.

Yet the very conventionality of their positions in the visiting room, which maintains an unspeakable love within the closet of disguise, suggests as well a

melancholy return to fixed identities and roles, underlined by the film's fade-out
to the music for "Stand by Your Man." Fergus's retelling of Jody's story of the
frog and the scorpion breaks down the binaries of white/other and English/Irish,
but it can also be read as a sign of the film's covert return to essentialist fixities.
This story, which Jordan adapts from Orson Welles's film *Mr. Akadin* (1955),
tells how the scorpion begs a fearful frog to carry it across the river and then stings
it anyway. To the frog's query as to why the scorpion stung him when it meant
their death, the scorpion can only answer, "I can't help it, it's in my nature" (196).
The fable's use of the term *nature* (changed from Welles's use of the term *character*) appears to contradict the film's performance of identity as cultural construction.[41] Its invocation of the nature/culture binary in the film's final speech appears
to halt the narrative's relational deconstruction of fixed identities and agonistic
narrative at a moment of proverbial conventionality. On the other hand, the fable
can be read as an insistence on keeping both poles of the nature/culture binary
forever in play. However conventional they appear at the end, Fergus and Dil are
not what they seem, subtly emphasized by the fact that "Stand by Your Man" is
sung by Boy George. Moreover, Jody originally recites the fable to suggest that
connection across difference is possible. As a speech act in a murderous context,
Jody's telling begs Fergus to act according to his "nature," which Jody intuitively
knows is not that of a killer but of a man capable of love across conventional
racial and sexual boundaries.

The film's deconstruction of gender and sexual binaries can also be read as
nonetheless caught up within a gynophobic economy of desire. Jude is the film's
only significant biologically female character. Her position initially shifts between the white woman used as a sexual object to seduce a black man for political
ends to the white woman who enjoys power over others, evident when she
smashes Jody's face with Fergus's gun. Jody's response to Fergus—"Women are
trouble" (199)—sharply evokes a fixed cultural narrative of evil female sexuality.
Jude's transformation from a blond in a traditional Irish sweater into a brunette
sophisticate can be viewed as a trope for the disguise and performance constituent
of all identities in the film. But it also functions as a revelation of her fixed malev-
olence. For the rest of the film, Jude remains singularly evil. Like Eve, Pandora,
and Mata Hari, this dragon-lady-as-IRA-terrorist uses her sexuality and gender to
seduce men into death. Just as *Mississippi Masala* retains the category of white
as fixed and monolithic, *The Crying Game* covertly leaves the binary of male
subject/female other in place. We are left with the message that the only good
woman is a dead one. Dil as transvestite fills the position of "woman," whose
exchange between men (first as photo, then in the flesh) cements their relationship, a homoerotic twist to the exchange of women identified as central to male
bonding by Eve Kosofsky Sedgwick in *Between Men*.[42]

However partial the film's deconstruction of fixed binaries, *The Crying Game*,
like *Mississippi Masala*, promotes an existential leap of love across the bridge of
difference. Although *The Crying Game* ends on a less euphoric note than does
Mississippi Masala, its appeal to cross-cultural bonding is nonetheless visionary
and utopic. Allusions to the Christian mythos of love and sacrifice abound in the

film, countering the forces of division. When Jody asks Fergus to tell him a story
to ease the tension of his captivity, an ambivalent Fergus responds by citing a part
of Paul's famous letter about love in 1 Corinthians 13:11: "When I was a child...
I thought as a child. But when I became a man I put away childish things" (202).
Fergus misappropriates the context of the quotation—Paul's advocacy of love—
to suggest that as an IRA soldier he can no longer afford such "childish things"
as love, although the irony is that his love for Jody makes him unable to shoot on
command. As figures of suffering, sacrifice, and revelation, Jody and Dil echo the
story of Christ to become the means through which Fergus recovers Paul's vision
about the necessity of love expressed in the opening of 1 Corinthians 13, the verse
that Fergus does not directly quote: "Though I speak with the tongues of men and
of angels, and have not love, I am become as sounding brass, or a tinkling cym-
bal" (13:1). Fergus, in turn, occupies the position of symbolic sacrifice for Jody
and Dil as he fulfills his promise to the doomed Jody and goes to jail in Dil's
place.[43]

Their race (black or white) and their national identity (British or Irish) alternately construct Jody, Fergus, and Dil as privileged on the one hand and as marginalized on the other. Their capacity to love across these racial and national boundaries signifies their ability to occupy a liminal borderland between fixed identities
of black/white, British/Irish, homosexual/heterosexual. Dil, as the androgynous
figure moving between all these binaries, functions as the mark and agency of this
love. Like the romantic narrative of love in *Mississippi Masala*, the religious
narrative of love in *The Crying Game* (which also screens a homoerotic one) can
be interpreted as a retreat from political critique. But it can also be read as a
narrative of a desire for connection that counters the urge to separate along racial
and ethnic lines.

CONCLUSION

For feminists seeking to move beyond the repetitive rounds of denial, accusation,
and confession in our discourses about race and ethnicity, the specifically romantic and religious forms of utopianism in *Mississippi Masala* and *The Crying
Game* are not in themselves compelling. Both films, however, present the desire,
however utopian, to make connection across racial and ethnic division as a fertile
and vital part of human existence. They also provide us with the narrativization
of a theory of subjectivity based in relational positionalities in which power circulates in complicated ways rather than unidirectionally, in which contradictory
subject positions allow for the possibility of connection across racial and ethnic
boundaries. I believe that our growth as a movement academically and organiza-
tionally depends in part on the continued search for such relational scripts and for
a common ground that acknowledges but is not erased by difference.

Scripts of relational positionality cannot, I hasten to say, provide a simple cure
for the politics of race within and beyond the feminist movement. Categories of
thinking do not by themselves erase the materialities of racism and ethnocen-

trism. My own brand of feminism is too materialist and historicist to believe that a revolution in the linguistic/symbolic order can, by itself, transform the world. But discourses do have power, even material consequences. Cultural narratives do help construct as well as reflect power relations within and beyond the academy. The categories in which we think do perform cultural work within a larger dialectical context in which language and material reality interpenetrate.

The agency necessary for ethical and political change begins in what S. P. Mohanty describes as the human capacity to reflect upon the meaning of our actions in relation to larger systems of the social order. To cross the divide between Us and Them, he insists, involves being able to imagine the agency of those other from ourselves, to assume their capacity, like our own, to reflect upon and negotiate the shifting confinements and privileges of their multiply constituted positions (" 'Us' and 'Them' " 19–21). And for this task, we need flexible and nuanced categories of positionality that do not assume an always already constituted status of fixed power and powerlessness. Exclusive reliance on binary models of domination—however much explanatory power they have in certain circumstances—may well retard instead of hasten cultural and political transformation.

There are dangers for feminists in using scripts of relational positionality. Like discourses of "multiculturalism" and "diversity," emphasis on contradictory subject positions can all too easily collapse into the pluralism against which S. P. Mohanty and Chandra Talpade Mohanty both warn us, a pluralism that obscures the inequalities of power for different groups in the social order (S. P. Mohanty, " 'Us' and 'Them' " 25–26; Chandra Mohanty, "On Race" 203). Moreover, stressing the endless play of contradiction runs the risk, as Radhakrishnan points out, of making relationality "a pure concept, an end in itself" (*Diasporic Mediations* 189). Such Derridean deferral (*différance*) can inhibit concrete political action, which requires some patch of terra firma from which to advocate change and exercise agency. Fluidity displaces fixity, but as the frog/scorpion parable in *The Crying Game* demonstrates, fluidity can also bring drowning and flooding. Furthermore, the discourse of relationality borders at times on the rhetoric of a complexity and cultural relativism that can obscure important power differentials between individuals and peoples. The politics of endless deferral and deconstruction is not inherently progressive and can function regressively depending upon the use to which it is put and the point at which the deconstructor stops the chain of deferrals.[44]

Finally, the insight that relational narrative brings to the discourse of race and ethnicity potentially carries within itself a blindness of its own. An exclusive focus on relational positionality runs the risk of obscuring the continuing necessity for the scripts of denial, accusation, and confession. The historical conditions that led to these three cultural narratives continue to exist and thus to compel their ongoing circulation. Just as the white/other binary has continued cogency in the beating of Rodney King and its aftermath, just as the white/people of color binary has important explanatory power in the Los Angeles upheavals and reports of them, so the binary of white women/women of color continues to have relevance in some contexts. Moreover, discourses of relational positionality should not deflect attention and resources from the critically important archaeological and theoretical work being done to recover, reflect upon, and transmit the often lost or repressed narratives of peoples whose history and culture have been marginalized by the dominant culture.[45] Commitment to multiculturalism in the academy involves ongoing efforts in what Anthony Appiah and Henry Louis Gates call the essential task of producing the "local histories" of different racial and ethnic groups ("Identities" 625).

In spite of these potential difficulties, however, I strongly believe that narratives of relational positionality can play a vitally important role in feminist discourse in the 1990s and on into the twenty-first century. Relationality does not have to be a pure concept existing as an end in itself but can be a conceptual cornerstone of a political teleology and practice. It can help to break the logjam of belligerence and apology that paralyzes so many of our classrooms, organizations, and conferences, that appears formulaically in so many of our writings. To move beyond the repetitive tropes of denial, accusation, and confession, we need a discourse about race and ethnicity that can acknowledge the differences and locate the connections in a complexly constituted global multiculturalism that avoids ethnocentrism of any kind. We need a discourse that does not (re)construct a multicultural other with a covert equation of the term *multicultural* with non-white. We need a narrative that does not reinstate white as center and multicultural as margin.

Relational narratives can form the basis for what Radhakrishnan calls a new kind of "coalitional politics" based on "relationality as a field-in-process" ("Post-Structuralist Politics" 311). They make possible the route to a genuine connection between different kinds of people that June Jordan identifies as essential for real change. As she argues, this kind of connection emerges neither out of appeals to universality (scripts of denial), refusals of similarity (scripts of accusation), nor out of expressions of guilt (scripts of confession) but rather out of unions based on common experience and need: "The ultimate connection must be the need that we find between us. It is not only who you are, in other words, but what we can do for each other that will determine the connection" ("Report" 47). The kind of coalitions that Radhakrishnan and Jordan call for, that movies like *Mississippi Masala* and *The Crying Game* reach for, are based on relational narratives. They are not bridges made between fixed differences. Rather they go beyond absolute categories of pure/impure and oppressor/oppressed to work instead with the location of shifting positions of privilege and exclusion in global perspective. As Gates writes in "A Liberalism of Heart and Spine," "The challenge is to move from a politics of identity to a politics of identification. . . . A politics of identification doesn't enjoin us to ignore or devalue our collective identities. For it's only by exploring the multiplicity of human life in culture that we can come to terms with the commonalities that cement communitas. . . . We may be anti-utopian, but we have dreams, too" (17). The epigraph from Proverbs that opens Lisa

Albrecht and Rose Brewer's hopeful collection, *Bridges of Power: Women's Multicultural Alliances*, articulates the vital necessity of such dreams: "When there is no vision, the people perish" (vi).

A feminist multiculturalism that is global in its reach and configuration needs scripts of relational positionality that can supplement and be enriched by thick descriptions and local histories of racial and ethnic difference. Without these relational scripts, feminist classrooms, conferences, organizations, and writing run the politically dangerous risk of promoting a fundamentalist identity politics that can easily regress into binaries mirroring hegemonic racism: pure/impure, us/them, self/other. We cannot afford to give up the utopian dream of coalition and connection. As the globe shrinks, as racially and ethnically inflected confrontations increase worldwide, as weapons become ever more deadly and available, as transnational economies further polarize wealth and poverty, as U.S. demographics (like those of many other countries) move toward an even more multiracial and multicultural society, our survival as a species depends on our ability to recognize the borders between difference as fertile spaces of desire and fluid sites of syncretism, interaction, and mutual change. As June Jordan reflects during her flight home from the Bahamas: "I look about the cabin at the hundred strangers drinking as they fly and I think even here and even now I must make the connection real between me and these strangers everywhere before those other clouds unify this ragged bunch of us, too late" ("Report" 49).

"Beyond" Difference:
Migratory Feminism in the Borderlands

The future of our earth may depend upon the ability of
all women to identify and develop new definitions of
power and new patterns of relating across difference.
—*Audre Lorde*, Sister Outsider

Difference exerts an uncanny fascination for all of
us. . . . Difference(s) from others are frequently about
forming and maintaining group boundaries. The brutal
and bloody nature of this maintenance work
is everywhere in evidence.
—*Henrietta L. Moore*, A Passion for Difference

As an organizing principle, difference
obliterates relation.
—*Linda Gordon, "On 'Difference' "*

I was born between 2 heritages & I want to explore that empty space,
that place-between-2-places, that walk-in-2-worlds. I want to do it in a
new way.

—*Diane Glancy,* Claiming Breath

THAT PLACE-BETWEEN-2-PLACES, that walk-in-2-worlds: this is the space "beyond" difference that I want to explore for feminist theory and praxis. The "new
patterns of relating across difference" that Audre Lorde called for in 1980 are still
urgently needed as we cross the millennial border. For Lorde, angry with the
exclusions built into the search so common in the 1970s for a universal sisterhood, those new patterns involved recognizing the creative possibilities embedded in difference. "How do we redefine difference for all women?" she asked. "It
is not our differences which separate women, but our reluctance to recognize

those differences" (*Sister Outsider* 122). I want to suggest, however, that we go beyond the correct naming of our differences as the *sole* pattern of developing new relations. There are other pathways just as vital for feminism and more generally for the survival of our earth, other ways to undermine what anthropologist Henrietta Moore calls the often "brutal and bloody" maintenance work of boundary building (*Passion for Difference* 1). I believe that Lorde's approach needs to be supplemented with attention to the processes of *relation* in the place of betweenness that poet Diane Glancy writes about in *Claiming Breath*. These are the migratory movements in the spaces between difference, the movements implicit in Lorde's own phrase, *relating across* difference.

Exclusive focus on difference tends, as feminist historian Linda Gordon argues, to "obliterate" the interactive mediations between difference. It obscures the blending as well as clashing that takes place in the contact zones between difference.[1] Glancy's double heritage as Sioux and German leads to her assertion that to "claim breath," she must deny neither side and must instead explore "in a new way" the borderlands between them that she inhabits (4). Similarly, my project is to move feminism "beyond" theorizing difference to theorizing the spaces in between difference. I do not regard this movement as originary, especially since many poets and novelists like Glancy herself have already led the way. Rather, I want to examine the implications of recent theorizations of borders, travel, migrancy, global flows, hybridity, and creolization for feminist debates about difference. These concepts—developed mostly within cultural studies, postcolonial studies, anthropology, and geography (including feminist versions of these fields)—constitute a new geography of movement, of intercultural contact within the context of shifting power relations. What has not been examined systematically is their significance for feminist theorizations of difference, specifically for the way the discourse of difference itself has become a space of theoretical and activist "stuckness." The explanatory power for feminism of this migratory geography of borders moves simultaneously in two directions: the descriptive, delineating networks of existing syncretisms (positive and negative) in everyday life; and the utopic, forging pathways of possible connection, affiliation, and reconciliation. Both directions represent alternatives to an ever more meticulous reassertion of differences, a strategy that has resulted in what Mary Louise Fellows and Sherene Razack call "the difference impasse" ("Seeking Relations" 1051), what Alice Kessler-Harris regards as a "crisis" in coalition feminism produced by "dichotomous modes of thinking" in a "fierce attention to differences," and I have described in chapter 2 as the repetitive scripts of denial, accusation, and confession. After reviewing the achievements and limitations of the feminist discourse of difference in the United States, I will examine the desire to go "beyond" this discourse, as reflected in theories of play and in the performances of playwright Anna Deavere Smith; map the theorization of intercultural encounter and hybridity in cultural, postcolonial, and anthropological studies; locate Gloria Anzaldúa's *Borderlands/La Frontera: The New Mestiza* within this discourse; and, finally, return in conclusion after these excursions to the special sense in which I invoke the term *beyond* and to the question of feminist theory and practice in the future.

FEMINIST PASSIONS FOR DIFFERENCE

What Henrietta Moore calls "a passion for difference" has been foundational for some twenty-five years in North American feminist theory, political organizing, and activism, including their pedagogical and scholarly manifestations in the academy.[2] By "passion," I mean not only the acknowledgment of difference but also the commitment to difference as a (if not *the*) major explanatory paradigm mediating all analyses of gender. This passion is not innate to feminism, has not always been in evidence, is not necessarily operative in other national or transnational feminisms, and takes a very particular form in the United States that reflects the specificities of racial and ethnic formations in American history.[3] As Edward Said points out in "Traveling Theory," theories are historically produced, traveling through time and space as transplanted and translating phenomena, changing significantly in the process of particularization. It is important to understand the production of the feminist discourse of difference and its subsequent hegemony in the United States in this context, particularly as it travels to and is influenced by other parts of the world for subsequent translation and adaptation.

The twin pillars of feminist difference discourse in the United States—women's difference from men and the differences among women—evolved in tandem, feeding off of each other, often more contentiously than harmoniously, but each necessary to the other. In her essay "On 'Difference,'" Linda Gordon (among others) has already provided the outlines of this story that I review here only to highlight its underlying privileging of difference. Broadly speaking, the initial stress on sexual or gender difference in the late 1960s and the 1970s gave way by the 1980s and 1990s to an emphasis on differences *among* women, a shift increasingly distinguished with the terms second and third wave feminism.[4] The result has been the development of a multicultural feminism that has seen its greatest effects in the transformation of knowledge in the academic and publishing arenas.

The first difference discourse in North American feminism arose out of the early exhilaration in defining common ground among women as the second wave of feminism erupted in the late 1960s. It quickly evolved into a full-scale critique of the sex/gender system and a theory of women's difference from men. Feminists did not agree on what produced this difference—whether it was biology, history, or some combination of nature and nurture. But across the spectrum of biological, materialist, and culturalist explanations, the axiomatic assumption of gender difference as primary category for analysis and activism prevailed.[5] The transplantation of French poststructuralist theory into the American academy in the late 1970s and 1980s both intensified and altered this emphasis on women's difference from men.[6] Various forms of poststructuralist linguistic constructivism shifted attention to the symbolic order, to the mediated processes and politics of representation, to "experience" as an effect (rather than producer) of discursive systems, and to the problematic instability of categories like woman/man, feminine/masculine, and identity. Lacanian, Barthesian, and Derridean versions of a "passion for difference" base their deconstruction of western humanism on a dismantling of the binary structure of language and thought preeminently (even transcendentally) represented by the gender pair of masculine/feminine. I risk homogenizing the rich array of French critical theory only provisionally, to make the point that its influence in American academic feminism in the 1980s—mediated particularly through the work of Hélène Cixous, Julia Kristeva, and Luce Irigaray—was to reinforce (and at times essentialize) the already dominant discourse of gender difference.[7]

Nipped in the bud by the rise of both American and French feminist discourses of sex/gender difference was an early formation of feminist humanism theorizing the yearning for or the ongoing existence of androgyny, by which second wave feminists meant some form of gender blending, fusion, or interplay of masculine/feminine. Evident in such widely influential texts as Woolf's rediscovered *Room of One's Own*, Adrienne Rich's poem "Diving into the Wreck" (1973), Carolyn Heilbrun's *Toward a Recognition of Androgyny* (1973), and Sandra Bem's psychological studies of existing androgynous behaviors, the feminist concept of androgyny emphasized the potential or real sameness of men and women, the capacity of each to fuse or combine elements of the masculine and feminine into a wholeness lacking in the purely masculine or purely feminine. But with the growing influence of the sex/gender difference discourse, the term androgyny became increasingly taboo, especially when former advocates like Rich publicly repudiated it. "These are the words I cannot choose again: / *humanism   androgyny*," Rich writes in "Natural Resources" four years after her poet-diver dove into the wreck of civilization to uncover her buried androgynous self. Insisting on difference, Rich abandons humanist androgyny: "Such words have no shame in them, no diffidence / before the raging stoic grandmothers" (*Dream* 66). What Rich and other influential theorists like Mary Daly and Elaine Showalter expressed through their attacks on the term was the historical necessity for feminism to organize politically around the nature and effects of sex/gender difference within the context of male/masculine domination.[8] This political imperative combined with the increasingly influential difference discourse of poststructuralism to establish the American feminist emphasis on sex/gender difference.[9]

The second feminist difference discourse in the United States, that emphasizing the differences among women, developed out of the belief that women's oppression and liberation could never be understood solely in terms of gender. This insistence on "double jeopardy" or "multiple oppression"—articulated particularly by black women—was present from nearly the very beginning of second wave feminism, although in tokenized and frequently ignored form, especially in arenas dominated by white and/or heterosexual feminists.[10] Racism, ethnocentrism, homophobia, and class bias remained pervasive in the sex/gender feminist difference discourse of the 1970s—whether intentional, unconscious, insensitive, ignorant, patronizing, or well meaning. What began as scattered challenges intensified into often angry and organized confrontations in which women of color, lesbian women, Jewish women, Third World women, and working-class women demanded attention to differences among women as a top priority for feminism. It is these differences that Lorde so eloquently theorized in a series of widely influential essays collected in *Sister Outsider*, insisting that differences of race, class, and sexuality should not be ignored, should not be reduced to the "problem" of feminism's "other," but should be treated as a source of creative empowerment for feminism. The early emphasis on women's shared identity based in their universal difference from men slowly gave way in the 1980s to an often conflicted and painful examination of the differences among women. Given the long and brutal history of racial stratification in the United States, this difference discourse has often developed its greatest intensity around issues of "color," as reflected in a central binary in U.S. feminism—women of color/white women. The urgency of racism as an issue in the American context has at times contributed to the marginalization or invisibility of other forms of difference, both in the United States and elsewhere.[11]

The way in which the sex/gender and multicultural threads of difference discourse in United States feminism were to weave uneasily and irregularly together in the 1980s and 1990s was symptomatically present in the 1980 collection edited by Hester Eisenstein and Alice Jardine, *The Future of Difference*, which patched together attention to both forms of difference discourse. The book's title was prophetic, even if its contents were heavily weighted in favor of sex/gender difference. By 1992, Christina Crosby could write in "Dealing with Differences" with a more integrated approach to poststructuralist, materialist, and multicultural theorizations of difference: " 'Difference' has become a given of academic feminism; feminism has been modified and pluralized. . . . It would seem that dealing with the fact of difference is *the* project of women's studies today" (131).[12] The achievements of this project are profound; its impact is everywhere apparent in the arena of academic feminism, the site where activism takes the form of the transformation and dissemination of knowledge. The discourse of sex/gender difference is institutionalized in the existence of women's studies in both its separate and mainstreamed forms; gender has become a legitimate field of inquiry across the disciplines to a degree that could scarcely have been imagined twenty-five years ago. The plurality of multicultural feminisms is pervasive not only in women's studies but also in cultural studies, postcolonial studies, ethnic studies, and gay and lesbian studies.

What concerns me is the shift in difference constituting *a* project to becoming *the* project of academic feminism—the development, in other words, of difference as *the* privileged or only legitimate lens through which to examine the cultural and material meanings of gender. What gets lost, forgotten, or suppressed in the exclusivity of the project of difference? In the feminist rush to delineate difference, the limitations of this strategy as an exclusive focus for feminist theory tend to be ignored. Alice Kessler-Harris's prescient warning in 1992 remains relevant to current debates: "I sense that we are facing a crisis. Stifled by an ill-defined but insistent wish to overcome our increasingly fragmented vision of women, our best energies are turned to self-examination. Our politics revolves around internal struggle instead of coalition against the nexus of sexism and racism that structures our world. . . . This fierce attention to differences leaves us vulnerable to vitriolic attacks from the neoconservatives" ("View from Women's Studies" 800–801). Like Kessler-Harris, I am not calling for a return to a theory of universal woman-hood, sisterhood, or gender. I agree profoundly with the foundational principle of multicultural feminism that gender must be interactively understood in relation to other societal stratifications and multiple constituents of identity. I still accept the basic premise of much feminist writing on difference that in order to build lasting coalitions, at least in the context of the United States, differences need to be examined and incorporated into the search for common ground.[13] The issue I raise, however, is how the exclusivity of difference discourse in feminist theory and practice inhibits or prevents us from examining the equally vital and real longings for connection in between difference and the everyday realities of how ever-changing cultural formations involve what is variously called hybridization, creolization, syncretism, or transculturalization.

By way of illustration, I want to consider the fascinating lyrical opening of the theoretical essay "On the Logic of Pluralist Feminism" (1991) by the Argentinian feminist philosopher María Lugones, who has lived in the United States since 1967. The essay itself is one among many eloquent calls for more attention to the differences among women produced in the past twenty years. But the preamble to this demand gestures at what she knows she has suppressed in the political need to claim attention for difference, particularly racial difference among women.

> I wrote this paper from a dark place: a place where I see white/anglo women as "on the other side," on "the light side." From a dark place where I see myself dark but do not focus on or dwell inside the darkness but rather focus on "the other side."
>
> To me it makes a deep difference where I am writing from. It makes a profound difference whether I am writing from the place of our possibilities as companions in play or from the place "in between," the place of pilgrimage, or true liminality; from the place of La Raza, la gente de colores, the place "within," or from across "the other side" where light and dark are highlighted.
>
> I inhabit the place from across "the other side" with anger, pain, urgency, a sense of being trapped, pounding the walls with speech that hurts my own ears. It is from across "the other side" that I want to explore the logic of pluralist feminism. ("Logic" 35)

Lugones's statement needs to be read carefully, like a poem, for its binary rhetoric depends not on the logic alluded to in her title but on a rhetorical pattern of images separated by an obscure semicolon in the middle and highlighted through quotation marks that undermine the fixity of the binary even as they affirm it. There are two places from which she could write, Lugones explains. One is the place where she sees the opposition of light and dark, the binary of white/

anglo women and dark women of color. From this standpoint, what she sees is racial difference between women, separating women into irrevocable "sides," specifically making white/anglo women "the other side," the "other" who enrages her "dark" self, makes it feel trapped, causes her speech to pound the walls of racial confinement. Such speech is a pounding that "hurts my own ears." This is in fact the place from which she writes the essay attacking the false pluralism of a (white) feminism that does not yet "get" the signficance of (racial) difference. This is "the place of La Raza, la gente de colores," the place from which the difference between "light and dark"—racial difference—is starkly etched.

What precedes the semicolon, however, what the lyrical preamble testifies to, is what Lugones has to suppress in the essay that follows: "the place of our possibilities as companions in play or from the place 'in between,' the place of pilgrimage, or true liminality." This site of open possibility, companionship, and play across the racial divide remains utopic for Lugones in this essay, a luxury she believes she cannot afford given the realities of racial power that separate white women and women of color. The binary of white women/women of color in the essay that follows remains absolute, without a liminal in between. Anger and the racism that causes her anger make the lyric possibilities of the space in between impossible, leaving her trapped in an echo chamber in which her words seem to bounce back in attack. The preamble expresses a lyric sense of loss for the utopic play she cannot risk, a nostalgia that functions as the countercoin side of regarding the space in between as miscegenation, a mixing that taints or pollutes.

But must we regard the liminal space in between difference as *merely* utopic, an unaffordable luxury, a lyric impossibility, a dream without realities, a myth without historical referent? The utopian aspect of "companionship" and "play" in the space between racial differences is undeniable. The realities of the unequal distribution of power based on group identifications construct a "fall" into difference that inevitably poses the liminal as a dream variously characterized as visionary, naive, or even traitorous to one's group (one's gender, race, nation, religion, class, and so forth). But what are the consequences of dismissing the visionary as irrelevant in a world through which power circulates unequally? "Nothing happens in the 'real' world," Gloria Anzaldúa writes, "unless it first happens in the images in our heads" (*Borderlands* 87). Utopic longing has a psychological reality that is a fundamental component of social change; it fuels the drive for a better world, the agency to resist. "I have a dream," begins Martin Luther King's most famous speech articulating the desire for social justice. Moreover, companionship and play are not the only possible positive interactions in the space between. There is also the desire for mutual understanding, for connections based on need, for coalition or affiliation, however provisional. As June Jordan warns apocalyptically in "Report from the Bahamas," human survival depends upon making connections: "I must make the connection real between me and these strangers everywhere before those other clouds unify this ragged bunch of us, too late" (49). Dreams and visions, however unlike the "real" world, can have powerful material effects and often serve as a force for resistance. They are not a luxury. Indeed, we cannot afford to abandon them.

Playing "Beyond" Difference

Passion for difference exists in symbiotic relation to a passion for mixing. Resistance to the impurity of the other is inseparable from desire to mingle with the other. In "On the Logic of Pluralist Feminism," Lugones's lyric longing to cross beyond the barrier of what Paul Gilroy calls "ethnic absolutism" in *The Black Atlantic* and her resistance to doing so encapsulates these competing passions. In a subsequent essay, "Purity, Impurity, and Separation" (1994), Lugones points out how the fear of and desire for mixing rests on a racialized binary of purity/impurity. In the complex metaphorics of this elusive essay, she turns to cooking with eggs to explain this opposition. Separating the yolk from the (egg)white represents the desire for purity, the fear of the colored other; mixing yolk with water and oil in the making of mayonnaise signifies the impurity of mixing, particularly when the oil-in-water emulsion curdles, refusing absolute fusion in a retention of the instability of mixing, in the production of "yolky oil and oily yolk" (459). *"This writing is done,"* Lugones explains in a preamble, *"from within a hybrid imagination, within a recently articulate tradition of latina writers who emphasize mestizaje and multiplicity as tied to resistant and liberatory possibilities"* (458). Claiming the privileged space of hybridity for people of color—specifically, latina writers—Lugones associates anglo/whiteness with desire for purity and control ("the categorical eye" [460]) and latina/color with *mestizaje* and resistance. In moving beyond pure difference, she ends up reinstating it, returning to the absolute barriers between white and color.

But what if we take the step Lugones is unwilling to take in this essay, to recognize with Gilroy (among others) that *all* groups, including racialized others, participate in a dialogic of difference and mixing, however various the motives and outcomes within the context of power relations? Lugones is insistent on separating her commitment to *mestizaje* and multiplicity from the postmodern, claiming that postmodern writing "goes against a politics of identity and toward minimizing the political significance of groups" (475).[14] But what if we embed postmodern theorizing on the play of signification in the construction of all identities in a thoroughly locational understanding of how such play interacts with the specificity of a given social order, including its structures of power? In resisting the ethnic or gender absolutism that often underlies the dominance of feminist difference discourse, we can, perhaps, begin to play with and thus "beyond" difference.

As a first step in such play, we need to restore the suppressed principle of sameness to a discussion of identity. The urge to imitate, anthropologist Michael Taussig argues in *Mimesis and Alterity* (1993), has too often been ignored in the critique of ethnography's formation around the binaries of self/other, civilized/savage. Ethnography's inscription of difference, he asserts, is inseparable from "the mimetic faculty" of imitation endemic to the human species: "the faculty to copy, imitate, make models, explore difference, yield into and become the Other" (xiii). Alterity—and its manifestations in the institutions of power—cannot be understood separate from its counterpoint in mimesis. One implication of Taussig's work for feminism is that theorizing difference (women from men; among women) has too often attempted to isolate difference from sameness.[15] This is, I believe, the import of Henrietta Moore's belief that sameness is undertheorized in feminist work, focused as it has been on the explosive issue of difference:

> This passion for difference seems to be linked to its unspoken and undertheorized pair, "the same" or "sameness." . . . Thinking about difference entails, then, thinking about identity and/or sameness. . . . Identity and difference are not so much about categorical groupings as about processes of identification and differentiation. These processes are engaged for all of us, in different ways, with the desire to belong, to be part of some community, however provisional. Belonging invokes desire, and it is in this desire that much of the passion for difference resides. (*Passion for Difference* 1–2)

Moore points to the contradictory nature of the term *identity* itself, a word that means "sameness", but that has often been put solely to the task of defining difference from the other or others, as in identity politics. As I have discussed in chapter 1, the term *identity* has a double and contradictory resonance. On the one hand, *identity* means sameness, as in the word *identical*, and involves the perception of common qualities. A person's identity as a woman, or a Chicana, or Jew, or Japanese, or lesbian—for example—emerges out of an identification with others in that group. This requires the foregrounding of one aspect of identity and a backgrounding of others in an emphasis on what is shared with others in that group. On the other hand, *identity* requires a perception of difference from others in order for the recognition of sameness to come into play. The category woman depends upon the category man for its meaning; knowing herself Chicana involves knowing herself as not Chicano, not Japanese, not Anglo; a Jew is not Christian, Muslim, Buddhist, or Taoist; a lesbian identity in 1997 develops in contrast to heterosexual and bisexual identities. None of these categories, of course, is fixed in a priori fashion; all are produced in history and undergo change. But the formation of any category of identity involves equally a symbiotic perception of sameness with some and difference from others. As Moore writes, "Deciding on difference is one way of delineating identities. Difference(s) from others are frequently about forming and maintaining group boundaries" (1). What this means for the hegemony of difference discourse in feminist theory (especially differences among women) is that attention focuses on communal identifications based on sexuality, race, ethnicity, nation, religion, or class (etc.) at the same time that it promotes the splitting apart of a group identity based on gender alone. In so doing, difference discourse tends to suppress attention to sameness produced in the liminal spaces in between racial, ethnic, sexual, class, religious, or geopolitical difference.

What I mean by playing with and beyond difference, then, does not involve abandoning the concept of difference in a rosy aura of imagined sameness or (feminist) sisterhood. It involves instead restoring the concept of sameness to a consideration of difference, recognizing the enmeshing of mimesis and alterity. It means traveling back and forth in the space in between difference, understanding how that space is charged with the magnetic energy (both positive and negative) of mixing and separation. Although such play may incorporate a Derridean *différance*, I do not want to suggest that playing with or beyond difference means merely the instability of sliding significations, where words refer only to other words in a chain of deferrals. A theoretical playing with signification that is cut off entirely from the referential aspects of language is in my view ahistorical and politically regressive. Rather, I am saying that the interplay of cultural markers of identity depends upon an oscillation of sameness and difference that is historically embodied within the context of complex power relations.

Curiously, María Lugones in an earlier essay articulates a notion of play and travel that moves well beyond ethnic or gender absolutism, beyond the isolated focus on difference. In "Playfulness, 'World'-Travelling, and Loving Perception" (1987), she allows herself to imagine the possibility of play across racial (and other) divides, basing her notion of play in the acknowledgment of how individuals occupy many "worlds" simultaneously and frequently "travel" through them and the partial identities they evoke. In defining what she means by play, she refuses an agonistic model in favor of a noncompetitive and thus potentially "loving" interaction that "involves openness to surprise, openness to being a fool, openness to self-construction or reconstruction and to construction or reconstruction of the 'world' we inhabit playfully" (401). Such an attitude is essential, she argues, for white/anglo women and women of color to interact lovingly. She also associates playfulness (here and in "Hablanda cara a cara" [1990]) with a form of Du Boisian double consciousness, an ability necessary for women of color to see "the double edges" of stereotyped and self-defined representations, to recognize "a plurality of selves" based in the different "worlds" through which they travel, and to activate intentionally the different voices and languages of their multidimensional selves. Recognition of how "I am a plurality of selves" (398) is the bridge that allows Lugones to imagine traveling to the worlds of others: "Without knowing the other's 'world,' one does not know the other. . . . Through travelling to other people's 'worlds' we discover that there are 'worlds' in which those who are the victims of arrogant perception are really subjects, lively beings, resistors, constructors of visions" (402). Even in this essay, Lugones tends to fall back into the binaries of pure difference (anglo/latina; white/color; oppressor/oppressed), to have difficulty imagining that a white/anglo other might also be a "world traveller," might also be a "plurality of selves," or might merit being "travelled" to. Nonetheless, her notions of play and travel are highly suggestive for feminists looking to move beyond the difference impasse.

Such play is performative as well as dialogic. The mimetic faculty, as Taussig reminds us, is based on a form of imitative play or representational performance of the other. Identification with a cultural group is acted out or performed through a repetition of the behaviors and beliefs associated with a collectivity. As an "imagined community" (to echo Benedict Anderson), groups contain individuals who reiterate the normative patterns of the group with which they identify. Additionally, intercultural encounters in the contact zone between differences often lead to forced or willing, conscious or unconscious repetitions of the other, as a kind of performance, often with a difference. As Homi Bhabha writes, "Terms of cultural engagement, whether antagonistic or affiliative, are produced performatively. The representation of difference must not be hastily read as the reflection of *pre-given* ethnic or cultural traits set in the fixed tablet of tradition. The social articulation of difference, from the minority perspective, is a complex, on-going negotiation that seeks to authorize cultural hybridities that emerge in moments of historical transformation" (*Location* 2). This negotiation takes place in a "restless movement," a "hither and thither, back and forth" (1) that plays out a dialogic of "difference and identity" (1). To Bhabha's formulation here, I would add that it is not only "minorities" that engage in such negotiations. Dominant groups also act out a ceaseless movement back and forth between separation from and imitation of others, often with more power to do so.

The performative nature of both difference and identity is a key component of much recent queer theory, a link that is particularly relevant to the difference impasse in feminism because of its dismantling or disruption of sex/gender fixities. Where Taussig and Bhabha begin with the question of cultural difference, queer theory originates in an interrogation of sexual difference, examining the interrelations of gender and sexuality as systems of alterity and the way that gender b(l)ending and non-normative sexualities can denaturalize and transgress such systems.[16] In *Gender Trouble* (1990), a book that pre-dates but nonetheless helped launch the sudden appearance of "queer theory" as a movement and field of inquiry in 1991, Judith Butler argues doubly for the performative nature of gender: first, for the way in which gender is constructed through a series of repeated performances compelled by the regulatory practices of gender ideology; second, for the way in which the parodic performance of gender, as in drag, undermines essentialist notions of sexual or gender difference. The first kind of performance is largely compulsory; the second, frequently intentional. Both, however, undermine notions of fixed or stable gender identities upon which the feminist discourse of sex/gender difference was often founded. Based on the deconstructive mimicry that Irigaray theorizes and paralleling Bhabha's concept of colonial mimicry, the performance of drag in particular does more than imitate gender; it "dramatize[s] the signifying gestures through which gender itself is established" (*Gender Trouble* x).[17]

As forms of gender play, such expressive phenomena as drag, transvestism, and camp function both literally and figurally in queer theory as a return of the repressed concept of androgyny, which reemerges with a decidedly antihumanist, poststructuralist twist. Gone is the notion of human wholeness; in its place is exhuberant pleasure in parodic mixing and juxtaposition of gender and sexual differences as acts of transgression. Like Bhabha's notion of colonial mimicry, queer hybridities—whether performed by gays and lesbians, bisexuals, heterosexuals, or people who refuse sexual categorization—call into question the "natural" authority of difference and highlight the constructedness of all identity. Occupying the borderlands between male/female, masculine/feminine, heterosexual/homosexual, queers act up, thus acting themselves out of the fixity or naturalness associated with normative gender and sexual ideologies based on difference. Playing "beyond" difference, once again, does not mean its abandonment, but rather its deployment in newly constituted combinations as a form of transgression.

THE TWILIGHT ZONE OF ANNA DEAVERE SMITH

By way of illustrating playing "beyond" difference, I turn now to a consideration of the performances of Anna Deavere Smith, the African American playwright, actor, and theater professor who has been engaged since the early 1980s in a multiplay project called *On the Road: A Search for American Character*. Well attuned to the performative nature of cultural constructs like race, class, ethnicity, religion, and gender, she remains sensitive to questions of power, not removing her play with signification from historical reference and material effects. She writes and performs against the hegemony of pure difference, without erasing the significance of difference for identity. Mimesis as a form of imitation and representation is central to her project, enacting on stage and in text (print and video) the dialogic of sameness and difference in the contact zone between differences. The importance of her work for feminist theory and practice lies not so much in what she does with gender issues (although her traversal of gender boundaries is significant) as in her vision of multiculturalism.

Two of her best-known plays, *Fires in the Mirror* (1992) and *Twilight: Los Angeles, 1992* (1994), take up the subject of multiracial and cultural violence as they erupted in Crown Heights, Brooklyn, in the wake of an accidental killing of a black child by the Lubavitcher rabbi's car and the retaliatory murder of a Hasidic student, and in Los Angeles, during the upheavals that followed the acquittal of the four white policemen whose beating of Rodney King was captured on video. Believing that theater epitomizes the desire for connection of one difference to another, Smith has developed a method of writing and performing that highlights the contact zone without obliterating difference. She interviews dozens, indeed hundreds, of people related to the incidents, closely observing their mannerisms, speech, clothes, and body language. Using only their words, she, as the sole actor in the play, performs a representative sampling of these people, inhabiting their bodies and speech. The stage metaphorizes the space in between difference. Delineating different perspectives on multiracial conflict, her performing body is itself the contact zone. This enactment of a connection between herself and others destabilizes the very differences she performs. For if she, as an African American woman, can suppress the racial/gender markers of her body to *become* in performance all these others—man/woman, rich/poor, white/black/

Korean/Chicano, professor/minister/rapper/truck driver, and so forth, then how fixed can these differences be? How unpassable is the chasm between?

In her introductions to the text versions of the two plays, Smith theorizes performance as a form of travel, a migratory back and forth reminiscent of Lugones's notion of "'world'-travelling" into the subjectivity of the other and Bhabha's advocacy of a "hither and thither" beyond difference. "The spirit of acting," she writes, "is the *travel* from the self to the other" (*Fires* xxvi). She opposes the foundational theory of "method acting," in which she was trained, the Stanislavsky method of teaching actors to express the other by thinking about the self—acting, for example, the sorrow of others by remembering one's own sadness. "To me," she continues, "the search for character is constantly in motion. It is a quest that moves back and forth between the self and the other" (xxvi–xxvii). In rejecting the "self-based" method for its reinforcement of difference, Smith "became increasingly convinced that the activity of reenactment could tell us as much, if not more, about another individual than the process of learning about the other by using the self as a frame of reference. The frame of reference for the other would *be* the other" (xxvii).

Embodying the dialogic between sameness and difference, Smith travels to and inhabits others who repeatedly insist on their difference. In so doing, she attempts to break down the rigid boundaries of identity. "Many of us who work in race relations," she explains in her introduction to *Twilight*, "do so from the point of view of our own ethnicity. This very fact inhibits our ability to hear more voices than those that are closest to us in proximity" (xxv). Her project is to make people hear and see the other through her enactments of the "twilight" limbo of the borderlands, thus encouraging all in the audience to travel to the other. She acknowledges the importance of boundaries, but insists on the urgency of crossing them as well:

> The boundaries of ethnicity do yield brilliant work, [providing] safer places . . . where we are supported and can support the works of others. . . . [T]hese boundaries have been crucial to the development of identity and the only conceivable response to a popular culture and a mainstream that denied the possibility of the development of identity. On the other hand the price we pay is that few of us can really look at the story of race in its complexity and scope. If we were able to move more frequently beyond these boundaries, we would develop multifaceted identities and we would develop a more complex language. After all, identity is in some ways a process toward character. It is not character itself. It is not fixed. (xxv)

Performatively speaking, Smith travels to the other, inhabits the other, but does not become the other. The play remains a performance, an acting out of others, an imitation of others in what performance theorist and director Richard Schechner calls the liminal, unstable, and frequently unsettling gap between the actor and the character being acted (*Performance Theory* xiv). Smith's performances are not seamlessly natural, pretending to a one-to-one correspondence. She sparingly uses clothes, makeup, hairstyle changes, and occasional props to suggest the tran-

sition from one class to another, one sex to another, one race to another, and so
forth. Since she is herself light in color, her literal body at times represents a
certain racial ambiguity as it passes through the social meanings of "white,"
"black," "brown," and "yellow." But she remains onstage, in the video, and in the
book's photographs ostensibly who she is in the context of a racially divided
America, a black woman performing the identities of many others. And as Richard Pearce points out, in the stage versions the audience actually watches her
migrate from speaker to speaker, donning the identity of others as she puts on
their clothes and mannerisms.[18]

Smith's reliance on accents, speech patterns, and body language to indicate her
migrations has contributed to the controversy attending her representation of others. Does she reproduce stereotypes of difference, undermining her own good
intentions by exaggerating the cultural expressivity of others, making them at
times the butt of laughter? (Smith's impersonations of professors like Cornel
West and Angela Davis gently parody the tendency toward abstraction, posturing,
and pomposity of academics, an occupational class to which Smith herself partially belongs.) Or does this parodic element in her performances function in
Bhabha's terms as a form of mimicry that denaturalizes cultural identities by
calling attention to the performer's artifice? Tania Modleski situates Smith's performances in the tradition of minstrelsy "because she plays so close to the edges
of caricature, sometimes pulling back in time and sometimes not" ("Doing Justice" 65). Such mimicry can be transgressive, Modleski writes in partial agreement with Bhabha, but she worries that it also "reduces people to stereotypes and
robs them of their complexity" (65).

I think in contrast that Smith's play with caricature draws attention to the styl-
ization and (stereo)typing that underlies cultural identity itself. Parody—and the
laughter it sometimes evokes—unsettles, disturbs, creates through irony a certain
distance between Smith-the-actor and her monologists. One effect of this mimicry
is to make visible the way in which the identities of difference to which people
often cling are performances. And performances, like culture itself, can and do
change.[19] As Pearce writes, "the dramatic changing from character to character"
especially evident in the stage versions literalizes the space in between difference.
"We see that she never really" fully inhabits or "becomes a character but is always
representing it, convincingly but with a difference." In her "travels" she always
retains "something of her original self."[20]

Structurally speaking, Smith's plays travel across boundaries between identities by tacking back and forth between sharply juxtaposed differences that often
emphasize the chasm of misunderstanding between sides at the same time that
they suggest parallels of sameness. For example, *Fires in the Mirror* opens with
a series of scenes about race and ethnicity in New York City that serve as a
broader context for the specific conflict between African Americans and Jews in
Crown Heights. One series of three scenes is entitled "Hair" and features the
monologues of an Anonymous Girl (a black high school student), the Reverend
Al Sharpton, and Rivkah Siegal (a Lubavitcher housewife). All reflect upon the
meaning of hair as a cultural marker of their identity. The Anonymous Girl talks

about hairstyles in her high school, reflecting the tensions among Puerto Rican, Dominican, and North American black girls who variously copy or refuse to copy each other's hairstyles and ape or resist the behavior of white girls. Sharpton explains why he straightens his hair, not to copy white people but to honor his surrogate father, James Brown, who took him one day to a beauty parlor to have it done. "So it's certainlih not/a reaction to Whites./It's me and James's thing," he insists defiantly (22). Rivkah Siegel comes next, explaining her pained ambivalence about her decision to follow the Lubavitcher tradition for women to hide their hair beneath a wig: "I mean, I've gone through a lot with wearing wigs and not/wearing/wigs./It's been a big issue for me" (25).[21] Thus, Smith performs the difference hair makes in the different individual, gendered, and ethnic/racial/religious groups to which the three speakers multiply belong. A common thread of anxiety about hair and its relation to their group identities runs through all three accounts, a parallel bond and potential basis of connection that actor and audience can experience, but not the characters themselves. Smith, and the audience along with her, travel back and forth to a multiplicity of selves, a journey the characters themselves do not take.

Smith's plays testify to the very power of fixed identity politics at the same time that her performance transcends that fixity by encompassing multiple others. In the imaginary space of a public theater (video or book), the liminal in between differences comes into being, moving beyond the ethnic absolutism or the isolated understandings of the people occupying historical space. The contradictory poetics underlying Smith's performative play with identities encompasses both a visionary hope for healing connection and testimony to real division. This migratory dialogic between identification and difference constitutes Smith's particular twilight zone, a limbo space built out of the interaction of differences. She concludes *Twilight* with the visionary monologue of a young man named Twilight Bey, an organizer of the gang truce that followed the L.A. upheavals. While he might seem an unlikely source of enlightenment to feminists, he names the space in between at which Smith's performances aim, giving voice to the necessity and real effects of the utopic yearnings I believe are essential for feminists to explore. To quote in part:

> So twilight
> is
> that time
> between day and night.
> Limbo,
> I call it limbo.
> So a lot of times when I've brought up ideas to my homeboys,
> they say
> "Twilight,
> that's before your time,
> that's something you can't do now."
> When I talked about the truce back in 1988,

that was something they considered before its time,

yet

in 1992

we made it

realistic.

. . .

I can't forever dwell in the idea,

of identifying with people like me and understanding me and mine.

(254–55)

THEORIZING CULTURAL HYBRIDITY

For Anna Deavere Smith, the twilight zone of interracial/intercultural reconciliation is largely visionary, a utopic longing that is essential to move the "real"
world outside her theatrical space of liminality beyond bitter confrontation and
misunderstanding. But we make a mistake, I believe, in conceptualizing the space
in between difference only in terms of desire. To be sure, the contact zone as a site
of repeated confrontations generates its opposite, the wish for a limbo where
peace and understanding are possible without erasing differences. Beyond the
binary of utopic/dystopic, however, lie the everyday realities of intercultural interaction in which power operates in complex, multidirectional ways, with both
good and bad effects. The question of desired or resisted healing—important as
it is—tends to obscure just how much different identities are experienced relationally and shaped through encounter. The space in between is the site of mutual
influence and intercultural intermingling, however unequally conditioned that exchange might be. As anthropologist Kamala Visweswaran writes, "Identities, because they cannot be located solely in the continuity of a culture or tradition, are
conjunctural and not essential" (*Feminist Fictions* 11). Primary focus on difference suppresses the conjunctural, the relational—the ordinary and extraordinary
ways in which cultural formation is an ongoing process in which the blending of
differences is fully as important as their clashing.

Current theorizing about what is variously called syncretism, hybridity, creolization, mongrelization, *mestizaje*, *métissage*, and *tahjien*[22] offers feminism
new ways of moving beyond the exclusive focus on difference. What these
terms encompass are different forms of biological and cultural mixing—just
what, how, when, where, and with what results such mixing occurs are hotly
debated. Particularly controversial and contested are the political implications
and consequences of the accelerating spread of "hybridity talk." As anthropologist Marilyn Strathern writes, "The huge critical onslaught against how to think
the way different 'identities' impact on one another has yielded a multitude of
hybridizing concepts such as amalgamation, co-optation and conjuncture. . . .
Yet despite the surfeit of terms, there are constant appeals to what this or that
writer leaves out; most regularly, appeals to power relations" ("Cutting the Network" 520). Overdetermined as it is, the term *hybridity* appears to have the most

currency in English to reference forms of intercultural mixing and is the term I will use, though I mean to encompass the other terms (with their different resonances) as well.

Gravitation to *hybridity* in English perhaps attests to the power highly charged, even predominantly negative, terms acquire in the revisionist reclamations of changing meanings, serving as a site for critique of the past.[23] Its original meaning in English is biological, referring to the cross-breeding of plant or animal species. Its common synonyms—*mongrel, half-breed, crossbreed, mixed blood*—have been largely derogatory, implying a degeneration from purebred or thoroughbred.[24] The rise of agricultural botany countered these negative notions with the development of new, often superior plant species. But as Robert J. C. Young shows in his history of the term in *Colonial Desire*, hybridity became a major (if not obsessive) preoccupation of nineteenth-century western racialism. Ideologically inseparable from the history of slavery and colonialism, hybridity was hotly debated in anthropology, religion, politics, popular culture, and the arts. Monogenists (believers in a single human species) and polygenists (believers in multiple human species) often used hybridity as the battleground for competing theories about race, arguing for the sterility or degeneration of mixed-race offspring or defending the common humanity of the species. Miscegenation became the taboo threat invoking both repulsion and desire, often forbidden by English and American law but widely practiced by white men with women of color over whom they had power.[25] As Young writes: "In the different theoretical positions woven out of this intercourse, the races and their intermixture circulate around an ambivalent axis of desire and aversion: a structure of attraction, where people and cultures intermix and merge, transforming themselves as a result, and a structure of repulsion, where the different elements remain distinct and are set against each other dialogically. The idea of race here shows itself to be profoundly dialectical: it only works when defined against potential intermixture, which also threatens to undo its calculations altogether" (19).[26]

In spite of, or perhaps partially because of, its complicity in the discourses of racism, *hybridity* has emerged explosively in the late-twentieth century as both rallying cry for antipurist ways of thinking about "race" and as a widely used term in postcolonial studies, anthropology, and cultural studies to suggest different forms of cultural mixing and interactive exchange. As an example of the former, Salman Rushdie defends his novel *The Satanic Verses* as an attack on the destructive "apostles of purity" and a celebration of hybridity as the creative force of change:

> Those who oppose the novel most vociferously today are of the opinion that intermingling with a different culture will inevitably weaken and ruin their own. I am of the opposite opinion. *The Satanic Verses* celebrates hybridity, impurity, intermingling, the transformation that comes of new and unexpected combinations of human beings, cultures, ideas, politics, movies, songs. It rejoices in mongrelization and fears the absolutism of the Pure. *Mélange*, hotch-potch, a bit of this and a bit of that is *how newness enters the world*. It is the great possibility that mass migration gives the

world, and I have tried to embrace it. *The Satanic Verses* is for change-by-fusion, change-by-conjoining. It is a love-song to our mongrel selves.

Throughout human history, the apostles of purity, those who have claimed to possess a total explanation, have wrought havoc among mere mixed-up human beings. Like many millions of people, I am a bastard child of history. Perhaps we all are, black and brown and white, leaking into one another, as a character of mine once said, *like flavours when you cook.* ("Good Faith" 394)

Rushdie's ringing endorsement of hybridity is not shared by all; many who agree with his critique of purism regard hybridity as neither inherently good nor bad per se. But what is widespread is the reliance on theories of hybridity and its more linguistically based cousin, creolization, to find ways of moving beyond the more common stress on difference to chart the very real effects of intercultural exchange. Just what hybridity means, however, is no less contested and volatile than the highly charged terms *modernity* and *postmodernity*, with which it is often associated. Meanings of the term migrate, encompassing differences and contradictions that are as important to the difference impasse in feminism as is the generalized notion of mixing itself. In the interests of precision, it is worth charting these movements schematically, with attention to debates about the types, functions, orientations, and politics of hybridity. (See fig. 1.)

The core meaning of hybridity in contemporary cultural studies shifts among three distinct but not mutually exclusive types of cultural mixing: fusion of differences, intermingling of differences, and mixing of the always already syncretic. The first alludes to the creation of something entirely new out of the mixing of two or more distinct phenomena. The second suggests that the differences that make up the hybrid remain in play, retaining some of their original character, although altered in the weaving. The third questions fundamentally the existence of pure difference and regards hybridity as the ongoing precondition of all cultural formations. Conflating the first and second types, Renato Rosaldo nonetheless usefully articulates the major distinction at stake:

On the one hand, hybridity can imply a space betwixt and between two zones of purity in a manner that follows biological usage that distinguishes two discrete species and the hybrid pseudo-species that results from their combination. . . . On the other hand, hybridity can be understood as the ongoing condition of all human cultures, which contain no zones of purity because they undergo continuous processes of transculturation (two-way borrowing and lending between cultures). Instead of hybridity versus purity, this view suggests that it is hybridity all the way down. . . . From this perspective, one must explain how ideological zones of cultural purity, whether of national culture or ethnic resistance, have been constructed. (Foreword xv–xvi)[27]

Language as both medium and site of cultural commerce provides ready examples of these three types. Within the terms of hybridity as fusion, the blending of many different distinct languages results in the formation of a new language like English (made up of Saxon, French, Latin, Greek, etc.) or Yiddish (German, He-

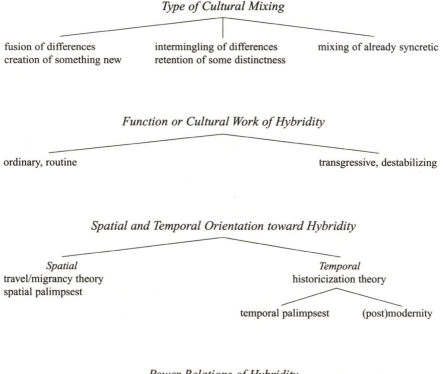

Type of Cultural Mixing

fusion of differences	intermingling of differences	mixing of already syncretic
creation of something new	retention of some distinctness	

Function or Cultural Work of Hybridity

ordinary, routine   transgressive, destabilizing

Spatial and Temporal Orientation toward Hybridity

Spatial   *Temporal*
travel/migrancy theory   historicization theory
spatial palimpsest

temporal palimpsest   (post)modernity

Power Relations of Hybridity

Oppression Model	*Locational Model*	*Transgression Model*
hybridity imposed	hybridity various	hybridity counterhegemonic
deculturation	transculturation	resistance
assimilation	negotiation	destabilization
co-optation	transfiguration	mimetic, parodic, creative

Fig. 1. Mapping Hybridity Theory.

brew, Slavic mixture). Within the framework of hybridity as intermingling, different parts of distinct languages (e.g., grammar, vocabulary, syntax) combine to produce a creole language in which the original languages remain recognizable, as in Spanglish, Tex-Mex, or Hawaiian and Jamaican pidgin. The third approach would stress that any given language is always in the process of hybridic formation through borrowings and adaptations of linguistic traditions with which it comes in contact—whether or not speakers are aware of or resistant to such syncretism. M. M. Bakhtin's distinction between "organic" and "intentional" linguistic hybridity in *The Dialogic Imagination* adds the important issue of agency. He defines organic hybridity as the melding of differences that occurs without conscious effort, as part of ongoing cultural evolution. Introducing notions of agency and creativity, he characterizes intentional hybridity as the conscious production of linguistic mixtures, especially in aesthetic artifacts.[28] Linguistic hybridity of all three sorts—whether organic or intentional—is not divorced from issues of power; indeed, power relations between people of different language and dialect groups condition the syncretic process. (A "standard" dialect is often defined in linguistics as the dialect backed by an army). These three types of linguistic hybridity translate well into other media of cultural commerce, sites of intercultural mixing such as religion, mass media, sports, food, fashion, epistemology, all the arts, and the body itself.[29] Since all these sites are also intense markers of cultural difference, discussion of hybridity clearly supplements rather than abandons the issue of difference.

Whatever the type of cultural mixing hybridity embodies, hybridity theorists tend to see the function or cultural work of hybridity in two distinct ways. Some regard hybridity as an ordinary, ubiquitous, routine component of any cultural formation—what Rosaldo refers to as the inevitable processes of transculturation (mutual and multiple borrowing and adaptation) that all cultures experience. As Stuart Hall writes: "I think cultural identity is not fixed, it's always hybrid" as the result of particular historical configurations ("New Ethnicities" 502). Others, like Rushdie, view hybridity as transgressive, counterhegemonic, resistant, interruptive. Homi Bhabha's concept of hybridity as "colonial mimicry" is an often cited example. Hybridity, he argues in "Signs Taken for Wonder" (1985), takes form in the imitations the colonized make of the colonizer, in which the very gap between the two calls into question the inevitability of colonial authority: "Hybridity intervenes in the exercise of authority not merely to indicate the impossibility of its identity to represent the unpredictability of its presence" (*Location* 156–57). In "Commitment to Theory" (1989), Bhabha broadens his concept to envision a double hybridity of colonized and colonizer produced through interaction (*Location* esp. 33–34). But like Rushdie, he also associates hybridity fundamentally with a resistance to purism and separatism of all kinds: "I want to take my stand on the shifting margins of cultural displacement—that confounds any profound or 'authentic' sense of a 'national' culture or an 'organic' intellectual—and ask what the function of a committed theoretical perspective might be, once the cultural and historical hybridity of the postcolonial world is taken as the paradigmatic place of departure" (*Location* 21). As Pnina Werbner writes in her introduction to *Debating Cultural Hybridity*, "The current fascination with cultural hybridity masks an elusive paradox. Hybridity is celebrated as powerfully interruptive and yet theorized as commonplace and pervasive" (1). How are we to make sense, she asks, of cultural hybridity being both "routine" and "transgressive" (1)?[30] In my view, we do so by recognizing that these two views of hybridity are not mutually exclusive any more than are the three types of intercultural mixing. We do not have to choose between or among them; rather, we can deploy these different meanings locationally, determining their suitability by context and project.

Notions of hybridity differ not only by type and function but also by spatial and temporal orientations. On the one hand, many represent the production of hybridity in geographical terms, stressing the significance of travel, migration, nomadism, global flows, border crossing, sea/air/roadways, cyberspace, and the like. On the other hand, some talk about hybridity in historical terms, stressing its development over time or under particular historical conditions. Since, as Adrienne Rich puts it, "a place on the map is a place in history" ("Notes" 212), geographical and historical modes of thinking about hybridity are ultimately necessary and inseparable. But the distinction in emphasis is significant.

Stressing geographically produced hybridity, migrancy theory looks at the function of travel in the formation of collective and individual identities—all forms of travel and the power relations that underlie it. As James Clifford writes in "Traveling Cultures," the study of cultural *roots* and traditions needs to be complemented by attention to intercultural *routes*, that is, the function of a culture's contact with other cultures through all forms of intercultural traffic (as I will discuss in more depth in chapter 6). In *The Black Atlantic*, for example, Paul Gilroy focuses on the ship as the major trope of the black diaspora—from the ships of the Middle Passage, through the geopolitical circuits of trading vessels, and on to the commercial and tourist lines that North American and Caribbean blacks took around the Atlantic triangle. Gilroy's spatial focus on the sea complements the land-based spatiality of borderlands that dominates fields like Chicano studies. Reflecting the greater reliance on airplanes by recent waves of Asian migrations, Bharati Mukherjee metaphorizes the surreal limbo space of the intercontinental migrant in her novel *Jasmine*: "There is the shadow world of aircraft permanently aloft that share airlanes and radio frequencies with Pan Am and British Air and Air-India, portaging people who coexist with tourists and businessmen. But we are refugees and mercenaries and guest workers; you see us sleeping in airport lounges, you watch us unwrapping the last of our native foods . . . , taking out for the hundreth time an aerogram promising a job or space to sleep. . . . We are the outcasts and deportees, strange pilgrims" (90). Another South Asian American writer, Meena Alexander, uses the image of the palimpsest in *The Shock of Arrival* (esp. 49, 69) to think through the hybridic layering of identities produced through crisscrossing travels. Born in Kerala, India, she spent most of her childhood in the Sudan, with frequent trips to Alexandria, Egypt, and summers back in Kerala. Educated in Khartoum and England, she married an American and moved to Manhattan, where she teaches and writes. Complicating each dislocation is the border of her female body and its shifting meanings in different cultural locations. "For a writer of the South Asian diaspora," she notes, "the radical nature of dislocation, not singular, but multiple" haunts; "so the shelters the mind makes up are crisscrossed by borders, weighted down as a tent might be by multiple anchorages, ethnic solidarities, unselvings" (7). "There is very little we can take for granted," she concludes, "as we etch ourselves in complex palimpsests of knowledge and desire" (69).[31]

Stressing historically produced hybridity, others emphasize how the mingling of different cultures and the formation of new ones takes place over time, constituting a temporal palimpsest of sedimentations. The history of conquest in particular produces a layering of different cultures that is especially intensified in areas of the world where great powers collide in their competition for resources, such areas as the Caribbean, where creole languages and cultures are particularly evident. In *The Aztec Palimpsest* (1997), Daniel Cooper Alarcón uses the image of the palimpsest (with its associations of partial erasure, superpositioning, and intertextuality) to theorize the hybridity of Mexican history, as well as the modern Mexican and Chicano constructions of that history. With its meanings of partial erasure and superimposition, Alarcón finds in the palimpsest "the nexus of power, empire, and discourse" (4), a way, in other words, of providing historical explanations for the mestizo culture of both Mexicans and Chicanos, combining in its histories of conquest the various strands of Mesoamerican, Spanish, and North American cultures (supplemented by the forced and willing migrations of Africans, Europeans, and Asians).

Another form of historicized hybridity focuses on hybridity as the result of a particular set of conditions at a specific moment in history. Writers like Rushdie and theorists like Gilroy, Arjun Appadurai, Ulf Hannerz, and Iain Chambers regard hybridity as inextricably linked with either modernity or postmodernity. The disruptive effects of modernity and the globalization of culture in the late-twentieth century, they argue, foster an intensification of intercultural contact and commerce, travel, migration, and nomadism of diverse populations. The subjects of the black diaspora, Gilroy argues, were the earliest "modern" subjects, experiencing the fragmentation and self-fashioning of identities that came to characterize modern subjects in general. Sailors of all races in the "black Atlantic" were "moving to and fro between nations, crossing borders in modern machines that were themselves micro-systems of linguistic and political hybridity" (*Black Atlantic* 12). Appadurai invents the term "global ethnoscape" to define the hybridic postmodern moment conditioned by the operations of power in "the landscape of persons who make up the shifting world in which we live: tourists, immigrants, refugees, exiles, guest-workers, and other moving groups and persons" ("Global Ethnoscapes" 191–92). Emphasizing the conjuncture of postmodernity and hybridity, Hannerz writes:

> The twentieth century has been a unique period in world cultural history. Humankind has finally bid farewell to that world which could with some credibility be seen as a cultural mosaic, of separate pieces with hard, well-defined edges. Because of the great increase in the traffic in culture, the large-scale transfer of meaning systems and symbolic forms, the world is increasingly becoming one not only in political and economic terms, as in the climactic period of colonialism, but in terms of its cultural constructions as well; a global ecumene of persistent cultural interaction and exchange. This, however, is no egalitarian global village. ("Scenarios" 107)

Whether this "global ecumene of persistent cultural interaction" is uniquely (post)modern or routinely present in human history is a point of contention among theorists of hybridity. Even more contested, however, are the questions of power that underlie hybridic formations, whatever their nature, function, or orientation. Who are the partners in the intercultural exchange that produces hybridity? To what multiple groups do they belong or represent? Is power distributed relatively equally or asymmetrically between them? Who or which side has more power? Is hybridization forced or embraced, hated or valued, limiting or empowering, destructive or creative (or some complex and/or evolving mixture of the two)? What role does agency play in the hybridizing process? How is it constrained, how negotiated? Who decides, sets the agenda? Who benefits the most and in what ways from hybridity? Are all groups (or individuals) equally hybridized and in the same way? Or is one side in an exchange more changed than the other? Can the same exchange produce benign hybridities on the one side and malignant ones on the other? Who has access to hybridity, especially when it is beneficial? How does hybridity relate to class/caste/gender stratifications within a given society? What is the cultural work of hybridity? How do all these circulations of power change over time, through space? The rhetorical force of the term hybridity for cultural mixing tends to obscure these questions of power because its origin in biological crossbreeding implies a mixture of equal parts (however different)—roughly equal in status and in proportion. But cultural hybridity is seldom the product of such economies or recipes of equality. It is this problematic of power that generates the most heated debate and to which feminists must pay particularly close attention in adapting the term.

Views on the politics of hybridity go in three basic directions. The first regards hybridity largely as an effect of oppression, focusing on intercultural contact as a process in which a dominant group forces some form of deculturation, assimilation, or co-optation upon a less powerful group and either expels or appropriates that group's cultural forms into its mainstream. To cite a few examples: the forced conversion or expulsion of the Jews in Spain in 1492 led to the formation of hybridic assimilation and Christianization (often only partial) in Spain and the various creolized forms of Sephardism among the Spanish Jews who scattered across Italy, North Africa, and the Middle East; the African slave trade to the American colonies severed Africans from their various traditions and forged syncretist cultural formations such as the Afro-Brazilians, the Afro-Caribbeans, and the Afro-Americans; the Dawes Act of 1887 in the United States instituted the infamous land allotments geared toward making English farmers out of American Indians, a policy supported by forced attendance at Indian boarding schools where native languages were forbidden; and the appropriation of African and other "primitive" art by modernists like Picasso resulted in the transformation of western art, but reinforced the ideology that African masks were not "art" until western masters transferred the images to canvas. Within this framework, hybridity is more often than not regarded as a negative, as a strategy of containment, regulation, policing, and control of those whose original cultures pose some sort of threat to hegemonic powers or figure as some sort of forbidden desire. Binaries of center/periphery, colonizer/colonized, First World/Third World, oppressor/oppressed predominate in this analytic mode, along with the assumption that hybridity leads to and is an effect of exploitation of the strong by the weak.

The second mode of political analysis does not reverse so much as deconstruct the first by suggesting that hybridity undermines authority and displaces the binaries upon which it rests. Representing the principle of mixing, the hybrid disturbs, intervenes, unsettles, interrogates, ironizes, denaturalizes, transgresses by refusing to "fit" established categories. The hybrid exceeds borders of the normative and expected, thus calling into question the inevitability of the status quo, the power relations of the social order. Within this framework, hybridity represents a liberatory, anti-authoritarian force for good, opening doors of possibility instead of regulating and confining. As in the work of Rushdie and Bhabha, this analytic mode does not suggest that hybridity is without pain, dislocation, suffering, or oppression. Rather, this stance toward hybridity emphasizes that within the context of power relations, hybridity performs progressive cultural work, as the force privileging genuine multiculturalism and heterogeneity, promising vitality, enrichment, and survival. As Ulf Hannerz writes in "The World in Creolisation," the "creolist point of view . . . identifies diversity itself as a source of cultural vitality; it demands of us that we see complexity and fluidity as an intellectual challenge rather than as something to escape from. It should point to ways of looking at systems of meaning which do not hide their connections with the facts of power and material life" (556). To cite a narrative example, Leslie Marmon Silko takes up the problematic of hybridity and power in *Ceremony* (1977), her novel about the World War II veteran Tayo, a "mixed-blood" Indian who seeks healing in the terrible aftermath of the war. The rigidly traditionalist healer, Ku'oosh, to whom Tayo first turns, cannot help him; the old rituals do not work. Instead, the medicine man who successfully initiates the healing process is Betonie, a syncretist figure who has traveled widely, speaks good English, lives on the edge of a tourist town, collects old calendars and other debris of American culture, and flexibly combines the traditional ways of the Indian past with new realities. Unlike that of Ku'oosh, Betonie's ceremony is part of a living, ever-evolving tradition formed through intercultural engagements, an Indianness that incorporates the resiliency and syncretist fluidity that Tayo needs to live in an oppressive world.[32] As Tayo's story illustrates, the view of hybridity as a social good tends to focus on individuals, while the notion of hybridity as an effect of oppression often looks primarily to systemic structures.

The third approach to hybridity and power does not assign an inevitable political effect to intercultural mixing, but rather asks for locational "thick descriptions" of historically and geographically specific situations. Where the first mode often assumes agency to reside with the dominant power and the second mode locates agency in the hybridic dissident, the third mode stresses mutual agencies on all sides, though not necessarily equally unencumbered agencies. (By agency, I do not mean autonomy or freedom to act but rather the assumption of human subjectivities that create meanings and act in negotiation with the systemic conditions of the social order, however circumscribed.) Within this third framework, power flows multidirectionally in the contact zone instead of unidirectionally. Consistent with a Gramscian perspective, hegemony contains within its normative systems contradictions that fuel resistance and change. Moreover, not all contact zones are structured around either the exploitation of the weak by the powerful or the resistance of the other against a dominant group. The third mode encompasses such plots of oppression and transgression, but is not restricted to them. It is just as likely to find good effects in creolization, even when the conditions engendering it are negative, as in the production of African American musical and dance forms, hybridized cultural effects born of suffering and the triumph of survival and creativity. It is more likely to stress interaction among heterogeneous others instead of action upon a monolithic Other. Terms such as transculturation, negotiation, and transfiguration replace deculturation, assimilation, and co-optation.[33] Insisting upon agency, subjectivity, and heterogeneity on all sides of an intercultural exchange, these terms assume the principle for which S. P. Mohanty argues in "'Us' and 'Them'": "'Culture' is thus best appreciated as defining the realm of human choice in (potentially) definable contexts, choices of individuals and collectives as potentially self-aware agents. . . . One specification we need to make . . . is through the conception of agency as a basic capacity shared by all humans *across cultures*. And in understanding the divide between 'us' and 'them,' it is this common space we all share that needs to be elaborated and defined" (20).

I propose these three modes of approaching the problematic of hybridity and power not to offer positions to which different usages can be attached but rather to distinguish among the analytic threads that are often woven together in different ways by different writers. In *Imperial Eyes*, for example, Mary Louise Pratt discusses hybridity only in the context of colonialism, focusing upon cultural exchanges in the contact zones characterized by asymmetrical power relations. However, she features the term *transculturation* in the book's subtitle, *Travel Writing and Transculturation*, and her adaptation of the term from ethnography emphasizes the agency of the colonized: "Ethnographers have used this term [transculturation] to describe how subordinated or marginal groups select and invent from materials transmitted to them by a dominant or metropolitan culture. While subjugated peoples cannot readily control what emanates from the dominant culture, they do determine to varying extents what they absorb into their own, and what they use it for" (6). Moreover, she acknowledges the way in which the dominant culture is itself hybridized in the processes of transculturation: "How are metropolitan modes of representation received and appropriated on the periphery? That question engenders another perhaps more heretical one: with respect to representation, how does one speak of transculturation from the colonies to the metropolis?. . . While the imperial metropolis tends to understand itself as determining the periphery (in that emanating glow of the civilizing mission or the cash flow of development, for example), it habitually blinds itself to the ways in which the periphery determines the metropolis" (6). Pratt thus weaves together the first and third modes of hybridic analysis of power in the contact zone, bypassing the second. Although Homi Bhabha, to cite another example, is most often associated with the notion of hybridic transgression, his complex and evolving theory of hybridity actually encompasses all three modes.[34] I am less interested in using these political modes to categorize theorists as I am in making distinctions that facilitate precise, thick descriptions of how hybridity works multiply in any given situation.

Critiques of what John Hutnyk calls "hybridity-talk" mostly revolve around questions of power and the dangers of abandoning identity politics, or what I would term exclusive emphasis on "difference-talk." A range of such critiques is included in Pnina Werbner and Tariq Modood's collection, *Debating Cultural Hybridity* (1997). Jonathan Friedman is the most dismissive in the volume, attacking use of the term as class-based, promoted particularly by "migrant elites" and "cosmopolitans" like Rushdie, Gilroy, Bhabha, and Anzaldúa. Peter van der Veer and John Hutnyk are less virulent, but raise objections to those who romanticize hybridity or divorce it from political movements devoted to change. Van der Veer concludes that however integral hybridity is to cultural change, "the hybridity celebrated in Cultural Studies has little revolutionary potential, since it is part of the very discourse of bourgeois capitalism and modernity which it claims to displace" ("'Enigma of Arrival'"104). Hutnyk objects to the fashionability and marketability of hybridity, wondering "why talk hybridity now rather than a more explicitly radical language? Another way to state this more bluntly is to ask why some 'post-colonial' discursive efforts seem to do very well at avoiding any discussion of Marxism" ("Adorno at Womad" 122). In his view "theorising hybridity becomes, in some cases [e.g., the work of Stuart Hall, Gilroy, and Bhabha], an excuse for ignoring sharp organisational questions, enabling a passive and comfortable—if linguistically sophisticated—intellectual quietism" (122). The danger in hybridity-talk, according to such views, resides in whether it contributes anything constructive to political activism beyond the classroom or the pages of publication. Related to this critique is the concern that hybridity-talk, whatever its intentions, ends up reinscribing the hegemony of a neo-imperialist West or other dominant groups who have the power to shape the agendas of intercultural contact. Much of the attack on the spread of hybridity discourse comes from those who remain committed to the epistemological and political imperatives of difference discourse, particularly in its most binarist forms (e.g., the West/the Rest, First World/Third World, white/other).[35]

What these critiques seldom take into account is the migratory and often contradictory meanings and deployments of the term *hybridity* across a wide spectrum of possibilities. Invoking Bakhtin's distinction between organic and intentional hybridities, Robert Young characterizes this linguistic nomadism by stating that hybridity "works simultaneously in two ways: 'organically,' hegemonizing, creating new spaces, structures, scenes, and 'intentionally,' diasporizing, intervening as a form of subversion, translation, transformation. . . . Hybridization as creolization involves fusion, the creation of a new form, which can then be set against the old form, of which it is partly made up. Hybridization as 'raceless chaos' by contrast, produces no stable new form but rather something closer to Bhabha's restless, uneasy, interstitial hybridity: a radical heterogeneity, discontinuity, the permanent revolution of forms" (*Colonial Desire* 25). My mapping of hybridity as a concept in contemporary discourse suggests a broader range of types (fusion/intermingling/always already syncretist), functions (routine/transgressive), orientations (spatial/temporal), and political modes (oppressive/oppositional/locational) than Young's dual model. But I agree with his statement that "There is no single, or correct, concept of hybridity" (26). What does remain a common denominator, however, is the use of the term hybridity to counter various forms of ethnic absolutism, cultural purism, and fundamentalist identity politics. "Hybridity here is a key term in that wherever it emerges it suggests the impossibility of essentialism," Young writes (26). Herein lies its particular relevance to a feminism caught up in the difference impasse.

FEMINIST MESTIZAJE: GLORIA ANZALDÚA'S BORDERLANDS

To explore the significance of hybridity-talk as supplement to difference-talk in feminism, I turn now to Gloria Anzaldúa's *Borderlands/La Frontera: The New Mestiza*. In "Traveling Cultures," James Clifford asserts the "need to conjure with new localizations like 'the border.' A specific place of hybridity and struggle, policing and transgression, the U.S./Mexico frontier, has recently attained 'theoretical' status, thanks to the work of Chicano writers, activists, and scholars" (109). Published in 1987, Anzaldúa's *Borderlands* has become one of the most influential and frequently cited of these Chicano/a texts to attain "theoretical status" among a wide range of multicultural, post-colonial, cultural, feminist, and gay/lesbian/queer scholars and activists. Its impact across the disciplines is not for its articulation of difference but rather for its complication of difference. Its broad appeal is centered in its variously angry, ironic, mythic, utopic, and postmodern exploration of hybridities, traveling identities, and contradictory interplays of power and powerlessness at "home" and in alien territory. As a self-consciously "literary" text focused on the autobiographical narrative of the writer's psyche in historical context, *Borderlands'* status as "theory" is itself hybridic, complicating the explanatory, system-building function of a generalizing theory with the rich allusiveness and unsystematic uniqueness of an imaginative text. As an overtly feminist and queer text that thematizes, plays with, and performs hybridity, *Borderlands* offers multicultural feminism a suggestive test case for the usefulness of hybridity-talk in confronting the issue of difference.[36]

Before turning to the text itself, I want to stress Anzaldúa's ongoing importance to the development of feminist difference-talk, especially through the pathbreaking achievements of *This Bridge Called My Back* (1981) and *Making Face/Making Soul* (1990). As an editor and essayist for these volumes, Anzaldúa has insisted upon difference, particularly the binary difference between women of color and white women in the United States. Much like Lugones's "The Logic of Feminist Pluralism," these books emphasize the impact of American racism in the formation of racialized gender identities, thus de-emphasizing the heterogeneity of gendered identities and multidirectional flows of power in both national and transnational contexts. As she writes in her introduction to *Making Face/Making Soul*:

"Diversity" and "difference" are vague, ambiguous terms, defined differently by whitefeminists and feminists-of-color. Often whitefeminists want to minimize racial difference by taking comfort in the fact that we are all women and/or lesbians and

> suffer similar sexual-gender oppressions. They are usually annoyed with the actuality (though not the concept) of "differences," want to blur racial difference, want to smooth things out—they seem to want a complete, totalizing identity. (xxi)

Anzaldúa's faint qualifications ("often," "seem to") do not alter her own totalistic homogenization of "whitefeminists" on the one hand and "feminists-of-color" on the other, a defense of difference that suppresses heterogeneity in favor of a fixed binarism.

As author of *Borderlands*, Anzaldúa does not abandon this commitment to difference discourse. Indeed, the categories of *white* and *Anglo* remain largely monolithic, unexamined, and morally condemned, even as she admonishes herself to accept her own Anglo elements, even as she gestures briefly to such white allies as the Holocaust survivor Irena Klepfisz and the working-class, lesbian poet Judy Grahn in dedications to various poems. But her visionary, historical, and autobiographical travels toward "the new mestiza" of her subtitle mark a pathway "beyond" difference: testifying to the force of difference but not limited to it; articulating both utopic longing for and recognition of already existing mestizaje; migrating through many forms and types of cultural, racial, gender, and aesthetic hybridity as a performative resistance to fixity. The scope and fluidity of mestizaje in *Borderlands* accounts in part for its wide-ranging influence; readers often ignore its nomadic and sometimes contradictory formations of hybridity, focusing instead on particular notions they either admire or want to critique.[37] For my purposes, however, this very fluidity is what has the most significance for feminism. Encompassing the full range of debate about hybridity, *Borderlands* attests to the multifacited meanings of the concept for feminism.

Borderlands' refusal of pure difference begins linguistically in what appears at a glance to follow the conventions of bilingual texts with alternations of English and Spanish. But a closer look quickly reveals a more complex, creolized text that goes well beyond translation of one "pure" language into another. *Borderlands* breaks down the boundaries between languages while retaining the flavor of their difference. At times, the text says the same thing twice in English and Spanish (as in the title), a repetition and two-way translation that privileges neither language. But at other times, Anzaldúa writes different things in English and Spanish, as if the freedom of the borderlands between languages exceeds the discipline of translation. At still other times, Anzaldúa weaves together different linguistic voices, intermingling English with Castillian Spanish, North Mexican Spanish, Tex-Mex, and "a sprinkling of Nahautl" (preface), a combination that she further characterizes in "How to Tame a Wild Tongue" as containing eight distinct linguistic strands (55). The English conjoins standard English and elements of what she calls "working class and slang English" (55). What appears to be "Spanish" in the text is actually a hybridized language based in Spanish, but reflecting its multicultural formation in new historical and geographical locations. Countering the view often internalized by Chicanos that they speak "poor Spanish," Anzaldúa calls this language Chicano Spanish, terming it a "bastard language," a "mestizo patois," a "living language," a "border tongue which developed naturally," and "a new language—the language of the Borderlands [where] at the juncture of cultures, languages cross-pollinate and are revitalized" (55, 58, preface). The language of *Borderlands* thus encompasses the three basic types of cultural hybridity theorized by others: the intermingling of different languages and dialects; the fusion of differences into a new language, Chicano Spanish; and the acknowledgment that language in the ongoing process of formation is always already syncretist. Moreover, the text's heteroglossia reflects what Bakhtin calls the "organic hybridity" of everyday linguistic mixture and the "intentional hybridity" of the writer's artistry. Readers who cannot understand Chicano Spanish experience the cultural impoverishment and exclusion of life within the boundaries of a single difference, an important reversal of the inadequacy Chicano/as are often made to feel in an English-only public culture. *Borderlands* clearly revels in the vitality, creativity, and transgressive politics of linguistic creolization.

This linguistic performance of playing "'beyond' difference paves the way for the text's generic hybridity. *Borderlands* is a nonlinear, (post)modern spiritual autobiography that pieces together fragments of personal, familial, communal, national, transnational, and mythic memories and ruminations. At a self-reflexive moment, Anzaldúa comments on the text's eclectic form, likening it to "an assemblage, a montage, a beaded work with several leitmotifs and with a central core, now appearing, now disappearing in a crazy dance" (66). In formal terms, *Borderlands* encompasses multiple binaries, insistently blending even as it acknowledges generic difference: poetry/prose, lyric/narrative, history/theory, and mythopoesis/realist mimesis. Transgression of what Derrida calls the "law of genre" depends upon expectations of distinction, a sense of the forbiddeness of crossbreeding as a kind of formalist miscegenation. Modernist and postmodernist experimentation often plays with and beyond difference in this way to reflect a dismantling of Descartian subjectivity and positivist epistemologies. *Borderlands* belongs to this hybridic tradition as much as it builds off specifically Chicano cultural forms.[38]

An elaborate structure based in a dialogic of difference and mixing orders the (post)modern, dialectical montage based in the overarching split between prose and poetry. Entitled "*Atraversando Fronteras*/Crossing Borders," the first half of the text contains seven prose essays that narrate personal, communal, and mythic histories, accompanied by a legitimizing section of notes documenting sources. These essays move from the oppression of Chicanos in the physical borderlands in the southwestern United States and northern Mexico to the pain and exhilaration of the "new mestiza consciousness" emerging out of her exploration of the historical, psychological, sexual, spiritual, and aesthetic borderlands. Under the rubric "*Un Agitado Viento/Ehécatl*, the Wind," six sections of poems follow. As lyrical and elliptical evocations of pain and spiritual searching, they counterpoint the prose narratives of part one. Different in aesthetic mode of address, they nonetheless go over the same ground again, as if they were a form of translation or linguistic transplantation. The six sections of lyric sequences move from memories of fearful confrontation to embrace of a simultaneously wounding and healing mestizaje in the final poems. Further blending the text's binary differences, the predominantly narrative, historical prose in part one contains excursions into the lyrical and poetic. Conversely, the lyrical mode of part two contains elements of prose. In formalist terms, *Borderlands* spans the three types of hybridity, just as its play with language does: mingling different modal voices and forms; fusing them into a new form akin to the expansive, often hybridic twentieth-century long poem;[39] and deconstructing the purity of binaries like poetry and prose, history and myth in the first place.

The border tongue and border form of *Borderlands* constitute the linguistic and aesthetic foundation for a double narrative of the writer's life in the geopolitical, psychic, spiritual, and sexual borderlands. Not a chronological narrative, the text tells a psychological story of search, moving once in prose and then again in poetry from the pathologies of oppression based on difference to the creativities of healing founded in revisionist mythmaking on the meanings of multiple borderland existences and histories. Like Audre Lorde, who subtitled her autobiography *A Biomythography*, Anzaldúa writes the story of her life in the form of "biomythology," not documentary history. As she warns her readers in the preface, "This book speaks of my existence. My preoccupations with the inner life of the Self, and with the struggle of that Self amidst adversity and violation; with the confluence of primordial images; with the unique positionings consciousness takes at those confluent streams; and with my almost instinctive urge to communicate, to speak, to write about life on the borders, life in the shadows." Since this Self is defined in and through the meanings of geopolitics, race, class, gender, and sexuality, Anzaldúa's individual narrative is also multiply communalist. But *Borderlands* remains a visionary story of self-healing through quest, not a blueprint for institutional change or revolution, not a historical analysis of Chicanas in general. The space of intercultural encounter in her text is interior and linguistic, the space of the self, of identity.[40]

This quest narrative depends fundamentally upon a migration through the different meanings and politics of hybridity. Too often identified only with "the new mestiza" consciousness articulated in the final sections of parts one and two or with a romanticized hybridity without pain, the borderland consciousness of the full text is actually shifting, nomadic, contradictory.[41] The underlying question of the text is how to move from the "old" to the "new" mestiza, from a shame-filled self-image of a "bastard" race to a shameless identity of a creative mestizaje. In exploring this question, Anzaldúa exhibits not only a nomadic subjectivity but also a mobile approach to mestizaje. Anticipating the spectrum of views about hybridity developed more abstractly in the academy in the late 1980s and 1990s, she resists a single model of cultural mixing. Instead, her narrative encompasses the various formulations of hybridity we have examined: its three types of hybridity; its dual function as ordinary and transgressive; its spatial/temporal orientations; its dystopic, utopic, and locational formations in relation to power. What she avoids above all is a simple romanticization of mestizaje as the transcendence of difference and the pain its structures engender.

The beginning point of narrative quest is the "physical borderland" (preface), the experience of oppression in the geopolitical contact zone between the United

States and Mexico, in the land occupied by Mexicans and Indians and conquered by the Americans in 1847. This spatial/temporal palimpsest or layering of differences is "not a comfortable territory to live in," she explains in the preface. It is a "place of contradictions. Hatred, anger, and exploitation are the prominent features of this landscape." Here, the politics of hybridity is dystopic; intercultural contact, predominantly exploitative and hostile. Here, borderland existence means splitting the land, the people, the body in two. In addition to fusion, Robert Young writes, hybridization "can also consist of the forcing of a single entity into two or more parts, a severing of a single object into two, turning sameness into difference" (*Colonial Desire* 26). The prose half of *Borderlands* opens with a searing lyric articulation of this severing in the contact zone:

> 1,950 mile-long open wound
> > dividing a *pueblo*, a culture,
> > running down the length of my body,
> > > staking fence rods in my flesh,
> > > splits me   splits me
> > > > *me raja   me raja*
> > This is my home
> > this thin edge of
> > > barbwire.

(2)

"The U.S.-Mexican border," she continues in prose, "es herida abierta [is an open border] where the Third World grates against the first and bleeds" (4). Conquest and oppression create and enforce difference between peoples, making of encounter and the hybridity it engenders a site for wounding, a space for the exercise of power over others and resistance against others. In its extreme form, the borderlands are the killing fields, quite literally in the three poems that open part two of the text: "White-wing Season," "Cervicide," and "horse." In the first, "The white-men with their guns / have come again / to fill the silence and the sky / with buckshot" as they kill the doves (102); in the second, the white game warden forces the Chicano family to kill its pet fawn (104–5); and in the third, the gringos kill a wild horse (106–7).

The geopolitical borderland between the United States and Mexico constructs a sense of absolute Anglo/Mexican difference with Chicanos occupying an uneasy and vulnerable space in between, racially and culturally mixing the white and brown, Anglo and Mexican, at home in neither, at "home" not even in their own bodies. Anzaldúa's answer to this painful hybridity is not ethnic absolutism, not an affirmation of "pure" Chicano identity. Rather, she insists upon dismantling binarist thinking, a task that requires a self-flexive and critical eye turned upon her Chicano and Mexican roots. She must come to terms with her status as outsider within a patriarchal, homophobic homeland, an act that encourages her to examine with a revisionist eye the shifting forms of hybridity and heterogeneity that have constituted Mexican and Chicano history and culture. (The hybridity of Anglo or western culture[s] remains mostly unexamined in *Borderlands*.) As she explains in the concluding section of part one, "At some point, on our way to a new consciousness we will have to leave the opposite bank, the split between the two mortal combatants somehow healed so that we are on both shores at once" (78). Reflecting the notion of hybridity as a force for social good, she notes that:

> The work of *mestiza* consciousness is to break down the subject-object duality that keeps her a prisoner and to show in the flesh and through the images in her work how duality is transcended. The answer to the problem between the white race and the colored, between males and females, lies in healing the split that originates in the very foundation of our lives, our culture, our languages, our thoughts. A massive uprooting of dualistic thinking in the individual and collective consciousness is the beginning of a long struggle, but one that could, in our best hopes, bring us to the end of rape, of violence, of war. (79)

This yearning for the healing transcendence of duality, of course, partakes of politically utopic hybridity, fed by the dystopic awareness of just how far inter-cultural relations have been from "the end of rape, of violence, of war." Nonetheless, the direction of the narrative is to move from the pain of home as "this thin edge of barbwire" (3) to acceptance of "psychological conflict, a kind of dual identity—we don't identify with the Anglo-American cultural values and we don't totally identify with the Mexican cultural values. We are a synergy of two cultures with various degrees of Mexicanness or Angloness" (63). The positivity of synergy, to the extent that she achieves it, arises out of a migratory exploration of hybridity in its many forms and functions.

Resonating with the early history of hybridity theory as a mixture of species, *mestizo* means, literally, mixed race, and Anzaldúa roots her meditations on mestizaje in the racial mixing of Spanish and Indian that produces the Mexican people, a history that she connects to an ideology of shame in both Mexican and Chicano/a imaginaries. For Anzaldúa, the foundational cultural narrative of Mexicanness revolves around a story of conquest and miscegenation, a pollution of the (masculine) Spanish by the (feminine) Indian, a humiliation of the Indian by the European. The originary narrative centers on Cortez's capture of the Aztec woman known as La Malinche, who became his translator, consort, and the mother of his children. Also derisively called La Chingada, the Whore, this mother of mixed-race Mexicans spans the divide between traitor and victim, the whore who betrayed her people by sleeping with the enemy and the woman taken in violence. Her betrayal and rape metonymically mythologize the violent conquest at the root of Mexican racial hybridity. The U.S. conquest of northern Mexico, the act of violent annexation that cuts off its indigenous inhabitants from their Mexican roots, repeats the initial Spanish conquest and initiates the cultural hybridity that differentiates the Chicano/a culture from the Mexican. The direction of the quest narrative is to move beyond the shame associated with this cultural narrative of racial hybridity. Adapting the revisionist Mexican philosopher José Vasconcelos in section 7 of part one, Anzaldúa suggests that this racial " 'crossing over,' this mixture of races, rather than resulting in an inferior being, provides hybrid progeny, a mutable, more malleable species with a rich gene pool" (77). Asserting the positive good of genetic hybridity involves revaluing the Indian and the woman represented by La Malinche, loving instead of scorning this racialized maternal matrix of Mexicanness.

The cultural hybridity of Mexicanness, she reflects, rests upon a similar pattern of superimposed conquests, going back even before the arrival of the conquistadores. Like Alarcón in *The Aztec Palimpsest*, she moves from consideration of the contemporary borderlands as spatial palimpsest to exploring Mexican (and Chicano) culture as a temporal palimpsest whose history of conquest involved a chain of cultural superimpositions. The Mexican blends the Spanish and the Aztec, but the Aztec Empire itself represents the conquest of other Tolpec and Indian peoples and the introduction of a violently stratified society of powerful elites and commoners.[42] She digs deep into the story of Mexico's syncretism by tracing the meanings of cultural icons in female form, particularly: la Virgen de Gaudalupe, the brown madonna, who, "like my race, is a synthesis of the old world and the new, of the religion and culture of the two races in our psyche" (30); la Chingada, "the raped mother we have abandoned"; and la Llorona, the wailing mother who seeks her lost children whom she killed, Medea-like, to punish the betrayal of her husband (30). These women, she finds, are descendants of Aztec fertility goddesses, particularly Tonantsi, the good mother, and Coatlicue, the sinister mother. This Aztec version of the Christian virgin-whore duality is a misogynist transformation of a Mesoamerican fertility deity, the Serpent Goddess Coatlicue, who bridges the duality of light and dark and serves in the text as Anzaldúa's muse and guardian spirit of the borderland state.[43] Movement toward "the new mestiza consciousness" beyond binarist thinking depends upon recovery of this hybridic palimpsest, this ongoing syncretism that mingles and fuses a succession of female figures central to both Mexican and Chicano identity.

The recovery of the power embedded within these layered cultural figures rooted in the Indian allows Anzaldúa to return without shame to the hybridity of Spanish and Indian that make up Mexican identity and the mixing of Mexican and Anglo that make up Chicano/a identity. In one sense, this "new mestiza consciousness" is utopic, beyond the binarist thinking that undergirds real relations of power. But in another way, this new consciousness resists being a romanticized end point, a stasis of reconciled healing through self-empowerment. Rather, Anzaldúa conceives of it as a migratory state of constant motion, ambiguity, and contradiction, immersed in "cultural collision," and ultimately inseparable from her feminism and queerness.

Relating the new mestiza consciousness to gender and sexuality leads Anzaldúa to migrate into yet another type of hybridity: the inherently transgressive, perpetually destabilizing, interstitial hybridity that Bhabha and Young theorize and that writers like Rushdie and Hanif Kureshi (*The Buddha of Suburbia* and screenplay for *My Beautiful Launderette*) narrativize. The mestiza as feminist, as lesbian, as androgyne becomes in *Borderlands* the principle that unsettles purism and absolutism of all kinds. As a liminal force, the new mestiza is also a pariah, a queer, a deviant, an outcast who, "like a turtle . . . [must] carry 'home' on my back" (21). The binary border between Anglo and Mexican or between each of these and Chicano is broken by the complex interplay of differences within each of these cultures—the differences of "multiplex identity," of contradictory and relational subject positions. In relation to the Anglo and the Mexican, the Chicano is scorned, but within Chicano culture the man has privileges denied to women, and though abused by her husband, the mother-wife has more respect than the single woman or the lesbian. As a woman and a lesbian living within the different patriarchal and homophobic formations of both Chicano and Anglo cultures, Anzaldúa is the figure of fluidity who challenges the fixity of all borders between difference. "I, like other queer people," she writes "am two in one body, both male and female. I am the embodiment of the *hieros gamos* [holy marriage]: the coming together of opposite qualities within" (19). To survive, she must develop "a tolerance for contradictions, a tolerance for ambiguity" (79). Crossing the borders of the conventional, "she has discovered that she can't hold concepts or ideas in rigid boundaries. . . . She learns to be Indian in Mexican culture, to be Mexican from an Anglo point of view. She learns to juggle cultures. She has a plural personality, she operates in a pluralist mode" (79). As androgynous, queer, India-Spanish-Chicana-Anglo, she migrates through all differences, her shifting hybridity calling into question their seeming fixity. She writes in the culminating prose chapter:

> As a *mestiza* I have no country, my homeland cast me out; yet all countries are mine because I am every woman's sister or potential lover. (As a lesbian I have no race, my own people disclaim me; but I am all races because there is the queer of me in all races.) I am cultureless because, as a feminist, I challenge the collective cultural/religious male-derived belief of Indo-Hispanics and Anglos; yet I am cultured because I am participating in the creation of yet another culture, a new story to explain the world and our participation in it, a new value system with images and symbols that connect us to each other and to the planet. (80–81)[44]

In its very migrations through multiple forms of mestizaje, *Borderlands* performs the resistance to fixed and rigid boundaries that the narrative thematizes. For Anzaldúa, the space in between difference ultimately unsettles the absolutism of difference itself, revealing the way that differences are formed, de-formed, and re-formed in history; the way they mingle or fuse over time and space; the way in combination they oppress and free, cause pain and foster healing. Like difference, the mestizaje she explores takes shape locationally—differently constituting itself in various spaces and times, its very fluidity in the text a mark of its necessity for creative survival. Although *Borderlands*' visionary scope repeatedly invokes the utopic mode, it is a mistake, I believe, to read it as a simple romanticization of an impossible hybridity. Anzaldúa's point is that everyday life—in all its physical, linguistic, psychological, and spiritual dimensions—insists upon the realities of hybridity, a mestiza condition that is both forced upon her as a mark of her oppression and embraced by her as a site of possible freedom. One of the concluding poems of part two recapitulates the multiple hybridities of the text as a whole and of the landscape of theory as it migrates rapidly through hybridity's oppression and liberation, pain and exhilaration, historical and geographical formations, biological and cultural dimensions, and multiple meanings and arenas of mixing. The poem names the borderlands of a multicultural queerness, encompassing race, ethnicity, gender, and sexuality in its articulation of clashing and blending. Its nomadic tone—spanning the tragic, comic, and ironic—echoes the text's migrations of meaning. I quote in part:

> To live in the Borderlands means you
>
>> are neither *hispana india negra españa*
>> *ni gabacha, eres mestiza, mulata,* half-breed
>> caught in the crossfire between camps
>> while carrying all five races on your back
>> not knowing which side to turn to, run from;
>
> To live in the borderlands means knowing
>> that the *india* in you, betrayed for 500 years,
>> is no longer speaking to you,
>> that *mexicanas* call you *rajetas,*
>> that den[y]ing the Anglo inside you
>> is as bad as having denied the Indian or Black;
>
> *Cuando vives en la frontera*
>> people walk through you, the wind steals your voice,
>> you're a *burra, buey,* scapegoat,
>> forerunner of a new race
>> half and half—both woman and man, neither—
>> a new gender;
>
> To live in the Borderlands means to
>> put *chile* in the borscht,
>> eat whole wheat *tortillas,*
>> speak Tex-Mex with a Brooklyn accent;
>> be stopped by *la migra* at the border checkpoints;
>
>> . . . .
>
> To live in the borderlands means
>> the mill with the razor white teeth wants to shred off
>> your olive-red skin, crush out the kernel, your heart
>> pound you pinch you roll you out
>> smelling like white bread but dead;
>
> To survive the Borderlands
>> you must live *sin fronteras*
>> be a crossroads.

$$(194–95)^{45}$$

MIGRATORY FEMINISM

Where, then, have these excursions taken us toward theorizing a migratory feminism in the borderlands, one that doesn't obliterate difference, but moves through and beyond it to the spaces of encounter and the processes of syncretism and intercultural hybridity? Robert Young has observed, "It is striking, . . . given the long history of cultural interaction, how few models have been developed to analyse it" (*Colonial Desire* 4). Nineteenth-century models such as diffusionism and evolutionism, he continues, "conceptualized such encounters as a process of the deculturation of the less powerful society and its transformation towards the norms of the West" (4). With the end of colonialism, more recent models "often stress separateness," constructing "two antithetical groups, the colonizer and colonized, self and Other . . . a Manichaean division that threatens to reproduce the static, essentialist categories it seeks to undo" (4). He seeks instead a model of mutual modification through intercultural exchange, "accounts of the commerce between cultures that map and shadow the complexities of its generative and destructive processes" (4–5). Something of what Young calls for in cultural studies, I have been looking for ways to articulate in feminist studies. And yet, I do not seek the model Young wants; I prefer the gerund to the noun. Theorizing: as an open-ended process continually criss-crossing all kinds of borders rather than the closed production of a model that sets up boundaries around human territories of experience. As a border-crossing activity, migratory feminism involves resisting the tendency of theory to fix, schematize, organize, taxonimize, and stabilize the fragmentation and fluidity of thinking and living. Even theories of transience and movement.

I am not entirely comfortable with the appropriation of the language of migration for metaphoric articulations of identity issues when the real conditions of involuntary movement, refugeeism, and homelessness are so desperate for so many people around the globe. The metaphor of migrancy may well be the luxury of the housed and relatively stationary. The attractions of migrancy, intellectual or material, are no doubt more evident to those located in spaces of relative power or privilege, like the academy. (I stress the *relativity* of this power because academic feminism and multiculturalism are extremely vulnerable in higher education, subject to marginalization and constant attack in the Culture Wars and university downsizing of the 1990s.) For all my attempts to integrate issues of power and the reality of difference, I may have done so insufficiently, leaving myself open to critique (justified or unjustified) for being just another privileged (white, middle-class, heterosexual, etc., etc.) academic feminist showing her ignorance of or insensitivity to the meanings of differences among women.

Nonetheless, I cling stubbornly to the belief that feminism needs to think *beyond* pure difference, especially beyond differences among women, but also differences between women and men. By using the term *beyond*, I do not advocate a *post*–difference feminism. Like *post-feminism*, such a notion suggests that we are past the need for difference-talk (been there, done that). Based as they are on such difference-talk, the achievements of multicultural feminism in the North American academy are profound. But the task of anchoring feminist theory and praxis in a comprehensive understanding of difference is not complete. Given the relative scarcity of people of color and the continued threat to uncloseted lesbians and gays in the academy, multiculturalist feminism is often fraught with the politics of tokenism, appropriation, bandwagonism, distrust, and envy. To have any lasting effects, the passion for difference needs to be ongoing.

By *beyond*, then, I mean the term in Homi Bhabha's sense of movement hither and thither, back and forth between our competing needs to understand difference and to chart the spaces in between difference. This is the dialogic between sameness and difference, between mimesis and alterity, that Henrietta Moore and Michael Taussig identify. It is the movement between "universalizing" and "minoritizing" discourses of sexuality that Eve Kosofsky Sedgwick advocates in *Epistemology of the Closet*. It is also the negotiation between "the Scylla of universalism and the Charybdis of differentialism" that Pnina Werbner advocates in her introduction to *Debating Cultural Hybridity* (1). She insists that "we recognize the differential interest social groups have in sustaining boundaries" (22) at the same time as we use the notion of hybridity to undermine "a politics that rests on a coercive unity, ideologically grounded in a single monolithic truth" (21). There is a "politics that proceeds from the legitimacy of difference," she argues, as well as one that acknowledges "the problems of cultural translation and reflexivity, inter-ethnic communication and cross-cultural mobilisation, hybridity and creolisation" (22, 6).

Similarly, I suggest that feminism, like other progressive movements, should refuse polarized choices between difference-talk or hybridity-talk. I advocate instead a dialogic negotiation between the two, allowing each approach to rein in the excesses of the other. The exclusivity of difference-talk fosters politically dangerous balkanization and suppresses both the utopic longing for connection and the visibility of the everyday realities of intercultural mixing. In the name of difference, binarist difference-talk suppresses heterogeneity. The exclusivity of hybridity-talk can in turn slip into a romanticization that elides the existence of collective identities on the one hand and the structures of power that construct them on the other. With its emphasis on constant movement, its effect can be to undermine the collectivity and stability often necessary for organized political opposition. What is necessary is a negotiation between the two, with a refusal of exclusivity for either side.

I have emphasized the theorization of cultural hybridity not to suppress the issue of difference for feminism but to supplement it with attention to the less acknowledged discourse of intercultural relation and mixing in the borderlands between difference. I have featured the work of María Lugones, Gloria Anzaldúa, and Anna Deavere Smith because each performatively negotiates the dialogic between difference and borderlands, embodying an aspect of the crucial issues facing feminism. Although both Lugones and Anzaldúa operate out of reductionistic racial binaries that suppress the heterogeneity of both "sides," both also insist upon their metizaje as Latinas, affirming the particular hybridity of people whose ancestry is Latin American and Mexican. Lugones articulates the dynamic of the need for difference in opposition to the desire for "'world'-travelling," a play beyond pure difference, and the transgressive nature of mixing. Anzaldúa moves with a dazzling fluidity through the multiple forms of life in the contact zone between difference, migrating between the different forms (intermingling, fusion, always syncretist), functions (routine, transgressive), orientations (historical, geographical), and political (oppression, resistance). Refusing fixed oppositions between white/other, victimizer/victimized, Smith questions more fundamentally the ethnic absolutism to which Lugones and Anzaldúa at times revert, developing her versions of "'world'-travelling" and mestiza consciousness, ones that potentially include all communities in her multicultural America. She performs difference as a way of traveling to the other, playing out both the gap between others and the urgency at efforts of mutual understanding and reconciliation. In significantly different ways, all three locate "that place-between-2-places, that walk-in-2-worlds" that Diane Glancy seeks in *Claiming Breath*.

I have defended the real effects of utopic desire for and performative play in between difference. And I have argued that the space in between is more than a longed for or resisted dream that transcends the realities of power. The contact zone where differences meet is as real and as significant a part of cultural formations, including the formations of identity, as the spaces of difference. Our theories of power and empowerment, our concepts of identity and subjectivity, need to spotlight the space of relational interaction as least as much as they examine the space of difference. I have mapped in some detail the landscape of cultural theory about hybridity because the very scope and fluidity of meaning along with the debates about the politics of hybridity offer feminism a way to articulate with some precision a migrancy in the borderlands between difference, in the borderlands beyond the difference impasse.

PART II

Feminism/Globalism

Geopolitical Literacy: Internationalizing Feminism at "Home"—The Case of Virginia Woolf

"De-Westernizing," then, could be seen to begin
at "home."
—*Caren Kaplan,* Questions of Travel

Worldliness is therefore the restoration to such works
and interpretations of their place in the global setting,
a restoration that can only be accomplished by an
appreciation not of some tiny, defensively constituted
corner of the world, but of the large, many-windowed
house of human culture as a whole.
—*Edward Said, "The Politics of Knowledge"*

ARGUABLY the newest initiative in academic feminism involves what is referred to in shorthand as the "internationalization of women's studies." Following fast on the heels of feminist difference discourse, the imperative to "globalize feminism" has emerged out of the convergence of multiple historical conditions: the accelerating transnational flows of people, commerce, culture, and information; the rise of grass-roots feminist movements setting their own distinct agendas for change in many parts of the world; the global spread and growing institutional presence of women's studies in research, higher education, and publishing; and the international movement to define basic human rights for girls and women in all societies in conjunction with the United Nations and other international organizations. Gender questions are regularly integrated with other issues in cultural studies, postcolonial studies, transnational or global studies, and area studies. Feminist scholarship in these new interdisciplinary areas is perhaps the "hottest" new area for academic feminism.

But what does it mean to internationalize women's studies or globalize academic feminism? As a start, it ought to mean resistance to feminist provincialism or pure localism, by which I mean the assumption (conscious or unconscious) that the nature of feminism at "home" and the sex/gender system out of which it emerges are replicated "elsewhere." In a global context, the pluralization of feminism into feminisms assumes that different regions of the world produce distinctive forms of feminism suited to particular sex/gender systems and their larger contexts. Internationalizing feminism surely includes, then, acknowledgment of and commitment to learning more about different parts of the world. This awareness of multiple local formations of feminism goes hand in hand with comparative analysis of similarities and differences in a global context and with mapping how feminism travels from one site to another, that is, with how feminism circulates globally, moving across lines of difference and changing in the process of transplantation.

The difficulties and dangers of such strategies of internationalization are significant. Unless one's field is itself comparative, learning about women and gender systems in other parts of the world from one's base of specialization requires a considerable time investment to acquire sufficient contextual knowledge about other societies and histories. Feminist bricolage or patchwork so beautiful and provocative in the arts is not so beautiful in theory and scholarship. Plucking bits and pieces of women's lives and gender systems from here and there is seriously ahistorical, oblivious to the local overdeterminations of cultural formations.[1] Moreover, *who* does the internationalizing and from what epistemological standpoint are significant issues. Gayatri Chakravorty Spivak has famously asked in "French Feminism in an International Frame," "What is the constituency of an international feminism?" Does it replicate the pattern of "the 'West' out to 'know' the 'East' determining a 'westernized Easterner's' symptomatic attempt to 'know her own world' . . . reversing and displacing . . . the ironclad opposition of West and East?" (*In Other Worlds* 135). In her well-known attack on what she calls the western feminist cult of *Jane Eyre*, Spivak warns against the feminist "'worlding' of what is now called 'the Third World,'" by which she means the reproduction of cultural imperialism as western feminism "discovers" and appropriates the Third World: "To consider the Third World as distant cultures, exploited but with rich intact literary heritages waiting to be recovered, interpreted, and curricularized in English translation fosters the emergence of 'the Third World' as a signifier that allows us to forget the 'worlding,' even as it expands the empire of the literary discipline" ("Three Women's Texts" 798).

As important as these strategies for, issues about, and critiques of globalizing feminism are, they are not my focus. Instead, I want to examine the epistemological issues underlying the attempt to acquire transnational knowledge about women and gender systems. That is, how might our categories for thinking about women and gender shift if we internationalize feminism? And I mean how we think about *any* women or gender system, including those of "home," not just those "elsewhere." How does thinking internationally change feminist thinking in general? What does it mean to internationalize feminist theorizing and critical practices in the knowledge revolution that constitutes the political work of academic feminism? What do "home" and "elsewhere" mean in relation to internationalization? Since neither are fixed, monolithic, or unproblematic categories, what impact do their migratory meanings have on interpretive acts of globalization? I will address these questions by first outlining the significance of geopolitical thinking for feminism, then examining in some detail how geopolitical categories can shift common readings of an influential feminist writer—namely, Virginia Woolf—and finally conclude with some brief reflections about what is epistemologically involved in feminist geopolitical literacy.

THE GEOPOLITICAL AXIS

Constructivist discourses of positionality and location sometimes resort to the rhetoric of axes to designate the different constituents of individual identity, cultural formations, and societal systems of stratification. Any given identity or practice can be read as the place where different axes intersect, axes such as race, ethnicity, gender, religion, class, sexuality, age, and the proverbial so forth. No one axis exists in pure form, but each is mediated through the others in the form of historically specific embodiments. In *Epistemology of the Closet*, Eve Kosofsky Sedgwick argues persuasively that sexuality requires its own distinct axis and that however closely sexuality is entwined with issues of gender, the two are not coextensive and therefore need separate discussion. Sexuality as a historically produced and changing axis of identity has a particular set of meanings for any "minority" sexual community, specifically for gays, lesbians, and bisexuals in a heterosexist society. But sexuality also has what Sedgwick calls a "universalizing" dimension, by which she means cultural notions, institutions, and practices that establish categories of sexuality affecting everyone in any given society. Just as "race" is a constituent of subjectivity for everyone in a racially stratified society, not just racial minorities, so sexuality has categorical cogency.[2] I want to make a parallel argument for the category of geopolitics as a distinct axis. Thinking geopolitically means asking about everyone and every cultural formation how the geopolitical constituents of identity and culture intersect and interact with other axes of difference. Just as we have learned to examine gender or racial or class or sexual inflection, so we need to seek the geopolitical as it inflects or mediates any given cultural identity or praxis.

But just what is the geopolitical axis? Like any term, *geopolitics* means different things to different people, variations related particularly to (inter)disciplinary locations and focuses. The term combines *geo*, the root for earth, with *politics,* the patterns and study of power relations. For some, geopolitics means international or transnational power relations; in these terms, geopolitical identity refers mainly to forms of national identity or origin. Feminists, however, have long insisted that the study of politics not be limited to government, let alone state formations. Thus for me, geopolitics invokes questions of power as they manifest in relation to space on the planet Earth.[3] What I am proposing for academic feminism and more broadly identity studies is a specifically *spatial* axis. I mean by space in this context not a static or empty essence, but rather the spatial organization of human societies, the cultural meanings and institutions that are historically produced in and through specifically spatial locations.[4] Thinking geopolitically means asking how a spatial entity—local, regional, national, transnational—

inflects all individual, collective, and cultural identities. We are used to critiquing ahistorical analysis, forms of thought that do not take into account historical specificity and change over time. Why don't we have a category of critique for the ageographical or the alocational? The geopolitical axis for analysis of difference is a form of geographical imperative, requiring vigilant attention to the meanings of space as they intersect with the meanings of time in the formations of identity.

Geopolitical and racial/ethnic axes are thoroughly entwined, as are the axes of sexuality and gender. We surely need to understand their complicity, but to do so effectively we also need to see them as distinct. Identity questions in Toni Morrison's *Beloved* and Bharati Mukherjee's *Jasmine*, for example, focus centrally on the question of race. In their American contexts, the dark skins of Morrison's (ex)slave Sethe and Mukherjee's Indian immigrant Jasmine trigger racist reactions based on ideologies of inferiority, alienness, bestiality, and/or exoticism. Although the forms of racism directed against women of African and South Asian descent are quite different, the axis of race within a system of white domination oppresses both women. While clearly related to the racial axis, the geopolitical axis in these novels is nonetheless distinct, evident most simply in the significance of Sethe's birth as a slave in the United States and Jasmine's origin in India and status as an illegal immigrant. Reflecting the racial axis, categories like "women of color" and "Third World women" stress the racial parallel between the women, but at the same time tend to elide their geopolitical differences, as well as the shifting complexities of their locational movements.[5] Both Sethe and Jasmine migrate through different locations whose geopolitical meanings define them differently—Sethe, a figure of the African diaspora, moves from South to North as an escaping slave; Jasmine, from Lahore before partition to the Punjabi village of Hasnapur, the provincial city of Jullundhar, Florida as a point of illegal entry, the immigrant enclave in Queens, the yuppie world of Manhattan, and the rural American "heartland" in Baden, Iowa. Local, regional, national, and international dimensions of geopolitical space intersect with race and gender, but are also separable from them. To understand those complex mediations, we must first distinguish among them. Bringing the geopolitical axis into sharp focus involves sensitivity not only to ethnocentrism but also to geocentrism.

So how do we go about thinking geopolitically, about identifying the political meanings of space as a distinct constituent of identity and societal systems? One component of such thinking is to "travel" elsewhere, a movement that can defamiliarize "home," teaching us that what we take as natural is in fact culturally produced and not inevitable. Another component is to begin "at home," bringing the issue of elsewhere to bear on home, locating the sometimes invisible traces of elsewhere in what is familiar. Yet a third dimension is implicit in the prior two—namely, to break down the geopolitical boundaries between home and elsewhere by locating the ways the local and the global are always already interlocking and complicitous. Such geopolitical strategies are already very much in play in the work of many theorists, a few of whom I will review for clarificatory purposes.

Edward Said's concept of "worldliness" as the restoration of a text's place in a global as opposed to purely local setting makes an important starting point, especially in challenging the tendency to remain categorically fixed within a single geopolitical location.[6] In *Culture and Imperialism*, his discussions of Jane Austen and other classically English writers combine examination of British inscriptions of travel elsewhere and the omnipresence of the colonial elsewhere at home. In Austen's quintessentially English novel *Mansfield Park*, for example, Said finds "an imperial map" "threaded through, forming a vital part of the texture of linguistic and cultural practice" (82–83). The way of life in Mansfield Park rests upon the slave trade, sugar, and the colonial planter class in the Caribbean, passing allusions to which appear throughout the novel. Rather than peripheral to the plot, this imperial foundation is central to it, for it is disorder in Antigua that removes Sir Thomas from England, which in turn leads to domestic disorder at Mansfield Park. "More clearly than anywhere else in her fiction," Said concludes, "Austen here synchronizes domestic with international authority. . . . She sees clearly that to hold and rule Mansfield Park is to hold and rule an imperial estate in close, not to say inevitable association with it. What assures the domestic tranquility and attractive harmony of one is the productivity and regulated discipline of the other" (87). This geopolitical reading of *Mansfield Park* shows how the political meanings of spaces outside England are always already present within its national, local, and domestic spaces, even when they appear incidental to a narrative focused preeminently on conflicts "at home." "De-Westernizing," as Caren Kaplan writes in a related way, "could be seen to begin at 'home'" (*Questions of Travel* 166). Or, as Simon Gikandi demonstrates in *Maps of Englishness*, the very self-fashioning of the western "home" (as in the national identity of Englishness) depends upon the existence of the colonial "elsewhere."

For Said, geopolitical thinking takes shape in strongly binarist terms that oppose the imperial West against the colonized and resisting Rest. His eurocentrism inhibits the full development of the geopolitical "worldliness" that he advocates. Nonetheless, his work laid a foundation for those who go well beyond it.[7] What is methodologically significant for my purposes are his related strategies of looking elsewhere for the imprint of the here and locating the elsewhere in the here. Such "worldliness" as an analytic process involves breaking the binary of global and local, of seeing how the global is always already present in the local; the local always already present in the global. As Roland Robertson writes, "the concept of globalization has involved the simultaneity and the interpenetration of what are conventionally called the global and the local," a notion of "interconnectedness" that he captures in the term "glocalization" ("Glocalization" 30). There is no such thing, he argues as a purely "local" culture, be it village, region, or nation. Rather, the local is "an *aspect* of globalization," and global forces are always at work in shaping the local (30).[8] What glocalization means for geopolitical thinking is attention to what Gayatri Chakravorty Spivak calls "the international frame" or the "transnational" conditions that inform any local cultural formations ("Scattered Speculations" esp. 262).[9]

Taking their cue from Spivak's call for "Transnational Culture Studies" in "Scattered Speculations," feminists Inderpal Grewal and Caren Kaplan theorize a transnational feminism beyond the reductionistic binaries of center/periphery,

First World/Third World, western/nonwestern in their introduction to *Scattered Hegemonies*. Transnational feminism is not, they argue, an ahistorical theory of worldwide gender oppression, a standpoint they associate with the term "global feminism" and a particular form of ethnocentrism that singles out gender from other systems of difference. Rather, transnational feminism examines the "relationship of gender to scattered hegemonies" throughout the globe based on various economic, legal, cultural, political, and sexual structures of power (17); it acknowledges the multidimensional patterns of stratification everywhere; and it insists upon the agency of people in all locations. Unlike a comparativist approach that looks for similarities among differences, they argue, the methodology of a transnational feminism looks for linkages and complicities in a global frame. Thus, the study of any historically specific gender formation—in other words, any local knowledge of gender—ought to be informed by the transnational. For them, the global is always present within the local; the local, within the global. Thinking geopolitically involves tracing these spatial interconnections as they constitute multidirectional flows and asymmetries of power.

Grewal's transnational feminist methodology goes well beyond finding a metanarrative plot of western dominance and nonwestern resistance. In *Home and Harem*, she explores the geopolitical interconnections of "home" and "abroad" by examining the discourse of travel within the national cultures and the travel writings of nineteenth-century Indians as well as British writers. She argues that "the 'contact zones' are everywhere and are contained in particular discursive spaces that embody and control the narratives of encounters with difference" (4). In this study of transculturation in the context of empire, both sides of the encounter localize and adapt to their own "domestic" culture what they find elsewhere or in the travel discourses about elsewhere. "Many other narratives of domestic culture, that is, culture within national boundaries," she writes, "must also be located within a transnational frame that is not reduced to a narrative of center and periphery or of globalization" (242). Transnational geopolitical thinking acknowledges, with Grewal, that *any* "domestic" setting serves as a site for absorption, appropriation, and transformation of cultural formations from elsewhere. In this context, a geopolitical analysis of power relations takes into account the scattered hegemonies produced by multidirectional flows of power and local as well as transnational stratifications.

Geopolitical thinking must be attentive to complex questions of power and hybridizing forms of transculturation in the context of empire and postcoloniality. But it should not be limited to tracking the effects of western conquest, imperialism, and dominance of nonwestern others since such an implicit prescription makes the eurocentric assumption that no other parts of the globe have engaged in such geopolitical activities. Moreover, it restricts the geopolitical too narrowly to questions of political, economic, and cultural hegemony, which, as important as they are, do not constitute the entire range of inquiry. Where Grewal, like Said, continues to work within the framework of western empire, James Clifford broadens the analysis of global/local interconnections by seeing them as inevitable and understudied elements of all cultures, including but not limited to those in the

contact zone of imperial encounter. In "Traveling Cultures," he argues that ethnography has been too focused on identifying the stable, localized centers of
culture, thereby missing how all cultures are constantly changing in response to
interactions along the syncretist borderlands with other cultures. He calls for a
shift from what he names the ethnography of dwelling places to an ethnography
of travel. He deconstructs the binary of anthropologist as observing subject traveling to study a static Other and proposes instead a recognition that movement and
travel are part of all cultures. The Other travels too; the Other observes the ethnographer, often from the perspective of having traveled or at least having been
influenced by intercultural encounters in the borderlands. "In much traditional
ethnography," he notes, "the ethnographer has localized what is actually a re-
gional/national/global nexus, relegating to the margins a 'culture's' external relations and displacements" (100). Attention to such nexuses of the local with the
national and transnational will right the balance and ultimately make possible an
ethnography that examines the interaction of dwelling and travel.

Arjun Appadurai's concept of the "global ethnoscape" extends Clifford's formulation by examining the demographic shifting and migratory patterns of people around the globe. No culture, he argues, is "pure"; all cultures are products of
intercultural transactions. By "ethnoscape," he means the shifting landscapes of
"moving groups and persons" whose travels unseat the fixity of home and elsewhere. "This is not to say," he explains, "that there are no relatively stable communities and networks, of kinship, of friendship, or work and leisure, as well as
of birth, residence, and other filiative forms. But it is to say that the warp of these
stabilities is everywhere shot through with the woof of human motion" ("Disjuncture" 7). Within Appadurai's framework, there is no purely domestic space.

In adapting the emphasis on travel and intercultural contact in the work of
Grewal and Kaplan, Clifford, and Appadurai for a feminist methodology of geopolitical thinking, it is important to highlight the important accomplishments of
and continued need for revisionist feminist work on power relations within the
home or the domestic. As ethnographies of dwelling, such work has usefully
troubled the concept of home, denaturalizing domestic space and showing that it
is anything but "stable," and is frequently a site of intense alterity, oppression,
marginalization, and resistance for women.[10] Moreover, access to travel and
movement is often a highly gendered phenomenon, mediated as well through
class relations (as Clifford himself acknowledges in "Traveling Cultures").
Grewal's equation of the domestic and "national culture" elides the distinctions
between nation and home, insufficiently addressing the tensions among the familial, local, regional, and national nexuses in its compensatory emphasis on the
transnational.

The continuing importance of domestic space for a geopolitically informed
feminism is paradigmatically clear in the much-discussed cover photo of Clifford
and George Marcus's *Writing Culture* (1986). Captioned "Stephen Tyler in the
Field. Photography by Martha G. Tyler," the photo focuses on a white, western
ethnographer thoroughly immersed in writing up his field notes in rural India.
Sitting on the front steps of a dwelling, his back is turned to a thoughtful Indian

man sitting on the porch just behind him, gazing at the scene of ethnographic writing. Clifford and Marcus use the photo to illustrate the "starting point of a crisis in anthropology" (3), the shift in focus from ethnography's object of study (the ethnos) to the process of writing (the graph). In "Traveling Cultures," Clifford updates this sense of crisis by arguing for greater attention to the intercultural contact accomplished through travel implicit in the photo. Feminist anthropologists have in turn noted what went unnoticed in Clifford and Marcus's initial discussion of the photo—namely, the presence of two Indian women in the doorway of and nearly inside the dwelling, women who are also gazing at the white man writing.[11] The lesson for feminist geopolitical thinking is that "the contact zone is everywhere," to echo Grewal, including *inside* the dwelling. In short, in our efforts to develop a systematic methodology for understanding the geopolitical axis of difference, the considerable body of feminist theory on the family, the home, and domesticity should not be abandoned. I am suggesting rather that we add to and revise what has been done by understanding the geopolitical dimensions that weave in and among the domestic.

I am similarly not ready to discard comparativist analysis as a component of geopolitical thinking, a move that Spivak, Grewal, and Kaplan partially suggest in their definitions of a transnational methodology.[12] Whatever the origins of comparative disciplines in the West, comparativist thinking is not in my view inherently eurocentric and bankrupt. In defense of comparativism, Clifford writes: "The comparative scope I'm struggling toward here is not a form of overview. Rather I'm working with a notion of comparative knowledge produced through an *itinerary*, always marked by a 'way in,' a history of locations and a location of histories" ("Traveling Cultures" 105). Susan Sniader Lanser argues effectively, I believe, for a revisionist feminist "cross-cultural comparative practice" that abandons the privileging of the West as the basis of comparison and attends as carefully to the specificities of difference as it does to the parallels based in similarity ("Compared to What?" esp. 296–300). Such "comparative specificity . . . embrace[s] both difference and similarity" without homogenization (297). I would add that cross-cultural comparativism effects a kind of categorical "travel" that denaturalizes "home," bringing to visibility many of the cultural constructions we take for granted as "natural." Sharp juxtapositions of different locations often produce startling illuminations, bringing into focus the significance of geopolitical mediations of other axes of difference. Comparativism and the "glocalization" of a transnational methodology are not mutually exclusive. Indeed, these practices complement each other as constitutive parts of geopolitical thinking.

UNCOMMON READINGS: THE GEOPOLITICAL WOOLF

Within my overlapping "home" bases of feminist theory, modernist literary studies, academic feminism, and the United States, Virginia Woolf has been a towering figure as a feminist thinker and writer. I would like to revisit some familiar aspects of her life and work within the less familiar terrain of geopolitical theory as a case study for internationalizing feminism "at home," for developing strategies to interpret the geopolitical axis of difference that threads itself throughout her work, always mediated by other axes of difference like gender, sexuality, and class. This involves attention both to the geopolitical dimensions of her writings and to the geographical dimensions of reading acts and practices. As reflected in a recent symposium entitled Virginia Woolf International, Woolf is an international, indeed transnational phenomenon.[13] But what has it meant and what should it mean to read Virginia Woolf International? How is the spatial and geopolitical imprinted in her work, nationally and transnationally? How has her work and presence circulated globally, subject to continual transplantation? In what way has she taken root and grown in different national soils? Should her point of origin as English constitute a privileged site for reading? Or, in leaving British soil, does Woolf lose her right to be read in her own national context? Is there a global Woolf, a transnational phenomenon or set of meanings? Or does the very effort to internationalize erase the specificities of different cultural readings? How does history—the passage of time and our stories about it—impact on Woolf's transfer through space? Just *who* is the geopolitical Woolf and how does she relate to the Woolf read through the distinctive or interactive lenses of gender, sexuality, class, race, and religion?

For academic feminists, these questions have special urgency, since Woolf's spatial transplantation involves crossing not only national borders but also institutional ones. Within the context of her England, Woolf would most likely have been amazed (if not hostile) to the way the North American academy has become a crucial site of feminist activism, with herself so often at the center of it. The fame she would have enjoyed, believing I think, against all anarchist tendencies to the contrary, that she deserved it. But politics and the university system? She was so used to thinking of the university in Oxbridgean terms as a walled-off enclave established to preserve patriarchal and class hegemonies that the whole notion of universities allowing or even fostering radical thinking in the form of feminist inquiry and academic activism would have been quite foreign to her. Screening her uncommonness behind the mask of the "common reader," Woolf anchored her oppositional consciousness in the position of outsider, including, preeminently, being outside the academy—true, with a touch of envy in her despisement, but nonetheless genuine disdain for the reactionary pomp and circumstance of elite scholarship and teaching.[14] And yet, the very internationality of Virginia Woolf locates her firmly in the center of an institution she scorned. For feminists of the U.S. academy, Woolf's significance to the oppositional project of academic feminism has been foundational. In her transatlantic transplantation, Woolf has moved from outside to inside the academy.

In the early 1980s, Woolf was already a site (sight/cite) caught in the crosshairs of two important and opposing formulations of the geopolitical Woolf: that of two North Americans, Hugh Kenner (originally from Canada) and Adrienne Rich of the United States. Both acknowledge Woolf's location at the interface between modernism and feminism. But Kenner attacks Woolf for her lack of internationalism, while Rich chastises Woolf for what she sees as her illusory internationalism. What they wrote in 1984 is telling. First, Kenner:

> [Virginia Woolf] is not part of International Modernism; she is an English novelist of manners, writing village gossip from a village called Bloomsbury for her English readers (though *cultivated* readers: that distinction had become operative between Dickens' time and hers, and Bloomsbury was a village with a good library.) She and they share shrewd awarenesses difficult to specify; that is always the provincial writer's strength. As she pertains to the English province, as Faulkner and Dr. Williams to the American: craftily knowing, in a local place, about mighty things afar: things of the order of *Ulysses*, even. It is normal for the writers of the Three Provinces to acknowledge International Modernism and take from it what they can. ("Modernist Cannon" 57)

Rich, in contrast, writes:

> I am to speak these words in Europe, but I have been searching for them in the United States of America. A few years ago I would have spoken of the common oppression of women, the gathering movement of women around the globe . . . the failure of all previous politics to recognize the universal shadow of patriarchy. . . .
>
> I would have spoken these words as a feminist who "happened" to be a white United States citizen, conscious of my government's proven capacity for violence and arrogance of power, but as self-separated from that government, quoting without second thought Virginia Woolf's statement in *Three Guineas* that "as a woman I have no country. As a woman I want no country. As a woman my country is the whole world."[15]
>
> This is not what I come here to say in 1984. . . . As a woman I have a country; as a woman I cannot divest myself of that country merely by condemning its government or by saying three times "As a woman my country is the whole world." Tribal loyalties aside, and even if nation-states are now just pretexts used by multinational conglomerates to serve their interests, I need to understand how a place on the map is also a place in history within which as a woman, a Jew, a lesbian, a feminist I am created and trying to create. ("Notes" 212)

While Kenner's refusal to consider Woolf a modernist writer is a maverick view, even within the conservative elite of modernist studies, his association of modernism with internationalism is widespread. But what do he and others of similar views mean by internationalism? We need to denaturalize the term *international*, understanding its particular ideological formation rather than assuming a fixed and inevitable meaning for the concept. Kenner characterizes "International Modernism" as a polyglot phenomenon built on ceaseless travel and movement, expatriatism, and the pastiche of many languages and cultures. Others as well stress its urban character, centered in what Malcolm Bradbury calls the great western "culture-capitals" of Britain, Europe, and the United States: especially London, Paris, New York, Berlin, St. Petersburg, and to a lesser extent, Vienna and Rome.[16] As these critics see it, the internationality of modernism means that lines of influence criss-cross the Atlantic and the European continent as writers pack their bags, often living in perpetual exile, creating an imagined *communitas* of fellows artists alienated from family and nation. Their material and aesthetic border crossings constitute them as a transnational elite, having more in common with each other than with people of their own nation—a reconstitution, if you will, of the medieval European cultural elite transcending local particularities.

Accepting as self-evidently true the construct of "the West" produced in the nineteenth century, Kenner and company regard modernist internationalism as a profoundly western phenomenon, its writers drawing from the palimpsest of grand traditions going back through the ages to Rome, Greece, and the cradle of civilization in the Middle East.[17] From this perspective, modernism disrupted its most immediate precursors—romanticism, Victorian realism, and the decadents—often through a return to and revitalization of the classics of western tradition. To break the stranglehold of the immediate past—so the story goes—many writers found inspiration in "primitivist" forms and nonwestern cultures in general, thus instituting massive appropriations of African arts, Asian religions, and indigenous American rituals. The empires of Britain and Europe provided more than raw materials and markets; their very difference fed the modernist shattering of nineteenth-century western hegemonies. International Modernism involved a form of cultural imperialism or theft, requiring what anthropologist Michel-Rolph Trouillot calls "the savage slot" occupied by the Other through and against which the West could define its own civilization as universal.[18]

Within the landscape of such an International Modernism, Woolf appears to be a homebody, limiting herself (and thus being limited by) her Englishness—in short, the "provincial" writer of Kenner's dismissal. Unlike so many modernists, she did not have to leave home in order to write. She never lived abroad, and compared with many other modernists, her travels were mainly brief holidays, perhaps because foreign travel early became associated with dire illness and death in her personal life. Her sister Stella's honeymoon on the continent coincided with her mother Julia's fatal illness; the family journey to Greece and Constantinople led directly to her brother Thoby's death; Vanessa's sudden illness during a later trip to Turkey brought an anxious Virginia all the way to Constantinople by herself; Woolf's own extended honeymoon journey to Spain and Italy was followed by several years of severe mental illness.[19] In aesthetic terms, Woolf also remained largely "at home," within the British tradition, only occasionally setting her novels outside Britain or writing about other national literatures in her essays.[20] The polyglot linguistic, stylistic, and intertextual citational strategies of *The Cantos*, *Ulysses*, and *The Waste Land* have no parallel existence in Woolf's oeuvre. Within the critical construct of International Modernism, Woolf appears to renounce transnational boundary crossing, to be largely content to remain within the confines of England.

Within the context of Adrienne Rich's feminist theory of the mid-1980s, however, Woolf exhibits a dangerous internationalism, one allied with rather than distinct from that of Kenner and company, one embodying the ethnocentrism of the West, which as an ideological formation takes all things western as the measure of the universal. What drives Rich's critique of Woolf's transnationalism is the pressing need she and many other feminists perceived in the 1980s to define a locational politics that did not erase the differences among women in the service of a false global sisterhood that potentially obscures the structure of power relations between different groups of women at home and abroad. In "Notes toward a Politics of Location" (1984), she was addressing a major theoretical and organizational issue in North American feminism—namely, the shift from an emphasis on women's gender difference from men to an understanding of the shattering differences *among* women. Her dissociation from Woolf's feminism in this essay also covertly screens a self-critique, her renunciation of her own previous calls in the late 1970s for just such a global feminism.[21]

The contrasting views of Rich and Kenner on Woolf's lack or excess of internationalism share at least one thing in common: a heuristic (mis)reading of Woolf's complex oeuvre and the place of the international and geopolitical within it. The proponents of International Modernism confine Woolf to the realm of the domestic and ignore entirely the multiple ways in which the local is for Woolf co-complicit with the national and international. Such blindness leads Malcolm Bradbury and James McFarlane, for example, to conclude their biographical entry on Woolf with the dismissive statement that "Mrs Woolf's can seem in some respects a domesticated Modernism, but it contains shrill undertones of disturbance and terror, dark insights undoubtedly related to her suicide in 1941" (639).[22] For them, the domestic is always already domesticated, not international. But for Woolf, as many Woolf critics have pointed out, geopolitical power relations begin at home in the patriarchal structure of the family.

The transcendental globalism to which Rich objects in *Three Guineas* depends upon wrenching Woolf's resonant lines out of their full context. In this section of the text, Woolf is not advocating the formation of a global feminism where gender oppression links women everywhere in a common sisterhood. Rather, she expresses a pacifist "desire for peace and freedom for the whole world," one that requires a self-conscious removal from "national self-praise" and military defense (109) and thus implicitly advocates a transnational oppositional identity that replaces patriotism. She regards women in some sense as a potential avant-garde for such a pacifism because they face, as a group, multiple exclusions that make their relationship to national identity significantly different from that of men, a point that many postcolonial feminist theorists have recently made.[23] Patriotism causes war instead of protecting against it, Woolf argues. Peace depends upon the renunciation of chauvinist patriotism in favor of a shared common humanity. In context, her ringing and often quoted line, "As a woman I have no country," suggests her refusal of nationalism and advocacy of a radical humanism. Like the rest of her work, *Three Guineas* does not erase local differences, but instead provides "thick descriptions" (Clifford Geertz's term for "local knowledge") of the interactions of gender with other systems of stratification within national contexts. Her work—materialist as it so often is—exhibits an early feminist formulation of a locational politics, not a repudiation of it, as Rich implies.

Although Kenner and Rich remain influential as readers of Woolf's internationalism, a different sort of geopolitical Woolf has begun to emerge, one beyond the limiting frameworks of a Kennerian International Modernism or a 1980s North American feminism fixated on differences among women. One approach has been to focus on the reception of her texts as they move through and into different national cultures. "In Passage to China: East and West and Woolf," for example, Melba Cuddy-Kean and Kay Li argue that scholars in China working on foreign writers in the aftermath of the Cultural Revolution and the death of Mao focus on Woolf's stylistics, ignoring her politics, in marked contrast to readers in the West. Historical conditions of location are powerful and complex determinants of different national interpretation, they argue (see also Chapman). There are two pitfalls to such reception studies, not insurmountable, yet nonetheless problematic. The first is the tendency to produce empirical summaries of what has been written about Woolf without regard to how these views reflect geopolitical location. The second is the temptation to homogenize what are actually heterogeneous reading practices by emphasizing those readings that fit some preconceived notion of national identity or interest. (The very difference between the views of Kenner and Rich about Woolf should alert us to the fact that a single national location does not ensure shared perspectives.) Both the absence of and the overemphasis on geopolitical determinants of reception can hamper the tracing of Woolf's geopolitical transplantations.

Challenged by postcolonial studies, some critics have begun articulating the geopolitical Woolf by examining the issue of empire in her life and work. Famously initiated by Jane Marcus's "Britannia Rules *The Waves*," readers have debated Woolf's critique of or orientalist participation in the rhetoric and power of empire, particularly in such texts as *The Voyage Out, Mrs. Dalloway, Orlando, The Waves*, and *Three Guineas*. Like Said's reading of classically English authors in *Culture and Imperialism*, Kathy Phillips, for example, argues in *Virginia Woolf against Empire* that British imperialism pervades Woolf's oeuvre; she differs from Said, however, in defining Woolf's stance as entirely critical. More in tune with Said's approach, Marianne Dekoven sees the place of empire in *The Voyage Out* as more contradictory, both attacking and reinforcing the discourses under critique and thus rupturing the ideological coherence of western imperialism.[24] Two problem areas have arisen in these geopolitical readings of Woolf and empire. First is the magnetic pull of binary analysis implicit in the category of western imperialism, resulting in overreliance on models of center/periphery and subject/other that all too often deny agency to multiple others in a rush to condemn the center. Second is the tendency of such binaries to enmesh Woolf critics in an unanswerable debate about whether to celebrate Woolf as critic of empire or to critique her as participant in and beneficiary of imperialism.[25] As vital as discussions of Woolf's relation to empire are, the geopolitical axis of Woolf's life, work, and reception is broader than the politics of imperialism. For an English writer born at the height of the British Empire and dying in its twilight, the story of empire is clearly central. But it is not the whole geopolitical story.

To broaden a geopolitical reading of Woolf beyond international reception and questions of western empire, I want to invoke the transnational and conjuncturalist methodologies of Grewal, Kaplan, Appadurai, and Spivak along with Clifford's call for an ethnography of travel. Attentive to questions of power, these theories offer a way to remove Woolf from the realm of the purely domestic or the purely English to show how the global is always embedded in the local. Adapting Clifford in particular, I ask that we shift our emphasis from reading Woolf's texts as ethnographies of dwelling—deconstructions of family plots; revisionings of domesticity—to seeing them as ethnographies of traveling. Just as ethnography borrows the narrative formations of fiction in telling stories about other cultures, so novel writing often inscribes the ethnographic gaze of a writer intent on representing a given cultural formation. Thus, in borrowing Clifford's theory of ethnography for a discussion of literary narratives, we can ask where and why do the tropes of travel and movement appear in Woolf's texts? Who and what moves in and out of domestic sites? In what way is home always already implicated in the regional, national, and global nexus of power relations? And vice versa. How do systems of power outside the dwelling perpetually destabilize the home? What is the dialectic between stasis and movement in Woolf's texts, and how does this process inscribe the geopolitical? In what way might the sites of home and travel be inflected by gender, class, sexuality, race, national origin, and so forth? To what extent do these questions enter into the self-conscious politics and experimental play of Woolf's writing, and to what extent do they remain as part of a geopolitical unconscious of the texts?

Such questions can refocus our readings of such oft-cited Woolfian moments as the description of Mrs. Brown in the railway carriage in the essay "Mr. Bennett and Mrs. Brown." Why does Woolf fictionalize her symbol of the mysteries of human character riding in a train instead of sitting indoors? Or think of the resonantly pre-oedipal moment that Woolf recalls as her earliest memory in "A Sketch of the Past": "This was of red and purple flowers on a black ground—my mother's dress; and she was sitting either in a train or in an omnibus, and I was on her lap. . . . Perhaps we were going to St Ives; more probably we were coming back to London" (64). The "woof of human movement" is woven throughout the warp of maternal stability, to echo Appadurai.

Even the fictional representation of St. Ives in *To the Lighthouse*, Woolf's most domestic of novels, is set not in Cornwall, but far away in the northwest of Scotland, in the Hebrides on the Isle of Skye.[26] In a later letter to Vanessa from Skye, Woolf emphasizes its foreignness: "Well, here we are in Skye, & it feels like the South Seas—completely remote, surrounded by sea, people speaking Gaelic, no railways, no London papers, hardly any inhabitants. Believe it or not, it is (in its way, as people say), so far as I can judge on a level with Italy, Greece or Provence" (Bell, *Woolf* 2:205–6). Such observations remind us that Britain, like all nations, has its own centers and peripheries, its history of internal conquest and colonization, its "foreigners" and "others" within national boundaries.

Mrs. McNab, it should be remembered, has an Irish name, a clear geopolitical marker within an English novel.[27] Why do we read her primarily in relation to class? She is certainly one of Woolf's relatively uncommon working-class characters whose subjectivity and agency are substantially represented. But as Mrs. McNab witlessly lurches, leers, and drinks her way through her first appearance in section V of "Time Passes," the English stereotypes of the drunken Irish and the Celts as an inferior race hover uncomfortably within the geopolitical unconscious of the text.[28] Countering this mode of representation is Mrs. McNab's second appearance in sections VIII and IX of "Time Passes." Here, Mrs. McNab is markedly different, the narrator having "traveled" from the exteriority of stereotypic symbol to the interiority of Mrs. McNab's consciousness sympathetically rendered in the same free indirect discourse used to represent English characters of a different class (135–41). One way to understand this shift is to see Woolf "traveling" from an ethnography of Otherness to one that begins in being able to imagine the agency of multiply defined others. The first fetishizes difference; the second attempts to bridge it.[29] Why, we might then ask, does Woolf so seldom cross this bridge—rejecting for the most part both the "savage slot" of modernist primitivism and the attempt to imagine the agency and subjectivity of geopolitical others?[30]

Despite the novel's "foreign" setting and servant help, Woolf travels primarily in *To the Lighthouse* into the interior heart of darkness within Victorian upper-middle-class domesticity through the figures of Mr. and Mrs. Ramsay.[31] As so many feminist critics have shown, Woolf's fictionalizations of Leslie and Julia Stephen deconstruct the gender binaries and rescript the oedipal family romance in revisionist transformations of home. But the geopolitical dimensions have been less visible. Let me suggest a transnational approach with a brief look at two familiar scenes from the opening sections of the novel: the preamble to Mr. Ramsay's demand for sympathy from Mrs. Ramsay as she sits Madonna-like, framed in the window with her son at her knee, in the opening sequence of the novel; and second, Mrs. Ramsay's solitary and restorative moment apart from her family, stolen after helping first one then another of her demanding family.

Clifford's opposition between the ethnographies of dwelling and travel can help us rethink Woolf's revision of the stereotypical Victorian gender plot, while Grewal and Kaplan's analysis of transnational glocalization help identify geopolitical dimensions of gender and class relations within the English family. Signifying the space of dwelling, Mrs. Ramsay is the stationary, fecund presence that nourishes, the beacon of light that preserves against shipwreck. Representing the space of travel, Mr. Ramsay is a figure of motion, pacing back and forth before the window with a sailboat's tacking pattern, booming lines of poetry before he finally approaches his wife for sympathy. He is the figure who moves in and out of the domestic space, having access to the world of public prestige unavailable to Mrs. Ramsay. The two seem as different as difference can be. But as Clifford's concept of the dialectics of dwelling and travel suggests, stasis and motion, the domestic and the foreign, are co-complicit and interpenetrating.

The poem that Mr. Ramsay spouts—Tennyson's "Charge of the Light Brigade" (1854)—brings the geopolitical realm of the Crimean War into the heart of domesticity, indirectly linking the geopolitics of states with politics of the home, much as Woolf was to do more directly in *Three Guineas* and *Between the Acts*. A watershed event for the English public "back home," the war was linked to geopolitical alignments far more complex than Said's master plots of an orientalist West versus East. Fought against Russia in alliance with the Ottomans, the war was part of Britain's long-term support of the Ottoman Empire as a way to resist the expansion of the Russian Empire into Iran and India. Tennyson wrote his famous poem after reading an editorial in the *Times* of London on 13 November 1854, based on the dispatch of its war correspondent, William Howard Russell. Russell's detailed accounts of the massive suffering, loss of life, and frequent stupidity or incompetence of military leaders appeared on the breakfast plates of a highly shocked civilian public, breaking down the separation between home and foreign places, between private domesticity and public aggression. More than any others, Russell's detailed dispatches ushered in a new role for a modern media in wartime, performing much the same cultural work as did the television cameras over a century later, feeding graphic scenes of the Vietnam War to an American populace along with their dinners. Fueled by Russell's accounts, the swirl of controversy about the war provided rich ground for Florence Nightingale, who made a cause célèbre of the soldiers' suffering, indirectly linking it to that of women of her class back home for whom she prescribed the cure of meaningful work in the Crimea and in the foundation of nursing as a profession in general (see figs. 2 and 3).[32]

Based on the suicidal charge of the British cavalry in Bakaklava, Tennyson's poem celebrates the heroism of the "noble 600" even as it calls into question the judgment of their leaders, who sent their men into a line of Russian guns and almost certain death for no good military purpose and as the result of a series of blunders and misunderstandings. Few survived the charge. An editorial in the *Times* editorial called it "some hideous blunder," a phrase that appears hauntingly altered in the poem as "Someone had blunder'd."[33] To quote in part:

> "Forward, the Light Brigade!"
> Was there a man dismay'd?
> Not tho' the soldier knew
>   Some one had blunder'd:
> Their's not to make reply,
> Their's not to reason why,
> Their's but to do and die:
> Into the valley of Death
>   Rode the six hundred.
>
>   .   .   .   .
>
> Cannon to right of them,
> Cannon to left of them,
> Cannon in front of them
>   Volley'd and thunder'd;
> Storm'd at with shot and shell,
> Boldly they rode and well,
>
>   .   .   .   .
>
> When can their glory fade?
> O the wild charge they made!

THE CARDIGAN CALOP.

BY

EARL HÖCHST.

Fig. 2. A contemporary cartoon of the Earl of Cardigan, who led the charge
of the Light Brigade at Balaklava in 1854 during the Crimean War. From
A. J. Barker, *The Vainglorious War.*

> Honour the charge they made!
> Honour the Light Brigade,
> Noble six hundred!

(289–90)

Tennyson's readers both then and now argue about whether the poem is stu-
pidly celebratory or intentionally ironic.[34] But for Woolf, it was clearly a caricature of its own bombastic patriotism, whether Tennyson meant it or not. Waving
his hands wildly, gesticulating, and shouting out first "Boldly we rode and well"
and then more despairingly, "*Some one has blundered,*" Mr. Ramsay is a parody
of a caricature as he charges toward Lily and Bankes, nearly knocking over her
easel (17, 18). Bearing down on his wife, he stamps his foot on the terrace and

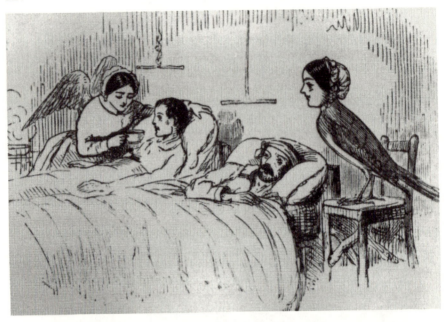

Fig. 3. A contemporary drawing of wounded soldiers and Nightingales, as Florence
Nightingale's nurses were called during the Crimean War. From A. J. Barker,
The Vainglorious War.

swears at her, "Damn you," presumably because she said the weather might allow
a trip to the lighthouse tomorrow after all (31–32). Once again he paces while she
knits: " 'Some one has blundered,' he said, striding off, up and down the terrace"
(33). The narrator, in words that waver ambiguously between external representation and the free indirect discourse rendering his consciousness, describes Mr.
Ramsay with rhymes, rhythm, and images taken directly from the poem:

> He shivered; he quivered. All his vanity, all his satisfaction in his own splendour,
> riding fell as a thunderbolt, fierce as a hawk at the head of his men through the valley
> of death, had been shattered, destroyed. Stormed at by shot and shell, boldly we rode
> and well, flashed through the valley of death, volleyed and thundered, straight into
> Lily Briscoe and William Bankes. He quivered; he shivered. (30)[35]

The effect of the Crimean War—or, to be more precise, Tennyson's rendition
of it—in the midst of intimate domesticity is surely mock-heroic, in best Popian
(if not Joycean) fashion, satirically diminishing through juxtaposition the heroism
of war and the folly of masculinist fantasy.[36] The joke, of course, is that Mr.
Ramsay has blundered—right into Lily and Bankes, right into cursing the woman
he desperately needs and will all too soon lose to unexpected death. But the
parodic mimicry of the Crimean War and the poem about it do more than dismantle murderous masculinist heroism and self-importance. To invoke Luce Irigaray's notion of feminine parody as a theoretical jamming of phallogocentrism,[37]

Woolf's exaggerated and repeated citation of both war and war poem discloses the interpenetration of the domestic, the national, and the transnational. Patriarchal folly at home is both a cause and a reflection of militarist and nationalist folly abroad. And vice versa. The geopolitical battles among nations—exacerbated by the stupidity and incompetence of their leaders—are both a cause and a reflection of gender politics in the home. This is, as so many have shown, the essential political lesson of *Three Guineas*, an internationalist lesson Kenner misses entirely and Rich misreads in her haste to rebuke Woolf.[38]

In soothing Mr. Ramsay's battered psyche, Mrs. Ramsay performs a function similar to what Tennyson's poem did for the British, but with a difference; for her role emphasizes how the domestic realm enables war, while seeming to be its opposite. To borrow from *A Room of One's Own*, "Women have served all these centuries as looking-glasses possessing the magic and delicious power of reflecting the figure of man at twice its natural size. . . . Whatever may be their use in civilised societies, mirrors are essential to all violent and heroic action. That is why Napoleon and Mussolini both insist so emphatically upon the inferiority of women, for if they were not inferior, they would cease to enlarge" (35–36). I carry this quotation beyond its familiar citation having to do with male/female relations to emphasize that the geopolitical Woolf goes beyond the psychopolitics of intimacy to show how the local is never purely local, but always belongs to "a regional/national/global nexus," to echo James Clifford. Woolf's representation of the domestic carries within an invocation of the international and geopolitical so that her notion of intimacy in the privacy of the family circle has a transnational valence.

Even Mrs. Ramsay's one moment of solitude participates in this geopolitical nexus. Having nourished the domestic space, Mrs. Ramsay "leaves home" for imaginary adventures as she becomes (we all know the passage)—

> a wedge-shaped core of darkness . . . , this self having shed its attachments was free for the strangest adventures. When life sank down for a moment, . . . [h]er horizon seemed to her limitless. There were all the places she had not seen; the Indian plains; she felt herself pushing aside the thick leather curtain of a church in Rome. This core of darkness could go anywhere, for no one saw it. They could not stop it, she thought, exulting. There was freedom, there was peace, there was, most welcome of all, a summoning together, a resting on the platform of stability. (62–63)[39]

Mrs. Ramsay, that fount of Victorian stability and domesticity, adventures imaginatively into the heart of the foreign: the Indian plains of the British raj; the forbidden Catholicism of Rome, surely an odd site for the atheistic Englishwoman. The reference is so brief, the fantasy so truncated, that we are left only with a sense of condensation in this transnational imaginary. Why India? Why the plains instead of, say, the Ganges, or Bombay? Or could this be the Plains Indians of the United States, long a symbol of freedom for many Anglo-American women? Why the Roman church? Is the church itself the "thick leather curtain" or is its doorway a hymenal "curtain of leather" for penetration? To what? The dark interior? The confessional box? What secrets does this core of darkness locate? To be experienced as "adventure," the foreign requires a domestic core of darkness—another kind of heart of darkness—that both travels and stays at home as a "platform of stability." For Woolf, the domestic—the local—is always already global and transnational. And vice versa.

Woolf's (inter)nationalizing of the domestic with allusions to the global is a common occurrence, with some references more overt than others. For covert references, we need a cryptographic approach for locating the geopolitical Woolf, looking well beyond the intentionalities and conscious play of a given text.[40] Just as Toni Morrison writes about race as the omnipresent "ghost in the machine" of American literature that must be brought to visibility ("Unspeakable Things" 11), the geopolitical must often be denaturalized in Woolf's texts, removed from what we simply take for granted. Where are the geopolitical ghosts in Woolf's texts, and how do they haunt them? By way of example, I want to suggest some uncommon readings of Woolf's metonyms in *A Room of One's Own* that are so commonly read solely in relation to gender: the food at Oxbridge and Fernham; the five hundred pounds a year; and a room of one's own—all most surely instances of the local, but containing often unacknowledged gestures at the geopolitical and transnational.

First, the food. We are used to reading the richly sauced sole-and-partridge luncheon topped with wines at the Oxbridge luncheon and the "homely trinity" of gravy-covered beef, greens, and potatoes with prunes for dessert at the Fernham dinner in relation to gender and class (10–11, 17–18). Clearly, the women's college, lacking the "gold and silver" of the men's colleges, served its students a poorer level of food, metonym for the paucity of material and figural nourishment for women's creativity. But what about the geopolitical resonance to these meals? Don't the "fancy" sauces and wines connote French food? Isn't 1066 and all that part of the text's political unconscious—that is, the French conquest of the English, and the class-related Frenchification of England (the higher the class, the more closely entwined the two material cultures in true postcolonial fashion)? At least, so it has seemed to me as an American teacher, continually attempting to re-create the full resonance of British cultural meanings for my students. When I mentioned this reading to a group of British feminists in Cambridge, England, explaining that I regularly presented this to my American students as an example of how important it is for them to cross (figuratively) the Atlantic when they read, these British women looked at me as if I were mad. Such a reading had never occurred to them. They saw only the class codes of the metonymic food transposed to gender. My attempt to re-create a British reading framework may after all be a reflection of my geopolitical position as an American reading an English text, sensitive to issues of conquest and colonialism in part because of the hegemonic pull things English retain in Britain's former North American colony, especially in English literary studies. Traveling to the United States, *A Room of One's Own* has become a different text. Geopolitics may reside as much in the reading process as in the text itself.

In any case, geopolitical ghosts reside less ambiguously in Woolf's use of five hundred pounds a year and a room of one's own as metonyms for what women need, both materially and psychologically, to write freely. The legacy of five hundred pounds a year as the measure of economic freedom depends upon a class-based system of banking that arose in Britain along with the development of the East India Trading Company and the other mercantile and agricultural institutions feeding off from colonies in the British Empire worldwide. Five hundred pounds a year represents interest income based on a much larger capital investment. Living on interest from an untouched capital investment was (and is) a mark of class, which in the Britain of Woolf's lifetime was inseparable from the economics of empire.

The biographical origins of Woolf's metonym confirm its geopolitical foundation through various condensations and displacements. As Jane Marcus points out, her father's sister, the Quaker reformer Caroline Emelia Stephen, left Virginia a legacy of twenty-five hundred pounds in 1909, which with other legacies produced an interest income of about four hundred pounds a year. Daughter of a man Marcus calls "a key 'architect of imperialism,'" Caroline is the aunt with whom Virginia stayed in the fall of 1904 after a severe episode of mental illness; here it was, at Caroline's Cambridge home, The Porch, that she wrote her first publication.[41] The five hundred pounds a year in *A Room of One's Own* contains a personal and political unconscious, condensing Caroline's financial, spiritual, and creative legacies with the British banking system and the colonialism rationalized and justified by Woolf's grandfather. These associational chains are compressed within Woolf's thoughts on seeing a ten-shilling note in her purse:

> I gave the waiter a ten-shilling note in my purse; I noticed it, because it is a fact that still takes my breath away—the power of my purse to breed ten-shilling notes automatically. I open it and there they are. Society gives me chicken and coffee, bed and lodging, in return for a certain number of pieces of paper which were left me by an aunt, for no other reason than that I share her name.
>
> My aunt, Mary Beton, I must tell you, died by a fall from her horse when she was riding out to take the night air in Bombay. (37)[42]

The automatic appearance of these shillings, the fact "that she had left me five hundred pounds a year for life," contrasts, the lecturer explains, to the kind of "cadging odd jobs" that had supplied her economic support prior to the legacy (37). "Free" money for life that appears without her own labor allows Woolf-as-lecturer to say "that five hundred a year stands for the power to contemplate" without worrying if one pleases or displeases (110). Woolf's figuration of women's intellectual and creative independence in both the literal and metaphoric fruits of investment banking within an imperial system exemplifies what Clifford means by the nexus of local/national/global and what Spivak, Grewal, and Kaplan mean by transnational complicities.

The "comparative knowledge produced through an *itinerary*," as Clifford articulates it, also illuminates the geopolitical axis at work in Woolf's texts. Woolf's metonym of a room of one's own with a lock on the door specifies the woman writer's need for material space free from interruption and family obligation, as well as the figurative "power to think for oneself" (110). Bringing the English writer "back home," Alice Walker engages in such comparativist thinking in her well-known interweaving of quotations from *A Room of One's Own* with brack- eted reference to the specific conditions of African American women in "In Search of Our Mothers' Gardens." In one such passage, Walker writes: "Virginia Woolf wrote further, speaking of course not of our Phillis [Wheatley], that 'any woman born with a great gift in the sixteenth century [insert "eighteenth century," insert "black woman," insert "born or made a slave"] would certainly have gone crazed, shot herself, or ended her days in some lonely cottage outside the village, half witch, half wizard [insert "Saint"], feared and mocked at'" (235). These sharp juxtapositions both testify to Walker's indebtedness to Woolf and inscribe a racial critique that makes visible the degree to which Woolf's image of a writer's freedom depends upon an unacknowledged enslavement of others.[43] But additionally, Walker performs a geopolitical grounding of Woolf as she "travels" in intertextual space across national boundaries to make her point about the more daunting material conditions that an American slave like Phillis Wheatley faced than did the middle-class woman in Britain who began to write at about the same time—to begin with, the lack of self-ownership, let alone possession of a room with a key (235).

Building on Walker's comparativist approach, I want to juxtapose Woolf's "room of one's own" with Harlem Renaissance writer Zora Neale Hurston's "store porch."[44] As Woolf penned *A Room of One's Own* in 1928, Hurston left Harlem and her anthropology classrooms at Barnard College to return to the South to collect Negro folklore. In her ethnographic and fictional work, porch talk serves as metonym for the verbal artistry, dramatic and figural expressivity, rhyth- mic asymmetry, hybridic originality, and racial health of the poetics that devel- oped syncretistically within a rural black southern culture rooted firmly in West African oral traditions—a poetics Hurston theorizes in her essay "Characteristics of Negro Expression" (1934), which ought to be read alongside of Woolf's "Mod- ern Fiction" (and Eliot's "Tradition and the Individual Talent") as a modernist manifesto.

In celebrating the poetics of porch talk, Hurston nonetheless shows how its progressive racial politics is regressive in relation to gender. The store porch is a distinctly masculine space, the site of black manhood denied by the white world and constructed through competitive talk like the dozens and through collective male gazing at women who pass by or through the porch but have no place upon it. In *Their Eyes Were Watching God*, Janie loves the porch talk and longs to participate, but is repeatedly silenced and denied access to the porch by her status- conscious and domineering husband, who makes clear that the porch is no place for ladies. As such, the porch represents the space of a specifically masculine linguistic and sexual authority within the culture. It signifies for an African American oral tradition what Leslie Stephen's library, Oxbridge, and the British Museum meant for Woolf in a lettered British culture: the site of dominant crea- tivity and desire from which women as cultural producers are largely excluded. Where Woolf argues that male writers have a solitary room of their own and women need one too, Hurston suggests that women need space on a communal porch to fulfill their creative genius. The narrative frame for *Their Eyes Were Watching God* significantly takes place on Janie's porch—not the store porch—but a porch where Janie tells her story to her friend Phoeby. A conjuncturalist, geopolitical reading of Hurston's porch with Woolf's room brings into focus the contradictory racial and gender politics of porch poetics.[45] It reveals what they share in their hindered longing for public creative expression and how the specificities of that desire differ.

My reason for this brief American detour is not to rebuke Woolf for ethnocentrism in proposing a room of one's own as a precondition for women's writing. She makes, after all, no universalist claims in *A Room of One's Own* and addresses quite specifically the link between women and written fiction in a British context. Rather, my point is to make visible the geopolitical inflections in the formulations of both Woolf and Hurston, uncommon readings that require a conjuncturalist approach that relies on spatial juxtapositions for insight and looks for structural parallels as well as locationally specific differences. Woolf's "room" heightens our reading of the interactive relation between racial and gender politics on Hurston's "porch." Conversely, Hurston's "porch" foregrounds the otherwise muted geopolitical dimensions of Woolf's "room." As readers, our transnational travel between *A Room of One's Own* and *Their Eyes Were Watching God* allows us to see elements in each text to which we might remain blind if our local readings are not enhanced by geopolitical considerations.

To triangulate this comparativist juxtaposition, I want to tell an unfinished story. I once spent an extraordinary evening a few years ago with an extraordinary woman—Memphela Ramphele, a South African anthropologist and anti-apartheid activist who was later to be appointed head of the University of Cape Town. Before the dismantling of apartheid, she had come to campus to lecture on apartheid, feminism, and the future of South Africa, making an argument unpopular back home that the new South Africa must address the issue of feminism as part of its efforts to avoid replicating the oppressive power structures of the old regime or following the road to dictatorship of many African nations after independence. She explicitly called for analysis of how British, European, and black South African forms of patriarchy have combined under apartheid. Later, as we sat before the fire for an evening of talk, she mentioned that she longed to write an autobiography, revisiting these issues in stories of the movement, her work on youth in the hostels and townships, the martyrdom of her companion Steven Biko, her single motherhood, her professional life. No time for such luxuries, she lamented. I urged her to write anyway, defending the powerful political praxis of stories. I asked her if she had ever read Virginia Woolf.[46] Her argument shared a great deal with *Three Guineas*, I told her, with Woolf's passion to root out the multiple causes of geopolitical violence, domestic as well as international. Ramphele wanted to know more about British patriarchal formations so that she could better understand their presence and transplantation into a South African context as they syncretically merged with indigenous patriarchal formations. I asked her if she had ever read *To the Lighthouse* or Maxine Hong Kingston's *The Woman Warrior*, another text that interweaves the story of gender with threads of differing patriarchal formations. She was curious; she was eager. So I sent her copies of the books. Our paths have not crossed again. Did she read them? Were they transplantable? What did they or could they have meant to her in the midst of her geopolitical and personal struggles? How might her locationally determined reading of Woolf (or Kingston) illuminate the blind spots in the eyes of Walker, myself, and any others?

In seeking the geopolitical Woolf, we have traveled far from the reductionisms of both Kenner and Rich about Woolf's lack (on the one hand) or excess (on the other hand) of internationalism, far as well from their differently limited meanings for the term *international*. Locating Virginia Woolf International, I have tried to show, involves more than determining the politics of empire in her work and more than charting the different readings of Woolf produced at different national sites—although both these approaches are vitally important parts of the whole story of Virginia Woolf International. It involves nothing less than tracing how the "warp of human stabilities is woven through with the woof of human motion," how the geography of travel is always already embedded in the geography of home, and how the reading in the time-space of one's position reflects geopolitical location.

GEOPOLITICAL LITERACY: A BRIEF SUMMATION

What we need, Gayatri Chakravorty Spivak argues, is to develop "transnational literacy" ("Scattered Speculations"). "Transnational feminism," she continues, "is neither revolutionary tourism, nor mere celebration of testimony" (284). Internationalizing or globalizing women's studies requires more than figurative or material "travel" elsewhere, though it certainly does require this commitment to learning from and about others. It involves much more than documenting the globe's multicultural heterogeneity. It also involves avoiding the reinscription of self/other centrisms, what Spivak calls the "worlding" of Third World others and what I call more broadly all forms of geocentrism, that is, of locational parochialism that occurs everywhere, not exclusively in the West in representations of the nonwestern. It involves fundamentally a change in the categories in which we think through difference, a form of intellectual labor that begins "at home." This work asks for an interrogation of how the geopolitical axis informs and inflects all cultural formations and identities, our own as well as that of others. It requires spatial, geographical thinking to complement temporal, historical analysis.

Fredric Jameson has famously commanded in the opening pages of *The Political Unconscious* "Always historicize!" (9). To this imperative, we need to add "Always spatialize!"—that is, always ask how locational and geographical specifics particularize any given phenomenon or interpretation of it. Alert to androcentrism, ethnocentrism, and heterocentrism (for example), we should become just as aware of geocentrism. The fact that terms of critique such as *ageographical* and *geocentric* do not have the conventional currency of their parallel mates, *ahistorical* and *ethnocentric*, is symptomatic of how far we have to go to foster the regular habits of geopolitical thinking. Ideally, such thinking would incorporate a number of related strategies I have tried to theorize, incorporate, or perform in suggesting uncommon readings of Woolf. First, there is the need to establish the analytic concept of the geopolitical axis, not to isolate it but rather to see its distinctness so as to better understand its interactions with other constitutive axes of cultural formations and identity. Second, there is the imperative to trace the structures and effects of spatialized power relations, understanding that the circuits of power flow multidirectionally, scattering hegemonies in complex ways. Third, there is the requirement to study localities other than our "home" base (both biographical and disciplinary), staying attuned to the ways others study us as well as how we study them. Fourth, there is the need to make visible the global woven into the local and the local embedded in the global—the transnational effects of glocalization. Fifth, there is the necessity of tracking how culture "travels," acquiring new forms and meanings in the process of transplantation and transculturation. And finally, there is the development of a comparativist/conjuncturalist perspective that juxtaposes different locations for the new light they shed on local formations at home and elsewhere. In sum, these are the forms of thinking and study that potentially produce geopolitical literacy.

Telling Contacts:
Intercultural Encounters and Narrative Poetics
in the Borderlands between Literary Studies
and Anthropology

Every story is a travel story—a spatial practice.
—*Michel de Certeau,* The Practice of Everyday Life

I will break open the story and tell you what
is there. Then, like the others that have fallen out
onto the sand, I will finish with it, and the wind
will take it away.
—*Marjorie Shostak,* Nisa: The Life and Words of a

!Kung Woman

SO BEGINS Nisa's "once upon a time," her formulaic opening of a story-to-come, her signal as storyteller to her listener that what follows is marked off and shaped as a separate entity that the "wind will take away" once her words are finished. So begins as well her reflection on the performance and passing of one of the many stories she tells to the North American anthropologist Marjorie Shostak, stories that constitute her life in the one-time gathering and hunting society of the !Kung as they subsist and face substantial change and possible annihilation in the Kalahari Desert of southern Africa. As Nisa's translator and editor, Shostak represents and re-presents Nisa's life and her tellings of it for a western audience curious about but far in every sense from the conditions of the story's production.

What interests me here is the potential for these scenes of storytelling to "break open" the nature of "story" itself. I mean by scenes of storytelling both the performative site of Nisa speaking to Shostak and the scriptoral site of Shostak reproducing that speech in a text for us to read. The first scene is one of intercultural encounter, one structured by unequal power relations and overdetermined by anthropology's history of hierarchical encounters, but one where Shostak's intellectual, psychological, and material intentions as ethnographer do not wipe out Nisa's subjectivity. Nisa is more than the anthropologist's Other. "Fix my voice on the machine so that my words come out clear," she instructs Shostak. "I am an old woman who has experienced many things and I have much to talk about"

(Shostak, *Nisa* 51). She exercises considerable agency and skill, seizing the chance to give textual permanence to the words that "the winds" would "take away," taking as well the opportunity to transform the anthropologist's desire for her words into material capital in the form of prized cattle. This scene is the site of exchange, not a one-sided expression of power. It is the site of double agendas, collaborative and interactive cultural work—though not by any means equivalent, let alone equal, as the first and last names by which the two storytellers are known metonymically signifies: Nisa and Shostak. Though highly mediated, Nisa's stories are there, here, have presence. They are not emptied, not ephemeral, not blown away by the winds.

The second scene of storytelling is the production of the text we read, the story of Nisa's performance and Shostak's translation, ordering, and contextualizing of it. This is the scene of ethnographic encounter in which the intercultural exchange between women, each with her own agenda and agency, becomes a scene of inscription: the anthropologist's transformation of performative orality into fixed textuality, Nisa's stories in the !Kung language into the English stories we read. Experimenting with ethnographic convention much as Zora Neale Hurston had done some forty years before, Shostak eliminates the invisible, omniscient, objective eye of the ethnographer, thus undermining to some extent the traditional ethnographic binaries of subject/object, self/other, civilized/savage. Instead, she foregrounds her own presence, narrating the story of ethnographic encounter alongside the stories that make up Nisa's life. She weaves different voices into a polyphonic, dialogic blend of multiple stories: the first person "I" of Nisa, telling her stories mediated through Shostak's transcription, translation, and shaping; the first person "I" of the young, recently married western woman seeking to learn what it means to be a woman from the more experienced woman in her fifties; and the mostly third-person, authoritative voice of the ethnographer who contextualizes Nisa's stories with anthropological theory and other studies of the !Kung. Like the first scene of storytelling, Shostak's (re)presentation of Nisa's life and words is the result of collaboration. As James Clifford argues, "Nisa's story is revealed as joint production, the outcome of an encounter that cannot be rewritten as a subject-object dichotomy. Something more than explaining or representing the life and words of another is going on—something more open-ended" ("Allegory" 107).[1] "Nisa gave her talk; I tried to keep the wind from taking its beauty away," Shostak reflects ("Wind" 234).[2]

How then do these two different scenes of storytelling—of intercultural and ethnographic encounter—"break open the story and tell us what is there"? In the borderlands between anthropology and literary studies, what might they suggest about narrative poetics? What they break open and expose, I believe, is the difference *difference*—specifically geopolitical and cultural difference—can make in our theorizations of narrative. A comparativist approach to narrative can illuminate ways in which narrative conventions are culturally and historically inflected—the agonistic, linear, and often teleological structure of much western narrative; the disruption of such linearity in some picaresque, epistolary, modernist and postmodern narrative forms; the episodic, digressional, or nonagonistic structures of some nonwestern narrative traditions.[3] However, I would like to focus on a different question—namely, the role of geopolitical and cultural differences in providing what generates, motivates, and fuels narrative. What kinesis, in other words, provides the narrative *donée,* the energy that keeps the story going, the listeners listening, and the readers turning pages?

Answers to these questions in narrative theory have largely developed within a psychoanalytic paradigm, originating in large part in Roland Barthes's assertion that all narrative is oedipal and others' subsequent affirmations, adaptations, or repudiations of his view.[4] Narrative theory has been preoccupied with questions of desire: oedipal desire; pre-oedipal desire; desire for plot; desire to transgress or dissolve plot; desire of *fort/da,* of Eros and Thanatos; desire to know, to solve the riddle, to detect; desire to oppress or repress; desire for order or disorder; desire for father, mother, or other. Whether observing, celebrating, critiquing, or revisioning—much psychoanalytically inflected narrative theory reads narrative desire within a paradigm of oedipal desires and post-oedipal discontents.[5]

To break open this story, I want for the moment to displace psychoanalysis and substitute anthropology—and the spatialization it engenders—for the insight it potentially brings to the issue of what generates, motivates, and fuels narrative.[6] Instead of centering narrative generatively within the family romance—that is, within the locus of the family and its revisitations in adult life—I want to see what happens to our understanding of narrative when we locate its motivation in encounters of self and other, specifically when those encounters are intercultural.[7] Narratives that perform and/or thematize such encounters partake of the ethnographic and thus invite readings within anthropological paradigms. Desire remains a part of such stories of contact—desire for the other, the different, the alien; desire to connect across or bridge difference; desire for difference as a mark of one's own lack or projection onto others of what is repressed in the self; desire propelled by curiosity; desire to fabulate, fantasize, dream, or create. Oedipal and post-oedipal configurations may well weave their way into such desires, though I would insist that heterogeneous forms of desire are not all reducible to oedipal and pre/post-oedipal plots. Rather than see self/other encounters solely as a function of desire, I want to posit intercultural encounter as the larger framework that incorporates the question of desire.

INTERCULTURAL LOCATIONS AND NARRATIVE SPATIALITY

What I mean by "intercultural encounters" requires some definition, since the word *intercultural* is deceptively simple, covering up and repeating all the instabilities and ambiguities of the word *culture* itself. I do not regard a "culture" as a static essence, a "pure" or even categorically definable entity, or an impermeable phenomenon outside history. Instead, I assume a "culture" to be historically produced, ever changing, and always reactively and syncretistically formed (and reformed) in relation to other cultures. Any culture, in other words, is always already intercultural and syncretist. I find it strategically useful to define a given culture in terms of a group of family resemblances, things more or less shared by members of the group, things such as history, material conditions, traditions, beliefs, stories, patterns of behavior, outlooks, values, epistemologies, fantasies, visions, and desires.[8] I further assume that cultures often posit an ideological homogeneity, even an essence, that obscures an actual heterogeneity and ongoing cultural re-formations and change. Moreover, cultures tend to erect boundaries between themselves and other cultures, defensively defining their own identity through assertion of difference from others. Such boundaries—often erected as a means of dominance over disempowered others or protection from more powerful others—obscure the syncretist borderlands of cultural exchange, intermingling, and mutual influence. (I am here making a sharp distinction between the words *boundary* and *borderland*, terms that are too often used interchangeably. By *boundary*, I mean a fixed line separating one side from another, often symbolically marking different sovereignties and loyalties; by *borderland*, I mean an indeterminate, potentially shifting and broad terrain across and through which intercultural traffic and transaction circulate.)[9]

Intercultural encounters, then, happen when people from different cultures meet and interact, making some form of connection across difference—whether that interaction is positive or negative; willed or forced; an embrace or a rejection. Such encounters are relatively easy to envision when people come from radically different societies, as Nisa and Shostak do. But they are less easy to articulate when they take place in the same society or when the different cultures at issue are based on constituents of identity other than "ethnicity" or "race"—constituents like class, gender, sexuality, religion, national origin, age, and so forth. I regard a "society" as a historically produced, changing, syncretist phenomenon that incorporates and intermingles many "cultures" simultaneously—as in the society of the contemporary United States, incorporating, for example, urban gay culture; white suburban women's culture; Korean immigrant urban culture; Orthodox Jewish culture; lesbian feminist culture; pink-collar working-class culture; Harley Davidson owners' culture; jet set, wealthy culture; midwestern farm culture; and so forth. Societies with any system of stratification—and this includes nearly all, if not all, societies—are inherently "multicultural," no matter what their own ideology of homogeneous identity might be. Further, all individuals within a society are "multicultural." Individuals belong to a number of overlapping "cultures," their identities (whether self-defined or not) partially based on multiple and continuously negotiated affiliations linked to class, sexuality, religion, gender, ethnicity, nation, age, and so forth.[10]

Within this matrix of intersecting cultures, an intercultural encounter between members of the same society might involve the meeting of multiple differences, even when a shared membership in one group tends to obscure or overwhelm those differences. Take, for example, an encounter between two hypothetical black people living in New York City—one poor, the other of a professional class; one Christian, the other Muslim; one female, the other male; one gay, the other heterosexual; one of West Indian/African descent, the other of southern

African American; the one driving a BMW, the other a nondescript, very much used American car. However much homogeneity of identity might be constructed either by white racism or by the notion of African diaspora, the encounter between two such individuals would nonetheless remain complexly intercultural, incompletely understood in categories of race alone. Or, for another example, consider a meeting between two Jewish women living in New York City—one lower-middle class and forty-five, Orthodox, wearing a wig, keeping kosher, working at home as the mother of five, living in Crown Heights, Brooklyn, in a rented brownstone flat, with many West Indian neighbors whom she fears; the other, upper-middle class and twenty-eight, secular, single, living on the Upper West Side in the "city" in a condo she purchased, sophisticatedly mingling in a cultural stew of multicolor hues. Faced with anti-Semitism, their shared Jewishness might create a bond; faced with misogyny, their common gender might make a connection possible. But an encounter between these two women would similarly be complexly intercultural, incompletely understood in categories of religion, ethnicity, or gender alone.

The endless multiplicity of stories that such intercultural encounters can generate is what interests me at the moment, stories well outside the framework of oedipal and post-oedipal plots. The marketability of this generative power in the United States is well-known to the television and film industries. The narrative *donée* of many a current television prime-time drama—from *N.Y.P.D. Blue,* *Homicide,* and *Brooklyn South* to *Chicago Hope* and *E.R.*—begins in an intercultural mix that sets in motion complex plots and poignant vignettes based in the confrontations and enticements of difference in both narrative lines (the ongoing stories of the repeating characters; the main, one-time stories of a given episode), as well as the mix between them. Talk shows from the daytime *Oprah* to the nighttime *Rivera Live* often stage intercultural encounters as a form of dramatic narrative to stimulate and keep television viewers tuning back in day after day. A spate of recent films focused directly around what happens when differences meet attest to the market power of intercultural plots. Self/other encounters fuel the narrative situation, drive, humor, and (melo)drama of films like *The Birdcage,* *Family Thing,* and *Big Night,* for example. Going back a bit further are hits like *Mississippi Masala, The Crying Game, The Wedding Banquet, The Piano, Grand Canyon, Do the Right Thing, Jungle Fever, Driving Miss Daisy, Dancing with Wolves, Pocahontas, E.T., My Beautiful Launderette, The Gods Must Be Crazy, The Brother from Another Planet.* I could go on. But the point is that plots based on intercultural blending and clashing pull in big audiences and underwrite at least partially a powerful culture industry with extensive global markets very important for both the production of the symbolic order and resistances to it. And yet, the field of narrative poetics has not theorized this phenomenon, nor taken fully into account the way in which narrative functions as a spatial practice. As Sabina Sawhney writes, "crossracial/ethnic encounter itself seems so knotty, so tangled with conflicting concerns and desires that it seems to demand a narrative unravelling, a fiction of explanation."[11]

Stories generated by intercultural encounters invite a strong shift in our reading strategies from a desire-centered, temporal paradigm that dominates much narrative theory to a more spatially oriented framework. In *The Dialogic Imagination*, M. M. Bakhtin, it should be recalled, invented the neologism "chronotope" to describe the coordinates of narrative, a sequence of events that take place in a given time and space, combining *chronos* and *topos*. But much narrative analysis privileges the temporal over the spatial axis, subtly turning Bakhtin's chronotope into chrono*type*.[12] "A story," E. M. Forster writes in *Aspects of the Novel*, "is a narrative of events arranged in time sequence"; and, "in the novel, the allegiance to time is imperative" (30, 29). For Paul Ricoeur, temporality and narrativity have a reciprocal relationship in which space drops out entirely: "My first working hypothesis is that narrativity and temporality are closely related. . . . Indeed, I take temporality to be that structure of existence that reaches language in narrativity and narrativity to be the language structure that has temporality as its ultimate referent" ("Narrative Time" 165).[13] Largely bypassing the spatial component of narrative, James Phelan highlights what he calls "progression"—namely, "narrative as a dynamic event, one that must move, in both its telling and its reception, through time"—as the basis of "how authors generate, sustain, develop, and resolve readers' interests in narrative" (*Reading People* 15). Within a psychoanalytic framework, Peter Brooks even more completely privileges the temporal over the spatial: "We might think of plot as the logic . . . that develops its propositions only through temporal sequence and progression. . . . And plot is the principal ordering force of those meanings that we try to wrest from human temporality" (*Reading* xi). For many narrative theorists, the nature of character as it unfolds within a sequence of causal events often takes center stage. Discussions of character are often exclusively temporally oriented, articulating themes of development, change over time that is schematized in organic or reactively disordered terms and interpreted through psychoanalytic lenses. Here, as themselves narratives of psychosexual development, oedipal and post-oedipal theories of desire shape readings of narrative along developmental lines—especially evident in narratives of *Bildung*, centered in temporal plots of the family romance, its repetitions and discontents.

Intercultural narratives, in contrast, foreground space and movement through space rather than time—the topochrone instead of the chronotope of narrative, if you will. Space often functions as trope for cultural location—for identity and knowledge as locationally as well as historically produced. Setting works as symbolic geography, signaling or marking the specific cultural location of a character within the larger society. A time-centered model of reading narrative fosters a figure/ground binary relegating setting to description that impedes narrative movement, the story of character development through time. (Thus, the phenomenon of skipping over long descriptions of setting in the Victorian novel for those who are "reading for the plot," to echo Peter Brooks; and thus the tendency of narrative theorists and critics to privilege action over setting.) A spatial model, in contrast, defines the figure in terms of the ground, describing character within and through cultural locations inscribed in spatial configurations. The growth or de-velopment—the *Bildung*—of a character might be seen not so much as a conse-quence of the play of desire but rather as the result of changing cultural interac-tions and locations. Thus the removal of the family in Elizabeth Gaskell's *North and South* from the agrarian south to the industrial north of Victorian England makes possible the expanding psychological horizons of the heroine in a narrative structured around a succession of intercultural encounters.

Ultimately, however, a spatial model should no more replace a temporal one than a time-centered approach should suppress a consideration of space. More-over, space is neither static nor given in an a priori fashion; rather, it is histori-cally produced and constructed. Space—at least in narrative—does not exist sep-arate from time any more than history can be removed from location. Space, as Henri Lefebvre asserts in *The Production of Space*, is historically produced, reflecting and constructing cultural meanings in the story of spatialization.[14] Shostak's intercultural encounter with Nisa—in both the performative and tex-tual scenes of storytelling—occurs in a moment subject to historical analysis as well as in a space that invites geographical interpretation. Narrative analysis needs, as Bakhtin writes, to examine the "intrinsic interconnectedness of tempo-ral and spatial relationships" (*Dialogic Imagination* 84). Because the spatial di-mension of narrative has been so relatively unexamined, I am provisionally em-phasizing location instead of time to see what aspects of narrative emerge more visibly.

This emphasis on space, in my view, allows us to see the role that intercultural encounter as a form of locational movement plays in generating narrative and structuring its progression. The case of Jean Rhys's *Wide Sargasso Sea* is instruc-tive. It is most certainly a story about the formation and deformation of desire, set within a clearly delineated historical period beginning shortly after the abolition of slavery in British colonies in 1832. But, foregrounding the spaces through which the narrative moves illuminates the intercultural motive of the text some-what differently. Narrative movement is not so much developmental, subject to psychoanalytic probing, as it is locational. The story moves from space to space, with each location delineating an identity for the characters: the impoverished plantation from which Antoinette flees as the site of bitter racial and class encoun-ter erupting in flames; the French convent where Antoinette is sequestered along with other "white" Creole children of the wealthy elite and groomed to marry an Englishman; the multiracial capital city of the English West Indian colony where Antoinette refuses to marry her "colored" cousin Sandi Cosway; the honeymoon home in the lush tropical forest where the Martinique "black" woman Celestine presides, where Antoinette first enthralls, then repels, and finally attempts to re-gain the Englishman's love; bleak Rochester Hall, where a caged Antoinette be-comes the beastly Bertha Mason. Each of these spaces represents a scene of inter-cultural encounter, threaded no doubt by desire. But it is the story of self/other confrontation, spatially located and articulated, that provides the narrative with its *donée*, momentum, and staging of desire. The story resides in its spaces, its sym-bolic geographies and the movement among them.

Although space is conventionally associated with stasis, I am suggesting that a spatialized reading of narrative based in intercultural encounter actually fosters a focus on narrative kinesis of a different sort, on spatial movement, travel, and passage—not passage through the psychosexual stages within the single locus of the family, but rather passage from one culture to another. How does the narrative get from one cultural location to another? What propels its motion, its travel? What role does the excitement, pleasure, and/or anguish of intercultural encounter play in this kind of movement? How does each space reflect the cultural production of spatialized meaning? Or, determine the nature of or changes in character? Or, provide the conditions within which the agency of the characters must maneuver?

Consider, for a moment, Toni Morrison's *Beloved*. The arrival of Schoolteacher to the plantation Sweet Home institutes a painful and murderously oppressive intercultural and ethnographic encounter between him and the slave Sethe that recapitulates what is in Morrison's view the racist origin of western science in general and anthropology in particular. Schoolteacher's measurement of Sethe's head and recording of her animal and human characteristics generates the narrative of travel: her decision to seek freedom; her capture on the barn floor, an "animal" ripe for rape and milking by Schoolteacher's henchman; her flight across the river; her journey first to the frosty Quaker kitchen then to her mother-in-law's warm/free hearth at 124; the pursuit of the slave catchers; Sethe's flight to the barn to kill her children; and all the travels that come after that act. Paul D.'s story enacts a parallel travel, differing by gender, moving through many spaces until he ends up at 124, where he cannot stop moving from room to room at the house and in the town until he can face the past as Sethe must do in the various spaces of desire for Beloved. For both Sethe and Paul D. each movement brings yet another intercultural encounter, episodes located in different spaces that symbolically inscribe different aspects of healing.

I mention the case of *Beloved* deliberately. Certainly oedipal and pre-oedipal readings of the novel have been plentiful and insightful, particularly in unraveling the complexities of love/hate, nurturance and destruction in the novel's mother/daughter plot. Desire is everywhere and variously present in the novel—desires of mother/child, husband/wife, man/woman, sister/sister, man/animal, human/divine; desires for freedom, Boston ribbon and velvet, human touch, memory and forgetting; and desire as a kind of knowledge that includes intellectual and bodily possession of a subject race/gender by a dominant one. I do not want to deny the presence of desire in *Beloved*, whose very title signals its importance. But I do want to suggest that oedipal and post-oedipal readings of desire, based as they are so centrally on gender and the family nexus in isolation from other constituents of identity and social stratification, are inadequate by themselves. They need to be supplemented by a very different kind of reading, one based in the spatial plotting of intercultural encounter. This framework fosters an understanding of the dangers and pain of intercultural borderlands, the offensive and defensive dynamics of intercultural boundaries, and the multiplicity of positionalities that make up any intercultural encounters.

Spatialized readings of narrative based in identification of intercultural encounters and movement through space can even "break open" the very Oedipus story and tell us what is there, what the oedipal and post-oedipal readings tend to obscure. Think, for a moment, of the full oedipal narrative out of which Freud plucked the paradigmatic story of male desire in the son's forbidden love for the mother and dread rivalry with the father. Oedipus grows up in Corinth, a port city with trading ties to the Middle East and Egypt. Oedipus flees his home in an attempt to escape the fate the oracle predicts for him. In his wanderings, he meets the Sphinx who guards the road into Thebes, the city he does not yet know to be his original home. The Sphinx herself is a transgressive, boundary-crossing figure. First, she devours all those who cannot answer her riddle about the enigma of humankind—what walks on one leg in the morning; two legs at noon; and three legs in the evening? Second, she is a wingéd creature, with the head of a woman and the body of a lion. As emblem of syncretism, she may well be an import from Egypt, where sphinxes were a regular part of the nonhuman pantheon of animal, part-animal, and humanlike creatures. As such, she embodies the Other; Oedipus's meeting with her is a prototypical self/other encounter generated by his travels: human meets alien; Greek meets foreigner (*barbaros* in Greek); male meets female. The Other not only poses the enigma; she is herself the enigma that Oedipus must solve before his travels continue. His journey back home, into the heart of uncanny Thebes (the familiar and the familial made unfamiliar through travel), takes place as a direct consequence of his meeting with the Sphinx. The story of oedipal desire that transpires unfolds within the larger framework of intercultural encounter.

I am not suggesting that desire plays no part in the Oedipus story. We can certainly read the story as it has so often been read as the play of interlocking and ultimately conflated desires: the son's desire to take his father's place as king and marry his mother; the desire of the son-as-king to know the truth; the desire of the wandering and blinded old man for the peace of home. Oedipus is a homebody, all right. But we can also read the story in a different way, one that emphasizes how the familiar story of desire is set in motion through travel, motion through space, and the intercultural encounters that result from such movement. In this story, Oedipus finds not only the alien Other in the figure of the Sphinx, but also himself, in the answer to the Sphinx's riddle: that is, the human being (male and female) who crawls in infancy, walks upright in the noon of life, and uses a cane in life's twilight. Oedipus's cane in Sophocles' *Oedipus at Colonus*, let us not forget, is his daughter Antigone, upon whom the emasculated old man leans. As his (phallic) cane, she is the introjected female Other, now become a necessary part of himself. What this spatialized reading of the oedipal story suggests is that the narrative of detection based in the desire for both carnal and intellectual knowledge of the maternal body and the father's law is not the only possible ur-text of narrative, as some narrative theory would have it. We might just as well look to travel writing as to detective fiction for the ur-plots of narrative cognition.[15]

ETHNOGRAPHIC THEORIZATION OF THE CONTACT ZONE

Modern and postmodern ethnography represents the genealogical descendant, as well as the professionalization, of post-Renaissance travel writing in the West.[16] Current ethnographic theory about the formation, problematics, and possibilities of the field has much to offer the formation of a narrative poetics of intercultural encounter precisely because ethnography is a form of travel writing in which the foundational narrative of the genre is the story of intercultural encounter in the contact zone between difference. I would like to review briefly this interdisciplinary borderland between anthropological and literary studies to identify theoretical formulations that have resonant possibilities for delineating a narrative poetics of intercultural encounter. The first of these is posed by James Clifford in "Traveling Cultures," in which he argues (as I have already discussed in chapter 4) that ethnography has been too focused on identifying the stable centers and unchanging essences of cultures, thereby missing how all cultures are constantly changing in response to its interactions along the syncretist borderlands with other cultures. Acknowledging that ethnography is always a spatialized project, he suggests that ethnographers stop looking only at the static, localized spaces of a culture and focus instead on the spaces of travel and intercultural connections. He calls for a shift from what he names the ethnography of dwelling places to an ethnography of travel. He deconstructs the binary of anthropologist as observing subject traveling to study a static Other and proposes instead a recognition that movement and travel are part of all cultures. The Other travels too; the Other observes the ethnographer, often from the perspective of having traveled. "In much traditional ethnography," he notes, "the ethnographer has localized what is actually a regional/national/global nexus, relegating to the margins a 'culture's' external relations and displacements" (100). The "sites of cultural encounter" upon which he focuses are parallel to the scenes of intercultural encounter I propose as motive for some narratives, removing us as readers from the oedipal and post-oedipal scenes of the dwelling (the localized family plot), and directing us to the intersubjective spaces of self/other interaction.

Even more radically, other anthropologists have variously questioned the notion of self/other encounter as a meeting based solely on difference. Much influenced by theorizations of cultural hybridity in postcolonial studies, James Ferguson and Akhil Gupta, for example, jointly critique this privileging of difference for its assumption that pure and distinctly different cultures exist prior to ethnographic encounters. (Pure cultural difference, they argue, is an ideological effect of ethnographic encounters, one that obscures patterns of cultural interaction.) Arjun Appadurai posits the construction of ethnic and national affinities as an effect, not the cause, of what he calls "cultural traffic" and "cultural transaction," both of which produce in an increasingly mobile and transnational world a "global ethnoscape" in which identity is never singular and fixed, but always multiple, overlapping, and changing as a syncretist process and production

("Global Ethnoscape"; "Disjuncture" 7). Another critique of the privileging of difference stresses the place of sameness in intercultural encounters, as both Henrietta Moore in *A Passion for Difference* and Michael Taussig in *Mimesis and Alterity* point out. Taussig argues that the practice of imitation or mimesis is as important as the experience of or insistence upon difference in intercultural encounters. Ethnography has been so focused on alterity, he suggests, that it has missed entirely the "mimetic faculty" of the human species and consequently has obscured the dialogic mimicry, mirroring, and aping processes of intercultural transactions.

For Lila Abu-Lughod and Kirin Narayan (among others), sameness enters scenes of ethnographic encounter through a politics of identification when one "side" in the exchange shares one or more constituents of identity with the other. What is variously called insider, "halfie," native, or indigenous ethnography breaks the pattern of early anthropological gazing at the exotic Other (Abu-Lughod, "Writing"; Narayan, "How Native"). Zora Neale Hurston had long ago raised this issue in her self-reflexive and experimental ethnography of her hometown, when she turned the "spy-glass of anthropology" on her own culture in *Mules and Men* and more problematically on other cultural formations of the African diaspora in Jamaica and Haiti in *Tell My Horse*.[17] Similarly, the conventional anthropological binary of western self/nonwestern other is disrupted by the contradictory subject position of the western female ethnographer, particularly when she writes about nonwestern women. Geopolitically privileged but marginalized by gender, she "unsettles the boundary between self and other" upon which the hierarchical politics of anthropology was founded (Abu-Lughod, "Writing" 137–38). Shostak's insistence on her shared gender with Nisa borders dangerously on the assumption of a universal "womanhood" that suppresses the different forms gender takes as it is inflected by class, race, national origin, and so forth. But the gender-based connection Shostak insists upon also exhibits the narrative strategy of "halfie" anthropology, where cultural difference is mediated through a shared aspect of identity. Narayan complicates this notion further by challenging the essentializing view of cultural membership and asserting the necessity of understanding the "shifting identifications amid a field of interpenetrating communities and power relations" of both anthropologist and the object of the anthropological gaze ("How Native" 671). "Given the multiplex nature of identity," she writes, "there will inevitably be certain facets of self that can join us up with the people we study, other facets that emphasize our difference" (680). She recognizes the multiple locuses of identity—including factors such as education, gender, sexuality, class, race, and geographical origin—some of which may align while others do not in the encounter between ethnographer and object of study.

Present in Narayan's account of multiplex ethnographic encounters is an assumption of agency at work on both sides of the anthropological gaze, a refusal of objectification that Michel-Rolph Trouillot and S. P. Mohanty theorize. Trouillot acknowledges the rise of anthropology as a codification of European conquest and construction of a "savage" Other begun in the Renaissance. He sees various feminist and "ethnic" ethnographers as the vanguard of an anthropology that dismantles the subject/object binary of anthropology's origins. He calls for a new anthropology that eliminates what he calls the "savage slot" of Otherness, that works on the assumption of subject/subject encounters, and understands that there is no singular Other, but only multiple and heterogeneous "others" existing in historically and geographically specific locations. "The 'us and all of them' binary, implicit in the symbolic order that creates the West," he writes, "is an ideological construct, and the many forms of Third-World-ism that reverse its terms are its mirror images. There is no Other, but multitudes of others who are all others for different reasons, in spite of totalizing narratives, including that of capital" ("Savage Slot" 39).[18] Mohanty argues in a related vein for the *commonality* among different human cultures, a common ground based in agency and subjectivity. "It is important," he asserts, "to go beyond a simple recognition of *differences* across cultures. For 'they' do ultimately what 'we' do, since they share with us a capacity for self-aware historical agency" (23). To understand "the divide between 'us' and 'them,'" he suggests, involves the acknowledgment of the "common space" or "shared ground" of human agency as the basis for the construction of difference and for the local specificities of alterity ("'Us' and 'Them'" 20–21).

Such ethnographic theorizations of the contact zone where different peoples meet have direct bearing on narratives generated by intercultural encounter in a number of ways. First, they reinforce the centrality of what I have already posed as the spatial coordinate of narrative. Second, they are aligned with the geographical, as opposed to developmental, rhetoric of identity that has become increasingly important in narrative studies—by which I mean the locational and spatial configurations of identity understood as forms of multiple, relational, and situational positionalities.[19] Third, they imply a spatial source of narrative energy—the engine that drives the story—one that exists distinct from the specular, temporal circuits of desire in the oedipal and post-oedipal plots of narrative theory. And fourth, they point to patterns that narrative might take in telling stories about intercultural contact—topoi such as the presence of movement or travel as opposed to stasis or dwelling (Clifford); syncretist blending and clashing of difference (Ferguson and Gupta; Appadurai); mimetic forms of cultural borrowing, assimilation, appropriation, and parody (Taussig); bonds of connection and disconnection established through multiple constituents of identity (Abu-Lughod; Narayan; Shostak; Hurston); and reciprocal agencies of heterogeneous others in subject/subject encounters (Trouillot; Mohanty).

These patterns of interaction, I would further suggest, arise out of a dialectical or dialogic oscillation between sameness and difference in the ethnographic encounter. Travel—a form of movement through space—brings about an engagement with the other or others in a liminal space materially, psychologically, or culturally in between. The ethnographic encounter in that space involves a further movement back and forth between alterity and mimesis, between the sameness and difference that is embedded in the double meaning of the term *identity* (meaning the same as, but also relationally different from).[20] This to-and-fro-ness—

what Homi Bhabha calls the "hither and thither, back and forth" of the interstitial, "'in-between' spaces" (*Location* 1)—also constitutes *a* (not *the*) propelling force in narrative. It can serve as the engine that drives the narrative forward. It helps explain the dynamics of and the kinetic work performed by scenes of intercultural encounter in narrative texts. Desire of some kind certainly underlies a part of this story. But the contradictory tensions between sameness and difference cannot be explained solely in terms of oedipal and post-oedipal plottings of desire, however much these stories may be a part of the narrative. Thus, a dialogic, spatial model of narrative displaces the exclusivity of developmental, temporal models that characterize some narrative theory. The interactive oscillations between alterity and mimesis supplement the kinetic force of *fort/da*, Eros and Thanatos, underlying the family romance plots of psychoanalytic theory.

The Contact Zone as Narrative Engine in *A Passage to India*

To move from the abstract to the concrete, let me demonstrate what I am proposing by re-visiting a well-known text that is often read in relation to desire—namely, E. M. Forster's *A Passage to India* (1924).[21] Certainly the novel exhibits the orientalist desire that replays and reconfigures the family romance of homoerotic and heteroerotic desire in the colonial context. Forster's unnarratable and unconsummated desire for his friend Syed Ross Masood, the Indian Muslim to whom he dedicated the novel, reappears in the text in double form: in the homoerotic relationship between the colonial college principal Mr. Fielding and the Muslim physician Dr. Aziz; and in the neurotic, sexually repressed longing of the English traveler Adela Quested, who wants to know "the real India," only to succumb to the colonizer's racial and sexual paranoia in her accusation that Aziz assaulted her in the mysterious womb/tomb of the Marabar cave. This psychoanalytic reading, however, does not suffice—even if we give the Freudian family romance enacted in this triangulation of desire a postcolonially queer twist. Just as the Oedipus story itself can be read differently, in relation to scenes of intercultural encounter, so too can Forster's novel.

Privileging space over time for the moment, we notice that the organizing principle of the narrative is located in a succession of scenes of intercultural encounter overdetermined most especially by the context of colonialism. The novel opens with a purely spatial discourse, the distant voice of the narrator locating the story geographically and geopolitically in the colonial space of Chandrapore and its environs. After this locational beginning, scene follows scene of intercultural encounters that oscillate dialogically between connection and disconnection, contact and refusal of contact, identity as difference and identity as sameness—from Dr. Aziz's opening experience of the racial snub at Major Callendar's house to the closing scene between Aziz and Fielding, where their horses swerve apart, figuratively representing the impossibility of friendship at this historical moment between two men who both "want" it, one British, the other Indian ("No, not yet. . . . No, not there" [322]). Sometimes the scene of encounter narrates the erection of boundaries that separate, sometimes the borderlands of syncretist intermingling, and sometimes the dialogic movement between the two. Mostly, these encounters confront British with Indian, but a significant number also juxtapose differences of gender, religion, and class as well. However much Forster reproduces—indeed contributes to—the discourses of orientalist colonialism, his satire of British racism and his longing for its transcendence underlie most of these scenes of intercultural encounter.

The encounter between Aziz and Adela at the Marabar caves—with its scarcely suppressed matrix of interracial seduction, assault, and paranoia—often dominates discussions of the novel. I would like to decenter this scene and suggest instead that it is one link in a chain of scenes whose narrative drive incorporates but is not fully explained in terms of desire, particularly an orientalized oedipal desire. The first two scenes of intercultural encounter in the novel, I want to argue, are definitive for the chain as a whole. They are linked encounters in which the intercultural pair is not Aziz and Adela, not even Aziz and Fielding, but instead Aziz and Mrs. Moore. What happens between them, I suggest, sets the whole narrative going and underlies much of what follows.

The first scene—Aziz's encounter with British racism at Major Callendar's house—sets up its opposite, the second scene—Aziz's meeting with Mrs. Moore in the mosque. Together, the scenes represent the erection of racial boundaries, followed by their momentary dissolution in the affirmation of common ground—in Taussig's sense, the move from alterity to mimesis; in Mohanty and Trouillot's sense, the move from subject/object to subject/subject relations; in Appadurai's sense, the move from a localized to a global ethnoscape; in Narayan's and Abu-Lughod's sense, the recognition of a bond rooted in shared marginalization based on gender or race. Humiliated and angered by the racism he encounters at Major Callendar's, Aziz walks away and soon finds himself in a beautiful mosque, still and peaceful as the moon that lights it. "Here was Islam," he thinks, "his own country, more than a Faith, more than a battle-cry, more, much more... Islam, an attitude towards life both exquisite and durable, where his body and his thoughts found their home" (19). Aziz's healing experience of pure difference—of Islam as home, as dwelling (to echo Clifford)—consoles him for the brutalities of difference that he experienced on the Englishman's veranda. An Englishwoman's sudden appearance enrages Aziz—how dare she intrude, even here, in the mosque? The intercultural encounter is multilayered, along many axes of difference: British/Indian, Christian/Muslim, colonial ruler by proxy/colonial subject, man/woman, young/old.

What begins as an experience of difference, however, ends in Aziz's insistence on similarity and shared ground. When he discovers that she has removed her shoes as required by religious law, Aziz's anger turns to amazement: "so few ladies take the trouble, especially if thinking no one is there to see," he tells her by way of apology for his sharp chastisement (20). She replies, "That makes no difference. God is here" (20). This assertion leads to a conversational chain, each link of which Aziz takes as proof of identity—not Islamic identity, but the identity between them. She, like he, does not fear walking at night in spite of the snakes. She, like he, is widowed and has two boys and a girl. She, like he, dislikes Mrs. Callendar, and is willing to admit it to him, thus breaking racial and geopolitical loyalty. "We are in the same box," he tells her. "You understand me, you know what others feel," he suggests in reference to his belief that she understands. When she demurs, saying, "I only know whether I like or dislike" people, he concludes, "Then you are an Oriental" (23). For a brief, epiphanic, and utopian moment, the multiple borders of religion, geopolitics, race, gender, and age dissolve in Aziz's experience of sameness.

The bond Aziz feels with Mrs. Moore at this point leads him to make what turns out to be a disastrous suggestion, that he host a picnic at the Marabar caves for Mrs. Moore and her daughter-in-law-to-be, Adela Quested. Certainly, we can read his gesture based in the desire to transcend difference as naive, seriously undermined by the events of the novel that demonstrate the powerful effects of the colonial context. He later repudiates this position and tells Fielding at the end that such friendship is impossible as long as the British raj continues (322). Without denying the novel's ironic dismantling of Aziz's enthusiastic bridge building in the mosque scene, I would nonetheless argue that the subsequent scenes of intercultural encounter in the novel continue a dialogic of alterity and mimesis and thus continue to question the fixity of ethnic, racial, geopolitical, religious, gendered, and sexual identities. However much Forster's novel underlines the impossibility of "friendship" across boundaries of difference in the temporal framework of the raj ("No, not yet"), it also more covertly charts the space of intercultural encounter as a syncretist borderland changing both sides of subject/subject contact.

Recall, for example, what happens to Mrs. Moore after her experience in the Marabar caves, dark interiorities in which sound bounds and rebounds apparently without origin or end, places of pure space seemingly outside of time that invoke the religion of Jainism, closely related to but predating Hinduism and Buddhism on the Indian subcontinent. The noise she hears in the Jainist caves looses the Anglo anchors of her identity, ushering her into what would seem from her formerly Anglican point of view to be a nihilist space beyond human caring and ethics akin to the consciousness of Jainist holy men who renounce the world. Mrs. Moore loses her English moorings and becomes Indianized. Or, to be more precise, since "India" is itself a fully heterogeneous, syncretist space where many cultures meet, she comes to mimic one aspect of "India," specifically, the epistemology and ontology of Jainism, with its removal from the joys and anguish of "ordinary" life.[22] In turn, the Indian populace turn her into a goddess after the trial, blending her, along with the mantra "God si love," into their pantheon, and many years later, into the festival of Krishna that dominates the final intercultural encounters of the novel.

Complementing Mrs. Moore's Indianization is Aziz's partial, and puzzling, Anglicanization. It takes place in the very midst of his retreat from Chandrapore for the relatively all-Indian environment of a maharajah's court in one of the Indian states. Although he refuses all contact with Fielding, although he has a "genuine hatred of the English" (293), Aziz devotes his poetry to one topic: the liberation of women from purdah, or seclusion. He who had "believed in the purdah," as he had told Fielding at an earlier moment of great intimacy between the men, now writes poems "all on one topic—Oriental womanhood":

> "The purdah must go," was their [the poems'] burden, "otherwise we shall never be free." And he declared (fantastically) that India would not have been conquered if women as well as men had fought at Plassy. "But we do not show our women to the foreigner"—not explaining how this was to be managed, for he was writing a poem. Bulbuls and roses would still persist, the pathos of defeated Islam remained in his blood and could not be expelled by modernities. Illogical poems—like their writer. Yet they struck a true note: there cannot be a mother-land without new homes. (293)

Indifferent to Indian nationalism, the Hindu Brahman Godbole likes these poems for what he approvingly calls Aziz's "internationality" (293). But Aziz's commitment to a western form of women's liberation (the ending of purdah) appears to exist in contradiction with his post-trial embrace of an Indian identity, an Indian motherland, and a rejection of all things English. Like Mrs. Moore's Indianization, Aziz's "imitation" of an English gender formation recalls Taussig's theorization of intercultural encounter. Cultural mimicry complements cultural difference in the dialogic exchange as each subject adopts and adapts elements of the other.

As with Mrs. Moore's metamorphosis, there is considerable irony in Aziz's assimilation of certain western forms of modernity. First, it is purdah of a different kind—Adela's enclosure within a form of sexual repression (in part, a screen for Forster's own closeted sexuality and repressed longing for Masood)—that leads her to imagine Aziz's supposed attack. The West, it seems, does not free its women no matter how its ideology claims modernity for itself. Second, it is Aziz's act of breaking his dead wife's purdah—by showing Fielding her hidden photo as a gesture of intimacy—that concludes part one of the novel, "The Mosque," and leads directly into its disastrous middle, "The Caves." And third, there is the editorial voice of the narrator in this passage, a judgmental voice that condescends to Aziz's syncretist embrace ("fantastical," "illogical"), thus revealing Forster's own complicity with the masculinist racism the novel so brutally satirizes. The somewhat unusual break in the novel's largely invisible omniscient narration and the use of free indirect discourse discloses a Forster unable to imagine that an anticolonialist movement might make the status of women a measure for societal freedom in general. In spite of his attack on British racism in India, Forster was unable to identify fully with the Indian nationalist movement led by Gandhi; in spite of his use of the sexually repressed Adela as a screen for his own closeted desires, Forster was unable to see the "logical" connection between modernity, women's freedom, and freedom in general.[23]

Nonetheless, the various ironies undermining the novel's unfolding reciprocal syncretisms in the colonial context do not entirely dismantle Forster's narrative of subject/subject encounters in the borderlands between British and Indian, male and female, Anglican and Hinduism/Islam/Jainism. The mimetic processes of imitation work to establish identity in sameness at the same time that the colonial plot intensifies identity as difference. Desire certainly plays a part in these scenes: desire for the other as different, even exotic and mysterious; desire for the security of one's own group; desire expressed, desire repressed; desire in its intergenerational and familial forms; desire along a continuum incorporating hetero-and homoeroticisms, hetero-and homosexualities, and androgyny and bisexuality; and queer desire. Across the boundaries of cultural, gender, and sexual difference, Forster replots the family romance of oedipal desire. But like the ur-story of Oedipus, the larger framework for these scenarios is the spatialized plot of intercultural encounter, a plot set in motion by travel through space, by *passage* to India and through India in scene after scene of telling contacts with heterogeneous and multiply constituted others.

Interfacing Disciplines: Anthropology and Literary Studies

Forster's *Passage to India* and Shostak's *Nisa* inhabit a borderland between seeming differences: fiction and ethnography, literature and social science. The differences are not just illusory, any more than the differences between Shostak and Nisa or Mrs. Moore and Aziz dissolve. Novel writing and ethnography are different social practices, involving different assumptions and expectations from readers about the empirical bases of the texts. Nonetheless, these stories of intercultural encounter represent an encounter on another level in which their differences coexist with syncretist borrowings from the other. Having traveled from England to India in 1912–13 (after which he began *A Passage to India*) and returned there to work as secretary to the maharajah of Dewas for nearly a year in 1921–22 (after which he finished the novel), Forster writes fiction thoroughly imbued with the ethnographic spirit.[24] Having traveled from the United States to Botswana's Kalahari Desert at the height of North American confessional feminism in its search for a common female language and voice, Shostak writes ethnography of !Kung culture thoroughly shaped by the conventions of the realist novel of female development and the fictional modes of women's autobiography in the West.

Both Forster and Shostak are indebted to a centuries-long western tradition of travel writing shaped by cultural narratives of self/other. Yet they write texts that resist the economy of the "savage slot" that underwrites much of that tradition. In an attempt to perform "thick descriptions" of life in Chandrapore (a fictionalized city near the Ganges) and the Kalahari Desert, both disrupt the tendency toward specular representations of exoticized or objectified Others. Forster does so through his representation of a heterogeneous India that resists totalizing generalities and through his scathing critique of British racisms. Shostak does so through her experimentation with multiple narrators and an implicit critique of the omniscient and invisible narrator of classic ethnography. In spite of these attempts, neither can fully escape complicity in the specular systems they employ in the context of unequal power relations. Forster's *Passage* retains a contradictory undercurrent of orientalist desire and rationalist epistemology that constitutes part of a colonial psychology.[25] Shostak's *Nisa* reflects a feminist desire for the sameness of sisterhood pervasive among western feminists of the 1970s and at the same time reinscribes anthropology's conventional tendency toward ahistorical representations of the nonwestern other. As a site for woman-to-woman bonding across vast difference, the !Kung culture as Shostak represents it is self-contained and isolate as a form of vanishing primitivism. She has largely removed it from the history of colonialism and from its contemporary intercultural clashes with its more powerful African neighbors.[26]

The encounter I have staged here between Forster's ethnographic novel and Shostak's novelistic ethnography metonymically represents the larger story of disciplinary interaction I have been telling. Telling contacts between literary studies and anthropology help to "break open" the nature of story itself. To expand the condensation of my title, telling the story of contact generates considerable narrative energy and drive; and, telling the story of contact is very telling, that is, very illuminative for understanding that generative engine. Ethnography always already embeds telling contacts; conversely, narratives of encounter always already partake of the ethnographic. Consequently, the encounter between anthropology and literary studies as agents of different disciplinary "cultures" within the academy produces a story of interaction, of reciprocal influence, and of an emergent syncretism in the borderlands of knowledge. Such interdisciplinarity does not erase the differences of the discursive disciplines; rather, it feeds off of them. To be transgressed, the boundaries between ethnography and literary studies must still exist. The interstitial borderlands between them require a dialogic symbiosis based in alterations of sameness and difference.[27]

As a literary scholar engaging with ethnographic theory, I have found in these disciplinary borderlands the theoretical basis for a spatialized approach to narrative poetics, one that fosters the significance of travel, movement, setting, cultural difference, and intercultural contact zones for the generation of story. This approach resists the conventional association of space with stasis and time with movement, positing instead the intercultural space in between difference as a dynamic terrain that makes things happen, as a space of travel and change—physical, psychological, linguistic, symbolic. It resists as well the reduction of story to sequence, to a temporal movement governed by the rhetoric of desire and development. The dominance of temporal paradigms for narrative poetics has led, I have argued, to an overemphasis on the oedipal and post-oedipal plots of desire as constitutive of narrative itself. In compensation, I have stressed the kinetic work performed by scenes of intercultural encounter as a common, significant, and often overlooked source of narrative drive. Desire of some kind certainly underlies a part of this story. My intent here has not been to deny the significance of desire for narrative drive, nor to deny the oedipal and post-oedipal plotting of desire and character development, nor to deny the status of time as a coordinate of narrative, nor to deny the importance of history and change through time. What I have attempted to do here is clear a space for the spatial and locational in our discussions of narrative, to mute for the time being the hegemony of temporal discourses of desire in the discussion of narrative drive. In the effort to make visible what has been largely invisible in narrative theory, I have insisted that the contradictory tensions between sameness and difference underlying intercultural encounters in the contact zone cannot be explained solely in terms of oedipal and post-oedipal plottings of desire, however much erotics play a part in such border-lands. I have proposed a dialogic, spatial model of narrative to displace the exclusivity of developmental, temporal models that characterize some narrative theory. Ultimately, we must examine the dialogic of space and time, location and development, encounter and desire as both together drive the narrative forward. As Adrienne Rich writes in "Notes toward a Politics of Location," "a place on the map is also a place in history" (212).

"Routes/Roots":
Boundaries, Borderlands, and
Geopolitical Narratives of Identity

We need to think comparatively about the distinct
routes/roots of tribes, barrios, favellas, immigrant
neighborhoods—embattled histories with crucial
community "insides" and regulated traveling
"outsides." What does it take to define and
defend a homeland? What are the political stakes in
claiming (or sometimes being relegated to) a "home"?
—*James Clifford, "Traveling Cultures"*

One is always on the run, and it seems I haven't
really had a home base—and this may have been
good for me. I think it's important for people not to
feel rooted in one place.
—*Gayatri Chakravorty Spivak,*
The Post-Colonial Critic

THINKING geopolitically about identity is a "spatial practice," to echo Michel de Certeau in *The Practice of Everyday Life*. It involves maps and mapping, routes and routing, borders and bordercrossings. As a form of relational spatialization, however, it incorporates the opposing dimensions of the homonym routes/roots. Traveling is a concept that depends upon the notion of stasis to be comprehensible. Routes are pathways between here and there, two points of rootedness. Identity often requires some form of displacement—literal or figurative—to come to consciousness. Leaving home brings into being the idea of "home," the perception of its identity as distinct from elsewhere.[1] Rootlessness—the sense that Spivak expresses of being "always on the run"—acquires its meaning only in relation to its opposite, rootedness, the state of being tied to a single location. Moreover, routes imply travel, physical and psychical displacements in space, which in turn incorporate the crossing of borders and contact with difference. Roots, routes, and intercultural encounter depend upon narrative for embodiment. What I plan to explore is the narrative poetics of geopolitical identity as the symbiosis between roots and routes and the encounters they engender as they are mediated through other particularities based on gender, sexuality, class, religion, and so forth. I will first discuss the dialogic pull of routes and roots in relation to narratives of identity and then turn to two texts for illustrative purposes—Julie Dash's avant-garde film *Daughters of the Dust* (1992) and Gish Jen's postmodern romp, the novel *Mona in the Promised Land* (1996).

Intercultural *Fort/Da* and Geopolitical Narratives

The emphasis on travel in Clifford's "Traveling Cultures"—reprinted as the lead essay in his collection *Routes*—is compensatory, to bring to visibility those aspects of cultural and individual identity that the conventional emphasis on home or "dwelling" has largely suppressed. Similarly, Paul Gilroy in *The Black Atlantic* affirms the significance of both roots and routes, but explores more fully what he believes has received insufficient attention: "Dealing equally with the significance of roots and routes, as I proposed in Chapter 1, should undermine the purified appeal of either Africentrism or the Eurocentrisms it struggles to answer. This book has been more concerned with the flows, exchanges, and in-between elements that call the very desire to be centred into question" (190). In a related fashion, Stuart Hall acknowledges the view of cultural identity that seeks to "discover, excavate, bring to light and express" the "common historical experiences and shared cultural codes which provide us, as 'one people,' with stable unchanging and continuous frames of reference and meaning," however much this rootedness belies "the shifting divisions and vicissitudes of our actual history" ("Cultural Identity" 393). But Hall clearly privileges the opposite approach to cultural identity, the one that stresses rupture, discontinuity, movement, "constant transformation," and "the continuous 'play' of history" (395). In her emphasis on rootlessness Spivak appears to do away with roots altogether. "If there's one thing I totally distrust, in fact, more than distrust, despise and have contempt for," she says to her interviewer in *The Post-Colonial Critic*, "it is people looking for roots. Because anyone who can conceive of looking for roots, should, already, you know, be growing rutabagas" (93). Spivak's scorn for seeking roots no doubt reflects the Derridean framework out of which she often works; it may also be related to the relative privilege she acknowledges as a nomadic intellectual from a well-off family, having had the wherewithal to remain diasporically "on the run" within global circuits of travel. Her despisement of roots is counterbalanced by those whose attachment to roots seems vital for survival, a psychological and material imperative evident in Alex Haley's *Roots*, to name one widely influential text.

In spite of compensatory emphases on routes and rootlessness in much cultural and postcolonial studies, theorists like Clifford, Gilroy, and Hall argue ultimately for a dialogic movement back and forth between routes and roots. Gilroy understands, for example, how the hybridity and heterogeneity of the "black Atlantic" is counterbalanced by how the effects of racism foster the "need to project a coherent and stable racial culture as a means to establish the political legitimacy of black nationalism and the notions of ethnic particularity on which it has come to rely" (*Black Atlantic* 97). And Hall writes that "we might think of black Caribbean identities as 'framed' by two axes or vectors, simultaneously operative: the vector of similarity and continuity; and the vector of difference and rupture. Caribbean identities always have to be thought of in terms of the dialogic relationship between these two axes. The one gives us some grounding in, some continuity with, the past. The second reminds us that what we share is precisely the experience of a profound discontinuity: the peoples dragged into slavery, transportation, colonisation, migration, came predominantly from Africa" (395). Roots and routes are, in other words, two sides of the same coin: roots, signifying identity based on stable cores and continuities; routes, suggesting identity based on travel, change, and disruption.

As an ongoing process of formation and re-formation, identity depends centrally upon narrative, whether it is an effect of rootedness or routedness. The specular, the visual, the figural, the metaphoric—all, of course, also contribute to the production of identity. But if we regard identity as a form of constant becoming (rather than a fixed point of origin or an end product), then we need to examine the several ways in which narrative poetics enters the process. First, identity is constructed through stories that communities and individuals tell about themselves. The "imagined community" that Benedict Anderson theorizes for national identity involves a state of mind or consciousness in which narrative and storytelling play a central role; the imagined boundaries of identity he proposes for nations are similar to the perceptual categories upon which all group identifications are based. Individuals develop a sense of self through acts of memory, reflexivity, and engagement with others, all of which require forms of storytelling to come into being. Second, the ongoing production of individual and communal identities constitutes a story itself, a psychological and cultural formation that is located in and moves through time and space. And third, cultural narratives of domination, resistance, desire, and their complex interplay constitute the intertextual web out of which individual and collective selves are woven within the context of asymmetrical power relations. As Carolyn Heilbrun writes about the stories we live by: "We live our lives through texts. They may be read, or chanted, or experienced electronically, or come to us, like the murmurings of our mothers, telling us what conventions demand. Whatever their form or medium, these stories have formed us all; they are what we must use to make new fictions, new narratives" (*Writing* 37).

How, then, does the geopolitical dimension of identity relate to narrative? How are roots and routes narrativized? What narrative patterns characterize the individual, communal, and cultural narratives that constitute identity? In prior chapters, I have already discussed ways in which the formation of cultural identity depends upon a dialogic of sameness and difference: the identification with others as a bond based in similarity that can be grasped only through a sense of difference from others. Within this framework, narratives of identity require some form of intercultural encounter, some form of contact with an other who is experienced as different. In terms of the roots/routes symbiosis, experiencing identity as roots requires some figurative or material engagement of routes through a contact zone of intercultural encounter. Conversely, identity developed through routes involves an experience of leaving roots, of moving beyond the boundaries of "home" (however that is defined or problematized). A geopolitical identity rooted in "home" insists upon sameness within the home circle; one formed through leaving home base involves interaction with others, which fosters the formation of hybridic combinations.

The narrative patterns that characterize these complex functions of mimesis and alterity seem endless. I do not want to propose a totalizing metanarrative, nor do I think it feasible to identify a deep structure that conditions heterogeneous narrative manifestations. What I will do is map one of these patterns: namely, the dialogic constituted by the bipolar pull between the erection of borders delineating difference and the dissolution of those boundaries in the formation of permeable borderlands of exchange, blending, and transformations. Narratives of encounter in the contact zone often exhibit a contradictory oscillation between the establishment of firm boundaries between self and other on the one hand and the transgression of fixed borders on the other. To invoke as I supplement psychoanalytic models of narrative drive, I call this oscillation the intercultural *fort/da* that underlies many plottings of encounter.

To define what I mean by intercultural *fort/da*, I'll start with a story—a geographic history—taken from Thongchai Winichukul's *Siam Mapped*, which examines how the encounter between Thai concepts of mapping and sovereignty evolved in contact with western epistemologies during the nineteenth century. Before the British and French entered Southeast Asia as colonial powers, Thongchai argues, the Thai had no fixed notion of a boundary line separating one region or nation from another and no technology for surveying such fixed boundaries. Instead, areas between different ethnic, regional, or national groups were spaces of overlapping sovereignty constituting broad borderlands across which people and goods moved continuously and freely in times of peace. The British concept of a fixed imaginary line constructed through measurement and enforcing separation was at first quite alien. Thai epistemology of mapping allowed for much greater fluidity. Only when tensions flared between different groups did a concept of a boundary line demarcating difference come into play. Enforced by armies, such borders were temporary, disappearing once relatively friendly relations were reestablished. Borderlands were spaces that expanded and contracted depending on relations between different power bases. In peacetime, the border areas were wide, with considerable cultural circulation and syncretist blending; in wartime, the borderland became boundary line, a space where encounters produced confrontations, not interminglings, of difference.

Gradually, in the mid-nineteenth century, King Mongkut (upon whom *The King and I* is based) adapted the British conventions of mapping with fixed boundaries, not because the British imposed western modes of thought but because he found them useful in his own attempts, on the one hand, to consolidate the central power of the Siamese state over regional powers and, on the other hand, to strengthen Siam's resistance to the West. Paradoxically, his syncretist adaptation of British epistemology was instrumental in the formation of Siam as a nation-state, a site of difference from the West and from surrounding Southeast Asian peoples. A partially mimetic relation to the West is precisely what fostered the formation of what Thongchai calls the Siamese "geobody," the national identity of the Thai tied to a map with borders and a set of stories about Thai history.

Thongchai's story narrativizes in complex ways what I mean by the contradictory dialogic of intercultural *fort/da*. *Fort/da*, it should be recalled, is the game Freud identified as the young child's first performance of the principle of signification or representation. As he explains the game in *Beyond the Pleasure Principle*, the child repeatedly throws down a toy in anticipated delight of having it returned, an act that recapitulates the absence of the mother and her return. The pleasure of the game resides in the child's agency: the control the child exercises over the oscillating presence/absence of the toy that symbolizes the mother's movements. Narrative theorists like Peter Brooks have found in Freud's play with *fort/da* and the related oscillations of Eros and the death instinct a theory to explain the unconscious energy that drives narrative as a form of representation, as well as the oedipal formations of subjectivity constituted through narrative representation.

In substituting an intercultural *fort/da* for the psychoanalytic game, I am shifting the grounds of encounter from the mother/child dyad of the son's desire—a kind of ethnography of the dwelling—to a more broadly conceived intercultural encounter in which both "sides" negotiate the borders between difference, however equal or unequal the power relations between them.[2] In tune with Clifford's notion of an ethnography of travel, I am locating story-producing encounters in the relational spaces between difference—all kinds of historically produced differences, those between societies and within societies; those formed by stratifications based on multiple axes of difference, such as gender, race, ethnicity, religion, sexuality, class, caste, national origin, and so forth; and those emergent in liminal borders between human and animal, human and machine, or matter and spirit.

Thongchai's narrative of the contracting and expanding borderlands in traditional Siamese epistemology facilitates the shift I am suggesting for narrative studies. The oscillation of an intercultural *fort/da* involves the alteration of impermeable and permeable borders between selves and other selves, both of whom have agency and subjectivity in the exchange.[3] At times, individuals or groups erect barriers separating themselves from others in a defense of their own difference. "Difference(s) from others," Henrietta Moore writes, "are frequently about forming and maintaining group boundaries. The brutal and bloody nature of this maintenance work is everywhere in evidence" (*Passion for Difference* 1). Such cultural formations come from both hegemonic and marginalized groups, the one defending difference as a form of its own superiority and power, the other insisting on its difference as a form of resistance and longed-for empowerment. The contact zones between such groups are often sites of bigotry, victimization, rage, and misrecognition. The dissolutions of the boundaries that sustain such group identities are sometimes simply ignored, sometimes repressed, or sometimes re-garded as a form of pollution, miscegenation, or betrayal of group solidarity. At other times, however, the borders between individuals or groups are not so fixed and function rather as a permeable borderland of cultural traffic where differences mingle, blend, and form new ways of being based on imitation and adaptation of the other. Such a borderland has the potential to be the site of connection and reconciliation, however ephemeral.

But wait. In invoking traditional Thai epistemology of borderlands, I have problematically aligned the erection of fixed borders of difference with oppres-sion and resistance, while linking syncretism with peace and reconciliation of differences. However, syncretism is not always the result of peace, as the tradi-tional Thai parable suggests, but sometimes constitutes the painful aftereffects of pacification. The cultural hybridity and creolization that mark all forms of cultural expressivity—language, food, art, customs, religions, and other social practices—are often the product of unequal power relations, forced assimilation, and cultural erasure of difference imposed by a stronger power. Sometimes embraced, syncre-tism is also sometimes imposed. Syncretism can enrich both sides of an encoun-ter, but it can also impoverish. In positing an intercultural narrative poetics, I need to avoid the all-too-easy idealization of hybridity as utopian panacea for the bru-talities that difference can sometimes exhibit.[4]

The second part of Thongchai's story, focusing on the king's formation of a Siamese national identity, provides the necessary corrective to a romanticized view of syncretism. King Mongkut, as Thongchai demonstrates in detail, adopted British notions of fixed boundaries in part to subdue restive regional powers in Siam. What happened to all those local peoples as they were absorbed into the national culture of Siam, which was able to resist western powers better than its neighbors in Burma and Cambodia? Internal colonization facilitated resistance to external colonization. Stratifications existed on both sides of the contact zone, complicating the story of differences meeting with other stories of intercultural heterogeneity and encounter.

An intercultural poetics of the contact zone needs both parts of Thongchai's story: first, the *fort/da* of contracting borders based in offensive or defensive assertions of difference and expanding borderlands based in recognition of cul-tural mixing and imitation; and second, the vigilant attention to questions of power relations that circulate in the contact zone and complicate the patterns of cultural hybridity. (I say circulate advisedly because I want to avoid reductionistic analyses of power that posit a unidirectional flow that reproduce center/periphery and oppressor/oppressed dualisms. Such binarist thinking, evident, for example, in much of Edward Said's theorizations of the contact zone, frequently ignores the heterogeneity of the other, the agency and subjectivity of the other, and the systems of stratification that operate on both sides of a border.) These two dimen-sions of borderlands are evident in Clifford's observation in "Diasporas" that "borderlands are distinct in that they presuppose a territory defined by a geopolit-ical line: two sides arbitrarily separated and policed, but also joined by legal and illegal practices of crossing and communication" (*Routes* 246). A narrative poetics of geopolitical identity requires attention to both activities at the border as they relate to roots and routes: the ethnographics of both dwelling and travel, stasis and movement, continuity and rupture, difference and hybridity.

ROOTS/ROUTES IN *DAUGHTERS OF THE DUST*

Let me turn now by way of illustration to Julie Dash's award-winning 1992 film, *Daughters of the Dust*, a surprise hit at the box office and video stores, a commercial success unanticipated at least in part because of its antirealist, experimental mode of mythopoetic narrative.[5] Breaking up linear narrative told by an authoritative filmic eye, the film presents a montage of fleeting images and juxtaposed fragmentary scenes to tell the story of a family reunion that takes place at Ibo Landing in 1902 in the Georgia Sea Islands of the Gullah people the day before most of the Peazant family joins the Great Migration of African Americans from the South to the North. Two members of the family long since gone return home to participate in the reunion picnic. Described in the script as the "new kind of woman" and a prostitute, Yellow Mary arrives at Ibo Landing accompanied by her lover Trula. Yellow Mary's cousin Viola has also been away for years, up north as a Christian missionary. She brings with her Mr. Snead, a dapper photographer who is eager to record the event. Nana Peazant, the matriarch of the family, fears for her family's spiritual survival and uses the power of her charismatic presence to bind one and all into a communal whole watched over by the ancestors who have passed on. *Daughters of the Dust* is about both roots and routes—about familial and communal bonds based in black ethnicity; about dispersals and migrations that produce the black diaspora.

The film's mode is nonrealist, organized around what Toni Cade Bambara calls in the preface its "multilayered unfolding" in the context of "dual narration, multiple-point-of-view camerawork," and "shared space (wide-angled and deepfocus shots in which no one becomes backdrop to anyone else's drama)" (*Daughters* xiii). The story unfolds through pictoral juxtapositions, layering vignettes and tableaux in a sequence that suggests simultaneity. Nonetheless, there is also a linear narrative that draws heavily on the conventions of agonistic plotting and resolution. The film's central conflict revolves around Nana's great-grandson Eli and his pregnant wife, Eula. She has been raped, and Eli fears the child is not his. She refuses to name the rapist, admitting only to Yellow Mary and Trula that if she did so, Eli would surely be lynched, thereby implying that the rapist is a white man. The painful division between husband and wife intensifies in the context of the rejection that the "ruint" Yellow Mary faces from all the Peazant women except Nana and Eula. As a fundamentalist Christian, Viola condemns Yellow Mary's sins, along with Nana's African religious practices—her ancestor worship, bottle tree commemorating the dead, and talismanic objects, like the swatch of her mother's hair, passed on to the child as her mother was sold down the river.

Roiling with angry undercurrents, the family fragments dangerously, until Eula vomits in the sand and delivers an impassioned speech, unveiling what she claims to be the secret self-hatred black women feel. Suspecting that their line of mothers are all fallen women ruined in the history of their sexual slavery, black women project their shame and self-hatred onto women they condemn like Yellow Mary. Eula's appeal for healing acceptance and self-love paves the way for a climactic bonding ritual in which nearly everyone, including Viola, participates. Nana Peazant winds a pouch containing her own and her mother's hair along with Yellow Mary's St. Christopher medal around Viola's Bible and asks each member of the family to kiss it as a mark of their communal and spiritual commitment to the survival of the family.

As mythopoetic history, the film presents a parable about the difficult formation of a diasporic identity for a people who were brutally cut off from their African home and nonetheless survived as an "imagined community" of black Americans rooted in African traditions. *Daughters of the Dust* is a filmic recovery of roots, a rewitnessing of past migration routes as a commitment to the survival of African Americans as they disperse even further in the future. This communal story of roots/routes parallels a personal quest as well, one that owes much to Haley's *Roots* in spirit (though not in form), one that demonstrates the entwining of the individual and the communal in diasporic identities. Dash writes about the project:

> The stories from my own family sparked the idea of *Daughters* and formed the basis for some of the characters. But when I probed my relatives for information about the family history in South Carolina, or about our migration north to New York, they were often reluctant to discuss it. When things got too personal, too close to memories they didn't want to reveal, they would close up, push me away, tell me to go ask someone else. I knew then that the images I wanted to show, the story I wanted to tell, had to touch an audience the way it touched my family. It had to take them back, take them inside their family memories, inside our collective memories. (*Daughters* 5)

Like Nana's hand-sewn pouch of memories, Dash's film patches "scraps of memories..... through them we came to know our mothers, grandmothers, & family history. And finally to know our own selves" (88).

With its shimmering celebrations of black cultural life, the film is easily assimilated into a generalized Afrocentric project about the claiming of African roots. Gilroy's general observation is applicable in this case: "modern black political culture has always been more interested in the relationship of identity to roots and rootedness than in seeing identity as a process of movement and mediation that is more appropriately approached via the homonym routes" (*Black Atlantic* 19). Bambara's preface, for example, aligns the film's experimental form with its "Africentric grounding," one "more in keeping with the storytelling traditions that inform African cinema" (*Daughters* xiii). Rather than associate Dash's filmic forms with modernist narrative technique or other traditions of western avant-garde film, she links them entirely with the Black Cinema Movement and other progressive Third World cinemas (xiii). Certainly, the film has been and can be interpreted only within the framework of what Gilroy calls "ethnic absolutism" in *The Black Atlantic* and which Hall associates with the "roots" approach to cultural identity. The film's loving visual and musical representations of black bodies and iconography, especially that of black women, performs a healing ritual of its own, binding diverse black viewers into a diasporic communal family watched over by their common African ancestors. As counterpoint to white racism, the film is a hymn to black difference and Africanness. Such a reading of the film, however, mutes its examination of syncretism as a foundational component of diasporic identity, the hybridity produced by migration, by "routes" in opposition to "roots." It suppresses as well the film's complex play with the dialogics of sameness and difference, fixed borders and permeable borderlands, roots and routes of identity—with, in short, the kind of intercultural *fort/da* and the circulations of power in the narrative poetics of the contact zone that I have been theorizing.

It is not difficult to make a case for the strong parallels between the film's experimental forms and that of some western disruptions of realist narrative and Hollywood conventions. But even the film's linear sequencing of scenes complicates exclusively Afrocentric interpretations. Fixed borders marking difference abound in the film's montage of visual tableaux, each moving in some form to a kind of permeable borderland by the end of the film. And I don't mean difference between black and white—that border remains fixed, uncrossed except for occasional allusions to the violent intrusions of whites into the world of the Gullah. I mean differences among the people at Ibo Landing, differences that highlight heterogeneity and undermine the presumed sameness of black identity. Borders between men and women; between married women and all the other "ruint" women like prostitutes, lesbians, or "new kind of women"; between light- and dark-skinned women; between Christian, African, and Muslim religions; between blacks and Indians; between North and South, island and mainland, Africa and America; between science and faith; between born and unborn, alive and passed on; between old and young; between past and present; between traditional and modern.[6]

Many of the film's scenes focus on the encounter of differences, often bitter in their fixities: the Peazant women refusing Yellow Mary's gifts; Eli rejecting Eula; Nana and Eli fighting over Eula's condition; Eli smashing Nana's bottle tree; Mr. Snead, the overdressed "Philadelphia Negro" (*Daughters* 79) enamored of western science, photographing the Gullah men; and so forth. On a metanarrative level, Julie Dash's handling of montage—the technique of filmic collage or editing—emphasizes these borders through heightened parataxis, or the juxtaposition of differences that form a series of visual encounters. For example, the image of Bilal Mohammed's performance of his morning prayer with his homemade Koran dissolves into the image of Viola holding her Bible, early in the film (77). Near the film's end, Mr. Snead snaps a portrait of Viola's mother, a scene that dissolves into an image of slave-community elders while Nana's voice over recalls the importance of the African Griot as the repository of family memory (146–47). The montage—a technique that Sergei Eisenstein, one of its earliest and most innovative practitioners, described as a dialectic—highlights the thesis and antithesis of African and western forms of memory.

As a dialectic, however, montage also suggests synthesis—the hybridic blending of differences that dissolves inviolate borders of difference as one scene fades to another. The four technical terms Dash uses in the screenplay to indicate different camera techniques related to montage—"cut," "angle on," "dissolve," and "fade in or out"—embody the dialectic of fixed and blurred boundaries. Consider, for example, the sequence that juxtaposes Mr. Snead's camera and the African Griot as different technologies of memory. The flashback to slavery times "cuts" back to Haagar's little son Ninnyjugs carrying a turtle with an African symbol for S.O.S. painted on its back. The camera then "angles on" to Daddy Mac explaining the connection of this game to slave times, when the ancestors used the turtle doubly: to communicate with African family and to symbolize their carrying that family with them wherever they wander. Another "cut" and "angle on" shows Nana and Haagar watching the photo session. As an "educated" woman who married into the Peazant family, Haagar is scornful of Nana's Hoodoo practices, including the bottle tree whose hanging glass signifies each of those who has passed on. "You're a natural fool, Haagar Peazant," Nana says. "Nobody ever said that the old souls were living inside those glass jars. The bottle tree reminds us of who was here and who's gone on. You study on the colors and shapes. You appreciate the bottle tree each day, as you appreciate your loved ones" (147–48). A final cut returns us to Mr. Snead sweating profusely as he adjusts his camera. On the one hand, this series emphasizes the difference between African and western forms of memory. But on the other hand, it also blends them in a filmic *fort/da*, an oscillation that weaves them together. As the most "African" of characters, Nana Peazant is also the one who articulates the syncretist message. Never the literalist, she understands the camera and bottle tree as different forms for the same activity of memory. The bracketed directions emphasize Nana's awareness: "Nana is curious, Snead is able to capture and hold 'memories' with his camera. Nana relied on her 'scraps of memories' and the 'bottle tree'" (148).

The message of the film's montage replicates the narratives of encounter, which move from staging difference to representing creolization, from borders to borderlands where differences mingle and change each other, where reconciliation and community become possible. In the powerful utopian drift of the linear narrative, most—though not all—chasms are bridged. The charismatic icon of creolization and reconciliation is the syncretist object that Nana Peazant creates, holds, and has her family kiss in the film's climactic ritual of community. The object is significantly not pure African, but a multicultural collection metonymically gesturing at the many locations of African American experience. Viola's Bible signifies her Baptist faith and more generally the black Christian spirituality of many Protestant sects. Yellow Mary's St. Christopher medal invokes Catholicism in the form of the patron saint of travelers. On top of these, Nana places the "charm bag" she has been making, saying "This 'Hand,' it's from me, from us, from them (the Ibo)... Just like all of you... Come children, kiss this hand full of me" (159). Inside the Hand mingle her slave mother's hair with her own, signifying not only Hoodoo practices of sympathetic magic but also the crime of slavery that denied a child her mother on the one hand and the reunion of that torn bond on the other. To complete the image of spiritual syncretism, Nana grips Bilal Mohammed's shoulder, bringing into the Peazant family the Muslim who was stolen from Africa, sold in the French West Indies, and then brought to Ibo Landing as a boy long after the slave trade was officially ended. This scene cuts to the image of Bilal saying his morning prayers at the seaside, facing Mecca, facing Africa.

This, however, is the positive syncretism of peacetime that Thongchai evokes in the Siamese example. How does it relate to the negative circulation of power in the borderlands? Complementing the regenerative syncretism of Nana's ritual and the film's ethnographic eye is its representation of African American identity as a hybrid grown in the bitter borderlands between black slaves and white masters. Representations of hybridity resulting from oppression and forced assimilation counterpoint the utopian strain of the film's mythopoetic syncretisms. For all its beauty, the world of the Gullah people is diasporic, marked by forcible removal and dispersion from various homelands in Africa. Nana's patched Hand represents this forcefully, since it contains as talismanic presence the metonymic body of the lost and violated mother in the form of her hair. The slave mother's bond with her descendants functions like an absent presence—absent not only through death but also through the slave markets; present not only in a piece of her body but also in spirit. So too the African motherland—the never-known, ever-longed-for absence/presence from which the slaves and their free descendants have been cut off but to which they connect themselves through spiritual and cultural bonds.

The use of the color blue in the film is the major visual figuration of how regenerative and oppressive dimensions of hybridity weave together. Flashbacks to slavery times on the Sea Islands focus on the production of the highly prized but poisonous indigo dye, which endangered the health of the slaves. Although working with indigo does not literally stain the body, as Dash well knows, the slaves in the film have hands stained with blue, a mark that appears very pronounced on the hands of Nana Peazant at various moments in the 1902 scenes. "I was using this," Dash explains to her historical adviser, "as a symbol of slavery, to create a new kind of icon around slavery rather than the traditional showing of the whip marks or the chains" (*Daughters* 31). These blue stains are metonyms for slavery's racial economy and human bondage. The indigo appears on more than hands, however. As reminders of slavery, Nana wears a faded indigo dress throughout the film, and Yellow Mary significantly dons a blue dress like Nana's after she decides to stay at Ibo Landing for a while (she does not depart with the family and Trula on the morning after the picnic). Eula's Unborn Child, who flits ghostlike in and out of scenes, doing many of the film's voice-over explanations, wears a vibrant indigo bow in her hair and sash around her waist, matched by the pale indigo buttons on her white dress. These indigo accents signal the presence of a painful past in a reborn future. The beauty of the indigo contains both victimization and agency, violation and survival. As the film's major icon, indigo functions doubly: as a mark of enforced hybridity inscribed literally on the body and as a sign of vibrant creolization signified by its dark beauty. African Americanness is a diasporic cultural identity, *Daughters of the Dust* argues, that transforms syncretism from enslavement into regeneration, a renaissance that incorporates without erasing bondage as the condition of its creativity.

The syncretism built out of the film's dialogic play with roots and routes in narrative and figuration operates also at the metalevel of Dash's relation with her audience, especially her African American viewers.[7] Nana's healing ritual binds not only the Peazant family together but also by example the black audience of the film, whose link to the family lies linguistically embedded in the family name (Peazant/peasant). As filmic icon, *Daughters of the Dust* stitches together "scraps of memory," fragments representing many intercultural differences within the African American experience. To do so, Dash borrows from multiple cinematic traditions, making of the film itself a borderland where genres of documentary, ethnography, history, avant-garde, and feature clash and blend. As contemporary filmmaker, Dash creates for her audiences the kind of record for posterity that Mr. Snead, the master of the modern technology for his time, makes for the Peazant family. Dash's ethnographic agenda to document the customs, crafts, rhythms, food, hairstyles, religion, and family relations of a vanishing culture reproduces the role that Viola plays in the film as Mr. Snead's native informant who can explain what he observes. (Like the native informant described in Clifford's "Traveling Cultures," Viola has traveled, which is precisely why she is able to explain what she can now see with both an insider's and an outsider's eye.) Supplemented by Viola's explanations, Mr. Snead's camera stands in for Dash's own filmic eye, her ethnographic gaze. Viola and Mr. Snead exist within the film to perform the functions of documentation, memory, and explanation for the Peazant family that Dash's film undertakes as its cultural work for audiences of today, especially (though not exclusively) African American viewers.

This parallel between Dash and her characters Mr. Snead and Viola proposes something of a paradox, one that the dialogics of intercultural *fort/da* and roots/routes helps to resolve. Because Mr. Snead and Viola are major figures of satire in the film, Dash's bond with them requires some explanation. In satirizing the photographer and the family ethnographer, Dash is in some sense satirizing her own activities, undermining the film's search for roots. Mr. Snead and Viola initially represent in the film the encounter of differences: his advocacy of western science and mastery of modern technology versus Nana's "root work" and the Gullah traditions; Viola's fundamentalist Christianity versus the Hoodoo and Islam of the Sea Islands. His suit and tie, her dress and watch fob, mark them as bourgeois, urban African Americans who have repudiated their African agrarian roots in their efforts to imitate white westerners. Where it exists in the film, humor emerges mostly out of the earnest awkwardness, out-of-placeness, and downright silliness that these two "educated," seemingly superior Negroes demonstrate in front of their country cousins. His faith in science and her literal-minded dependence on Jesus are naive in relation to Nana's greater cultural adaptability and more powerful spirituality. As this encounter of difference evolves, Nana is entirely privileged, while Mr. Snead and Viola are entirely discredited. The boundary between self-loving blacks in touch with their African roots and "westernized" blacks who either exoticize or condemn those roots is permanently fixed. Or so it seems. So an Afrocentric interpretation of the film would assert.

However, several major elements of the film undermine an exclusive association of the film with roots, particularly an essentialist view of a blackness rooted solely in Africa.[8] First, Nana's own syncretism symbolized by the ritual she presides over reintegrates the "modernized" African Americans back into the family. In kissing Nana's Hand, Mr. Snead and Viola abandon their own fixities—the photographer with more eagerness; Viola with more fear and reluctance. In so doing, they can both return North and bring something of the Gullah culture with them. Second, Dash's own identification with modernity through her manipulations of the camera and loving ethnographic representation reinforce the film's subtle blending of African and western forms of memory. What begins as borders of difference ends as the space of intercultural mixing. Rather than condemn everything western, as the satire of Snead and Viola appears to suggest that viewers should do, Dash insists that African Americans claim western technologies of memory for themselves, adapting them in hybridic combination with African forms.

Third, the film exhibits a kind of deconstructive play with whiteness that Homi Bhabha calls "colonial mimicry," by which he means the imitative practices of the colonized whose adaptation of certain western modes undermines the ideology of "natural" western superiority through a performance of constructivism.[9] Bhabha introduces the concept in part as a way of going beyond the notions of internalized racism, resultant self-hatred, and the racial pathology of the colonized proposed by Frantz Fanon in *Black Skin, White Masks.* Emphasizing the agency of the colonized, Bhabha interprets some forms of cultural imitation as hybridic resistance to the colonizer's ideology of natural racial difference and white superiority. Within these terms, Viola's and Snead's adaptations of western religion and science stake a claim to black participation in the formation of "the West." Where Audre Lorde asserts that "the master's tools" will never "dismantle the master's house" (*Sister Outsider* 110–13), the colonial mimicry represented by Viola, Snead, and Dash herself suggests that the tools of ethnography and photography can be appropriated to recover and hold on to a history that might otherwise be lost.

The same argument can be made about the function of the color white in the film. Among its many filmic appearances, the dresses of many of the women are a dazzling white, which contrasts with the rich array of black/brown/tan shades of skin, most especially with the darkest of these. The film presents a visual feast of black and white: not only the skin tones and dress but also the white sand of the beach dazzling in the sun, the moving shades of the ocean cresting in white waves against darkness, and the blackness of the river in its heavily shaded banks. The film's chiaroscuro—its constant play of light/dark oppositions—deconstructs an absolute binary to emphasize syncretist interaction. Moreover, the white dresses worn especially by the young girls look positively Victorian, or more properly speaking, Edwardian, especially that of the Unborn Child. White lace, pleats, buttons, ribbons, and embroidery forcefully claim "western" dress as their own, their "Sunday best" donned to celebrate the reunion and parting. Even Nana's indigo bodice is trimmed in delicate lace, the kind women traditionally tatted in places like Belgium and Ireland. As the black children dance in white Edwardian clothes on the beach, they indirectly "mimic" in Bhabha's sense white children who cavort on other beaches—like the Ramsay children on the Isle of Skye in Virginia Woolf's novel *To the Lighthouse*, or the young Virginia Stephen who loved to run about on the beach of St. Ives during her childhood summers in Cornwall. Pictures survive of Virginia dressed much as the children of Ibo Landing are garbed in Dash's film. The hairstyles of the women in the film hark back to African traditions, but their clothes are decidedly western and bourgeois, not African. In claiming these clothes in her mythopoetic rendition of the Gullah people, Dash challenges the natural authority of western whiteness and insists upon the creative agency of Gullah creolization, and by extension, the syncretism of the African diaspora, of what Gilroy calls "the Black Atlantic."

Black diasporan identity, *Daughters of the Dust* suggests, is made up of many cultural strands. Not a pure, static, or absolute difference, it is continually in the process of being made and remade; it is always already syncretist, the product of travel through space and time. The way to find black roots is through revisiting all the routes of black life in diaspora. In this sense, the film makes a clear distinction between African and African American experience and identity at the same time that it affirms their connection. "Africa" remains in the film largely an undifferentiated and longed-for Other in the African American imaginary born of the Middle Passage and slavery. African Americanness *is* differentiated, heterogeneous, multicultural. No melting pot, its creolization is like the gumbo the women make on the beach—full of many ingredients that blend and change each other without losing some distinctiveness in the syncretist cookpot of cultural formation.

Left out of Dash's cultural stew for the most part are the diasporas, dispersions, and migrations of other peoples in the United States. The film remains within the framework of a search for African American roots through a tracing of black routes. Within this framework, the film represents black Americans as heterogeneous and multicultural. But the focus on a family reunion at Ibo Landing in 1902 deals largely and for good reason with the race issue in terms of black and white. I say largely, because there are three characters in the film who gesture at other "others": Haagar, Trula, and St. Julian Last Child, a Cherokee Indian and the last of his people on the island. Significantly, none of the three participate in Nana's healing ritual, an exclusion whose resonances lie in the film's political unconscious. Haagar and Trula refuse to kiss the Hand binding the family together. And St. Julian Last Child is not present. The largely repressed meanings of these exclusions involve an intercultural *fort/da*, the dialogic of roots/routes.

Trula's reason for not kissing the Hand remains unnarrated. As the family members go up to Nana one by one, Trula sadly leaves the scene, walking alone into the fields. This sadness is repeated when the family leaves next morning, with Trula on the boat gazing mournfully at Yellow Mary on shore, now dressed in blue. Why can't Trula participate in the ritual? Why are the lovers separated? Trula never speaks in the film, serving mainly as an exotic and foreign object of everyone's gaze. A figure of racial ambiguity, she has the lightest skin tones of any character in the film. Where Yellow Mary is clearly presented as bisexual (a mother, a prostitute, and a lover of women), Trula is Yellow Mary's companion and lover. Must the lesbian be expelled from the family group? Does the light-skinned woman have no home in a film rooted in the aesthetic of "black is beautiful"? The film doesn't say. In her dialogue with hooks, Dash reveals that Trula was originally meant to be Asian American (66) and was only later made African American. Does a trace of her earlier racial configuration remain in her "yellow" skin? (Yellow Mary is a dark-skinned woman, but travels with what is often called a "high yeller" woman.) Trula's Asian American origins certainly remain as trace in one of the most beautiful of the beach scenes, where Trula, Eula, and Yellow Mary find an Oriental umbrella washed up on shore. They open it up, walk, and sit beneath its tattered wheel. The routes of Asians in the Americas—important not only in the United States but also in the Caribbean's different racial mix—reside hidden within the film's focus on African American roots.

St. Julian Last Child does not attend the family reunion, but ultimately, he joins the family as a future son-in-law. He is in love with Iona, one of Haagar's daughters, and at the end of the film, he appears dramatically on his horse and convinces Iona to gallop away with him instead of leaving with her family for the North. This marriage, which ensures the continuation of his line through absorption into the lineage of African Americans, metonymically represents the largely hidden or forgotten but often mythologized presence of Indian ancestry among African Americans. With their original homeland in the South, the Cherokee in particular had close ties, often family relations, with escaped or freed slaves in the nineteenth century. As a diasporic nation, the Cherokee were forced west to the Oklahoma Territories, but a few stayed behind. Dash's implication is that they became "black," through absorption into the African American family. While there is a certain historical foundation for Dash's symbolic marriage between St. Julian Last Child and Iona, there are also some troubling implications. Dash (unintentionally, I believe) participates in what she satirizes, the mainstream fascination with "vanishing" cultures, especially those of the "noble savage" in the Americas, thereby ignoring the very real existence, suffering, and creative survival of American Indian peoples on the continent, including the Cherokee in the Oklahoma region where they were forced to relocate. Her focus on African American roots/routes involves a concomitant insensitivity to the roots/routes of American Indians.

Haagar's reason for refusing to join the ritual is clearly narrated, but its full political resonance is buried, I suspect, hidden within the repressed memories of the slave trade. Considering herself an "educated person," Haagar announces defiantly that "I'm tired of Nana's old stories. Watching her make those root potions... and that Hoodoo she talks about" (130). Identifying completely with western norms and epistemology, she rejects the cultural hybridity that even Viola and Mr. Snead learn to accept for its binding effects on family and community. Dash's decision to personify this particular black response to Gullah and African traditions in the figure of a woman she names Haagar is puzzling. The biblical Hagar is Abraham's concubine and the mother of Ishmael; Sarah's jealousy leads to the expulsion of mother and babe into the desert, where they become (according to later traditions) the progenitors of Arab peoples. Why does Dash give the woman who refuses to be included in the story of roots the name of a woman who symbolizes female servitude, unjust expulsion, and nomadic routes of North African and Middle Eastern peoples?

One possible answer lies in the extensive involvement of Arabs in the slave trade to the American colonies, a participation that does not "fit" into a racial epistemology that sees things in black and white. A hint of this history appears in Haagar's anguished cry to her daughter as she helplessly watches the galloping horse from the boat. "Iona! Iona!" she screams. "I...Own...Her!" (163). The ebonic homonym Iona/I Own Her directly picks up on Viola's earlier explanation to Mr. Snead of what she fondly regards as the islanders' "'primitive' naming habits" from slavery times: "It's fifty years since slavery, Mr. Snead, but here, we still give our children names like 'My Own' (Myown), 'I Own Her' (Iona), 'You Need Her' (Unita), 'I Adore Her' (Eudora)" (138). Reflecting slavery's terrible breakup of families, these names invoke the power of words to keep families together before emancipation and the celebration of self and family "ownership" after emancipation. However, Iona's decision to remain at Ibo Landing with St. Julian Last Child represents another kind of family separation, one produced by her right to decide her own future. Haagar's transition from calling out "Iona" to "I Own Her" has a double resonance: the pain of mother/child separations during slavery; and the unlawful ownership of another human being that her desire to control Iona's future invokes. In this context, the suppressed echoes of the biblical Hagar, ancestress of Arab people (including their slave traders in West Africa), in the name Haagar make some sense. Rooted in the history of American slavery is a multicultural routing of many peoples, not just the black/white narrated in *Daughters*. In telling the story of African diaspora, Julie Dash, much like Paul Gilroy in *The Black Atlantic*, remains largely within a black/white binary framework that suppresses a more diverse narrative of intercultural mixing and hybridity.

ROUTES/ROOTS IN *MONA IN THE PROMISED LAND*

I would like to turn now to Gish Jen's postmodern play with cultural roots and routes in her best-selling novel *Mona in the Promised Land* (1996). In contrast to Dash's film, the novel appears to abandon all roots in a celebration of a playful engagement with routes, an embrace of rootlessness and change across fluid terrains of cultural identity. The novel's four epigraphs set the stage for Jen's satiric attack on what Gilroy calls "ethnic absolutism." The first cites Richard Rodriguez: "I'm becoming Chinese, I know it." The second quotes David Mura, a Japanese American, who says he learned more Yiddish than Japanese growing up in Skokie, Illinois. The third recalls Ovid: "all things change. The cosmos itself is flux and motion." And the fourth selects from the *I Ching*, linking "supreme good fortune" with he who "dissolves his bond with his group. . . . Dispersion leads in turn to accumulation." But just as Dash's search for roots leads to the traveling routes of a heterogeneous diaspora, so Jen's revel in the changeability of ethnic, racial, and geopolitical identities repeatedly bumps up against the intransigence of multidirectional racism and the powerful continuities of communalist identities. Like *Daughters of the Dust*, *Mona in the Promised Land* requires close attention to the interplay of roots and routes; the narrative moves back and forth in an intercultural *fort/da* as it negotiates between identity's fixity and changeability, borders and borderlands, and difference and hybridity.

Jen, however, casts her cultural nets more widely than Dash, moving well outside a binary racial grid. She represents not only the heterogeneity of Asian Americans but also that of Asians in general and of Americans of European, Jewish, and African descent. As a Chinese American writer, Jen examines Chinese roots and diaspora, but not as the primary focus of the novel. Rather, the plot develops out of the multicultural stir-fry of differences as they interact with each other to form a diverse America. What drives the narrative is the question of difference itself as it plays out in a nation built mostly by waves of immigrants and their descendants. How do cultural differences come into being? Why do they resist change? How do they change anyway? How do they remain? How do they reflect and shape the American mythology of itself as the promised land, as the land of the free and the home of the brave where anything is possible? What does it mean to be "American"? Set in the wealthy New York suburb Scarshill (clearly based on Scarsdale), the novel opens in 1968 shortly after the Chang family leaves the city for the "promised land" of the suburbs at a time when "the blushing dawn of ethnic awareness has yet to pink up their inky suburban night" (4). But the sensibility of the novel is thoroughly postmodern, governed by the trope of change on the shifting global ethnoscapes produced by constant migrations of peoples and intercultural mixing.

Mona in the Promised Land challenges the pieties of fundamentalist identity politics in a tone of spirited irreverence quite consistent with Spivak's observation cited above that "anyone who can conceive of looking for roots, should, already, you know, be growing rutabagas" (*Post-Colonial Critic* 93).[10] No group is exempt from Jen's biting wit. Unlike the lyrical mythopoesis of *Daughters*, *Mona* is playfully ironic throughout, using the colloquial easy-talk of teenage America to establish distance between the tongue-in-cheek writer, her less sophisticated narrator, and her wisely naive protagonist. The novel narrates the *Bildung* of Mona Chang, following her life from eighth grade through her high school graduation, with an epilogue that takes place after college and the birth of her child, just before her marriage to her high school lover.[11] With her best friend, the wealthy Jewish girl named Barbara Gugelstein, Mona grows up Asian American in Scarshill, where her immigrant parents have opened a House of Pancakes restaurant (a play on the stereotype that all Chinese Americans not working in laundries are involved in the Chinese restaurant business). In her search for an adult American identity distinct from that of her parents, Mona has a crush on a boy from Japan, then decides to convert to Judaism after Sherman Matsumoto rejects her, falls in love with Seth (a Jewish high school grad who acts out his rebellion by living in a tepee in his parents' backyard), tries to help Alfred (the homeless African American cook at her family's restaurant) and his friends, and leaves home when conflict with her parents worsens. Angry with her father's favoritism of his Chinese staff and discriminatory treatment of his black employees, Mona breaks family loyalty and tells Alfred why he doesn't get the promotion he deserves. Complicating the scenario of secrets and confessions, Alfred carries on a secret affair with Barbara's cousin Evie while he lives hidden in her house. An old tunnel from the Underground Railroad allows him to move in and out of the house undetected. When Barbara's parents return from a summer abroad to uncover the multiple plots, Mona's father fires Alfred, who promptly sues the family, armed with information Mona has given him. Mona's mother slaps and rejects her for betraying her family ("Fort Chang"), which leads Mona to run away, hide out in her sister Callie's dorm room at Harvard, pretend to her parents that she is in France, and wander out to California for a visit with her nonconformist Aunt Theresa. Upon her return, she convinces Alfred to drop the suit by apologizing to him for her own and Barbara's racism in suspecting him of stealing, and goes home with relief, only to find her mother refusing to acknowledge her presence. Here, on this completely unresolved note, the novel ends. The epilogue supplements the story of family fragmentation with a conventional comedic scene of reconciliation and marriage. Only here, the restitution of the social and familial order is intercultural. Alfred marries Evie, and Mona marries Seth, after the birth of their daughter Io. Just as the wedding begins, Mona's estranged mother appears, her presence signaling her acceptance (if not her blessing) of her Chinese/Jewish/American daughter. The mother-daughter plot overwhelms the marriage plot as Mona and Helen embrace with a clapping baby Io at their side. As a product of cultural and biological mixing, Io signifies the new American, the future.

The plot is elaborate, convoluted, improbable—a clear transgression against the conventions of verisimilitude at the same time that it borrows from popular culture clichés of family melodrama and racial/ethnic stereotyping. The familiar linear story of young adult love, rebellion, and initiation holds the narrative together. But the plot's underlying *donée* is the question of identity, particularly ethnic, racial, religious, and geopolitical identities as these are mediated by gender and class.[12] Scene after scene either stages a performance of intercultural encounter or makes those differences the focal point of dialogue and action. As I have argued in chapter 5 about the function of setting in intercultural plotting, the various locations into which the story moves signal different identity formations and encounters: the Chang restaurant; the Gugelstein estate; Seth's tepee; the Wasp resort; the Harvard dorm; the Califo pad; and so forth. The conventional tropes of teenage *Bildung*, the transparent simplicity of the narrative voice, and the linear chronology borrow heavily from the conventions of the realist novel. But irony, satiric exaggeration, and mimicry of stereotypes give the novel a decidedly postmodern flair. The text both thematizes and acts out the performative dimensions of communal identities.

The novel's seeming disavowal of roots calls into question the binary of "us" and "them" that underlies group identities of all kinds. Well outside the racial grids of white/other or white/black, the novel insists upon the heterogeneity of each group represented. We meet different kinds of Jews, different kinds of blacks and Asians, different enough to call into question the viability of the familiar ethnic/racial categories of the "gorgeous mosaic." Moreover, the novel is awash in relational thinking, juggling multiple axes of difference and hierarchy in its representation of everyone occupying contradictory subject positions. The love-hate relationship between Jews and blacks of the past thirty years is satirically and metonymically present in the relationship of Barbara and Alfred—she, with her strong social conscience alloyed with unacknowledged racism and incomprehension; he, with his dependence on her largesse, resentment of it, and refusal to take her experience of anti-Semitism seriously. In class terms, Barbara has the most money, though less social status than the Ingles, the token Wasp family. Alfred, kicked out of his house by his West Indian wife, is homeless, initially grateful to accept Barbara's well-meaning but insensitive desire to help; but he repeatedly utters familiar anti-Semitic lines (discounting the Holocaust, calling her father a "Jew-daddy," making fun of her nose). And he reiterates the black/white checkerboard of American racism in his continual inability to see Mona as anything but white. When Alfred and his male friends mock Barbara's "nose job," Mona explains how many Asians have eye operations to look "white," thus exposing the mediations of race and gender as they affect Jewish and Asian women in a culture where women face the external and internalized male gaze that privileges white female beauty. In relation to Scarshill Jews and Wasps, Mona's parents are mere restaurant immigrants, but as the employers of the largely black kitchen crew, they exhibit considerable racism in their efforts to protect themselves and other Chinese. Their insecurity is in turn related to their impoverished background in Shanghai, exacerbated by having lived through war, revolution, and diaspora. No one is exempt from racial, ethnic, gender, or class stereotyping—in being either the perpetrators or victims of the othering process. Everyone at some points erects barriers of difference against the other.

At the center of this identity whirl sits Mona, trying to figure out who she is and what being "American" means. Although the narration is in the third person, the novel clearly plays off of Mark Twain's *Adventures of Huckleberry Finn* as a quintessentially American novel that uses a naive teenage narrator (an American version of the wise fool in Shakespeare) as the vessel for the author's satire, critique of inhumanities of all kinds, and appeal for change.[13] Mona has bought into the American dream of freedom and repeatedly acts as if the dream were reality, not understanding the gap between ideology and the conditions it masks. When she is put in charge of Sherman, the visiting student from Japan, at her school, she answers his puzzled question about whether she is American by saying: "Sure I'm American. . . . Everybody who's born here is American, and also some people who convert from what they were before. You could become American." To his denial, she answers: "Sure you could. . . . You only have to learn some rules and speeches." "But I Japanese," he answers, to which she replies:

"You could become American anyway. . . . Like I *could* become Jewish, if I wanted to. I'd just have to switch, that's all" (14). Just as Huck's naiveté contains a kernel of truth and core value for Twain, Mona's explanation reflects the profound difference between Japanese and American concepts of citizenship in 1968. In Japan at that time, citizenship resided in paternal lineage: a child was considered Japanese only if he or she had a Japanese father.[14] In the United States, in contrast, not only parentage but also birth within the boundaries of the state could confer citizenship, a possibility that deemphasizes biological lineage as determinant of geopolitical identity.

As Jen's satiric attack on ethnic absolutism, Mona's innocent belief in the American power to "switch" represents a denial of both biology and history to determine identity. She interprets her family's immigration and the American promise of freedom quite literally, much to her mother's dismay. To her mother's outrage over her conversion to Judaism, Mona says, "You are the one who brought us up to speak English. You said you would bend like bamboo instead of acting like you were planted by Bell Telephone. You said we weren't pure Chinese anymore, the parents had to accept we would be something else." "American, not Jewish," her mother replies. Mona answers: "Jewish is American, . . . American means being whatever you want, and I happened to pick being Jewish" (49). During her final break with her mother, Helen attacks Mona's attendance at the High Holy Day services:

"That's enough Jewish," she says. "Forget about services. Not funny anymore. You know where all the trouble started? All the trouble started from you become Jewish."

"Mom," Mona says. "It's a free country. I can go to temple if I want. In fact, if I wanted to, I could go to a mosque. . . ."

"Forget about free country," she says.

"What do you mean? This is America. I can remember what I want, I can be what I want, I can—"

"You want to be something, you can leave this house, don't come back," says Helen. (248–49)

Echoing mass media clichés, Mona embodies the principle of routes, representing American metamorphosis, the cultural narrative of American freedom to pick and choose whatever identity one wants. After all, "it's a free country." "Tell them this is America; anything is possible," Barbara advises Mona on how to deal with her parents' insistence on Chinese ways (84). Even the family name, Chang, with a slight alteration, becomes the word *change*, carrying with it resonances with money, trade, exchange, and the cultural commerce associated with routes. Marking her embodiment of "switching," Mona's conversion brings her a new name—from Chang to Changovitz—first in jest, the nickname her friends call her, and then more seriously in the epilogue, with Mona's fantasy that she, Seth, and Io would all change their names to Changovitz to reflect their particular American hybridity.

Mona's desire for the name that would publicly announce and legitimate her sense of hybridity represents a kind of end point for her *Bildung*, one that she arrives at in part through resistance not only to her mother but also to the figure who represents the search for ethnic roots: namely, Naomi, the statuesque and charismatic black woman who is Callie's roommate at Harvard. With a background more bourgeois than that of working-class Alfred and his friends, Naomi doesn't just "have" her roots; she must find them and insist in the process that others find their own roots as distinct from her own. Naomi takes first Callie and then Mona under her wing to teach them proper respect for their authentic roots and politically correct views of white imperialism. Much as the black nationalist daughter in Alice Walker's story "Everyday Use" (a canonical text of second wave feminism) is the butt of Walker's satire on essentialist racial authenticity, Naomi represents the ethnic absolutism that Gilroy attacks in his insistence on cultural heterogeneity and hybridity. Under her influence, Callie takes Chinese in college, returns home to discover that she cannot understand her father's working-class Shanghaiese accent and that he thinks her Chinese class is a waste of time. Naomi tells Callie, "*Forget your parents*" and "be in touch with" your "ancestry." A puzzled Callie asks, "But aren't my parents my ancestors?" (129). "How come you're turning Chinese?" Mona asks her sister; "'I thought you were sick of being Chinese.'... Callie is indeed sick of being Chinese, but there is being Chinese and being Chinese..., saying she didn't understand what it meant to be Chinese until she met Naomi" (168). Naomi's celebration of heritage even involves the pursuit of "authentic" Chinese food that Mona finds to be "so genuine" that eating it is "an encounter" (186). The contrast between Naomi's privileging of different ethnic authenticities and the Chang family's syncretism is heavily ironized in the narrator's bland account: "Naomi, for example, has learned to do an authentic tea-smoked duck that involves burning tea leaves in a wok and smoking the duck in it for sixteen hours. (Mona, meanwhile, shares Helen's most recent favorite duck dish recipe—namely, Peking duck, Westchester style. The whole secret is soaking the duck overnight in Pepsi-Cola.)" (186).

The Chang family's culinary transculturation celebrates a cultural hybridity that Chip Kidd successfully captures in his design for the cover of the cloth edition of the novel. He images American identity not as a melting pot of acculturation into homogeneity but rather as a simmering soup of distinct but ambiguous ingredients (fig. 4). This is not the gorgeous mosaic made up of different ethnicities clinging to their roots, but instead a syncretist site of individual heterogeneity and blending. The photocollage superimposes a bagel (is it whole wheat?) on top of a dish of soup noodles. The eyes and nose of an East Asian woman peek through the bagel hole. The author's Chinese name on the bagel makes one think both woman and soup must be Chinese too. But the noodles are actually Japanese *udon*, not Chinese, and the face—whose is it? Its racial marking as "not white" is clear, but its cultural marking? Chinese? Japanese? Korean? Or "just plain" American? A back-cover photo clarifies that the woman is actually Gish Jen herself, but on the cover only enough of her eyes show through to metonymically mark the body as East Asian. The soup plays off the familiar image of the melting pot and the more recent images of American multiculturalism like stir-fry. But like the novel, it has fun with the possibility of new hybridities and the always

Fig. 4. Cover design by Chip Kidd for the cloth edition of
Mona in the Promised Land, by Gish Jen.

already hybridized nature of identity. The cover design sets the stage for the epigraphs and narrative governed by change and the power to switch.[15]

Counterbalancing the novel's postmodern play with identity as chosen performance, however, is Jen's representation of the return of repressed histories as determinants of identity. Freedom to switch, to choose, may be part of the American mythos, but however much Mona embraces protean routes of change, her story reveals the ongoing persistence of cultural roots. In scene after scene of intercultural encounter and debate, the satire is double-edged: mocking not only ethnic absolutism but also blindness to the effects of history. Biological essentialism remains the butt of mockery, but Mona's dismissal of history—and by

extension, America's ideology of individual freedom and even perhaps postmodernity's tendency to valorize the free play of the signifier cut off from the signified—is heavily ironized. The dialogic of routes and roots in the first chapter,
"Mona Gets Flipped," functions as a foreshadowing microcosm of the whole
narrative. Here is where Mona first expresses the American principle of switching, which she explains to Sherman Matsumoto. But the events in the chapter
repeatedly undermine her innocent faith in protean freedoms. The most prescient
of these is the history lesson Mona learns after the school pairs the Chinese
American girl with the boy from Japan as if there were a natural alliance between
them, ignoring the bitter history of Japanese imperialism and widespread Chinese
hatred of the Japanese for such events as the Nanking Massacre of 1937–38.
Largely unaware of this history that shaped her parents' lives, Mona develops a
huge crush on Sherman, urging him to become American. His response is to plan
for her to become Japanese so that they can marry and return to Japan. Such
dreams of switching come to a screeching halt when Mona's mother comes into
the kitchen as Sherman recounts the victimization of the Japanese at Hiroshima
and bows to a picture of the Japanese flag he places on her refrigerator. Helen's
response reaffirms the powerful and lasting effects of history on identity and calls
into question (while ironically invoking the language of) the American mythology of personal freedom:

> When Helen comes in, her face is so red that with the white wall behind her, she looks
> a bit like the Japanese flag herself. Yet Mona gets the feeling she'd better not say so.
> First her mother doesn't move. Then she snatches the flag off the icebox. . . . She
> crumples up the paper. She hisses at Sherman, *This is the U.S. of A., do you hear
> me!"* (15)

In response to Mona's puzzlement, Helen "explains that World War II was in
China too. 'Hitler,' Mona says. 'Nazis. Volkswagens.' She knows the Japanese
were on the wrong side, because they bombed Pearl Harbor. Helen explains about
before that. 'What Napkin Massacre?' says Mona. *'Nan*-king'" (15). Cut off from
her historical roots, Mona has learned very little about World War II outside of
Europe. Helen's history lesson, one not provided in the schools, suggests that
relations between people of Chinese and Japanese descent in the United States are
heavily overdetermined by history, one that cannot and should not be easily forgotten. The chapter's conclusion confirms Helen's message. As Sherman and
Mona engage in initiatory sexual activity, Mona unbuttons her blouse to encourage the progression, a form of sexual initiative that offends Sherman's masculinity and Japaneseness. He responds angrily by violently flipping her onto the
ground and later writing to her that *"You will never be Japanese"* (23). Mona is
left wondering about, but refusing to give up on, the possibility of "switching." In
this multilayered satiric text, the reader absorbs more of Helen's history lesson
than Mona does. Historical roots matter.

The double-edged satire that undermines but affirms the necessity of both roots
and routes is even present in the portrayal of Naomi. Like Helen, she is intent
upon teaching Mona about history, and for the most part, her history lessons,

based as they are on a belief in an authentic essential blackness, are undercut. But the ironized lesson she teaches about racial categories is also the occasion for satirizing Mona's naiveté about the material effects of ideological discourses. As the butt of Jen's irony, Naomi's biological explanation of race clearly mirrors the hegemonic racialism she opposes, but Mona's attempt to understand it discloses to the reader (though not to Mona) the powerful effects of racial constructivism. The neutral narrator sets the stage for the doubly directed irony:

> But as it happens, pretty soon Mona worships her, just like Callie. She does every-thing Naomi says. She strives to think the way Naomi thinks. In terms of *white folk*, for example. Naomi never says they're out to get your ass, the way Alfred does. She talks about them in a gentler way that makes them seem involuntarily stuck to one another by a special invisible but all-weather glue. This makes Mona and Callie and Naomi stuck together too, by virtue of their being colored folk. Mona has never thought of herself as colored before, though she knew herself not to be white. *Yellow*, says Naomi now. *You are yellow. A yellow person, a yellow girl.* It takes some getting used to, this idea, especially since Mona's summertime color is most definitely brown, and the rest of the year she is not exactly a textbook primary. But then Naomi is not black either; she claims to be closer in color to a paper bag. If she were a cabinet door or a shade of hair dye, people would have a name for her exact shade. But as she is only a person, she is called black, just as Mona and Callie are called yellow. And as yellow is a color, they are colored, which is how it is they are working together on the project. (171)

In socializing Callie and Mona to accept the labels "yellow" and "people of color" as natural, Naomi appears unaware of how race is a cultural construct—a phonemic code that makes certain parts of the body (and not other parts) bear the social meaning of biological difference. (In borrowing the linguistic term pho-neme, which refers to a sound that carries meaning within a given linguistic system, I am suggesting that human bodies differ in a near infinite series of grada-tions around the globe just as sounds do, but that cultures assign specific mean-ings to a finite number of specific physiological differences just as languages associate particular meanings to a set of sounds.) For Callie, objectified by other races for her skin color, skin is the body part that carries the powerful cultural code of race. For Mona, the body parts that operate as part of a phonemic racial code to make her feel "different" are not skin but eyes, body hair, and breasts (75–76, 92).[16] With a turn of the comedic screw, Jen makes this point by satiri-cally invoking the language of imperialism in her use of body changes during puberty to interrogate biological racialism:

> Mona was the first one in her entire grade to get her period. Plus she surmises by the population problems of the Far East that she is appropriately equipped. But she doesn't look like, say, Barbara. If her friend is a developed nation, Mona is, sure enough, the third world. Barbara's is the body Mona is still waiting to grow into: Her breasts, for example, are veritable colonies of herself, with a distinct tendency toward independence. Whereas Mona's, in contrast, are anything but wayward. A scant

handful each. . . . Even her nipples seem somehow dietary, smallish brownish nubs—
areolaless. . . . Later Mona will realize how in the popular conception Orientals are
supposedly exotically erotic, and all she'll want to say is, But what about my areolaless nubs?. . . . And no billowy, Brillo-y bush, alas. How should she have one when
she does not even need to shave her legs. . . . Her underarms too—actually she boasts
a few wisps there. If only she didn't have to put her hands on her head for anyone to
notice! Hair, hair, hair, she thinks. And especially facial hair, body hair.(76–77)

For all her faith in the ability to switch, for all her difficulty in relating to categories like "yellow" and "people of color," for all her refusal to accept binary thinking about people, Mona *does* experience the effects of racial thinking and its
institutionalization as racism. Consequently, she forgets her parents' geopolitical
origins in China at her own peril; to suppress these historically determined roots
leaves her open to a racialized invisibility and self-rejection based in the phonemic meanings of her body within a system that privileges norms based on "white"
eyes, body hair, and body shape.

The pernicious intransigence of racism against African Americans in a multiracial American grid is also the lesson that Mona (and by extension, the reader)
learns by listening to Alfred and his friends and by watching what happens in the
aftermath of disclosure. The history of slavery and its aftereffects can no more be
ignored than the Holocaust or the Nanking Massacre, particularly when it is mediated by class. Where Naomi's education and upward mobility make her the
(exotic) toast of Harvard, the Wasp resort, and the publishing world, Alfred's
position as a skilled cook dependent on each paycheck cannot protect him from
discrimination at the restaurant or Barbara's suspicion that he stole her father's
silver flask from the Gugelstein house. When Barbara and Mona hold up Mona's
conversion to Judaism as an instance of American freedoms open to him as well,
Alfred answers with the bedrock of race for African Americans. The instrument
of satire elsewhere, Mona is here its object in her suggestion that Alfred "switch":
"You can have a big house and a four-bay garage and a gardener too" (137);
"'We're never going to have no big house or no big garage, either,' explains
Alfred. 'We're never going to be Jewish, see, even if we grow our nose like Miss
Mona here is planning to do. *We be black motherfuckers*'" (137). The combined
racist actions of the Gugelsteins and the Changs confirm Alfred's perception. The
echoes of *Huckleberry Finn* that hover throughout the text become particularly
resonant in the parallels between the antics of Tom and Huck playing games with
Jim's freedom in the disturbing final section of the narrative and the machinations
of Barbara and Mona to secrete Alfred in the Gugelstein house, using the
remnants of a tunnel from the Underground Railroad. Jen's intertextual play on
the problematics of the precursor text both complicates the representation of
American racism but also attests to the persistence of racial othering and the
particular victimization of African Americans in the "promised land" of the New
Eden.

Even the novel's main trope for change—Mona's conversion to Judaism—is
subject to irony, demonstrating the continuities of communalist thinking about

identity in its fundamentalist forms. Underlining the racial tribalism of traditions about "who is a Jew," the rabbi who oversees Mona's conversion is fired and basically forced out of the rabbinate. The briefly sketched story of Eloise Ingle makes a related point. Brought up in a quintessentially Wasp family, she discovers that her dead mother was Jewish, which leads to her immediate welcome into the Jewish community, even though she has not studied Judaism for months as Mona has done. The lesson the reader learns through Mona's puzzlement is that birth through the mother, not belief, confers real membership in the Jewish community, even when a person has no historical ties to a Jewish identity.

Moreover, the connection between Mona's Chinese and Jewish identities—figured in the blended hybridity of her name, Changovitz—is not so arbitrary as it first seems. What Jen does in linking Jewish and Asian American identities in the figure of Mona is to signify on the hegemonic treatment of Asian Americans (especially those of Chinese, Japanese, and Korean ancestry) as the "model minority" who play the role in the current wave of immigration that the Jews played early in the twentieth century. As David Polumbo-Liu has shown, Asian Americans often fulfill the function of honorary "whites" in the mass media, with the success of some rendering invisible the suffering of other Asian Americans and covertly being used to blame other racial minorities for their "failure" to succeed (see his "Los Angeles" and chapter 2 in this volume). Jen signals this historically produced association on the novel's opening page, where the narrator announces that the Chang family has newly moved to the suburbs, as "the New Jews, after all, a model minority and Great American Success. They know they belong in the promised land" (3). Jen may also have in mind the conventional association of Jews and "overseas Chinese," who are often known in Southeast Asia as the "Jews" of Asia through their association with commerce and education.[17] In any case, the novel directly plays off how Asian Americans have complicated the black/white racial binary in America, which has a rich association between blacks and Jews (historical and cultural) through their shared narratives of slavery, exodus, and diaspora. In *The Black Atlantic*, Gilroy reviews that special bond and its divergences. *Mona in the Promised Land* adds to his account by alluding to the covert ways Asian Americans (particularly of Chinese descent) have supplanted Africans Americans through their status as a "model minority," as honorary whites, almost, but like Jews never quite fully assimilable.

Ultimately, Jen's multidirectional irony reaffirms the historical production of both roots and routes, both the persistence of traditional group identities based in a belief in difference and the inevitability of change and cultural blending. Notions of ethnic absolutism and of absolute freedom are both undermined as the novel moves back and forth in an intercultural *fort/da* based in the assertion of difference and the dissolution of pure difference in the syncretist borderlands. As Mona wonders when she imagines calling Rabbi Horrowitz "just to say hi, or maybe to ask why it is that now that she's Jewish, she feels like more of a Chinese than ever," "Is there some great explanation—Hegelian perhaps?" (66). Later in the novel, the rabbi provides her with an answer, one that insists upon the reality of both roots and routes: "It's not so easy to get rid of your old self. On the other hand, nothing stands still. All growth involves change, all change involves loss" (268). What she also learns from him and her mother is that she does not even want to get rid of her old self completely. What becoming "Changovitz" means in the end is not switching or flipping, but a hybridic blending of the one with the other. Like Anzaldúa's "new mestiza consciousness," Mona's creolized identity often leaves her feeling as if she never belongs: "not Wasp, and not black, and not as Jewish as Jewish can be; and not from Chinatown, either. . . . I'm never at home" (231). But also like Anzaldúa, Mona's multiple strands constitute a vital source of energy and creativity.

GEOPOLITICAL COMPARATIVISM

I have juxtaposed the dialogical performances of roots and routes, borders and borderlands, in *Daughters of the Dust* and *Mona and the Promised Land* as a metalevel staging of the interplay of alterity and mimesis in the geopolitical formations of cultural identity. The lyrical film about roots and the ironic novel about rootlessness appear at first glance to embody difference. The chasm between an African American and an Asian American representation of geopolitics, race, and ethnicity mediated by gender and class seems unbridgeable. The cultural work that each text potentially performs appears equally different. Dash's film aims to heal, binding its black viewers both to their ancestral past and a diasporic imagined community. Jen's novel sets out to dismantle all ethnic pieties, including those of American multiculturalism. But a closer look at both texts and their potential effects tells a more complex story, one that brings the two into mimetic relationship. Dash's narrative of roots proves to be inseparable from the story of routes, from the migratory subjectivities and syncretisms produced by identities always in the process of becoming through the various terrains across which people travel. Conversely, Jen's tale of routes returns inevitably to evocations of roots, facing up to the evidence and necessity of historically produced legacies out of which group identities are formed. Moreover, just as difference can only be understood in the context of sameness, both texts set in motion narratives that oscillate back and forth between roots and routes. The erection of borders between difference and their dissolution in hybridic borderlands means that their narratives operate "beyond" difference without erasing it. "We need to think comparatively about the distinct routes/roots" of peoples, Clifford writes in the epigraph that opens this chapter ("Traveling Cultures" 108). Moving through the geopolitical locations and origins represented in *Daughters of the Dust* and *Mona in the Promised Land*, I have attempted to do just that: track the interplay of routes/roots within each text and between the two texts as they represent and perform intercultural encounters.

Race plays a defining role in the encounters narrated in the texts and in the narrative of textual encounter in this chapter. In part, this reflects how in the United States race has long functioned as the major lens through which institutional systems of stratification have been understood, even when such asymmetries of power and status are clearly more multiplex than the discourse of racial hierarchy alone can explain. The interactions of race with gender, class, and religion in *Daughters of the Dust* and *Mona in the Promised Land* insist upon the kind of relational, situational analysis of identity that I have discussed in earlier chapters. The production of racial and ethnic identities encompasses a dialectic of sameness and difference and the multifarious forms of hybridity theorized in chapter 3. But the conjuncture of Julie Dash and Gish Jen does more than confirm the significance of race and ethnicity for understanding cultural identity, especially in the context of forced and voluntary immigration to North America. This conjunctural comparativism also calls into question the adequacy of categories like "people of color" that elide the differences produced by spatial location. In both literal and figural senses, where people come from and where they travel to are constitutive of identity. As I have argued in chapter 4, the geopolitical axis of identity is closely related to racial/ethnic ones, but is not absolutely coextensive with them. Geopolitical comparativism requires a form of spatial practice, a kind of geographical thinking that addresses the meanings of location and itinerary in the production of cultural identities. As such, geopolitical thinking is attuned to questions of borders and their transgression—all kinds of borders and all kinds of transgressions. Stories in and about these borders and borderlands narrate the dynamic doubleness of all thresholds. As Madan Sarup points out, "All frontiers, including the frontiers of nations, at the same time as they are barriers are also places of communication and exchange" ("Home and Identity" 98). So, I believe, are the frontiers between all differences: the locations of movement in which routes produce roots and routes return to roots.

PART III

Feminism/Poststructuralism

Negotiating the Transatlantic Divide:
Feminism *after* Poststructuralism

WHEN I first wrote this chapter, we were on the cusp of the nineties, and I sense the winds of change circulating in the universities and colleges, as well the streets of the world—a longing for the nineties to be different, a looking ahead to the twenty-first century. The eighties, dominated in the United States by the Reagan presidency, bottled up the active commitment for social justice, marginalized those who refused to forget, and drove the wedge ever more deeply between those in the mainstream and society's outsiders. Of course, there continued to be critical voices—engaged, political voices—throughout the eighties, but what I sensed at that moment was a shift in the critical mass toward commitment, vocation, social responsibility. For us as scholars, teachers, and students, this shift has meant a growing legitimacy (once again) for questions of ethics and politics, of agency and action, of intention and meaning. It has meant (once again) the insistent return of urgency, of a sense that our intellectual work matters—or at least that it should matter, must matter in the arena of cultural production and social change.

In titling a 1989 Modern Language Association session "Feminist Engagement after Poststructuralism," Celeste Schenck and Lisa Ruddick took a bold step by (re)introducing the term "engagement" into critical discourse (a wonderfully overdetermined term for feminists, I might add, with its history in the cultural scripts of courtship and political activism) and by doubling the phenomenon of *after* by inserting the word "after" before "*Post*structuralism." "After" suggests with seeming neutrality that we are beyond poststructuralism, that *post*-structuralism is *past*, still inevitably part of our present, but present differently than it was before, present as a significant vestige of our immediate past, but fundamentally altered by its new context in the present. Sparked by their title, my own title asserts that historically, we in the academy are situated in a post/ poststructuralist moment. By this I particularly mean to suggest that after nearly two decades of the growing power of poststructuralist theory as the most authoritative and prestigious discourse of the profession, this developing hegemony is being called into question by a wide range of critics—from those who advocate a return to an ideal realm of canonical classics and fixed meaning; to those who attack intellectual elitism and exclusionary power relations endemic in the sheer difficulty of poststructuralist discourses; to those who insist that what Barbara Christian calls "the race for theory" involves a retreat from the insistent and growing presence of women, people of color, and Third World people on the literary and critical scene; and to those writing *within* a poststructuralist framework who are increasingly critical of poststructuralism's tendency to ahistoricism, indifference, and disengagement on the one hand and, on the other hand, to totalizing orthodoxies and master-disciple psychodynamics.

The shift *within* poststructuralism itself, the result at least in part I believe of critiques from without, helps especially to define this post/poststructuralist moment. Two books, published nearly ten years apart, capsulize the change. I am thinking of Catherine Belsey's explication and advocacy of poststructuralism in *Critical Practice*, published in 1980, and Thomas Kavanagh's poststructuralist anthology entitled *The Limits of Theory*, published in 1989. These two books—I could have chosen others—frame the decade.[1] Embodying the antihumanist project of poststructuralism, Belsey celebrates the liberating effects of "the death of the Author" and lionizes what she calls the "scientific" criticism of theorists like Roland Barthes, Jacques Lacan, and Pierre Mucherey. Echoing the claim to "science" made by Marxism as well as by I. A. Richards in the early days of New Criticism, Belsey's call for poststructuralist "critical practice" aims to place criticism on a "scientific" basis: "a scientific criticism . . . distancing itself from the imaginary coherence of the text, analyzing the discourses which are its raw material and the process of production, which makes it a text, recognizes in the text not 'knowledge' but ideology in all its inconsistency and partiality" (128).

At our end of the decade, Kavanagh, in his introduction to *The Limits of Theory*, alludes to an earlier poststructuralist faith in "this brave new science" (5), but argues that poststructuralist theory has gone beyond its proper limits. Instead of freeing a multiplicity and infinity of readings, it has hardened into a hegemonic orthodoxy that deadens readings into a repetition of the same. "What we had introduced," he writes self-critically, "as a discourse of the radically Other seems to have produced only the most resolute sameness and orthodoxy" (5). Theory, he asserts, shifted attention from the "author" to the "text" in foregrounding the problematic nature of linguistic representation. Echoing Freud, Richard Machin and Christopher Norris "put it nicely," Kavanagh says: " 'Where once the author was now shall the text be' " (7). In the "banishing of language's mimetic function"—referentiality and "the real"—theory also made itself "the site of an unfettered *performance*, a performance in no way limited by any preexistant script," one "cut off from all possible authentification by a meaning situated within the work independent of the theorist's discourse" (10). In real terms, this "self-justifying performance of the critic as theorist" led to the formation of a "master-disciple dialectic" within the university. What began as a "brave new science" has become "an arcane science accessible only through diligent apprenticeship," a system that commands allegiance and exerts control through admission and expulsion. "It is clearly a question here of a politics," he writes, "a politics demanding the brutal disqualification of all who would remain outside or speak against the mutually sustaining dialogues of masters and disciples" (12). Moreover, this politics enacted on the site of theoretical performance has made "the real itself . . . at best irrelevant," "held resolutely outside the symbolic system sustaining a given theory" (15). To bring "theory" back within the limits it should respect, Kavanagh calls for an end to orthodoxy, "the freedom of reading, the elusive presence of the real, and the challenge of a voice speaking outside the

various rhetorics of mastery" (17). In effect, Kavanagh advocates a poststructuralist recuperation of some of the concepts that poststructuralist theory had orgi-
nally suppressed.

Kavanagh, I want to suggest, is inscribing the post/poststructuralist moment
from *within* the framework of poststructuralism. Nor is he alone; he is exemplary
of a change within poststructuralism that is symptomatically present in the growing influence of Bakhtinian dialogism, Foucauldian analysis of discourse and
power relations, the proliferating readings of the postcolonial subject and texts,
and the attempt by some to assimilate the analysis of Otherness generated by
feminist, Afro-Americanist, Asian Americanist, Native Americanist, Chicano/a
and Hispanicist, and lesbian and gay theory and criticism. Kavanagh himself does
not acknowledge—indeed seems blindly ignorant of—the critiques outside
poststructuralism that have sparked the direction of his critique. But I am struck
by what his critique shares with the powerful theoretical attack on poststructuralist theory launched by Barbara Christian from a non-poststructuralist, Afro-
Americanist, and feminist position in her 1987 essay "The Race for Theory." She,
like he, objects to the "hegemony" of the "reigning academic elite" in poststructuralist theory (227). She, like he, believes that this power structure within the
profession leads theorists to repeat what it is they claim to oppose: "For I feel that
the new emphasis on literary critical theory is as hegemonic as the world which
it attacks. I see the language it creates as one which mystifies rather than clarifies
our condition, making it possible for a few people who know that particular language to control the critical scene" (229). She, like he, focuses on poststructuralist
theory's erasure of the author and of "the real" as particularly dangerous: "Now
I am being told . . . that authors are dead, irrelevant, mere vessels through which
narratives ooze, that they do not work nor have they the faintest idea what they are
doing; rather, they produce texts as disembodied as the angels" (229–30). His
disturbance that critics in their performative self-display displace the literary texts
they discuss is matched by her resentment that "theoretical criticism" has "di-
verted so many of us" from the important work of reading literature (231). His
concern that theory has become an orthodoxy enforcing correct thinking mirrors
her anger at its "tendency towards monolithism" and the establishment of a "monologic," "authoritative discourse" (233).

Of course, there are important differences in the critiques of Kavanagh and
Christian. In particular, his analysis of politics focuses on the master-disciple
dynamic, while she emphasizes the production of a theoretical elite at precisely
the time "when the literature of peoples of color, of black women, of Latin Americans, of Africans, began to move to 'the center'" (229). For her the question of
canonicity is paramount, where for him the issue of who we read and why is not
even on the horizon. Christian distrusts the poststructuralist enterprise in its en-
tirety, whereas Kavanagh is attempting to establish responsible limits for "theory" and in no sense repudiates poststructuralism. But my point in drawing these
two critics of poststructuralism together is to suggest that what they have in common helps to characterize this post/poststructuralist moment when the urgent
question of political "engagement" is once more on the agenda. That two such

different critics would unknowingly echo each other signifies something about the times.

By "the times," I mean first the historically specific conditions within the profession, where the internal dynamics within various critical schools have led to change and where the differences between schools have clashed and blended into a new intertextual grid. Secondly, I mean that the world beyond the academy is also fostering change within the profession. Resurgent activism around the globe is forcing people within the academy into the *experience* of history, into an awareness of how the public invades and pervades the private—whether this consciousness of "history" develops out of direct experience or out of mass media representation of global events. The possibility of change is in the air, and along with it the recognition that change is not always "good." The post/poststructuralist moment is a particularly self-reflective one when many are asking, along with Christian, "'For whom are we doing what we are doing when we do literary criticism'?" (235). And why? to what end? we might add.

For feminist scholars, the post/poststructuralist moment raises again the issue of "feminist engagement"—its nature, its origin, its arena, its direction, its objectives, its alliances, its effects, its contradictions. Feminism in all its global manifestations—and they are as myriad as the differing conditions of women—is both under siege and on the rise. For women in the United States, the recent threat to women's reproductive rights from the Supreme Court, state legislatures, and anti-choice activists has led to widespread demonstrations, political organizing by advocacy groups, and a growing recognition that the rights won a decade or two ago could be lost. The Montreal massacre of fourteen women gunned down as "feminists" because they were women in an engineering class hammered home the message that women, as women, are not safe because they are women. This terrorism profoundly disturbed many not just because the killer was a lone, demented man, but also because his hatred of women, scapegoating of feminists, and resort to violence pervades our culture, putting millions of women at physical and emotional risk. He represents momentarily the most visible tip of the iceberg in this world which is emphatically not "post-feminist."

For many feminists within the academy, these and related events compel the question of political engagement. How and in what arena can and should we be engaged? What is the locus of our political work? Where should we exert our energies and time? Especially when these become, I hasten to insist, ever more precious and fragmented and pressured, subject to burnout and stress that often make the tug between work and personal lives unbearable and pleasures a fantasy. Where can our impact best be felt?

In the Women's Studies Program at the University of Wisconsin-Madison, of which I have been a faculty member since 1975, we are discussing these questions with an urgency that has not been felt since the seventies. For a large, well-established and funded program like the one at Wisconsin, important generational issues complicate the questions. The resurgence of national and regional feminist activism has suddenly given many younger feminists a taste of the political engagement out of which women's studies grew in the late sixties and early seventies. Of course, the major difference here is that in the early days of women's studies, there wasn't an older generation of feminists in the academy who were our teachers from whom we could learn and would have to separate in order to "grow up" as intellectual activists. There was instead the old boy's network of the academy, the often terrorizing hostility of the men who were our teachers and senior faculty (and there were, thankfully, a few curious and sympathetic allies among senior male and female faculty). And there was instead the feminist movement outside the academy to which many of us belonged, bringing the activism of the streets back into the universities and colleges. Now the large numbers of graduate students who come to Wisconsin to study women's history and feminist criticism face a well-established network of largely female feminist faculty. For the younger feminists, the questions of political engagement form initially in relation to their feminist faculty. Tension and conflict have been inevitable as feminists of different generations debate the questions of political engagement.[2]

The resurgence of feminist activism outside the academy has changed the texture of these intergenerational relationships. Earlier in the eighties, many students (particularly graduate students) experienced feminism largely in intellectual and theoretical terms, in contrast to most of their older teachers, who had brought their activism into their intellectual work. Today, many students are involved once again with grass-roots organizing and demonstrating outside the academy. Some pressure their feminist faculty to take to the streets again, to become "politically engaged" as individuals and as women's studies programs outside our universities and colleges. The question of "feminist engagement" at this post/poststructuralist moment forces us to ask anew where and how we can be politically engaged as academic feminists.

I am deeply opposed to prescriptive answers to these questions. I would echo the lessons Christian learned from the Black Arts Movement of the sixties about the dangers for activists of what she calls "monologic" thinking or "monolithism." I am opposed to any unit such as a women's studies program mandating the shape and nature of anyone's individual political activism; and I am equally opposed to any totalizing tendency within feminist theory and praxis that would elevate any one direction or stance as "politically correct" or the "true feminism" or the truly "radical" position. For me, the issue of feminist engagement is as complex and multifaceted as the differences among women and the differences of the historically specific conditions in which women find themselves. Moreover, as has become increasingly evident from the feminist theory produced by women of color, women are themselves multicontexted; gender can never be experienced in "pure" form, but is always mediated through other categories like race, ethnicity, religion, class, national origin, sexual preference, abledness, and historical era. This multiplicity of contexts, of the components of any woman's identity, suggests that any monolithic theory or praxis is doomed to privilege one set of contexts over another, one kind of feminist agenda over another, one kind of woman over another.

For me, the academy is my site for "feminist engagement." I do not accept the all-too-frequent binaries of academic versus political; intellectualism versus ac-

tivism; ivory tower versus the "real world." I take seriously the founding statement of the National Women's Studies Association: that women's studies is the
academic arm of the women's movement. The writing I do, the classes I teach, the
committee meetings I attend, the administrative jobs I perform are my political
work. To do these things effectively, I can in no sense promote a propagandistic
"line" of "the" feminist truth. Nor can I give in to the prevailing epistemology of
the academy—that politics and academics must remain separate, that knowledge
should be "objective" and "value free." In asserting the political nature of the
construction and dissemination of knowledge, I acknowledge that my academic
work is an effect of and affects the political organization in society. To be an
effective feminist within the academy has meant, for me, the development of a
dialectical, dialogic engagement with my field, my discipline, my department, my
institution. Sometimes this dialogue has been openly combative, other times more
collaborative. Flexibility, fluidity, and openness have been as important as a commitment to feminism.

Always, I feel that I work on the border, that it is the dialogic movement back
and forth across that border that sparks my creative and political endeavors. This
means, I realize, that feminist engagement in the academy is and must perpetually
be a site of contradiction. There is always the threat of a slide into careerism, into
co-optation, assimilation, collaboration in the negative sense; the danger of tip-
ping the delicate balance toward reinforcing instead of challenging the ideological and institutional formations of knowledge. The basic contradiction of academic feminists is that we must "make it" somehow within the arena we are
committed to transforming. This places us fundamentally not in the imagined
"Society of Outsiders" of Virginia Woolf's *Three Guineas*, but rather in a dialogic relationship with the symbolic and institutional order we are trying to
change.[3]

Having sketched what I mean by a "post/poststructuralist" moment and "feminist engagement," I want to turn more specifically to the connection between the
two. It should be evident that my views of feminist engagement presume the
existence of both "agency" and "identity," terms that have been deconstructed as
humanist illusions and largely erased from respectable poststructuralist discourse.
As a feminist in the academy, I have been saying, I have an identity that is self-
consciously constructed and maintained in a state of contradiction. This identity
is by no means fixed or unitary, but is rather split and fluid in multiple ways and
is (re)formed in ways of which I am both aware and unaware. Particularly because
language is the primary tool of my trade, this identity is surely made and remade
in language, within and through a system of competing discourses. Moreover, my
academic identity is both expressed and perpetually (re)created through what I
say and do in my work—that is, it has agency, which means, fundamentally, "to
act, to do." However language is implicated in this agency, what I have done in
the academy has a reality that cannot be reduced to just words. Agency involves
action that is not separate from, but also not reducible to, language. "The real"
that Kavanagh now finds missing in poststructuralist theory exists in the things
that I, in a complex web of relations with others, have made happen—a feminist

book, a women's studies program, a student awakened, a woman hired, and so forth—and also in the difficult negotiation I must perform everyday on the ideological and institutional borders of my profession. These are "real" acts, the flesh of a perpetually (re)formed identity.

It should be equally evident, however, that the "identity" and "agency" that I have just asserted show the influence of poststructuralism on my thinking, especially in my recognition of the role of language. Blending as it does poststructuralist and non-poststructuralist discourses, this affirmation of identity and agency partially characterizes what I mean by the post/poststructuralist moment for feminists in the academy. To use affirmatively the terms "identity" and "agency" breaks the silence poststructuralism has attempted to impose by declaring them illusory constructs of humanism. To emphasize the significance of language and the fluidity of what Julia Kristeva calls the *subject-in-process* is to bring the insight of poststructuralism to bear on concepts that were produced in the discourses of the Enlightenment.[4]

"Identity" and "agency" are not the only such terms that are undergoing such an intertextual reformation. Poststructuralism has made taboo in critical discourse a number of other terms—such as "self," "author," "work," "experience," "expression," "meaning," "authority," "origin," and "reference." Poststructuralism is itself not a monolithic discourse—there are important differences among the major masters. But poststructuralists generally share the view that such terms are tainted by their association with what they regard as a bankrupt, defunct, and hopelessly naive humanism. All supposedly operate within a false assumption of the transparency of language, naively unaware of the materiality and mediation of language.

Several essays by Roland Barthes in the late sixties and early seventies both epitomize and were very influential in articulating this view. "The Death of the Author," published in 1968, proclaims the "author" as a construct whose "empire" in critical discourse must be overthrown. "The *author*," he writes, "still reigns in manuals of literary history, in biographies of writers, magazine interviews, and in the very consciousness" of those "eager to unite person and work" (50).[5] This concept of a preexisting "individual" who intends a meaning should be replaced with "the modern *scriptor*," who "is born *at the same time* as his text," who does not originate meaning, but rather "contains . . . that immense dictionary," that "fabric of quotations, resulting from a thousand sources of culture" (52–53). In "To Write: An Intransitive Verb?" (1966), Barthes further attacks the ideology of writing as expression, in which "the agent" is "*anterior*" to the process of writing (*Rustle of Language* 19). Rather, he says, the "subject," which "is constituted as immediately contemporary with the writing" replaces the "agent" who preexists the writing. In his 1971 essay "From Work to Text," Barthes adds that in talking about literature (or more accurately, "writing"), we should move from discussion of "the work" to "the text." The "work," he writes, is "a traditional notion . . . conceived in what we might call a Newtonian fashion," one that focuses on a fixed "meaning," the signified (*Rustle of Language* 57, 58). "The work," he continues, "is caught up in a process of filiation," as the "expression" of the "author," who "is reputed to be the father and the owner of his work" as well as of its "declared intentions" (61). The "text," on the other hand, is "a methodological field," an "irreducible" "plurality" of signifiers, a "fabric" that is woven anonymously out of many other intertexts. The "death" of the "author" and "agent," in Barthes's view, makes possible the "birth" of the "subject," the "text," and the "Reader," in whose act of reading the text is finally constituted. Liberated from the tyranny of the "Author," the "Reader" no longer attempts to decode a work's fixed and intended meaning, but rather plays endlessly with the circulation of signifiers that refer only to other signifiers, not to "the real" of "experience."

The impact on critical discourse to which Barthes's formulations greatly contributed was the creation of a constellation of forbidden terms that could be used only in dismissal. From a poststructuralist perspective, use of the discourse of the *author*, the *self*, *expression*, or *experience* marks the critic as an outsider, a foreigner who has not learned the lingo. From a poststructuralist perspective, the critic should say *text*, not *work*; *subject*, not *self*; *scriptor*, not *author*. Many graduate students experience their early professionalization as the process of stumbling in a foreign tongue that they gradually learn to speak, hopefully without too much of an accent. The most fluent speakers tend to get the "best" jobs. I heard from one young feminist critic that she was taught early in her graduate student career never to use the word *self* by a professor who crossed out *self* and substituted *subject* throughout one of her first graduate papers. Of course, much more is involved in the substitution of one term for another than a mere change in lingo would suggest. From *work* to *text* and from *self* to *subject*, as Barthes makes clear, involves a reconceptualization of what stands behind each term within its larger philosophical discourse. But these linguistic transitions are also, I believe, overdetermined by a psycho/political dynamics of the forbidden. Certain terms—such as *self*, *work*, and *author*—have become taboo, tainted, impure. They certainly do reflect different philosophical assumptions, but they also serve as linguistic markers that signify who is outside (and therefore inside) on the current poststructuralist scene.[6]

Moreover, underlying these anxieties about forbidden terms and poststructurally correct translations may well be a playing out of a postcolonial dynamic in which the "theoretically sophisticated" terms are produced by the European "father" countries (especially France) for proper consumption in the culturally "naive" former colonies. Europeans have been dismissing North American culture as "pragmatic," "naive," "unsophisticated" for some two hundred years; and American intellectuals have been responding for an equally long period with various forms of defiance, defensive self-justification, and postcolonial inferiority complexes. The conflict over poststructuralism on the American cultural scene can in part be interpreted within this larger context of European imperialism and its discontents as it has been played out in the difficult formation of a specifically American culture.

Whatever the political unconscious of these critical narratives in this post/poststructuralist moment, the tabooed terms I have been discussing are coming back—a return of the repressed that has great import for feminist criticism. The word widely used for this process is *recuperation*. The *author* is being resurrected; *agency* is once more on the agenda. *Self* and *experience* may even one day be rehabilitated (that may be going to far). However, in being recuperated, these terms are not reappearing as they once were. Battered and buffeted in the poststructuralist storm, they have a different, more self-conscious and self-critical texture, one that weaves aspects of poststructuralist discourse with other threads. For feminist criticism in particular, this has often been figured in the attempt to heal the so-called split between American and French feminism, an opposition that should more accurately be called poststructuralist and non-poststructuralist feminisms.[7] By now, the intertextual weave of these feminisms is everywhere evident in feminist literary theory and criticism. Patricia Yaeger's *Honey-Mad Women*, for example, self-consciously recuperates for feminism key terms suppressed by poststructuralism. Entitled "The Bilingual Heroine: From 'Text' to 'Work,'" chapter 2 challenges Barthes as "a brief manifesto to other feminist critics" that is "a call to abandon our commitment to the concept of 'text' as Roland Barthes defines it and begin to consider women's writings as 'works,' as 'texts' that do the work of reinventing culture" (29). But in considering women's texts as the "work" of emancipation, Yaeger throughout highlights the textuality and intertextuality of women's writing, a concern and terminology that owes a great deal to Barthes's formulations.

Nancy K. Miller's collection of essays entitled *Subject to Change* has both led the way for and epitomizes what she calls a "political intertextuality" within poststructuralist feminism in the United States (111). Her theoretical essays on the politics of identity and the subject (Miller does not usually use the word *self*) have argued, since they first began to appear in 1982, that "the death of the author" and the supremacy of the text and reader have suppressed the agency of women writing, the significance of gendered subjectivity, and the conditions of cultural production. The text, Miller writes in agreement with Barthes, is indeed a woven textile, but a web, she counters, has a weaver who produces within historically specific material conditions. Reading women's writing involves interpreting how "the question of identity—the so-called crisis of the subject— . . . is irreducibly complicated by the historical, political, and figurative body of the woman writer" (*Subject to Change* 107). The poststructuralist erasure of the Author and "subjective agency along with him," she continues, "prematurely forecloses the question of identity for them [women]. Because women have not had the same historical relation of identity to origin, institution, production, that men have had, women have not (I think collectively) felt burdened by too much Self, Ego, Cogito, etc." (106). This foreclosure, she argues, does not "work" for women because "only those who have it [the status of subject] can play with not having it" (52). Yet in recuperating the concepts of agency, identity, subjectivity, and the "author" for feminist criticism, Miller in theory and practice retains a poststructuralist emphasis on textuality.

The recuperative gestures of post/poststructuralism, however, have themselves a politics within the profession that needs to be examined in this particularly self-reflexive moment. The word *recuperate* means to "recover from sickness or exhaustion," to "regain health or strength," to "recover from loss." Embedded in the term is a notion of disease, lack. In needing "recuperation," terms like *identity*, *self*, and *agency* are presumed to be in a state of weakness or illness, with poststructuralism as the restorative force. The subtext of the term, in other words, inscribes an unequal binary that subtly reinstates the hegemony Kavanagh critiqued. *Recuperation* potentially means assimilation, even co-optation, rather than a more balanced dialectic of equally viable intellectual terms. Within the concrete politics of the profession, this may mean that poststructuralists who engage in recuperations of the terms (and embedded concepts) that poststructuralism initially suppressed will retain their authoritative positions of prestige and power.

Paul Smith's *Discerning the Subject* (1988) illustrates both the positive and negative aspects of this recuperative process and politics. Like Kavanagh, Smith presents a post/poststructuralist critique of "theory" from within a poststructuralist framework. Although he seems completely unaware of Miller's critically important essays, he focuses specifically on the crisis of the subject in several currents of poststructuralist theory. He argues that in its various discourses, poststructuralism has created an "abstract," "passive" subject that tends "to foreclose upon the possibility of resistance" (xxx). Concepts of hegemonic ideology have precluded the recognition that subjects "simultaneously exist within and make purposive intervention into social formations" (5). In his critique of deconstruction, for example, Smith says that Derrida's deconstructed subject erases the possibility of human agency and resistance. "Derrida's view of human agency," he writes, "is limited in such a way that it could not be adapted to *any* oppositional politics"; it "requires that subjectivity be construed in such a manner that it cannot take responsibility for its interpretations, much less for the history of the species" (51). Indeed, "Derrida's work often derides the very notion of responsibility" (55). Smith's reading of deconstruction helps to explain the conflict within poststructuralist ranks about the significance of Paul de Man's anti-Semitic writings during the war. Is there a link, many wonder, between the refusal to acknowledge past responsibility and deconstruction's erasure of the concept of meaningful social action and agency?

In *Discerning the Subject*, Smith calls for a new poststructuralist theory that will recuperate an active, engaged subject he calls "the human subject." He foregrounds feminist criticism as the avant-garde of a shift toward a "responsible" poststructuralism—not because feminism is "the only—or even the sufficient—contestatory discourse and practice," but rather because the debates within feminism have articulated the problem and suggested directions for change that he thinks will be more broadly fruitful for poststructuralism. In particular, he champions the contradictions in feminism—represented by what he calls "humanist" and poststructuralist feminism—as a productive site for the formation of the concept of the subject-as-agent and for a "responsible" criticism. Outlining what he sees as the two branches of feminism, he says that feminist criticism has now reached the point of "collaboration" instead of "problematic tension" (138).

Smith's critique of poststructuralism is a powerful one, and his positioning of feminist criticism at the avant-garde of needed change strikes me as both refreshing and sincere. But his discussion of feminist criticism also demonstrates the hierarchical subtext of recuperation that I noted above. His presentation of "humanist," largely American feminist criticism scarcely encompasses two pages, names only two critics, and quotes three passages as exempla of dismaying tendencies. His discussion of poststructuralist feminists, on the other hand, takes up the bulk of the chapter, some thirteen more pages with specific overviews of various theorists and positions. Although he critiques the poststructuralist feminists, his respectful analysis of their work contrasts markedly with his scarcely contained disdain for the "humanists." "They," he says, promote "the positive valorization of women's *experience*"; their "underlying assumptions about the nature of the human 'subject' here are at first sight depressingly familiar ones, relying upon a set of demonstrably humanist values and ideologies" (135–36). Their reliance on humanist concepts of "identity," "expression," "communication," "truth" (etc.) inevitably compromises them, returns them to the "masculinist" and "humanistic economy, the economy of the same" (137). He is aware of the counterargument—that women excluded by patriarchy from having an identity outside Otherness need to claim one and have always done so. He acknowledges that the "pragmatic strain" of "humanist" feminism has "nonetheless produced significant political effect" (138). He demonstrates his sympathy for "American" feminism by asserting that Toril Moi's *Sexual/Textual Politics* is a "relentless critique—even a rejection—of feminist theory in most of its recent forms" (134). But he really cannot bring himself to identify a single worthwhile idea in "humanist" feminism.[8]

It would be misleading to suggest that Smith's repetition of the hegemonic claims of poststructuralism is idiosyncratically his or even that his privileging of European theory reflects his status as a man discussing feminism. I think, in fact, that the reverse is true. He has accurately reproduced the accent with which poststructuralists in general frequently dismiss the work they associate with "humanism," a language that many poststructuralist feminists have in turn used on feminists they associate with "humanism." Words like *humanism, essentialist, unsophisticated, naive, simple, pragmatic, empirical, experience-based,* or *expressive* are frequently used as descriptors by poststructuralists for non-poststructuralist work. But such terms have long ago lost any descriptive meaning, if indeed they ever had any. Instead, like gang insignia, they have become the fashionable tropes of poststructuralism, figures that function covertly to establish the critic's place inside the poststructuralist club. We can chalk some of this up to the intellectual sparring that is endemic to the academy. Moreover, poststructuralist arrogance is often matched by an equally dismissive know-nothingism and resistance to anything new by some non-poststructuralist critics (a stance to which I am as opposed as I am to the cliquishness of some poststructuralists). But partic-

ularly within the multifaceted community of academic feminists, this poststructuralist language of dismissal has been deeply divisive, experienced by many non-
poststructuralist feminists as a betrayal of a common feminist project in the
re-formation of knowledge.[9]

Smith's invocation of these dismissive tropes helps to uncover the problems of
a recuperative model for a post/poststructuralist moment. Recuperations can potentially reinstate the original hierarchy, privilege poststructuralist theory, and
trivialize the contributions of non-poststructuralist feminist theory and praxis. I
see four particular forms this problem can take. First, recuperation often conflates
poststructuralist theory with all theory, thereby delegitimating other theoretical
frameworks. This happens when so-called American feminism is labeled "empirical," in contrast to "French feminism," which is constituted as its opposite, that
is, "theoretical." Such a false binary positions one kind of theory as "the" instance
of theory (as when someone says "I do 'theory'" to describe his or her work in
poststructuralist or critical theory). It does not recognize the potential multiplicity
of theoretical perspectives and languages. Adrienne Rich, Audre Lorde, and Alice
Walker, for example, have written essays as powerfully theoretical as those of
Hélène Cixous and Luce Irigaray. To make this point to my students, I like to
teach Cixous's "The Laugh of the Medusa" alongside Lorde's "The Erotic as
Power." As Barbara Christian writes about the different rhetorical modes of "theory," "people of color have always theorized—but in forms quite different from
the western form of abstract logic. And I am inclined to say that our theorizing
(and I intentionally use the verb rather than the noun) is often in narrative forms,
in the stories we create, in riddles and proverbs, in the play with language" ("Race
for Theory" 226).

Second, a recuperative gesture that covertly dismisses what it appears to assimilate often represents the claim to political correctness, to the "true" cultural radicalism. Widely known in many branches of "the left," this rhetorical move delegitimates the position of the other by asserting the other's regressive tendencies.
Theoretical formulations of progressive "stages" often succumb to this kind of
appeal to orthodoxy—whether it is Betty Friedan's *The Second Stage*, dismissing
lesbian feminism; or Julia Kristeva's "Women's Time," a three-stage vision of
feminism that sees it moving from humanism, to essentialism, to a mystical individualism. Stagist formulations frequently pose synchronic theoretical arguments
in diachronic drag. Within the context of poststructuralist debate, non-poststruc-
turalists are often dismissed as caught in the snares of "humanism," the main
tyrant to be overthrown. Poststructuralism thus stakes its claim as the avant-garde
of revolution, of politically correct thinking.[10]

Third, the kind of recuperative analysis that Smith's book represents—and I
stress that he is not alone—posits a fixed and monolithic humanism that bears
little resemblance to the fluid and multifaceted traditions of western philosophy
as they have taken shape in different cultures and historical moments. It is surely
beyond the scope of this essay to demonstrate my sense that the antihumanist
project of poststructuralism tends to construct a straw man or woman out of its
precursor in the best of Bloomian fashions. But within the context of feminism,

poststructuralist critiques of so-called humanist feminism are frequently very inaccurate, based on little actual (dare I say "empirical"?) reading, especially of work by women of color. What Smith—and Moi, Chris Weedon, Catherine Belsey, Rita Felski, Alice Jardine, and many others—overlook in discussions of non-poststructuralist feminist criticism is the self-consciously revisionist stance much of it took in relation to humanism from the very beginning.[11] Both Rich's 1971 essay "When We Dead Awaken: Writing as Re-Vision" and Walker's 1974 essay "In Search of Our Mothers' Gardens," for example, launched a major attack on humanism as the founding gesture of feminist reconstructions of literary tradition. These, along with many other early feminist critical texts, asserted the role of ideology *and language* in the patriarchal construction and feminist reconstructions of women's identity, agency, and writing. In various ways, this work stressed the necessity of a materialist analysis of women's cultural production and reception. The frequently leveled charge of essentialism and a belief in a preexisting womanhood outside patriarchal construction does not hold up with a careful reading of these texts. The focus on women's "experience" often went hand in hand with a recognition that this experiential identity was inseparable from women's struggle within and against patriarchal norms for femininity. That the language of this work is not poststructuralist should not prevent us from seeing, as Nancy K. Miller writes, that it challenges "the confidence of humanistic discourse as *universality*" (*Subject to Change* 70).

Fourth, the very notion of recuperation ignores that many non-poststructuralist feminists never gave up the concepts that poststructuralism now wants to recuperate. Within the framework of various feminist theoretical positions, concepts such as the *author, identity, agency,* and *language* underwent major re-visions, but retained their legitimacy in critical discourse. Many poststructuralist feminists followed Kristeva, Irigaray, and Cixous in asserting that language is inherently phallogocentric. Such a view, one that frequently valorized the mute speech of the hysteric's body, claimed that women cannot be represented in language (or narrative), that women's past writing could inscribe only their Otherness within phallogocentric discourse, that women have, in short, been denied access to the status of subject within the symbolic order. But other feminist critics explicitly or implicitly refused to accept this victim view of women's writing and examined the various forms of women's agency exerted often in the face of enormous ideological and institutional constraints—a point that is central to Elaine Showalter's *A Literature of Their Own*, Barbara Christian's *Black Women Novelists: The Development of a Tradition*, Sandra M. Gilbert and Susan Gubar's *Madwoman in the Attic*—to name a few influential feminist literary histories from the 1970s. Increasingly in the 1980s, these and other feminist critics doing what Showalter has called "gynocriticism" borrowed concepts and interpretive strategies from poststructuralism, especially feminist forms of it. But they retained revisionist versions of such concepts as the *author, identity, self, agency,* and so forth. Rachel Blau DuPlessis's widely influential book, *Writing beyond the Ending: Narrative Strategies in Twentieth-Century Women's Writing* (1985), is exemplary of this kind of work, especially for its adaptation of narrative theory, psychoanalysis, and materialist analysis to a reading of women's various *strategies* for writing within and beyond prevailing cultural scripts. Her title is echoed in Yaeger's subtitle for *Honey-Mad Women: Emancipatory Strategies in Women's Writing* (1988), which uses Cixous's manifesto for a new feminine language as a paradigm for reading the difference of women's past "sextual" discourse. Alicia Ostriker's *Stealing the Language: The Emergence of Women's Poetry in America* (1986) plays on Cixous's famous pun calling for women to "*voler*," but rather than a utopian figure, Ostriker's "theft" is one that she sees women poets having already achieved. In *Reconstructing Womanhood: The Emergence of the Afro-American Woman Novelist* (1987), Hazel V. Carby "explores how black women intellectuals reconstructed the sexual ideologies of the nineteenth century to produce an alternative discourse of black womanhood" (6). Although Carby critiques some prior black feminist theorists, such as Barbara Smith and Deborah McDowell, for what she terms their tendencies toward "bourgeois humanistic discourse," she asserts that "my basic premise is that the novels of black women should be read not as passive representations of history but as active influence within history" (95).[12] In these and many other critical works, some form of agency is assumed, often symptomatically present in the frequency of such words as *revision, reconstruction, strategy, project, intervention, insertion, positioning, situating,* and *negotiation.*

It is this last word—*negotiation*—that I would like to propose as a substitute for the problematical term *recuperation* to describe post/poststructuralist feminist criticism. *Negotiation* carries the double connotation of "mutual discussion and arrangement" (as in negotiating a treaty) and maneuvering to clear or pass an obstacle (as in negotiating a mountain pass). It also holds out in the way *recuperation* does not at least the possibility of mutual respect between equals. It is a negotiation, not a recuperation, that Miller accomplishes in her three essays on the subject (*Subject to Change* 65–121). In "Changing the Subject," for example, she juxtaposes the theoretical contributions of Rich with Barthes and holds in dialogue a number of poststructuralist and non-poststructuralist critics (102–21). It is a negotiation as well that Margaret Homans maneuvers in *Bearing the Word: Language and Female Experience in Nineteenth-Century Women's Writing* between Lacanian psycho-linguistics and a gynocritical examination of women writers' experience and inscription of language.[13]

This kind of negotiation does more, it seems to me, than move back and forth between poststructuralist and non-poststructuralist poles, more than weave the discursive threads together, more even than hold the contradictions in dialogic suspension—though it certainly does all of these. Negotiation at this post/poststructuralist point in time involves a commitment to self-consciously historicizing theory and theorizing history. Since at least the time of Plato and Herodotus, "theory" and "history" have been ideologically represented in western culture as a binary that is more or less polarized depending on a multiplicity of factors. (In practice, of course, "theory" and "history" have not in reality been nearly so dualistic.) "Theory" is often set up as a set of interlocking principles that have explanatory power in different times and places. It is supposed to be fundamentally synchronic, making its claim to "truth" on its ability to explain the fixed structure underlying myriad phenomena. It has a tendency toward totalizing generalization and utopian assertion. Like a geometric theorem, it presents itself as an abstraction beyond space and time. "History," on the other hand, has been most often represented as fundamentally diachronic, making its claim to "truth" on its ability to collect and order "facts." It is often set up as a reproduction of what already happened in the past, with its objective to explain the process of change within the coordinates of a specific space and time. It has a tendency toward the experiential, and like a chronicle, it binds itself to the empirical as the necessary building blocks of its reconstruction of the past.

Such an ideological binary is of course ripe for deconstruction. It underlies, I would argue, a lot of the conflict and misreadings on both "sides" of the poststructuralist divide in the profession. And it is based on a false notion of both "theory" and "history." For "theory" cannot abstract itself from the story of its own production. It too has a "history," a space and time within which it emerges, changes, disappears, and returns. This "history" of "theory" is present in some form within the "theory's" abstractions, no matter how far removed it appears to be. Conversely, "history" cannot separate itself from the theoretical. It can never be an absolute likeness of "what happened," of "fact," because it is a re-presentation of the past based upon a selective and shaping perception. The story of a given space and time that "history" tells is just that, a narrative whose ordering principles reflect the implicit or explicit theories of its narrator. Whether overt or covert, some kind of "theory" is invoked for its explanatory power—such as the theory of periodization, the theory of organic change, the theory of random change, the theory of the state, and so forth.

The negotiation I increasingly see taking place in the work of many feminist critics—I will call them post/poststructuralist feminists—theorizes history and historicizes theory by examining how each is present in the other. Theorizing history involves the critic's self-conscious examination of his or her underlying premises in the construction of a literary historical narrative—whether it is an author's oeuvre, a literary school or movement, the evolution of a genre, and the like. It requires resisting the temptation to read texts and narrate a history as if the language of each were a transparent medium communicating meaning unproblematically. In relation to poststructuralism, theorizing history in particular means the willingness to use poststructuralism's rich insight into language for an analysis of writing and reading as processes that are constructed within a complex set of cultural scripts.

As historiographers, Hayden White and Dominick LaCapra have led the way in asking historians to understand the degree to which writing "history" is an interpretive act based on explicit or implicit theoretical assumptions. Literary historians have increasingly done the same. Among feminist critics, it has become a common practice to open a book or article with an exposition of the main theoretical presuppositions underlying the study and a self-reflexive situating of the critic's approach to debates in the field. Moreover, interpretation of a literary text is frequently acknowledged as one among many possible interpretations—

not as a pluralist gesture, but rather as a recognition that different critical frameworks lead to the production of different "readings." The historian's traditional
search for "the" story is often replaced by an acknowledgment of multiple stories,
each one of which reflects the hermeneutics of the critic-as-narrator. This kind of
negotiation between "history" and "theory" requires the critic to be familiar with
various theoretical traditions, including, but not limited to, poststructuralist ones.
In a post/poststructuralist age, poststructuralist theory exists on the ever-expanding landscape of the profession. Because of its wide-ranging presence in literary
studies, it can not be dismissed out of hand (as some feminists have attempted to
do), any more than the new knowledge about women writers, gender, and writing
by people of color should be ignored by those whose field is white, male, canonical literature. As teachers and members of the profession, we all have a responsibility to read—and often teach—beyond the boundaries of our specific fields. And
for non-poststructuralist feminist critics, this involves some form of dialogic engagement with poststructuralism.

Conversely, historicizing theory takes at least two forms for engaged post/
poststructuralist feminist critics. First, it involves understanding the underlying
historical conditions of theory's production. Abstract as it is, "theory" is formed
and disseminated in a given space and time. The "death of the author," the erasure
of the subject, the deconstruction of agency, for example, are concepts marked by
their European origin and changed fundamentally as they were introduced into
the United States. Poststructuralism's particular despair, it seems to me, reflects
the fallout from two massive wars fought on European soil in this century and the
widespread sense among intellectuals that western humanism was irredeemably
bankrupt. Existentialism, poststructuralism's immediate precursor on the French
cultural scene, had valorized the "transcendental ego," the "I" whose leap into
agency could be taken despite the meaninglessness of the universe. Poststructuralists in France rejected the transcendental ego (and its existential act) in
favor of what they perceived as a more radical transformation of western phallogocentrism.

In American culture, however, the euphoria of victory and the global power of
the United States fostered the intensification of traditional American individualism, even among intellectuals. The year 1968, a watershed of radical activity in
many parts of the world, was not the same in France and the United States.
Poststructuralism in its French form was launched, if not actually born, on the
Parisian barricades, at least in part as a repudiation of Sartre and existentialism.
But in the American left, Sartre remained influential, a fact that may account for
the adaptations that American feminism made of Simone de Beauvoir's existential feminism, with its concepts of Otherness and authenticity, immanence and
transcendence. Moreover, the ideology of the "Self"—as individualistic, independent, self-reliant—is deeply rooted in American history and culture. Groups who
have been denied the agency and status of the "individual" for reasons of race,
class, gender, religion, ethnicity, sexual preference (and so forth) have traditionally felt excluded from the promise of the "American Dream." Appropriation of
the discourse of the "Self," however redefined, has been and still is a central

characteristic of cultural and political movements of the marginalized in the United States.

These cultural and historical differences between France and the United States changed the nature and function of key poststructuralist concepts as they flowed across the Atlantic to take root in strange soil. Intertextuality, for example, lost its anonymity as many American critics reintroduced the concept of the author and agency into a discussion of the blend and clash of discourses. As Miller writes, "Feminist critics in the United States have on the whole resisted the fable of the author's demise on the grounds that stories of textuality which trade in universals—the Author or the Reader—in fact articulate marked and differentiated structures of what Gayatri Spivak has called masculine 'regulative psychobiography'" (*Subject to Change* 107).[14] Miller's own concept of "political intertextuality" and the importance of a reconstituted author in her feminist reading practice reflects at least partially the ongoing importance of the American discourses of agency and the "self," however redefined. Similarly, Yaeger's use of French feminist theory to read the "emancipatory strategies" in already existing women's poetry demonstrates the feminist resistance in the United States to "the fable of the author's demise."

Second, historicizing "theory" can involve the transformation of a given theory from a totalizing abstraction into an interpretive tool that is used within a different framework. Instead of appearing as "scientific truth," a given theory can be adapted as a technology for a reading that also takes historical analysis into account. Deconstruction, for example, is increasingly being used as an interpretive strategy for readings that also perform historical analysis. Like New Criticism, deconstruction is becoming part of the craft of a critic's task. Within a feminist context, Homans's *Bearing the Word* demonstrates this kind of negotiation in her use of Lacanian psychoanalysis. As she explains in her introductory chapter, she finds Lacan's theory of language to be a particularly coherent instance of "the dominant myth of language" that was "already at the heart of nineteenth-century European literary culture" (5). Consequently, his theory is useful for understanding the ideology of language within which nineteenth-century British women had to write. "The Lacanian view of language is not a universal truth," Homans insists, "but the psycholinguistic retelling of a myth to which our culture has long subscribed. I believe that a woman writer could be affected by this myth without my believing in its truth" (5–6). *Bearing the Word* examines how a number of nineteenth-century women negotiated the anxiety of language they experienced as a result of the "dominant myth of language" that Lacan himself articulates and thereby helps to explain. For Homans, women writers exist as "authors" and "agents" who forge a different relationship to language in the face of an ideology that would deny them access to the status of subject.

Both these forms of historicizing "theory" involve the refusal to grant "theory" the status of "fact." Foregrounding the historical specificity of "theory" and adapting it as an interpretive tool, both resist theory's tendency to proclaim itself as scientific law, synchronically "true." Historicized, a given theory becomes a generalization with explanatory power, a system of interlocking ideas that may coexist with many other systems, all of which are subject to the test of usefulness. Within this epistemological framewok, a theory that loses its capacity to explain can be discarded. Instead of being mastered by the hegemonic power of master-discourses, the critic exercises agency—her or his own subjectivity, expressive of a specific positionality within culture—in relation to "theory."

I will close with a recollection of a heated exchange I once had with an excellent poststructuralist feminist critic who insisted that Lacanian and Derridean theory had established that women could not be represented in language because the system of signification was inherently phallogocentric. Poststructuralism, she told me, was a plane that had already taken off; there was nothing we could do but go along with the ride. Struck by the determinism of her plane imagery, I tried to articulate a different view—that this was just one "theory" of language; that if it was not "good" for women, then we should abandon it. What I was somewhat clumsily trying to say in my invocation of the proverbial "if it's good for the Jews..." was that a "theory" is just a "theory," no more, no less, that new "theories" replace old ones all the time, and that no "theory" should make a claim to absolute "truth."

After the heat of the exchange cooled down, I realized that as an engaged, academic feminist in a post/poststructuralist moment, I have found it necessary to avoid getting on any one "plane," but have rather attempted to negotiate a number of intersecting "planes." In refusing to remain locked in the poststructuralist "plane," I have reclaimed an agency denied by the discipleship that Kavanagh critiques. For me, the *negotiation* among competing and often divisive discourses most fruitfully characterizes feminist engagement in the academy "after" poststructuralism. *Negotiation* connotes a dialogic exchange, where *recuperation* covertly reinforces the hierarchy of "theory" over "history." Created by both the internal dynamics within the profession and the global tenor of the times, post/poststructuralism (which I realize I may have named in order to nudge along its difficult birth), involves a deconstruction of the extreme polarization of "theory" and "history" and a reconstruction of discourses that combines the two in a multiplicity of creative and often contradictory ways.

Making History:
Reflections on Feminism, Narrative,
and Desire

. . . Women have always been making history, living it
and shaping it.
—*Gerda Lerner,* The Majority Finds Its Past

. . . All historicizing is narrativizing—putting in the
form of a story.
—*Gayatri Chakravorty Spivak,* Outside in the
Teaching Machine

The dream of a "total history" corroborating the
historian's own desire for mastery of a documentary
repertoire . . . has of course been a lodestar
of historiography.
—*Dominick LaCapra,* History and Criticism

What has surfaced is something different from the
unitary, closed, evolutionary narratives of
historiography as we have traditionally known it: . . .
we now get the histories (in the plural) of the
losers as well as the winners, of the regional
(and colonial) as well as the centrist, of the unsung
many as well as the much sung few, and I might
add, of women as well as men.
—*Linda Hutcheon,* The Politics of Postmodernism

MY REFLECTIONS begin with the contradictory desires within contemporary
American feminism revolving around the question of history, particularly what is
involved when feminists write histories of feminism. On the one hand, a pressing

urgency to reclaim and hold on to a newly reconstituted history of women has fueled the development of the field of women's history as well as the archaeological, archival, and oral history activities of feminists in other areas of women's studies outside the discipline of history, inside and outside the academy. On the other hand, there has been a palpable anxiety within the feminist movement about the possibility that our activities as feminists—including the productions of our own history—run the risk of repeating the same patterns of thought and action that excluded, distorted, muted, or erased women from the master narratives of history in the first place. The first impulse is outer-directed and has channeled phenomenal energy and excitement into the interrelated projects of the de-formation of existing history and re-formation of new histories of women and the place of gender in all cultural formations as they change over time. The second impulse is inner-directed and has applied the brakes to the new enthusiasms and in sober self-reflexivity insisted on problematizing the project of feminist history writing. With some exceptions, the reflexive impulse has found expression not so much in the field of women's history itself as in the discourses of feminist theory and activism. Feminism, particularly as it attempts to construct the stories of its own production, is caught between the desire to act and the resistance to action that threatens to reproduce what poststructuralists like Luce Irigaray call the economy of the same.

In this essay, I intend to explore the political necessity and creative possibilities of both the outer- and inner-directed activities by drawing on the debates about and histories of the encounters between French poststructuralism (including feminist forms of it) and American feminism. As well, I hope to show how the insight of one involves a blindness to the insight of the other, and how ultimately, both are necessary to the larger agenda of feminists "making history." I will first examine the underlying epistemological issues and then defend both the problematization of feminist history writing and the political necessity of this enterprise. Additionally, I will discuss how the competing needs to narrate and problematize the history of feminism reflect the desire for empowerment and fear of the will-to-power, the one affirming women's agency, the other muting it. And finally, I will suggest that feminists can be engaged in a dialogic, not monologic, project of writing feminist histories—in the plural—in which the politics of competing histories need not paralyze the need to tell stories about feminism.

FEMINIST EPISTEMOLOGIES AND MAKING HISTORY

The contradictory desires of feminists "making history" reflect the epistemological issues embedded in the double reference of the term *history* itself: first, to history as the past; and second, to history as the story of the past. The first meaning of history—what has happened—posits a base reality whose totality can never be fully reconstituted. The second meaning of history—the narrative of what has happened—foregrounds the role of the narrator of past events and consequently the nature of narrative as a mode of knowing that selects, organizes, orders, interprets, and allegorizes.[1] These two dimensions of *history* in turn reflect the double reference in my title, "making history." The feminist desire to "make history" entangles the desire to effect significant and lasting change with the desire to be the historian of change. As a heuristic activity, history writing orders the past in relation to the needs of the present and future. The narrative act of assigning meaning to the past potentially intervenes in the present and future construction of history. For feminists, this means that writing the history of feminism functions as an act in the present that can (depending on its influence) contribute to the shape of feminism's future.[2]

The heuristic and interventionist dimension of history writing—historiography as an act in the present on behalf of the future—raises the question of epistemology, central to understanding the inner- and outer-directed energies of feminist history writing, whether inside or outside the academy, whether within the field of women's history or more broadly within women's studies in general. For those working out of a positivist epistemology, the goal of history writing is to construct an objective account of the past based on thorough immersion in the empirical data and an unbiased assemblage of that data into an accurate sequence. The positivist belief in history writing as the production of objective truth may no longer be very prevalent in its purest form, although it served as the philosophical bases for the formation of history as a discipline in the nineteenth and early-twentieth centuries. But the notion of history writing as the best possible reconstruction of the past in a seamless narrative by an omniscient, invisible narrator nonetheless continues to underwrite many projects, including feminist ones.[3] Within this framework, the heuristic and interventionist dimension of history writing tends to be unacknowledged or overtly denied, and thus covertly operative.

For those working out of a subjectivist epistemology, the Real of history is knowable only through its written or oral textualizations.[4] The past is therefore triply mediated—first, through the mediations of those texts, which are themselves reconstructions of what "really" happened; second, through the fragmentary and partial survival of those textualizations that are dependent upon the politics of documentation and the luck, skill, and persistence of the historian-as-detective who must locate them; and third, through the interpretive, meaning-making gaze of the historian. From this perspective, the excellence of history writing depends not upon the level of objectivity but rather upon the cogency of interpretation. And interpretation, as Hayden White and Dominick LaCapra preeminently theorize, introduces the mediations of language: the meaning-making of tropes, rhetoric, and narrative. Within the subjectivist epistemology, this dimension of historical discourse is often openly acknowledged as a source of speculation or even commitment.[5]

Both epistemologies have been at work in women's studies as feminists from a variety of fields engage in "making history"—in the writing about feminism's past and the performance of feminism's present and future. Some feminists work within a positivist framework, emphasizing the "truth" of what has been recovered; others function within a subjectivist framework, foregrounding the interpretive dimension of their narratives; and still others combine aspects of each episte-mology. This diversity of historiographic assumption reflects, I believe, the con-tradictions built into the foundations of women's studies itself, contradictions that continue to underlie and permeate most work in the field, whether acknowledged or not. On the one hand, women's studies developed out of the need to counter hegemonic discourses about women that ignored, distorted, or trivialized women's history, experience, and potential. Women's studies consequently for-mulated compensatory and oppositional histories that told the "truth" about women—whether it was about women's status in the so-called Renaissance, the production of women's writing in the nineteenth century, or the sexual brutaliza-tion of black women slaves. This search to discover of the "truth" of women's history that could shatter the "myths" and "lies" about women in the standard histories operates out of a positivist epistemology that assumes that the truth of history is objectively knowable.

On the other hand, the early insistence in women's studies that hegemonic knowledge was produced out of and in the service of androcentrism necessitated a subjectivist epistemology that insisted on all knowledge as value based, emerg-ing from a given perspective or standpoint. No knowledge is value free, many feminists claimed, including feminist knowledge. Thomas Kuhn's *The Structure of Scientific Revolutions* (1962) was widely used to promote women's studies as a "paradigm shift" of dramatic and revolutionary proportions within the institu-tions of knowledge.[6] The goal of writing history within this epistemological framework was not to discover the true history, but rather to construct the story of women's experience out of a feminist paradigm. Feminist histories countered hegemonic histories not with the objective truth, but with stories produced from a feminist perspective.[7]

Both feminist epistemologies developed out of and have continued currency because of the urgently felt political agenda of women's studies: to engage in the de-formation of phallocentric history and the re-formation of histories that focus on or integrate women's experience and the issue of gender. Why political? Be-cause what we know of the past shapes what becomes possible in the future. Because the repositories of human knowledge constitute the building blocks of the symbolic order. Because knowledge is power, ever more increasingly so in what is coming to be called the Information Age. As much as my own work and sympathies operate primarily out of the subjectivist epistemology, I believe that both are necessary to the enterprise as moderating influences on the potential excesses of each. On the one hand, the positivist epistemology can lead toward fundamentalist assertions of truth that obscure the interpretive perspectives of historical narrative. On the other hand, the subjectivist epistemology can lead toward the paralysis of complete relativism in which the Real of history vanishes into the play of story and discourse.[8]

It would be easy, but misleading, to align the positivist epistemology with the outer-directed, action-oriented desire to "make history" and the subjectivist epis-temology with the inner-directed, self-reflexive problematizing of feminist history writing. Certainly, the anxiety about the potential for replicating the master narratives of hegemonic discourse assumes the subjectivist model and foregrounds the role of the narrator in an interpretive ordering of the past. But to associate feminist history writing (whether in women's history or other fields of women's studies) with positivism would obscure the diversity of epistemologies present in these histories—some of which are positivist, some subjectivist, and some a combination, with the contradictory presence of both epistemologies underlying the endeavor as a whole. Moreover, it would too simply replicate the dismissive gesture that consigns everything but the act of poststructuralist problematizing to a bankrupt and naive humanism.

Instead, the epistemologies underlying feminism should aim for a negotiation between objectivism and subjectivism, between the search for the Real and a recognition that all access to the Real is mediated through discourse. As LaCapra writes, "extreme documentary objectivism and relativistic subjectivism do not constitute genuine alternatives. They are mutually supportive parts of the same larger complex" (*History* 137). He insists that his critique of positivist historiography does not mean that he abandons the empirical. He argues instead for a "dialogic and mutually provocative" relation between the empirical and the rhetorical as equally necessary parts of history writing ("Intellectural History" 433).

This interplay encompasses the kind of dialogue Shoshana Felman and Dori Laub advocate in *Testimony: Crises of Witnessing in Literature, Psychoanalysis, and History*. They use the Holocaust as touchstone for theorizing a kind of history writing that acknowledges history as a form of representation and of testimony to the Real. On the one hand, history writing bears witness to "the encounter with the real" (xvi). On the other hand, this Real is not transparently present, but is rather "reinscribed, translated, radically rethought and fundamentally worked over by the text" of history (xv). The "empirical context," they argue, "needs not just to be *known*, but to be *read*" (xv). The Real to which we have access only through texts of various kinds must be read with an eye to the processes of textualization and interpretation. If the Real of the past is always mediated, then history writing should not only "encounter the real" but also reflect upon those forms of mediation. As Stuart Hall writes: "There is a past to be learned about, but . . . it has to be grasped as a history, as something that has to be told. It is narrated. It is grasped through memory. It is grasped through desire. It is grasped through reconstruction. It is not just a fact that has been waiting to ground our identities. What emerges from this is nothing like an uncomplicated, dehistoricised, undynamic, uncontradictory past" ("Local and the Global" 38).

In Defense of Problematizing (Feminist) History

Recognizing the contradictory and mutually interdependent epistemologies underlying women's studies introduces the necessity of problematizing feminist history writing. But how does the need to problematize go beyond the issue of competing epistemologies and into the politics of writing feminist history, especially the history of feminism? And what models for problematization have been developing within feminism in the past twenty years?

To answer the first question, I want to move outside the discipline of women's history proper to an example of less rigorous feminist history writing published in the *New Republic* in October 1992: "Sister Soldiers" by Christina Hoff Sommers, a professor of philosophy at Clark University and the author of the heavily marketed, sensationalist *Who Stole Feminism?*[9] Billed as "Live from a Women's Studies Conference," this article narrates a partial "history" of the 1992 National Women's Studies Association convention in Austin, Texas, by way of introducing a brief history of academic feminism in the United States. Sommers writes overtly from the perspective of what she calls "an older 'First Wave' kind of feminism whose main goal is equity" (30). As a feminist, she engages in a historiographic project whose covert agenda is to attack what she calls the newer "'Second Wave' gynocentric feminism, which since the early '70s has taken center stage in the universities" (33). Most academic feminists would recognize her article—in spite of its self-identified feminism—as consistent with the phenomenon of current attacks on women's studies coming from such media heroes as Charles Sykes and Dinesh D'Souza and organizations like the National Association of Scholars. Sommers uses historiographic discourse—first, of the NWSA convention, then, of the development of women's studies—to condemn wholesale the project of contemporary academic feminism. Her stories of the past represent her attempt to intervene in the present—to halt the march of what she opposes within feminism.

Sommers's diachronic discourse is easily unveiled as synchronic discourse in drag. Her narratives of the NWSA convention and the development of women's studies collapse quickly into figural representations of a demonized feminism. She practices a kind of metonymic historiography in which the telling anecdote of feminist excess stands in for the multifaceted phenomenon of academic feminism. Substituting a part for the whole, she characterizes all women's studies through narrative recitation of single incidents that determine guilt by association. This metonymic smear begins with the title, "Sister Soldiers," which foreshadows her attack in the article on "gynocentric feminism" by echoing the name of the Afrocentric rap singer Sister Soljah, from whom candidate Bill Clinton distanced himself during his presidential campaign. The implication of this allusion is that just as the liberal Clinton was right to separate himself from black ethnocentrism, she as liberal feminist is correct to distance herself from a gynocentric feminism that promotes "sisterhood." Whatever one thinks of Sister Soljah, Sommers's analogic figuration of academic feminism as Afrocentrism parallels the evocation of racist paranoia in the Willie Horton commercial during the Bush-Dukakis presidential race in 1988.[10]

Sommers establishes her authority as historian by amassing narrative detail about the conference for the first third of the article. She carefully sets the scene of the conference and narrates its opening events, detailing Eleanor Smeal's late arrival for the initial address and the panelists who filled in until she came: "To pass the time, we were introduced to an array of panelists. . . . Still no Smeal. A panelist named Angela took the floor. . . . A weary Eleanor Smeal finally arrived" (30). This narrative detail functions to produce what Roland Barthes calls the "reality effect," that is, the effect of reality, of objective history achieved through the piling up of "facts."[11] Detail establishes verisimilitude, which then lends credibility to her point of view, which seems to emerge objectively out of the data. She reports, for example, that "Louise and I were relieved when the proceedings were interrupted by a coffee break. Half-and-half was available—though perhaps not for long. The eco-feminist caucus has been pushing to eliminate all meat, fish, eggs, and dairy products at NWSA events" (30). Sommers's manipulation of the reality effect in her narrative of the conference establishes her credibility for her accounts of feminist conferences and classrooms around the country. Metonymies of feminism appear throughout the rest of the article as characterizations of the norm: the women's studies program directors who joined hands in a "healing circle" and "assumed the posture of trees experiencing rootedness and tranquility"; the introductory women's studies course at Rutgers that requires students to perform "some 'outrageous' and 'liberating' act outside of class" and then share feelings about it in class; the "heady claim" by Elizabeth Minnich that " 'What we are doing is comparable to Copernicus shattering our geo-centricity. . . . We are shattering andro-centricity' "; and so forth (31–32). "Ouchings and mass therapy," she asserts, "are more the norm than the exception in academic feminism" (30).

Operating out of a positivist feminist epistemology, I could respond to Sommers's attack by saying that her history is "not true," that she is a "bad historian," and then I could offer counterstories that are more accurate and have greater objective truth value. I could demonstrate that she exhibits no skill in handling her data, in assessing and demonstrating with evidence just how characteristic her anecdotes are of academic feminism in all its complexity and multiple formations. I might ask, for example, why she left out the massively influential presence of feminist scholars in professional associations and their conferences—such as the Modern Language Association, American Historical Association, American Psychological Association, American Political Science Association, and so forth. Shouldn't she have examined feminist activities at conferences within the traditional disciplines as well as at NWSA? It is not difficult to show, especially in the humanities, that academic feminism has permeated and altered (if not transformed) many traditional disciplines. But for historically specific reasons having to do with the formation of academic feminism in the United States, the place to see such change in process is not primarily NWSA conferences, but rather discipline-based feminist conferences, journals, and research, much of which is influenced by interdisciplinary feminist theory and knowledge, but retains a methodological and substantive "home base" in a preexisting discipline.

From a subjectivist feminist standpoint, I might counter Sommers's history by critiquing the bias that shapes her narrative at every point—her claim to greater objectivity than that of the "Second Wave"; her metonymic substitutions of the part for the whole; her stagist designation of "First Wave" and "Second Wave" feminism, where the second is represented as a degeneration and betrayal of the first; her invocation not only of racial paranoia in the title but also more generally of conspiracy theories rooted historically in anti-Semitic discourse ("These women run the largest growth area in the academy"; "They are disproportionately represented"; "They are quietly engaged in hundreds of well-funded projects" [30]). Indeed, the disdain she exhibits for academic feminism seems to operate on a binary of pure/impure in which she laments the contamination of reasonable feminism by the destructive distortions of irrational excess. Both positivist and subjectivist critiques of Sommers have merit. Sommers's history is both wildly inaccurate and anything but value free.

Sommers's "Sister Soldiers" is easy to critique as historical discourse. But her self-identification as feminist should warn us that the critical gaze we so willingly turn upon an attacker of academic feminism we must be ready to turn upon the historical discourse of its defenders. The danger of an exclusively positivist response to Sommers is that in posing a counter-"truth," such a critique can easily remain blind to its own potential use of historiographic discourse as a power play in current feminist debates. The need for reflective problematizations suggests that we be aware of the ways in which feminist histories can narrativize the past of feminism in ways that discredit or discount other feminist histories.

Sommers's "history" of academic feminism does more than provide an occasion for epistemological analysis. It also reminds us that at any given moment in the history of feminism there are many feminists competing to tell the history of feminism and shaping their histories in relation to the politics of feminism's present and future. In general historiographic terms, James C. Scott raises this question of the politics of competing histories in "History According to Winners and Losers," in which he uses the different histories that landed and landless peasants tell about the "facts" of Malaysia's "green revolution," the system of double cropping introduced in 1972. He likens the histories of "winners" and "losers" in the green revolution to two groups of carpenters building competing edifices. Imagining them each to have comparable skills, training, and material, he notes that the houses they build "are, to mix metaphors, different stories told in the same language" (169). "Events," he writes, "are not self-explanatory . . . they do not speak for themselves" (167). The events are similar but the meaning given those events differs markedly. The narratives of those who benefited and those who lost out in the green revolution reflect their different class positions.

Similarly, Jeannine DeLombard makes the same general point about feminist history in her review of Elizabeth Lapovsky Kennedy and Madeline D. Davis's *Boots of Leather, Slippers of Gold*:

> History is written by the winners. If any winners have emerged from the lesbian community's internal struggle for self-representation, they are the predominantly white, well-educated lesbian feminists who have had access to the bullhorn and the media, including the publishing houses, since the late 1960's.
>
> Their depiction of 20th-century lesbian life before . . . 1969 as a gay Dark Ages is a familiar one in which lesbians eked out a dreary existence in seedy bars, their

> internalized homophobia and sexism betrayed by their heavy drinking, barroom
> brawls and butch-femme role playing. ("Buffalo Gals" 24)

DeLombard praises *Boots of Leather, Slippers of Gold* for eluding that hegemonic lesbian narrative to construct a different history of Buffalo's lesbian community before the gay and lesbian rights movements of the 1970s.

Scott's and DeLombard's discussions of the competing histories of winners
and losers raise a further question about the politics of representation. What access do winners and losers have to the construction of written histories that maintain visibility on the cultural terrain? Who controls the means for the production,
reception, and dissemination of history? Scott and DeLombard both suggest that
the history that gains currency in the economy of ideas belongs to the "winners."
It's not that the "losers" don't create their own historical narratives, but rather that
marginalized, "muted," or subaltern people often produce histories that are
ephemeral—in oral form, undocumented, unpreserved, difficult to locate, or hard
for an "outsider" to interpret.[12]

It has surely been a cornerstone of feminist critique that hegemonic histories
tell the stories of "winners," namely, of powerful men and masculinist ideas. But
shouldn't we also as feminists turn a self-reflective eye upon ourselves to recognize that feminist histories of feminism are not exempt from the politics of historiography? Feminism too has its "winners" and "losers," its stratifications and
contested terrains. Whose story of feminism gains currency? What interests does
it serve? Whose story is lost, marginalized? Why? The same questions feminists
have asked of masculinist history about the erasure and distortion of women's
lives must be put to feminist histories.

But *how* should such questions be framed? From what perspectives have such
feminist problematizations been formulated? In the United States, the first feminists to ask such questions were those who felt marginalized within the feminist
movement and women's studies by white, middle-class, heterosexual feminists.
Women of color, lesbian women, and Jewish women in particular challenged the
meaning of "woman" and assumptions about the unified subject of feminism. The
emergence of Second Wave feminism beginning in the 1960s led among academic feminists to the early radical breakthrough of establishing the categories of
"woman" and "women" as fully legitimate sites of intellectual inquiry. The initial
emphasis of American feminism in the 1970s was on sexual difference—the different nature of women's experience, history, traditions, and culture from that of
men. But if sexual difference dominated early feminist discourse, a groundswell
of angry critique and institutional challenges from women marginalized by this
hegemony within feminism led to a gradual change in emphasis.

By the late 1970s and through the 1980s, differences *among* women became
increasingly a central focus of American women's studies and feminism more
generally, due to the pioneering essays by writers like Alice Walker, Audre
Lorde, Barbara Smith, Adrienne Rich, Johnetta Cole, Bonnie Zimmerman, Rachel Blau DuPlessis, Gayatri Chakravorty Spivak, Cherríe Moraga, Gloria Anzaldúa, Alice Chai, and Chandra Talpade Mohanty—to name a few—and edited

collections such as *This Bridge Called My Back: Writings of Radical Women of Color* (Moraga and Anzaldúa); *All the Women Are White, All the Blacks Are Men, But Some of Us Are Brave: Black Women's Studies* (Gloria T. Hull et al.); *Nice Jewish Girls: A Lesbian Anthology* (Evelyn Beck); *Lesbian Studies* (Margaret Cruikshank); and *Third World Women and the Politics of Feminism* (Mohanty et al.).

The impact of these challenges to feminism from within its boundaries was to problematize gender as *the* determining factor in women's lives.[13] Other forms of alterity and systems of stratification intersect with the gender system to disrupt analysis of women's lives solely in relation to gender. Discourses of multiple oppression, intersection, positionality, standpoint, and contradictory subject positions have to a large extent supplanted the monolithic category of "woman" in academic feminism in the United States.

Women's Words: The Feminist Practice of Oral History (1991), edited by Sherna Berger Gluck and Daphne Patai, brings this framework for problematization directly to bear on the methodology of feminist oral history. Oral history, the editors explain, was quickly adopted by feminists in the 1970s as an ideal feminist methodology that could make available "in accessible forms the words of women who had previously been silenced or ignored" (2). Representing a range of disciplines using oral history, the feminists in *Women's Words* have discovered that doing women's oral history is "more problematic" than they "had imagined" and requires moving "beyond celebration of women's experience to a more nuanced understanding of the complexities of doing feminist oral history" (2, 3). Differences between the researcher and the researched as well as the power relations structuring the oral history exchange mediate between the reality of women's lives and the feminist history constructed by the research for dissemination in the academy or the media at large. The problematic of competing narrative authorities, for example, is the subject of essays by Katherine Borland and Sondra Hale. Borland's feisty grandmother did not like the feminist interpretation Borland provided for her life, while Borland did not want to yield all her narrative authority to the woman whose life she retold (63–76). Hale, a white American anthropologist of working-class background accorded the status of "honorary Sudanese" was frustrated in her attempt to get the life story of one of the Sudan's leading feminists because this Third World woman from a relatively elite family wanted to use the researcher for her own political ends in the factional politics of her country (121–36). Patai and Gluck in their own essays on their respective research in Brazil and the occupied West Bank raise ethical and political questions about how national, ethnic, and class differences between researcher and researched inevitably problematize the processes and products of feminist oral history.[14]

The second major framework for problematization has come from poststructuralism. Beginning sporadically in the late 1970s, especially in French departments, and accelerating in the 1980s throughout the humanities, the arrival of European poststructuralist feminism, which emphasizes the theoretical and linguistic meanings of sexual difference, focusing particularly on the role of language in the construction of femininity. Influenced by theorists like Jacques

Lacan, Jacques Derrida, Roland Barthes, Julia Kristeva, Hélène Cixous, Luce Irigaray, Louis Althusser, and Michel Foucault, many feminists in the United States began to problematize feminism's essentializing or totalizing gestures and its roots in Enlightenment humanism.[15]

Although not all forms of problematization are poststructuralist, it is generally true that all poststructuralist theory aims to problematize. Echoing Jameson's command to "Always historicize!" (*Political Unconscious* 9), we might identify the poststructuralist imperative—if there is one—in a countermanifesto: "Always problematize!" As R. Radhakrishnan writes, "post-structuralist thought" has an "indefatigable capacity for problematization and protocols of vigilance" ("Feminist Historiography" 192). "Poststructuralism," Judith Butler writes, "is not strictly speaking, *a position*, but rather a critical interrogation of the exclusionary operations by which 'positions' [including feminist positions] are established" (Butler and Scott, *Feminists* xiv). In writing "against the grain of individualism, novelistic discourse, and personal testimony," Linda Kauffman asserts the foundation of poststructuralist critique: "I want continually to cast doubt on the status of knowledge—*even as we are in the process of constructing it*—a perpetual project" ("Long Goodbye" 129, 143). And as Peggy Kamuf argues, the "erosion of the very ground on which to take a stand" is necessary for feminist critical practice ("Replacing Feminist Criticism" 42).

For many poststructuralist feminists, feminism is doomed to repeat the binarist structures of the phallogocentric symbolic order if the most basic categories of feminism are not thrown open for question. *Woman, women, gender,* and *identity* are cultural constructs, the "effects," not the preexisting causes, of discourse, especially for feminists influenced by the early work of Foucault. The formation of feminist positions and standpoints should not be exempt from metatheoretical interrogations just because they are feminist. We make a mistake, Butler warns in *Gender Trouble*, if we keep seeking what she calls "the subject of feminism" (2–3). As an expression of identity politics, the subject of feminism is just as much based on "foundationalist fictions" as is the universal male subject of humanism (3). "Feminist critique," she writes, "ought to explore the totalizing claims of a masculinist signifying economy, but also remain self-critical with respect to the totalizing gestures of feminism" (13).[16] From this perspective, poststructuralist problematization of feminism itself is essential to avoid the erasure of heterogeneity and difference upon which the universal subject of humanism is based.

Historical narrative should itself be problematized, in the view of many poststructuralist feminists, because of what they see as its epistemological naiveté, its ideological formations, its association with the symbolic order, and its failure to acknowledge its allegorical and rhetorical foundations. In the field of women's history, Joan Scott is perhaps the foremost proponent of poststructuralist problematizations, of moving historical discourse away from the referential and toward the rhetorical (in de Manian terms), away from narratives of agency and toward the analysis of discursive effects (in Foucauldian terms). In *Gender and the Politics of History*, Scott advocates for feminist historians "politics that are self-consciously critical of their own justifications and exclusions, and so refuse an absolutist or totalizing stance" (9). She promotes poststructuralist historiography as the only way to avoid a regressive objectivist epistemology that can do little more than reify the very notions of sexual difference that should be under question. "Women's history written from this [objectivist] position," she writes, "and the politics that follow from it, end up endorsing the ideas of unalterable sexual difference that are used to justify discrimination" (4). To avoid such repetitions, she advocates a "more radical feminist politics" based on the "more radical epistemology" of poststructuralism (4). Like Foucault, who warns in *The Archaeology of Knowledge* against "classical history" as a coercive discourse and promotes a "new history" that is synchronic rather than diachronic narrative, Scott wants to shift feminist historiography away from a reconstruction of the past and toward an analysis of how meanings are constructed and function ideologically: "The story is no longer about the things that have happened to women and men and how they have reacted to them; instead it is about how the subjective and collective meanings of women and men as categories of identity have been constructed" (6).[17]

Poststructuralist feminist problematizations of historical narrative are situated within the larger field of historiographic debate represented particularly by the work of White and LaCapra. This debate in turn draws heavily on the more general (post)structuralist critique of narrative itself for what various theorists see as its dangerous alliance with mimesis and representationalism. Barthes, for example, in "The Discourse of History" attacks historical discourse as ideological narrative that obscures its own status as figuration behind the veil of representationalism. The discourse of history institutes "narration as a privileged signifier of the real" (140). The construction of the historian as "objective I" creates the illusion that history tells itself, that the Real speaks for itself (131–32). Historical discourse elides the distinctions between the signifier (the narrative), signified (the concept), and the referent (the "real" event). It does so by amassing facts that reproduce not reality, but "the reality effect" (139), a signifying practice he defines in more detail in "The Reality Effect." "History" and "narrative" serve ideological functions in part by veiling or naturalizing their own construction as an ordering discourse.[18] Introducing gender into this kind of critique of narrative and historical discourse, Kristeva and Cixous variously associate narrative—particularly representational narrative—with an oedipal discourse that institutes and enforces the Law of the Father.[19] The poststructuralist critique of historical narrative begun in Barthes's structuralist work has extended into a widespread suspicion of narrative in all its forms as a discourse that is allied to the social order and serves an ideological, coercive, even authoritarian function.[20]

Other theorists are not so much hostile to narrative as they are suspicious of its tendency to obscure its own foundations in rhetoric. Paul de Man, for example, regards narrative—including historical narrative—as an allegory of temporality, a figuration of duration that is unaware of its own dependence on rhetoric. However much it presents itself as diachronic, narrative can be deconstructed to show its allegorical formation. "A rhetorical trope serves as the ground of a historical system," he writes in "Reading and History" (67).[21] In relation to historical discourse in particular, de Man's approach suggests that chronological accounts may be governed less by the succession of events and more by such metaphoric structures as linear progress or regression, salvation or damnation, stagism, organicism, dualistic or even Manichaean conflict, the dialectic, the Weltanschauung, the war of the sexes or races, class struggle, sexual degeneracy, and so forth. Diachronicity potentially collapses into synchronicity, as Sommers's stagist historical narrative so clearly demonstrates.

Poststructuralist theory provides many important strategies for problematizations of feminism and feminist history writing, especially those that highlight linguistic effects and textual mediations. But poststructuralist problematizations should not be set up as the *only* route to the continual interrogation of the basic categories of feminist analysis and history making. Joan Scott, for example, relies upon a reductionistic binary of objectivist and poststructuralist epistemologies, retaining for poststructuralism a unique radicalism that comes out of a distinctive "emphasis on its variability, its volatility, and the political nature of its construction" (*Gender* 5). She does not acknowledge the many feminists before and parallel to poststructuralism who work out of subjectivist epistemologies that stress the constructedness of meaning and the politics of meaning making. Like many poststructuralists, Scott accepts without question that feminists who are not poststructuralists remain caught within a "naive" humanism.

The other framework for problematizing that I have identified—the discourses of positionality and differences among women—is equally important, especially with its insistence on the multiple, interactive, and relational facets of identity. Moreover, these two frameworks are not in the least mutually exclusive. Their sites of "origin" are different—primarily European, particularly French, philosophy and psychoanalysis; primarily North American feminism. But the fertile mixing of these discourses, which began in a substantial way in the 1980s in the United States, has created an arena of overlap so that problematizations of linguistic mediation and positionality are often mutually reinforcing.

Whatever the framework for critique, the problematization of feminist history writing represents a thoughtful and necessary brake on the excesses of feminist "truth telling." We need to recognize the way in which any history represents *a* history, all the more dangerously if it assumes itself to be *the* history. If we can easily recognize that Sommers attempts to establish her own kind of feminism as *the* future of feminism through her heuristic narrative of the NWSA conference and the spread of women's studies programs, then surely we must be ready to turn a critical eye inward to ask how our own histories of feminism might also engage in such play. Who are the winners and losers of our feminist histories of feminism?

In Defense of Feminist Narrative History

Interminable problematization of history writing poses a number of dangers that in themselves constitute a defense of feminist narratives of feminism. The first danger is the problem of paralysis, the kind of infinite regress and fetishization of indeterminacy that can develop out of constant navel gazing. Perpetual self-reflexivity—particularly with its continual focus on linguistic construction—contains within it the potential of dangerous inaction—or, to be more precise, action that in its constant inward turn inhibits an outer-directed energy for social change. As Daphne Patai writes in her problematization of feminist oral history across boundaries of difference: "It is a mistake to let ourselves be overwhelmed by these problems. The fact that doing research across race, class, and culture is a messy business is not reason to contemplate only our difficulties and ourselves struggling with them" (150). Indeed, to abandon the oral history of multiply oppressed women because of the researcher's mediating privilege would displace the women whose stories need to be told to focus attention all over again upon the problematic of the historian.[22]

This danger is more broadly endemic in poststructuralism itself and has been articulated by many within and outside the broad umbrella of poststructuralism.[23] In his efforts to define the limits of poststructuralist theory, Thomas Kavanagh argues that the banishing of language's mimetic function detaches literary studies from referentiality and delegitimates any concern for the "real" and "experience" (*Limits of Theory* 10, 15, 17). In his related critique of the political limits of Derridean deconstruction, Paul Smith argues that Derrida's continual effacement of subjectivity limits the possibility of agency "in such a way that it could not be adapted to *any* oppositional politics" (*Discerning* 50–51). The "*desiring* subject/individual has no place in deconstruction," he writes, and thus "cannot take responsibility for its interpretations, much less for the history of the species" (50–51). Although their attempts from within a poststructuralist framework to return poststructuralist theory to history and politics are directed mainly at literary studies and theory, the implications of their argument for history writing are self-evident. Indifferent to the Real of women's lives, without intentional agency and political responsibility, feminist history writing potentially loses its subversive raison d'être, its oppositional bite.

Michèle Barratt brings this poststructuralist erasure of the Real and effacement of subjectivity to bear directly on poststructuralist feminism, here represented by the British journal *m/f*:

> The exclusive emphasis [in poststructuralist theory] placed on discursive practice . . . [is i]n some respects proper and valuable. . . . Yet the critique of feminist slogans elaborated in successive articles in *m/f* is surely politically inappropriate to the point of being destructive. One by one the campaigning slogans of women's liberation—"The personal is political," "A woman's right to choose," "Control of our bodies"—is found to rest on errors of epistemology. . . . This critical exercise . . . fails to appreciate the grounding of such slogans in particular historical struggles. More importantly, perhaps, it leads us to ask what alternative political strategy is being offered. . . . Fundamentally, it is unclear that the project to deconstruct the category of woman could ever provide a basis for a feminist politics. (72)

Political struggle, Barratt suggests, depends upon establishing a historical ground from which to act.[24] The political problem with endless problematization of the ground on which we stand is the elimination of any position or standpoint from which to speak, organize for social change, or build coalitions based on common objectives. This applies as well to history writing as a form of feminist activism.

The second danger also represents a more general tendency within poststructuralism as it has been institutionalized in the academy. The constant undermining of feminism's discourse threatens to become its own hegemonic gesture, offering a totalizing dismissal of any activity not based in a critique of the grounds of discourse. Instead of opening up possibilities for feminist multivocalities, poststructuralist problematizations of feminism's so-called essentialism and humanism potentially constitute a new and exclusive orthodoxy, a new hierarchical power structure within academic feminism in which the theoretical problematizers often occupy the most prestigious and powerful positions. As Kavanagh writes, "What we had introduced as a discourse of the radically Other seems to have produced only the most resolute sameness and orthodoxy" (5). The hegemony of (poststructuralist) theory in the academy—not in any sense absolute but nonetheless influential—establishes theory as the "site of an unfettered *performance*," a "self-justifying performance," "freed from any referential function" (*Limits of Theory* 10). Rooted in a master-disciple system of theoretical proficiency and loyalty, poststructuralist theory can exhibit a politics of inclusion/exclusion based upon the binary of sophisticated/naive. "It is clearly a question of politics here," Kavanagh concludes, "a politics demanding the brutal disqualification of all who would remain outside or speak against the mutually sustaining dialogues of master and disciples" (12). Although Kavanagh does not specify further, the potentially gendered and racialized inflections of such binaries as master/disciple and theory/experience reinforce existing power structures in the academy.

From outside the poststructuralist umbrella, Barbara Christian's analysis in "The Race for Theory" parallels Kavanagh's. She writes that "it is difficult to ignore this new take-over [because] theory has become a commodity that helps determine whether we are hired or promoted in academic institutions. . . . Critics are no longer concerned with literature, but with other critics' texts, for the critic yearning for attention has displaced the writer and has conceived of himself as the center" (225). Her remarks about literary criticism can be adapted to history writing. The privileging of theory often rewards those who problematize feminism and focus their research not on what happened in the past but on other historians' texts. This power structure in the academy functions all the more insidiously because of the way poststructuralist theory potentially veils its own ideological power, obscures its own stoppage of the endless deferral of meaning by insisting on the "truth" of its own formulations and its dismissal of others deemed "humanist" or insufficiently un-self-reflexive.[25] In relation to feminist history writing, this means that those engaged in continual problematization run the risk of establishing their critique, freed as Kavanagh says from any concern for the referential, as hegemonic, as *the* meaning of feminism itself.

The third danger is implicit in the perpetual questioning of feminist history writing itself. This kind of critique covertly threatens by extension the whole multidisciplinary enterprise of writing women's history, of which writing the history of feminism is just one part. Writing women's history does not, of course, focus exclusively on women's experience, but begins with this compensatory center and then broadens to question the formation and operation of the gender system as its intersects with other systems of social organization based on race, class, sexuality, religion, national origin, and so forth. Much of the work in women's history aims to recover and/or analyze anew lost, forgotten, never-examined, or phallocentrically understood aspects of women's experience and the gender system. Poststructuralist attempts to redirect women's history writing toward discourse analysis carry with them a dismissal of history writing as, in Joan Scott's words, the "story . . . about the things that have happened to women and men and how they have reacted to them" (*Gender* 6).[26]

As Molly Hite writes in reference to literary studies as a form of history writing: "Being a feminist literary scholar seems more and more to be a matter of keeping abreast of the current repudiations. We're always killing off the Mother and riding sternly into the future on our newly phallicized hobbyhorses, call it modernity" ("'Except thou ravish me'" 125). Gayle Greene reflects even more provocatively:

> I sense a self-defeating tendency in all of this, a critical implosion that has the sound of a grinding halt. I wonder, also, if turning in on ourselves with this fierce self-scrutiny isn't a form of self-erasure, an analogue to our obsession with thinness, a way of assuring ourselves and others that we'll take up less space—a kind of professional/pedagogical anorexia. ("Looking at History" 16–17)

Deflecting the attention away from the Real of feminist history carries with it a broader displacement away from the Real of history itself, however mediated our knowledge of reality always is. The political consequences of this displacement threaten to return the dominant structures of history writing within the academy to what it was before the advent of women's studies. This danger brings us back to the political imperatives that underlay the founding of academic feminism in the 1960s and 1970s, however much later developments have altered, nuanced, and broadened those early manifestos for an activist feminist historiography. Writing about women's past represents a way to claim it, to assert the authority to interpret its meanings for the present and future. "What is new at this time," Gerda Lerner writes in *The Majority Finds Its Past*, "is that women are fully claiming their past and shaping the tools by means of which they can interpret it" (166). The premise of such statements is that making history in the present and future depends in part on the writing of women's past history.

What are the political consequences if the focus of feminist histories of feminism and women's history more broadly shifts entirely away from stories and analysis of (mediated) past realities and exclusively toward discourse analysis, constructivism, and critique of feminist historiography? Such an exclusive displacement would vacate the arena of writing about historical *women* (as opposed to *woman* as a discursive effect) to nonfeminists and antifeminists. Like boycotting an election, an act designed to bring attention to the illegitimacy of the electoral process, such a withdrawal from writing about the "real" lives of women and historical configurations of gender leaves the field of narrative history entirely in the hands of the patriarchal mainstream, but just how much attention this withdrawal brings to the structure of the academy is not clear.

It is vitally important, I believe, for feminists to stake our claim, to insist on our presence, within the academy as producers and teachers of new knowledge, which should include new stories about how women and men lived, new interpretations as well of the events and meanings in the history of feminism. Do we want the Christina Hoff Sommerses of the world to have free rein in constructing the stories of academic feminism? Certainly, it is a valid enterprise to critique the discourse of her history—indeed, much influenced by poststructuralist problematizations, that is just what I attempted to do. But, it is equally valid and important for alternative histories of academic feminism to be written, histories (however mediated) that attempt to get at the "real" events, ideas, and meanings of the formation, spread, and contradictions within women's studies. As Annette Kolodny writes, we must "take responsibility for recovering our history, lest others write it for us" ("Dancing" 464).[27]

The survival of feminism—of feminism as an ongoing history-in-process with a future—depends in part on our ability to reproduce ourselves in subsequent generations and to pass on what we have learned so that the wheel does not need to be reinvented every generation. As Elaine Showalter writes about women writers denied access to histories of women's writing, "each generation of women writers has found itself, in a sense, without a history, forced to rediscover the past anew, forging again and again the consciousness of their sex" (*Literature* 10). I am not suggesting that women's history and more specifically the history of feminism are fixed "truths" that must be handed down like precious heirlooms or that succeeding generations should be clones of their feminist foremothers (and occasional forefathers). Indeed, such fixity would induce stagnation and rebellion. History, as a result of multiple interpretive acts, is necessarily fluid, ever changing in relation to the heuristic needs of the present and the future. Moreover, in the family romance of political movements, new generations of feminists will inevitably resist as well as build upon the authority of the old in order to clear a space for new stories impelled by new historically specific conditions.[28] This fluidity and need for change, even conflictual change, should not obscure the politics of history writing as a form of memory. The loss of collective memories, of myriad stories about the past, has contributed greatly to the ongoing subordination of women. The unending, cumulative building of broadly defined histories of women, including histories of feminism, is a critical component of resistance and change. As Leslie Marmon Silko writes in *Storyteller*, "with these stories we will survive" (247).

I invoke Silko's celebration of the political imperative of storytelling on purpose. The final danger of perpetual problematization is its implicit attack on narrative in general and on history writing as a narrative act in particular. The poststructuralist critique of narrative as inherently authoritarian or totalizing implicitly condemns narrative history writing as part of the economy of the same, as the reproduction, not the transgression, of the symbolic order. However, the insistence of many minority women on the centrality of narrative to communal survival ought to call a halt to any wholesale condemnation of narrative as a reactionary or totalitarian epistemological mode. Louise Erdrich, for example, says in an interview, "I'm hooked on narrative. . . . Why is it that, as humans, we have to have narrative? I don't know, but we do. . . . The people in our families make everything into a story. They love to tell a good story. People just sit and the stories start coming, one after another" (Schumacher, "Marriage" 29–30). Toni Morrison in some sense answers Erdrich's question: "Narrative is one of the ways in which knowledge is organized. I have always thought it was the most important way to transmit and receive knowledge. I am less certain of that now—but the craving for narrative has never lessened, and the hunger for it is as keen as it was on Mt. Sinai or Calvary or the middle of the fens" ("Memory" 51). In writing the history of her mother Rose Chernin, the well-known communist organizer, Kim Chernin recalls how "Very softly, whispering, I say to her, 'Mama, tell me a story.' . . . And yes, with all the skill available to me as a writer, I will take down her tales and tell her story" (*Mother's House* 17). Poet Irena Klepfisz in *Keeper of Accounts* faces the painful gaps in her memories of the Holocaust:

> So much of history   seems
> a gaping absence   at best a shadow
> longing   for some greater
> definition   which will never come
> for what is burned   becomes air
> and ashes   nothing more.
>
> (90)

And yet her long poem is a sustained effort in which lyric and narrative collaborate, however haltingly and inadequately, to testify to the history that has become "air," to recover the knowledge of what was lost as a precondition for living fully in the present and the future.[29] To forget the Holocaust is to risk its return.

The insistence on narrative as a mode of knowing essential for survival is not restricted to minority women whose cultural ties to the oral tradition remain strong. In her prose/poem/essay, "It Was a Dark and Stormy Night," for example, Ursula LeGuin argues that telling stories fulfills the needs of and for memory, testimony, and survival. Narrative staves off fear of the "dark and stormy night," of all the unnamed horrors of history, of death itself. "It remains true," writes Gayle Greene, "that stories, stories about the self, stories about women and about women's selves, had enormous power and continue to have power in the creation of feminist consciousness" ("Looking at History" 11). In *The Pleasures of Babel*, Jay Clayton sees the "turn to story" in American minority writers as the avant-garde of a return to narrative in many contemporary postmodern writers. The proliferation of what he calls, after Lyotard, multiple "local narrative communities" constitutes a kind of postmodern resistance to the "grand narratives" produced by the Enlightenment and its aftermath. Narrative serves in this regard as a localized site for the productions of multiple meanings. Narrative can serve ideological and authoritarian ends, Clayton asserts, but it can also function as a meaning-making discourse of resistance for many different kinds of communities, including feminist ones.[30]

Clayton's perspective on narrative provides the basis for a strong defense of narrative as an interpretive discourse that feminists can use for telling stories about the history of feminism itself. Narrative history is one of a number of transgressive strategies feminists can use to resist or subvert the stories of feminism told by various sectors of the dominant culture. To counter ideological narratives of feminism's alterity, feminists can tell counterstories that chart their exclusions, affirm their agency (however circumscribed or complicit), and continually (re)construct their identities as feminists. Morrison's defense of narrative for African Americans can be adapted to the project of feminist history writing of feminism: "We are the subjects of our own narrative, witnesses to and participants in our own experience, and, in no way coincidentally, in the experience of those with whom we have come in contact. We are not, in fact, 'other.' We are choices" ("Unspeakable" 9). Feminist history writing of feminism can be topical and spatial, as Giana Pomata has shown.[31] But narrative discourse can also represent the "choice" to formulate not *the* but many "subjects of feminism," many identities and stories, as an inscription of the desire to insist upon a feminist presence in the making of history.

THE QUESTION OF DESIRE IN AND FOR HISTORY

Thus far, my discussion of feminist history writing has put aside an important issue: desire. What does desire have to do with either the dangers or the necessities of feminists writing history, specifically histories of feminism? Theorists of narrative from Laura Mulvey to Teresa de Lauretis, Leo Bersani, Hayden White, Peter Brooks, and Jay Clayton have written positively and negatively about the entanglement of narrative and desire as a mode of knowing. Brooks in *Reading for the Plot*, for example, examines "the nature of narration as a form of human desire," one in which the "need to tell" functions as "a primary human drive that seeks to seduce and to subjugate the listener, to subjugate him in the thrust of a desire that never can quite speak its name" (61). Clayton in *The Pleasures of Babel*, on the other hand, refuses to see desire in narrative as a process of inevitable subjection. Rather, he regards the power of narrative desire as neither good nor bad, policing nor liberating in and of itself. He argues for the historicization of narrative desire, for an analysis of how it works in given situations as a positive or negative force, whether as a disciplining structure or as a means of empowerment.[32]

To consider the implications of this linkage between narrative and desire for feminist historiography, let us take *desire* out of the realm of the purely erotic wherein it is mostly confined in theoretical discourse (Clayton is an important exception). "To know," in the biblical sense, means to encompass or possess sexually, a conflation of perception and sexuality that serves as a cornerstone of psychoanalytic configurations of oedipal desire as a foundation of subjectivity, as Brooks's *Reading for the Plot* particularly illustrates. But recall that the appeal of knowledge in another, muted biblical sense impels Eve's tasting of the apple from the Tree of Knowledge of Good and Evil. Eve's desire for knowledge prefigures the drive for literacy, for access to books and education, that runs as a powerful current through the long history of intellectual women, as well as of women who struggle for the basics of literacy.[33] Harriet Jacobs powerfully configures another desire, the longing for freedom in *Incidents in the Life of a Slave Girl*, while feminists like Sheila Rowbotham have articulated the desire of any oppressed group to "shatter the self-reflecting world which encircles it and, at the same time, project its own image onto history" (*Women's Consciousness* 27).

The debates, divisions, and contradictions within feminism as it projects its own image onto history reflect different formulations of the politics of desire and its relation to historical narrative. On the one hand, the outer-directed, shattering, and projecting gaze of feminism embodies a will-to-empowerment, a desire to overturn patriarchal hegemonies and to make its mark on and in history. On the other hand, the critical inner gaze of feminism fears its own will-to-power, its capacity to repeat the power structures it sets out to transgress.[34] The insistence on making history, on narrative as a potentially transformative mode of knowing, expresses the desire to transfer power to those who have not had it. The problematizing of history making reflects the dangers of empowerment as a reestablishment of power over others. The one affirms the political importance and possibilities of agency and, by extension, of the "subject of feminism." The other finds in the notion of agency a naive unawareness of how subjectivity is always already constructed within ideology, within the hegemonic discourses of the symbolic order.

These contradictory desires and differing notions of agency play themselves out in the debate between Linda Gordon and Joan Scott in a 1990 issue of *Signs* in which the two prominent feminist historians review each other's books (*Heroes of Their Own Lives: The Politics and History of Family Violence* and *Gender and the Politics of History*) and respond to each other's reviews. Since the publication of *Woman's Body, Woman's Right: A Social History of Birth Control in America* (1976), Gordon has been widely known for her resistance to a "victim" paradigm of women's history and her advocacy of a complicated notion of social control that encourages the analysis of how women maneuver within the specific constrictions they face. In her response to Scott's attack, she writes that she uses "gender to describe a power system in which women are subordinated through relations that are contradictory, ambiguous, and conflictual—a subordination maintained against resistance, in which women have by no means always defined themselves as other, in which women face and take choices and action despite constriction" ("Response" 852). Scott, on the other hand, has been known for her advocacy of poststructuralism as a basis for writing history, particularly for Foucauldian concepts of coercive discursive systems and subjectivity as an effect, not a autonomous cause, of discourse. Scott argues for a "different conceptualization of agency," which "would see agency not as an attribute or trait inhering in the will of autonomous individual subjects, but as a discursive effect" ("Review" 851).[35]

Scott praises Gordon's *Heroes of Their Own Lives* for its account of an area of women's experience that has not been much explored: "she conjures up something of the experience of neglect, abuse, battering, and incest for those involved" ("Review" 848). She is more enthusiastic about Gordon's analysis of how certain elements of this experience were constructed as "social problems" in the period from the 1880s through the 1960s, constructions that ironically "frequently contributed to the dissolution of the very households that, in principle, were supposed to be saved" by the social workers (849). But she faults what she sees as Gordon's "reading strategy," which she thinks "does not try to analyze closely the case-workers' accounts" (850).

Moreover, Scott is not persuaded by what she sees as Gordon's secondary argument for the agency of these victimized women. Not the "will of autonomous individual subjects," this agency should be regarded, Scott believes, as a "discursive effect, in this case, the effect of social workers' constructions of families, gender, and family violence" (851). Although Gordon nowhere equates agency with autonomy, Scott identifies Gordon's book with a humanist feminism that regards women as autonomous subjects who resist the forces of social control. The "major achievement of the book," Scott believes, resides in its presentation of "the story of this process" that "constructs possibilities for and puts limits on specific actions undertaken by individuals and groups" (852). But she thinks the "book would have been even better . . . if it had explicitly articulated in a more sophisticated conceptual frame, one that refused the oppositional thinking of overly simple theories of social control (either domination or autonomous action) and thus moved beyond the individualistic notions of heroes and their agency implied by the title of the book" (852). Gordon's title, in Scott's view, marks the book as unsophisticated, caught up in "more [of] a wish than a historical reality, more [of] a politically correct formulation than anything that can be substantiated by the sources" (850).

Scott's lukewarm praise for and attack of Gordon's book, as well as her response to Gordon's review, recapitulate many of the conventional themes of poststructuralist problematizations of feminist history writing. There is the belittling of history that presents a *story* of women's experience, with its implicit attack on narrative itself as an inferior mode of historical writing. There is the insistence on problematizing everything, on linguistic and discursive analysis. There is the reduction of agency and subjectivity to *effects* of discourse, a Foucauldian emphasis on the construction of policing discursive formations, a dismissal of notions of empowerment, and a disregard for forms of opposition. There is the charge of naiveté and fear of reproducing the economy of the same. Above all there is the privileging of poststructuralist theory as *the* radical ground of feminist activity. Echoing, perhaps unconsciously, the familiar and unanswerable defense of psychoanalysis (if you don't agree, it's because you are resisting), Scott concludes her response by reducing Gordon's statements to a resistance to poststructuralist theory:

> Where does this resistance to poststructuralist theory come from? Why is there such resistance at a moment in the history of feminism when—if we are to formulate new kinds of political strategies—we need to understand how, in all their complexity, collective and individual differences are constructed, how, that is, hierarchies and inequalities are produced?. . . Since it is the nature of feminism to disturb the ground it stands on, even its own ground, the resistance to theory is a resistance to the most radical effects of feminism itself. ("Review" 859)

Whereas Scott's underlying agenda appears to be the promotion of poststructuralist feminist history, Gordon's review and response argues for the empowering effects of different theoretical perspectives and methodologies for feminism. She praises Scott's challenge to objectivism and her demonstration that "studying language is vital" to the historical enterprise ("Review" 854–55). But she is not convinced by what she sees as the more ambitious aim of Scott's book: to establish "that language is and must be the only subject of history and that through linguistic analysis gender will be revealed" (854). Gordon locates the strengths of the book in the essays on French history and its weaknesses in Scott's critique of historiography that assumes a "'reality' 'behind' the language" (856–57). Ultimately, she remains unpersuaded that poststructuralist theory is the *only* social theory that can write nonobjectivist history sensitive to the linguistic structures of meaning. Gordon stresses the importance of a subjectivist epistemology, linguistic analysis, and the use of many kinds of social theory, including (but not exclusively) poststructuralist theory.

Instead of advocating a history that collapses into the metanarrative of how "hierarchies and inequalities are produced," Gordon argues for complicating the "top-down" model of social control with one that acknowledges societal constructions of power relations, but does not reduce women to effects of discourse. Rather, she proposes a notion of agency that emphasizes women's negotiations within constriction—not a belief in women's always already autonomous empowerment, but instead a notion of women's struggle within the terms of a patriarchal system to survive as more than passive victim. In doing so, she theorizes a kind of history writing that acknowledges subjectivism and linguistic constructionism, but embraces the power of narrative as a form of feminist activism and does not reduce the Real to language. She stands by her references to "'real' family violence" as something beyond the "competing understandings of those assaults" ("Response" 853). "One of the things I like about writing history," Gordon concludes in her response, "is drawing meaning from stories, in the ambiguous, metaphorical, narrative language of daily life" (852).

WRITING FEMINIST HISTORIES: IN THE PLURAL

The *Signs* debate between Linda Gordon and Joan Scott demonstrates more than the oppositions between agency and its critique, between the will-to-empowerment and resistance to the will-to-power. It also acts out a contemporary struggle within feminism for the authority to "make history." *Who* will speak for feminism? In what way? Gordon makes no claim for exclusive authority. Her praise of Scott's book, so different from her own, invites the multiplication of feminist historiographic methodologies—what I am calling feminist histories *in the plural*. Scott, on the other hand, insists upon a singular methodology, her own poststructuralist one. Her denial of the subject of feminism, of agency, ultimately takes the form of a performative insistence on her own subjectivity and agency, one that dismisses other voices as naive, as poststructurally incorrect, and as insufficiently radical. Scott bases her defense of poststructuralist historiography in a critique of a feminist "politics that sets and enforces priorities, represses some subjects in the name of the greater importance of others, naturalizes certain categories, and disqualifies others" (*Gender* 9). But ironically, her attack on Gordon's non-poststructuralist historiography takes the form of enforcing a set of (poststructuralist) priorities and repressing other social theory in stressing the importance of poststructuralist theory. However much Scott warns against the politics of priority and dismissal, her own theorizing about historiography engages in a politics of dismissal and the suppression of heterogeneity.

Scott is not alone in this contradictory impulse to establish poststructuralism—which often promotes heterogeneity, multiplicity, difference, and open-ended *differánce*—as the single pathway to revolutionary Truth. Other advocates of poststructuralism, particularly in literary studies, all too often perpetuate the binary of winners and losers in their attempt shape the future of feminism. This performance of a poststructuralist will-to-power jars wildly against poststructuralist problematizations of hegemony. But poststructuralist feminists, of course, are not alone in the performance of monologic advocacy. In "The Race for Theory," Barbara Christian is as relentlessly dismissive of poststructuralist theory as Scott is for it. The promotion of feminist histories *in the plural* requires vigilance, not only openness to others but self-reflective interrogation of one's own premises.

Feminist histories of the conflict between "French poststructuralism" and "American feminism" are a case in point for the tendency of history writing to fall unself-consciously into allegorical narratives of winners and losers, as well as for the urgency of problematizing such reductionisms. This conflict has achieved near-formulaic status in the scores of essays that address the meeting, opposition, and mingling of these different feminist traditions. The allegorical trope that governs these narratives is the agon, the dualistic struggle that is overdetermined by a (post)colonial discourse in intellectual history about the influence of continental theory on the naive, empirically oriented Americans.[36] By way of example, I want to focus on three such accounts, in all of which Kristeva figures curiously as invisible presence, feminist hero, or demon: Elaine Showalter's "Women's Time, Women's Space: Writing the History of Feminist Criticism" (1983/84); Toril Moi's *Sexual/Textual Politics: Feminist Literary Theory* (1985); and Gayatri Chakravorty Spivak's "French Feminism in an International Frame" (1981).

Both Showalter's and Moi's accounts of the conflict use historical markers that create what we might call, after Barthes, a "history effect." Phrases in Showalter's essay like "in the second phase of this history," "in 1968," "since 1975," "since the late 1970s, "within the past year or two" punctuate the loose narrative, creating a sensation of chronological progression, and establishing an overall effect of historicization. Similarly, Moi's discussion of Anglo-American feminist criticism (chapters 2–4) carefully follows the chronology of publication and passage through the decades from the late 1960s into the early 1980s, with the arrival of poststructuralist theory in the United States. Both writers borrow the generalizing discourse of periodization from history to characterize evolving phases in feminist criticism. Like historical periodization in general, these chronologies tend to erase the heterogeneity of feminist criticism at any given point in time. Moreover, their historical narratives dissolve into allegorical representations of their own theoretical positions within the field whose history they purport to tell. Consequently, the effect (though undoubtedly not the conscious intention) of the "history effect" in their narratives is to intervene in the debates of the present as a way of shaping the future of feminist criticism.

The allegorical foundation of Showalter's "Women's Time, Women's Space" begins in her unacknowledged displacement of Kristeva's "Women's Time," to which her title alludes. Showalter's chronology of stages covertly invokes and revokes Kristeva's dialectical progression of feminism in France, which she sees beginning in the humanist project of inserting women into the "men's time" of history, moving on to a terrorist assertion of feminine difference in "women's time," and heading in a utopian direction of individual mysticism beyond men's time or women's time. Where Kristeva's "women's time" is a space outside history (which is constituted in and through the phallocentric symbolic order), Showalter's "women's time" is the separate *history* of women, which is distinct from the history of men, but just as much a part of history as the story of men. Traditional periodizations of literary history do not work for women writers, Showalter asserts, because the patriarchal exclusions of women from the public sphere constituted historical conditions that made their writing different. Paralleling the critique of traditional periodization in the field of women's history,[37] gynocriticism develops a separate periodization based in "women's time." Showalter's title and its related argument thus function to assert her position within an unstated agon between herself and Kristeva, between an American feminist criticism and a French feminist theory.

Showalter does openly acknowledge, and even gestures generously toward, the importance of French feminist theory within the evolving history of American feminist criticism. Indeed, in narrating its arrival, she rejects the all-too-prevalent binarist accounts of French/American conflict: "In writing the history of feminist criticism, I want to avoid, however, such a hostile polarization of French and American feminist discourse, arid theory and crude empiricism, obscurantism or essentialism. In formulating or endorsing such hierarchical binary oppositions, we not only fall into the old dualistic traps, but genuinely misrepresent the much more complex and nuanced reality of feminist critical practice" (36). She argues instead for a historical narrative that recognizes how French and American feminist discourses in the United States have been "enriched by dialectical possibilities," mutually influencing each other as they established two modes of feminist critical discourse: gynocriticism (the historically oriented study of women writers) and gynesis (the theoretically oriented analysis of the feminine Other in discourse, especially in male texts).

In the final portion of her narrative, however, when she recounts how feminist criticism "since 1980" has in general "moved inexorably . . . back into standard critical time," Showalter's implicit privileging of gynocriticism becomes evident. By the end of the essay, "standard critical time," "men's time," and poststructuralist theory have conflated into a single category, "modern criticism," to which she opposes "feminist criticism." "What is the relationship between feminist criticism and modern criticism?" she asks (41). Her answer is that fear of and resistance to the feminine and feminism fueled the rise of "modern theory." Paradoxically, "modern theory" has more recently turned in desire toward feminist criticism, to feed off its energy and ability to lead the "way out of the labyrinth of indeterminacy, non-interference and self-referentiality post-structuralism has built for itself" (42). Her narrative concludes with a warning to feminists: "Insofar as the production of theory is now the business of modern criticism, there will be increased pressure on feminist criticism to accommodate itself more and more to prevailing terminologies and systems, abandoning in the process the political priorities and concerns for the personal that have made it effective in the past" (42).

What interests me here is not the accuracy or inaccuracy of Showalter's history, but how her own theoretical position within feminism heuristically governs the narrative. Her final opposition between feminist criticism and modern criticism subtly aligns feminist poststructural theory (gynesis) with "modern criticism" and thereby removes it from the category of "feminist criticism," which is implicitly represented by gynocriticism. The "dialectical enrichment" she promoted earlier in the essay between gynocriticism and gynesis recedes, displaced by the binaries of feminist criticism and modern theory, women's time and men's time, feminism and poststructuralism. History becomes synchrony, narrative becomes allegory in a chronological account of feminist criticism that overtly legitimates gynesis along with gynocriticism, but covertly promotes one kind of feminism over another.

Moi's openly polemical narrative of feminist criticism has none of the attempted pluralism of Showalter's narrative.[38] Like Joan Scott's, Moi's advocacy of poststructuralist heterogeneity inscribes a performance of singularity—her history as an erasure of any one else's. Moi's book opens with a feminist parable that demonstrates the need to "rescue" Virginia Woolf for feminism by reading her within a poststructuralist rather than a realist framework. This introduction openly allegorizes the agonistic binary of French and American feminisms in the form of an attack on Showalter's chapter on Woolf in *A Literature of Their Own* as a demonized metonymy of the reactionary humanism of American feminist criticism. Moi aligns what she sees as Showalter's preference for bourgeois realism over Woolf's modernism with "Lukács's Stalinist views of the 'reactionary' nature of modernist writing" (6). Showalter, and by extension the American feminist criticism she represents, is trapped in the "totalizing, humanist aesthetic" characteristic of realism, naively holding on to a belief in the unitary self and the referentiality of language. "What feminists such as Showalter and Holly fail to grasp," Moi writes, "is that the traditional humanism they represent is in effect part of patriarchal ideology" (8). Poststructuralism, represented especially by Kristeva, offers the only escape from this "crypto-Lukácsian perspective implicit in much contemporary feminist criticism" (8).

Moi's introduction thus announces in advance the teleological direction of the historical narrative that follows. Her diachronic narrative of the evolution of Anglo-American feminist criticism is heuristically governed by the allegory of progress. The Anglo-American feminists, caught in the economy of the same, repeating the patriarchal ideology of bourgeois humanism, await the revelations of poststructuralism, which starts coming across the Atlantic in the late 1970s. The four chapters on Anglo-American feminist criticism proceed chronologically, beginning with those who worked for social and political change in the 1960s, moving through the "images of women" criticism and gynocriticism of the 1970s, and ending with the inklings of "theoretical reflections" in the late 1970s, which paved the way for the introduction of poststructuralist feminist theory.

Moi does not actually narrate the influx of poststructuralist feminism into Anglo-American feminist criticism. Rather, the structure of the book itself suggests the book's promotion of poststructuralism. Part II, which consists of four chapters, one each on Lacan, Cixous, Irigaray, and Kristeva, contains far fewer markers of historical discourse. Not a chronology, it is rather a presentation of theorists in ascending order of Moi's approval. Although she provides something of a materialist critique of Kristeva, Kristeva's work comes the closest to what Moi herself advocates and thus occupies the climactic position in Moi's teleological narrative governed by the allegory of progress. Part II of the book functions to rescue the Anglo-American feminism surveyed in Part I from its reactionary tendencies. "The central paradox of Anglo-American feminist criticism," she writes, "is thus that despite its often strong, explicit engagement, it is *in the end* not quite political enough . . . in the sense that its radical analysis of sexual politics still remains entangled with depoliticizing theoretical paradigms" (87). In Moi's agonistic narrative, French feminist theory carries not only the day in feminist criticism but also the torch of true feminist radicalism. Even more overtly than Showalter's account, Moi's history of feminist criticism collapses into allegories of struggle and progress in which poststructuralist feminism is the winner and what she calls bourgeois humanist feminism is the loser, a victory that her own historical narrative attempts to ensure.

Spivak's "French Feminism in an International Frame"—a set of theoretical reflections that makes no attempt at historical narrative—uses fragmentary stories as allegories that contain a critique of western feminism and a demand for a genuine discontinuity and heterogeneity. Stories of a Sudanese woman writing about clitoridectomy, of herself "choosing" English as a profession in Bengal, of the washerwomen on her grandfather's estate, of Kristeva traveling in China serve as occasions that probe the relation between history and identity, between historically specific social orders and the destinies available to women within them. The allegorical function of these fragments is to disrupt the discourses of western feminism, particularly the agon between French and Anglo-American feminist criticism. Within an international frame that includes the Third World, the great debates in western feminism appear homogeneous, particularly in their inability to incorporate the "excess" of excluded Third World women (141, 152). This "inbuilt colonialism of the First World against the Third World" (152) is allegorically evident in Kristeva's *About Chinese Women*, a book based on a short trip to China in which she reports a millennia of Chinese history, with "sweeping historiographic scope," with "no encroachment of archival evidence," with "the most stupendous generalizations" and "no primary research" (137–38). Spivak's critique of Kristeva's primitivist orientalism is scathing, all the more so because it uncovers how the poststructuralist unraveling of unitary identities that Kristeva directs at the West vanishes in the face of her desire for a totalized identity for Chinese women throughout the millennia. The very insight of French feminism in its critique of humanism—its insistence on discontinuity, heterogeneity, and excess—is lost when the First World faces the Third World.[39]

What Spivak's critique of Kristeva and western feminism in general helps bring into view is how historical narratives about the clash between Anglo-American and French feminisms function covertly as theoretical arguments whose telos is to defeat other perspectives. Feminist histories of feminism can, in other words, all too easily become a narrative of winners and losers rather than a story of multiple, heterogeneous voices. In the spirit of Spivak's critique of western feminism, the reduction of feminisms to a single feminism in any historical account erases differences, obscures heterogeneity, and effectively denies voice to those who have less power.

Spivak's deconstruction of agonistic narratives of western feminism, however, falls into the same trap she critiques by replacing the binary of Anglo-American and French feminisms with the binary of western and Third World Feminisms. As in the accounts of Showalter and Moi, Spivak ignores the many voices of American feminists—particularly those of women of color, lesbians, and Jewish women—who have since the 1970s been insisting on the multiple positionalities of women in relation to different systems of alterity. Showalter names such influential gynocritical feminists as Alice Walker, Barbara Smith, Audre Lorde, and Bonnie Zimmerman, but her history of feminist criticism does not acknowledge how these feminists launched a major problematization of gynocriticism for its homogenization of women. Moi justifies their absence from her account with a gesture of double dismissal: "Some feminists might wonder why I have said nothing about black or lesbian (or black-lesbian) feminist criticism in America in this survey. The answer is simple: this book purports to deal with the theoretical aspects of feminist criticism. So far, lesbian and/or black feminist criticism have presented exactly the same *methodological* and *theoretical* problems as the rest of Anglo-American feminist criticism" (86). And Spivak herself does not even mention the "Third World" and lesbian challenges *within* the West to feminist racism, classism, and heterosexism. Her (poststructuralist) refusal of narrative allows her to identify certain theoretical positions within western feminism and drop out other voices whose existence would complicate her own allegorical binary of western and Third World feminisms.

What lesson does the cluster of texts by Showalter, Moi, and Spivak hold for feminist historiography? It demonstrates the difficulty of and necessity for feminist histories *in the plural* instead of feminist history. Rather than seeking *the* definitive narrative of feminism, or of any given moment in feminism, we must acknowledge the potential for many localized narratives of feminism, none of which can claim to represent the totality of feminist history. This means that we need not only to foster the existence of many voices engaged in the dual tasks of making feminist history but also to acknowledge in our own histories the possibilities of other voices (re)telling the stories we have told. Linda Hutcheon argues for history *in the plural* in her notion of postmodern narrative history, which she sees located in the "paradox of the desire for and the suspicion of narrative mastery—and master narratives" (*Politics of Postmodernism* 64). In postmodern history writing, "the narrativization of past events is not hidden; the events no longer seem to speak for themselves" (72), and the "seamlessness of the join between the natural and the cultural, the world and the text" is always open to interrogation (53). This awareness of the historian as narrator makes possible "the histories (in the plural) of the losers as well as the winners, of the regional (and colonial) as well as the centrist, of the unsung as well as the much sung few, and I might add, of women as well as men" (66).

Hutcheon's "histories (in the plural)" needs another turn of the screw, however, to avoid the construction of winners and losers. We need to extend the necessity of heterogeneity to histories written by the marginalized (whether postmodern or not). We need what Radhakrishnan calls a kind of "totality" based not on the narrative totalization of any given history but rather the totality of different narratives about that history:

> My objective here . . . is to suggest both that no one discourse or historiography has the ethicopolitical legitimacy to represent the totality, and that the concept of "totality" should be understood not as a pregiven horizon but as the necessary and inevitable "effect" or function of the many relational dialogues, contestations, and asymmetries among the many positions . . . that constitute the total field. (*Diasporic Mediations* 189)[40]

For Radhakrishnan, such totality requires a negotiation between poststructuralist problematization and feminist praxis. Without poststructuralist theory, "feminist historiography . . . is in danger of turning into a superficial reversal of forces of power that would leave untouched certain general and underlying economies of meaning and history" ("Feminist Historiography" 189). But feminist historiography also needs an "affirmative programmatic," a "determinate politics" based in "the intentional/agential production of meaning as change" (189, 203). Feminist historiography is different, he concludes, "precisely because it is still interested in creating and transforming history," with "making and doing history" (202–3).

The hegemonic posturing of some poststructuralist feminists, however, demonstrates that poststructuralist theory by itself is not sufficient protection against the production of histories of winners and losers in feminism, as the texts I have discussed by Joan Scott, Moi, and even Spivak illustrate. The "totality" of histories Radhakrishnan advocates requires not only the "affirmative programmatic" of feminists producing histories *in the plural* but also the widest possible range of self-reflective problematizations, which would certainly include but not be limited to poststructuralist interrogations.

The promotion of multiple feminist histories runs the risk, of course, of pluralism, of obscuring the structures of power within and outside the academy that constitute some histories as "more equal" than others in the brave new world of feminism. "Pluralism," Linda Gordon warns, "was never merely a recognition of variation but a masking of inequality" ("Review" 858). Which histories of feminism become canonical? Which fall into obscurity? Which stories do the media pick up and disseminate? Which do they ignore? Who tells the story and what is her/his position?

In spite of the risks of pluralism, however, I believe that negotiating the active and reflective modes of feminist historiography opens up the potential for feminists to engage in constructing histories *in the plural*, for recognizing that no single history can encounter the full dimensionality of the Real, and for reflecting upon our own processes of mediation. I have defended two positions that are all too often set up as mutually exclusive oppositions: the need to make history by writing history as a political act; and the need to problematize that activity so as to avoid the creation of grand narratives that reproduce the totalizing histories of winners in which the stories of losers are lost. Instead of *either/or*, I promote *both/and*, where the active and reflective supplement each other in creative negotiation. Feminist histories (in the plural) of feminism (in the plural) are essential for negotiating the interplay between action and reflection and between the Real and its textualizations.

Craving Stories:
Narrative and Lyric in Feminist Theory
and Poetic Practice

Narrative is one of the ways in which knowledge
is organized. I have always thought it was the
most important way to transmit and receive
knowledge. I am less certain of that now—but the
craving for narrative has never lessened, and the
hunger for it is as keen as it was on Mt. Sinai or
Calvary or the middle of the fens.
—*Toni Morrison, "Memory, Creation, and Writing"*

[It] is in this atmosphere of doubt and conflict
[in the modern age] that writers have now to create,
and the fine fabric of a lyric is no more fitted to
contain this point of view than a rose leaf to envelop
the rugged immensity of a rock. . . . It may be
possible that prose is going to take over—has,
indeed, already taken over—some of the duties
which were once discharged by poetry.
—*Virginia Woolf, "The Narrow Bridge of Art"*

THE NECESSITY of narrative—indeed the hunger for it—evident in these epigraphs resonates with the work of narrative theorists such as Robert Caserio and
Peter Brooks, both of whom identify narrative as an essential mode of understanding reality. But curiously, their insistence on narrative is out of tune with the
views of a number of poststructuralist theorists such as Roland Barthes, Julia
Kristeva, and Hélène Cixous as well as those whom they have influenced. These
theorists have variously suggested that what they loosely call "poetry," the "poetic," or the "lyric" is the avant-garde of modernity's disruptions of the symbolic
order. They often associate narrative (and often the novel or prose), on the other
hand, with a regressive representationalism or mimesis, with, in other words, the

tyranny of the symbolic order. For many feminist poststructuralists in particular, the lyric mode and poetry (especially avant-garde poetry) are tied to the repressed feminine, maternal, and pre-oedipal whereas narrative and the novel (especially the mimetic novel) are linked to the repressive masculine, paternal, and oedipal. None of these poststructuralists imagines doing away with narrative; rather, the point is that for many, a revolutionary poetic involves a transgressive disruption of narrative. Narrative may be necessary, inevitable, but its mode of discourse is to be resisted.

Not everyone, however, centers transgressions of the symbolic order in the lyric. Jay Clayton notes the widespread "turn to narrative" by many novelists of color, a phenomenon that challenges the prevailing association of the postmodern with a repudiation of narrative ways of knowing ("The Narrative Turn"). I would like to bring this insight back to the question of poststructuralist privileging of the lyric. The chasm between this craving for narrative and the refusal of it by some poststructuralist theorists suggests a blind spot on race and ethnicity that leads to a universalizing of an ethnocentric view of narrative as an authoritarian mode. Writers rooted in cultures where the oral tradition remains vital are more likely to regard narrative as food for the hungry rather than as the tyrant to be resisted. As Leslie Marmon Silko writes in her autobiographical prose/poem *Storyteller*:

> The storyteller keeps the stories
>   all the escape stories
>
>   she says "With these stories of ours
>   we can escape most anything,
>   with these stories we will survive."
>   (247)[1]

Moreover, some writers based in cultures for which the written predominates over the oral also exhibit the "turn to narrative" evident in many writers of color. In her prose/poem/essay, "It Was a Dark and Stormy Night," Ursula LeGuin argues that telling stories fulfills the necessities of memory, testimony, and survival. Associating narrative with comfort and survival, she says: "Tell me a story, great-aunt,/so that I can sleep./Tell me a story, Scheherazade,/so that you can live" (188). She highlights as well the function of tales to "bear witness" in citing the statement made by Primo Levi, an Auschwitz survivor: "Even in this place one can survive, and therefore one must want to survive, to tell the story, to bear witness" (193). Where LeGuin bases her defense of narrative in invocations of the oral tradition, Marjorie Perloff in *The Dance of Intellect* argues that postmodernism brings back into poetry the prosaic and narrative elements that had been suppressed in the modernist privileging of the lyric.[2] In postmodern poems, this "return of story" does not, Perloff hastens to add, mean a return of the linear plot, but the often fragmented, collagelike narratives expose the equation of poetry with the lyric as an ideological construct and deconstruct a modernist separation between the poetic and the everyday, between the timeless lyrical moment and the historical.

To these debates about narrative, I want to add the hypothesis that the need for narrative also reflects issues of positionality and marginalization. A historically produced cultural imperative exists that creates a need for narrative to resist or subvert the stories told by the dominant culture. Oppositional, transgressive discourses often embrace narrative as one among many strategies of resistance. To themselves, people made peripheral by the dominant society are not "marginal," "other." But to counter the narratives of their alterity produced by the dominant society, they must tell other stories that chart their exclusions, affirm their agency (however complicit and circumscribed), and continually (re)construct their identities. Morrison's defense of narrative for African Americans articulates a broadly defined "craving for narrative" that exists for many others: "We are the subjects of our own narrative, witnesses to and participants in our own experience, and, in no way coincidentally, in the experience of those with whom we have come in contact. We are not, in fact, 'other.' We are choices" ("Unspeakable Things" 9). Narrative can represent "choices," the insistent subjectivity of the "other," for marginalized groups in highly literate domains where the oral tradition is but a trace of a memory.

I will test this hypothesis by examining first the poststructuralist privileging of lyric over narrative and, second, women's poetic practice in the contemporary long poem. As a descendant of the epic and the autobiographical long poems of William Wordsworth and Walt Whitman, the twentieth-century long poem has been a defining genre for male poets—from the modernists through the "confessionals" and the postmodernists.[3] Before the current wave of feminism, however, epics and long poems by women were relatively uncommon, particularly for poems written by women who achieved any stature in the world of poetry. In the first half of the century H.D., Mina Loy, Gertrude Stein, and Gwendolyn Brooks were key pioneers in the twentieth-century women's long poem.[4] Since the 1960s there has been a phenomenal outpouring of poetic sequences and long poems by women. However much the twentieth-century long poem by both women and men has broken the conventions of narrative poetry through a reliance on lyric sequencing, fragmentation, and paratactic juxtapositions, narrative has remained a central issue for the long poem. I will suggest that the dialectical play between narrative and lyric in the women's long poem is overdetermined by a need for narrative based in traditional western exclusions of women from subjectivity and from the discourses of both myth and history. The result, I believe, has been a re-vision of narrative convention rather than a totalizing association of narrative with the tyranny of the social order.

PRIVILEGING THE POETIC AS TRANSGRESSIVE

In spite of a deconstructionist resistance to binaries, a number of poststructuralist theorists have reinstated preexisting and overlapping polarities between narrative and lyric, novel and poem, prose and poetry, representationalism and nonrepresentationalism, realism and surrealism, humanism and modernity. Such binaries are often asserted in ahistorical terms, without regard for the diachronic and synchronic variations in historically produced modes, genres, and discourses. Moreover, there is often an inexact slippage between modes (lyric, narrative) and genres (lyric poem, novel), or between broad discourses (poetry, prose) and specific forms (poem, fiction). What remains relatively constant in these formulations is the inevitability of an oppositional binary in which the lyric/poetic/nonmimetic continuously disrupts the narrative/novelistic/mimetic. In spite of the emphasis on process—the motion of textual practice—the revolutionary potential of language is statically located at the site of this lyric transgression of narrative.

This poststructuralist fixity is rooted in structuralism, a continuity evident in the evolution of Roland Barthes's work. In *Writing Degree Zero* (1953), for example, Barthes writes that "poetic language and prosaic language are sufficiently separate to be able to dispense with the very signs of their difference" (43). "There is no humanism of modern poetry," he continues. As the site of modernity, "This erect discourse [of modern poetry] is full of terror, that is to say, it relates man not to other men [the subject of prose], but to the most inhuman images in Nature: heaven, hell, holiness, childhood, madness, pure matter, etc." (50).

In *Mythologies* (1957), Barthes defines "myth" as "a mode of signification," a "type of speech" closely associated with a "signifying consciousness," history, and bourgeois ideology (109–11). He sets up poetry, especially contemporary poetry, as the discourse that exists in opposition to myth. Because myth is coercive, Barthes theorizes, "Poetry occupies a position which is the reverse of that of myth" (158). As "motivated" speech, "myth has an imperative, buttonholing character. . . . I am subjected to its intentional force" (124). As "interpellant speech," myth summons subjectivity, occupies it. Barthes's rhetoric sensationalizes the "I"'s battle against myth: "It thus appears that it is extremely difficult to vanquish myth from the inside: for the very effort one makes in order to escape its stranglehold becomes in its turn the prey of myth: myth can always, as a last resort, signify the resistance which is brought to bear against it" (135). "Revolutionary language proper," he warns the left, "cannot be mythical" (146). Poetry, he concludes, aids in his search for "the best weapon against myth" (135).[5]

In *Revolution in Poetic Language* (1974), Kristeva is perhaps less apocalyptic than Barthes, but no less "revolutionary" in her call for transgression against the symbolic order. However, for her, narrative and lyric remain inevitable aspects of all discourse, ever present but varying considerably in prominence. Weaving Lacanian psychoanalytic theory with semiotics, she regards the text as a "signifying practice" in which the two modalities of language—the semiotic and the symbolic (or thetic)—engage in dialectical interplay. With the semiotic, she associates the lyric, the feminine, the pre-oedipal; with the symbolic (thetic), she associates narrative, the masculine, the oedipal (23–30). Poetry tends to foreground the semiotic; prose, the symbolic. The revolutionary potential of modernity, she believes, resides most especially in the avant-garde writers whose experimentations with the semiotic register of language hold out the promise of disrupting the symbolic order and the Law of the Father.[6]

Revolution in Poetic Language works out this dialectical semiology in some detail in a series of chapters that interconnect textual practices, subjectivity, pre-oedipal and oedipal configurations, (male) avant-garde writers, and the revolutionary potential of the semiotic. In opposition to "poetic language" (also "modern poetic language" and "poetic practice"), Kristeva associates narrative, "whether theatrical or novelistic," with "verisimilitude" and "classical mimesis," with "denotation" and "meaning," with "systems of science and monotheistic religion," and with "political and social signifieds" (58–59, 88). Narrative genres in which the signifying function of the thetic/symbolic dominates include "mythic narratives, the epic, its theatrical substitutes, and even the novel (including its stage or screen adaptations), news reporting, newspaper columns, and other journalistic genres . . . legends, sagas, myths, riddles, idioms, cases, memoirs, tales, jokes" (92). In all these forms, the oedipally constituted structure of the family serves as the foundation for the "social organism" and for the "I" or "author" it signifies (90–93). As the thetic function of the text, narrative is "a projection of the paternal role in the family" (91). In *Powers of Horror*, Kristeva adds: "Narrative is, in sum, the most elaborate kind of attempt, on the part of the speaking subject, after syntactic competence, to situate his or her self among his or her desires and their taboos, that is at the interior of the oedipal triangle" (165).

While Kristeva associates narrative with the oedipal complex, she connects poetic practice, in contrast, with the pre-oedipal and the *chora*, the maternal body. Poetic language unleashes the semiotic's transgression of the symbolic order, initiates a "breach of the symbolic" (62–63). The semiotic cannot itself stand alone; rather it exists as a dimension within the symbolic in a state of perpetual opposition: "Though absolutely necessary, the thetic is not exclusive: the semiotic, which also precedes it, constantly tears it open" (62). As the avant-garde of revolutionary linguistic practice, "poetry is the *chora*'s guerilla war against culture," in the words of Calvin Bedient's summary of Kristeva's revolutionary poetic ("Kristeva and Poetry" 809).[7]

In "The Laugh of the Medusa" (1975), Cixous makes explicit what is largely implicit in Kristeva's formulation: namely, the connection of these binaries to the repression and liberation of the feminine and of women through *écriture féminine*. "Only the poets—not the novelists, allies of representationalism," she writes, can wield "the anti-logos weapon" and "blow up the Law"; for "poetry involves gaining strength through the unconscious and because the unconscious, that other limitless country, is the place where the repressed manage to survive: women" (250). Cixous's early work on Joyce (*The Exile of Joyce*) and her more recent work on Brazilian novelist Clarice Lispector suggest that the kind of *écriture féminine* she promotes in her essays is precisely what she finds in the avant-garde novels of these writers. It is not the novel per se to which Cixous objects, but rather the novel's tie to representationalism, which she in turn links to narrative. What she applauds in the novels of Joyce and Lispector is precisely their lyric resistance to narrative.

Barthes, Kristeva, and Cixous all variously associate narrative and the novel with a repressive social order that the lyric and the poem can potentially disrupt.

Their resistance to narrative is matched by much poststructuralist narrative theory. Leo Bersani, for example, argues in *A Future for Astyanax* (1984) that narrative is inherently authoritarian, allied to the state through its connection to mimesis and subject to perpetual disruptions from unruly desires. Representing a feminist/poststructuralist critique of narrative, Teresa de Lauretis suggests in *Alice Doesn't* that narrative is inseparable from an oedipal configuration of desire in which subjectivity is constituted as masculine. Many other feminist critics have focused on the pre-oedipal and/or the lyric as a site of past or potential disruption of oedipal narrative patterns.[8] Here, I would include my own essay, "Lyric Subversion of Narrative," in which I assumed the relationship between narrative and lyric in women's writing to be essentially conflictual and implicitly privileged lyric as the more subversive mode.

Writing *Penelope's Web: Gender, Modernity, H.D.'s Fiction* has made me rethink my own resistance to narrative and to that of much poststructuralist theory in general. Here I argued that the innovative lyric discourse H.D. forged in the imagist period to write herself out of the cultural script of sentimental poetess was intentionally impersonal and seemingly ungendered. During World War I, she began to write experimental narrative fiction that anticipates *écriture féminine* precisely so that she could represent herself as a woman, flagrantly gendered, in the text. Narrative—with its insistent representationalism and location of subjectivity within the coordinates of historical space and time—was essential to this experimental discourse. Where her early lyric had denied story, narrative invited the inscription of female identity as it is forged through engagement of the self with the social order. These narrative self-constructions in lyric prose made possible the complex symbiosis of narrative and lyric in H.D.'s epics and long poems of the 1940s and 1950s. In her prose, as well as in her later poetry, narrative and lyric are allies, not enemies—a play of different voices, not a war.

The implications of this turn to narrative for poststructuralist privileging of lyric as the site of subversion has its corollary in the debate about identity politics in current feminist theory. Some poststructuralist feminists such as Alice Jardine and Peggy Kamuf have seen great potential for feminist theory in the death of the Cartesian subject and modernity's dispersal of "identity." But others, such as Nancy K. Miller, have argued that it is premature to erase the issue of identity for those who have been denied the status of subject by the symbolic order. "Only those who have it [the status of subject] can play with not having it," Miller writes (*Subject to Change* 75).

It is similarly premature, I believe, to dismiss narrative for those who have been denied the authoritative voice and position of the storyteller by the dominant symbolic order. The poststructuralist need to shatter the "meaning" and "coherence" that narrative constructs may well originate in the privilege of those who have traditionally controlled the production of literate meanings. The attack on narrative's representationalism and mimetic reference to "real" experience risks ethnocentric cultural erasure of those writers who come from marginalized cultures rich in narrative traditions—like Silko's and Morrison's. Moreover, to miss the radical potential of narrative for writers of any group that has been absent in or trivialized by hegemonic historical discourses "prematurely forecloses the question of agency for them," to borrow Miller's formulation (*Subject to Change* 106).

Having defended narrative, I hasten to say as well that just as "identity" has often undergone revisionist transformation in women's writing, so narrative has often been subject to many forms of deconstruction and reconstruction. Many women writers have, for example, resisted what Virginia Woolf called in "Modern Fiction" the "tyranny of plot . . . *in the accepted manner*" (154, my emphasis)—that is, narrative conventions that replicate the ideological scripts of the social order. Secondly, as Rachel Blau DuPlessis demonstrates in *Writing beyond the Ending*, women writers have often reconfigured conventional narrative patterns so as to tell stories new to literary tradition, ones suited to the historically produced narratives of women's experiences and dreams. Thirdly, women writers whose cultures rely on a living oral tradition have transformed literate narrative by weaving strands of oral and written narrative conventions. And finally, as Morrison suggests in "Memory, Creation, and Writing": "Still, narrative is not and never has been enough, just as the object drawn on a canvas or a cave wall is never simply mimetic" (388). She argues that narrative does not preclude—in fact, it positively requires—other modes of knowing, modalities such as the metaphoric, the visual, the musical, and the kinesthetic. We might recognize in her evocation of the non-narrative the realm of the lyric, even the dimension of language that Kristeva identifies with the semiotic, the *chora*, the maternal body. Many women writers have engaged in a revisionist reconstitution of narrative by setting in play a collaborative dialogue between narrative and lyric.

CLAIMING THE DISCOURSES OF HISTORY AND MYTH

The contemporary women's long poem provides a rich testing ground for the relation of narrative and lyric in women's writing. At first glance, both generic convention and twentieth-century poetic practice suggest that women poets would readily disrupt narrative and foreground lyric discourse. The generic grid within which contemporary long poems are written and read includes the epic, a genre whose conventions largely precluded a woman occupying the place of bard in the community. Women would have every reason, one would suppose, to resist conventions of epic narrative within which WOMAN often functions without subjectivity as muse, booty, occasion for masculine quest, or idealized symbol.[9]

Moreover, influential twentieth-century long poems such as Pound's *Cantos*, T. S. Eliot's *The Waste Land* and *Four Quartets*, William Carlos Williams's *Paterson*, and Hart Crane's *The Bridge* broke with the narrative conventions of the epic through a variety of structural patterns based in the juxtaposition of lyric sequences. As Margaret Dickie puts it: "The long public poem has traditionally thrived on narrative or on argumentation for development, and the Modernists had no enthusiasm for either mode of expression. They intended to start the long poem with an image, a symbol, a fragmented translation, a mode of ecstatic affirmation. In short, they began to write the long poem as if it were to be an extended lyric" (*Modernist Long Poem* 11). M. L. Rosenthal and Sally M. Gall further argue that the modern poetic sequence (the term for the type of long poem they privilege) "usually includes narrative and dramatic elements, and ratiocinative ones as well, but its structure is finally lyrical" and "progressively liberated from a narrative or thematic framework" (*Poetic Sequence* 9, 11).

Other critics stress the modern long poem's existence within a horizon of expectations based in the epic (see Dembo, Michael Bernstein, James Miller). They consequently find narrative to be at least implicitly present, frequently as an interior quest narrative that underlies lyric juxtapositions. But whatever their differences, critics regularly see the foregrounding of lyric and muting of narrative as a consistent feature of twentieth-century long poems.[10] This feature, pioneered by the avant-garde practices that Kristeva favors, thus invites a reading of women's long poems in relationship to the poststructuralist privileging of lyric as a transgressive discourse.

The scores of long poems published by women since 1960 certainly confirm a widespread resistance to narrative as it had been formulated in the epic tradition and a frequent reliance on lyric juxtaposition and sequencing as structuring devices. But I am also struck by the positive and frequent presence of narrative in these poems as part of a project to assert female identity and agency in a world that would contain that subjectivity into forms of alterity. Narrative in these long poems takes different forms; to be aware of them, we need to understand the genre in its broadest sense.[11] Sometimes, the narrative function is direct—the poet tells a story, a sequence of events that occur within recognizable coordinates of space and time. Sometimes, the narrative dimension is indirect—the reader (re)constructs an implicit story in the ordering or juxtaposition of often loosely connected lyric sequences. And sometimes the narrative exists tenuously at the borderland between the long poem and a collection of discrete but related poems as a structuring principle that suggests a progression from one section or poem to another.

Whether narrated by the poet or the reader, these narrative functions may be mimetic or nonmimetic, may borrow heavily from or disrupt conventional narrative forms. In all cases, narrative, in Toni Morrison's words, "is not enough." Narrative and lyric (along with related pairs of prose and poetry, story and figure, mimetic and nonrepresentational, symbolic and semiotic) coexist dialogically—sometimes supportively or conflictually; sometimes both cooperatively and oppositionally; sometimes in a simultaneous play of voices or in a distinctly bifurcated text of prose and poetry. Whatever the shifting forms and dynamics of this collaboration, narrative and lyric cannot be accurately said to exist in a fixed binary where lyric is (always) the revolutionary force that transgresses (inherent) narrative tyranny. Rather, they coexist in a collaborative interchange of different and interdependent discourses.

In general, narrative functions in two main ways in women's contemporary long poems: first, as a claim to historical discourse and, second, as a claim to mythic discourse.[12] As the Greek roots for both *history* and *myth*[13] suggest, history and myth were initially not polar opposites—the one narrating fact, the other fiction. Both terms, moreover, are inseparable from narrative, and specifically, the kind of narrative associated with the epic tradition. As *story*, both history and myth are forms of human knowing that narrate movement (whether external or internal) through space and time (whether material or spiritual). Taken separately or together, both history and myth have provided the dominant modality of western epic poetry.

Long poems by men often use historical and mythic discourses,[14] but women's claim to these discourses in their contemporary long poems is overdetermined by their predominant exclusion from such discourses in the past, exclusions that have been identified and reversed by numerous feminist scholars in recent years. Women have always had a history, of course, but it is only in recent years, as a result of feminism, that women have begun to narrate that history in a systematic, sustained, and cumulative way—in a field ambiguously known as "women's history," incorporating both the past events of women's lives and the telling of those stories as a field in which women are the pioneering and predominant (though not exclusive) voices. The development of "women's history" in the academy parallels the reclamation of historical discourse in the contemporary women's long poem—compelled by similar reasons: a conviction that the lives of women have been systematically erased or trivialized in the dominant historical discourses; an insistence on the necessity for women to participate in the construction of history, so that women's stories, as well as women-as-storytellers, will not be lost and forgotten.

Women's exclusion from myth in many cultures is tied to the religious authority men have systematically claimed as an inherent function of their maleness. Women have always been, in one form or another, active participants in the religion of their cultures. But positions of sacred authority within the community have been (with a few exceptions) reserved for men in western tradition—at least in part because of the patriarchal repression of maternal deity and the gynophobic perception of women's bodies as polluted—to be feared and adored, desired and loathed.[15] The development of feminist theology and growth of movements to open positions of religious leadership to women in recent years parallel the reclamation of mythic discourse in the contemporary women's long poem—compelled by similar reasons: a belief that sacred texts have degraded or repressed the feminine; an insistence on the need for women to experience and narrate the sacred.

Derridean deconstructions of history and myth—of the metaphysics of Presence, of the "real" and referentiality—lie behind much of the poststructuralist resistance to narrative and privileging of lyric. But for those who have been excluded from the discourses of history and myth, such deconstructions, without corresponding reconstructions, are potentially regressive, accomplishing in the realm of theory the silencing that has already been a foundation of their historical positionalities. Derridean *différance*—the endless play of signifiers without reference to signifieds, the endless deferral of reference itself—is a concept that is richly useful for the deconstruction of representation. But by itself, as an end point, it has little to offer those whose survival depends upon the reconstruction of their own histories, the reclamation, through language, of their experience of the "real." Lacanian *jouissance*—the mystical/sexual pleasure beyond representation—is equally suggestive for the identification of revelatory moments that are unnarratable, unspeakable. But as teleological utopia, *jouissance* is not enough for those who need to (re)claim the religious authority to tell the sacred stories that have been appropriated, stolen, or erased. Both mythic and historical claims on the discourses of the "real" and the sacred require narrative—not as a mode of knowing to be resisted, but rather as one that empowers.

Focusing on the overdetermined function of narrative discourse—both historical and mythic—suggests three broad categories within which we can read the interplay of lyric and narrative in contemporary women's long poems. The first type of long poem is the one that claims a historical discourse, whether that history is personal or societal, in past time or present time, or some combination of the two. The second type is the kind that claims a mythic discourse, whether this involves revisionist or new forms of mythmaking. The third type is the poem that refuses the binary of history and myth to construct a fusion or intermingling of the real and the sacred. I suggest these categories not as fixed or intentional types, but rather as useful descriptors that facilitate an examination of the presence and function of narrative discourse in these poems.[16]

IRENA KLEPFISZ'S *KEEPER OF ACCOUNTS*

By way of example I will discuss the dialogically collaborative relation between narrative and lyric in a poem that makes a powerful claim to both historical and mythic discourse: Irena Klepfisz's *Keeper of Accounts* (1982), a long poem in four parts made up of discrete poems and sequences that cohere around the poet's project of survival in diaspora, specifically in the exile of the post-Holocaust world.[17] Narrative and lyric, prose and poetry, mimesis and fable, history and religion conjoin in a mosaic of discourses in which the different components cooperate dialogically in an inscription of the poet's subjectivity. To echo Kristeva's *"sujet en procès"* (*Revolution* 37), the textual practices of the poem construct a subject very much in process and on trial—caught in the processes of retrieving forgotten histories of a childhood in Poland, on trial as a Jew who survived the Holocaust by "passing" as a Polish child, who must now reclaim her Jewish legacy and identity.

Part I, "From the Monkey House and Other Cages," is a two-part narrative poem in which two female monkeys tell the story of their captivity in the timeless space of an unnamed zoo: the first, a daughter separated from her mother, forced into sex, and then separated from her baby; the second, a lonely monkey touched momentarily by the arrival and death of a rebellious monkey. Part II, "Different Enclosures," gets its title from the last line of Part I (24) and contains three poems in which the poet tells about her enclosure in the monotonies of clerical work and her dreams of freedom: "It is a story, I tell myself, at least/a story" (31). Part III,

"Urban Flowers," contains eight poems that center on the poet's efforts to grow flowers in the "inhospitable soil" of modern American urban life: "It is the stuff of mythology/both old and new. . . . now/we must burst forth with orange flowers/with savage hues of our captivity" (56, 49, 57). Part IV, "Inhospitable Soil," contains three lengthy sequences that, from the heuristic perspective of the poet's present life in rural Cherry Hill, New York, return to Poland before, during, and just after the war to tell the stories of capture, death, escape, and survival of the poet's family and friends. The poem, then, moves in circular fashion back in time from one kind of enclosure to another. Its repetitive rhythm is the interlocking imagery of and narrative movement from captivity to freedom, from sterility to regeneration, from death to survival.

Keeper of Accounts has a strong narrative drive in both its discrete parts and its overarching project, a drive that claims historical, mythic, and religious discourses. Many of the poems tell or contain powerful stories. The monkey narrators in Part I tell riveting tales of intimacy, separation, loss, rebellion, and death. These two stories prefigure the poet's (re)telling of events from her childhood in Part IV: the death of her father in the Uprising of the Warsaw Ghetto; the separation of mother and daughter, who was left first at a Catholic orphanage and then with a Polish peasant; the mother's struggle to survive alone in the woods; her friend Elza's escape, American adoption, and final suicide; her aunt's "passing" so as to help the Jews in the Ghetto and her courageous claim to Jewish identity in death.

These stories (and others—of office work, dreaming, and gardening) cohere into the larger narrative projects of the poem: the recovery of a forgotten past, the exodus from captivities, the reclamation of a Jewish identity and destiny. "So much of history," the poet writes in her final poem, an elegy for her aunt, "seems a gaping absence   at best a shadow/longing   for some greater/definition   which will never come" (90). As poet-historian, Klepfisz attempts to fill that gap, to locate the "vestige of one history forgotten and unattended" (63). While gardening, she thinks, "In the earth   are buried histories/irretrievable" (95). But her poem, written over a six-year period (1976–82) gradually retrieves the irretrievable, speaks the unspeakable histories of the Holocaust and its aftermath.

The return of this repressed history is gradual and painful, won through difficult discipline. It begins with the indirect displacement of fable: the story of the caged monkeys, animals who speak and feel as women and foreshadow the women who are treated as animals. Elements of the Holocaust story are present— the enclosure, the separation of mother and daughter, death of the beloved—but this zoo story does not yet trigger the memories of Poland. The poet must first understand her bond with the monkeys through an examination of her life as a clerical worker in Part II and then initiate the indirect process of regeneration by seeking the insistent urban flowers in Part III. Gardening in Cherry Hill and her mother's visit in the first poem of Part IV ("Glimpses of the Outside") bring about the first surfacing of painful childhood memories, which then follow in a rush of events in the next poem, *"Bashert."* As the Yiddish word for "inevitable, (pre)destined," *bashert* inscribes the poet's entrapment in history and her claim to freedom by acceptance of her Jewish identity. No longer must she deny who she is to survive, as she and Elza had to do in Poland; now she can accept the inevitability of her destiny, one tied to both the death and courage of her Aunt Gina, eulogized in the final poem, "Solitary Acts." "History," she writes, "keeps unfolding and demanding a response" (81). Her poem is that response, one that gradually allows her to confront the past that she and the present moment had forgotten. The larger narrative of the volume, consequently, is a therapeutic one.

Contributing to this healing process are the mythic and religious narratives that permeate the historical. *Keeper of Accounts* emphasizes Judaism's strong tie, as a religion, to history.[18] The Bible, especially the Torah, narrates the history of the Jewish people in relation to their God. Without explicit allusion, biblical resonances nonetheless abound in Klepfisz's "history." The Garden of Eden—with its narrative of desire, expulsion, and exile—exists within the poem's urban and rural gardens as an image of paradise lost and to be imperfectly regained in the poet's solitary labor. "I have been a dreamer   dreaming/of a perfect garden," the poet muses in the final poem (96). The story of the exodus from slavery to the promised land governs the poem's oscillations between captivity and freedom. The displacements of diaspora resonate throughout the poet's rootlessness. God's demand for the sacrifice of Isaac and the questions of Job echo within the poet's stories of loss and injustice. The lonely discipline, visionary scope, and moral fervor of the prophets undergird the poet's harsh portrait of the modern landscape. The poet's political history evokes the condemnation of oppression and the call to freedom evident in some of the prophets, especially Amos and Isaiah. The existential hope in the face of the "mortal wounds" of history with which the poem ends—"I need to hope. And do" (95)—repeats in secular terms the faith in God's special covenant with his people that sustains the ancient Hebrews in all their many exiles. And finally, the poem performs the ritual of Kaddish, the prayer for the dead that is the obligation of those who survive.

The claim Klepfisz makes on historical and mythic discourse does not preclude a strongly lyrical, even semiotic, dimension in the poem. In contrast to Kristeva's notion of narrative and lyric in fixed opposition and transgressive interplay, the poem establishes a mosaic of lineations, dictions, tones, repetitions, rhythms, and stanzaic configurations that fluidly collaborate rather than disrupt each other. The narrative modality of the poem is not allied with the symbolic order; rather, it takes both lyrical and prosaic form to construct mythic and historical discourses that transgress the social order's silence about the Holocaust. The poet's recovery of the past and survival in the present emerges from a multiplicity of forms, each of which is necessary to the project of the poem.

"Work Sonnets with Notes and a Monologue," for example, is the central poem in Part II, the section on the poet's clerical work as an enclosure that stifles dreams. The captivity/exodus theme appears in multiple discourses separated into three parts, the first in "poetry," the second in sketchy note form, the third in a "prose" monologue that reports on a dialogue. Part I, titled "Work Sonnets," with its alternation of discourses, is a useful example of how narrative and lyric modes collaborate in Klepfisz's text. "Work Sonnets" is a highly schematized sequence of nine sections, each of which (except viii) is fifteen lines. Sections i, iv, vii, and ix are short-lined, highly lyrical poems centered on a succession of objective correlatives for the poet's subjectivity: iceberg, volcano, rock, and dust. Repetition is the unifying device as each section begins and ends the same way. For example, "iceberg/I dream   yearning/to be fluid" (33) opens the first section, followed by "volcano/I dream   yearning to explode" in section iv (35). Each section ends with the line "and day breaks." In contrast, sections ii, iii, v, vi, and viii are mimetic, prosaic diarylike entries of the poet's activities and feelings on successive days in the office. Each begins with a summary of the day. For example, the lines "today was another day.first i typed some/letters that had to get out.then i spent/hours xeroxing" open section ii, followed by "today was my day for feeling bitter.the xerox/broke down completely   and the receptionist/put her foot down" in section iii (34). The imagistic and prosaic discourses are dialogic, but their opposition is collaborative rather than conflictual. The mimetic sections ground the lyric sections' images in history; the lyric sections free the representational scenes from the purely material. Each adds a dimension that the other lacks.

"From the Monkey House and Other Cages" (Part I) and "*Bashert*" (the central poem of Part IV) represent another instance of paired discourses that dialogically collaborate to tell the story of captivity. The monologues of Monkey I and II tell stories in imagistic, elliptical, gap-filled lyrics that focus on sensation, color, and sound patterns based in alliteration, syntactic parallelism, and rhythmic prosody—elements that Kristeva associates with the semiotic, the *chora*, and the linguistic vestiges of desire for the maternal body. For example, Monkey I's monologue begins in pre-oedipal bliss marred only by the sterility of captivity:

> from the beginning
> she was always dry   though
> she'd press me close
> prying open my lips:
>
> the water warm
> the fruit   sour   brown
> apples bruised and soft.
>
> hungry for dark   i'd sit
> and wait   devour dreams
> of plain sun and sky
>
> large leaves   trunks   dark
> and wet with sweet thick sap.

(5)

Her monologue closes—after narrating the life cycle of separation, sexuality, reproduction, and separation—with a memory of that lost mother-daughter union in a discourse that repeats the child's rocking in the arms of the mother:

> and i can see clearly
> the sky   the bars
> as we sat together
> in a spot of sun

and she   eyes closed
moved me
moved me
to the sound of the waters
lapping
in the small   stone pools
outside.

(15)

These passages both thematize and perform a Kristevan semiotic—not to transgress the narrative, but rather to underscore its story of loss and longing.

"From the Monkey House and Other Cages" is a displaced, lyrical version of what the poet speaks in prose stanzas in *"Bashert."* After opening with two lyrical prayers—for those who died and those who survived—*"Bashert"*'s first prose sequence ("Poland, 1944: My mother is walking down a road") begins with another story of separation, one that grounds Monkey I's lyrical monologue in the matter-of-fact discourse of material history:

My mother is walking down a road. Somewhere in Poland. Walking towards an unnamed town for some kind of permit. She is carrying her Aryan identity papers. She has left me with an old peasant who is willing to say she is my grandmother.

She is walking down a road. Her terror in leaving me behind, in risking the separation is swallowed now, like all other feelings.

(77)

As in "Work Sonnets," the lyrical does not disrupt the journalistic; rather both discourses work together to deconstruct the binaries of animal/human, captivity/freedom, separation/union as a foundation of the poet's *bashert*, her capacity in the final sequence of *"Bashert"* to say: "I do not shun this legacy. I claim it as mine" (86).

The spatial gaps Klepfisz uses throughout *Keeper of Accounts* demonstrate another way the poem establishes a cooperative dialogue between semiotic and symbolic discourses. These gaps slide imperceptibly between functioning as syntactic markers of grammatical pauses (a function of the symbolic modality) and as spaces that resist language as a system of signification (the semiotic modality). Some gaps, in other words, mark off grammatical units, while others function as a kind of stutter, a performance of the poet's hesitations in attempting to speak the unspeakable pain and yearnings of the Holocaust. This interplay of semiotic ellipsis and symbolic syntax is not a fixed opposition, but rather a fluid mingling that both thematizes and performs the poem's double discourse. The poet's Kaddish for Gina Klepfisz in the second sequence of "Solitary Acts" demonstrates how the pause and the stutter reinforce rather than resist each other:

So much of history   seems
a gaping absence   at best a shadow
longing   for some greater

definition   which will never come
for what is burned   becomes air

and ashes   nothing more.

So I cling   to the knowledge of your
distant grave   for it alone
reminds me   prods me   to shape that shadow.

(90)

CONCLUSION

In *Feminism and Poetry*, Jan Montefiore argues that "strategies of storytelling are not, finally, effective in overcoming the paradoxes of exclusion" (56). With some qualifications, she follows the French theorists who privilege lyric over narrative in her examination of women's poetry. But my review of some contemporary long poems by women suggests that the transgressive and revolutionary potential of women's poetry does not lie in a fixed rejection of narrative, whether mimetic or experimental in form, or in a negative association of narrative with the social/ symbolic order whose task it is for the poet to dismantle, disrupt, and (in Kristeva's formulation) tear open. Instead, the insistence on *story*, on narratives that claim historical and mythic discourse as the right and necessity of women poets, permeates the interplay of lyric and narrative in women's contemporary long poems. *Story*, however (re)defined and (re)constructed, is a precondition of agency. "Such will to be known," Klepfisz writes, "can alter history" (88). As Silko says: "There have to be stories" ("Conversation" 29); "with these stories we will survive" (*Storyteller* 247). And as Joy Harjo writes in her poem "The Book of Myth":

> When I entered the book of myths
>   in your sandalwood room on a granite island,
> I did not ask for a way out.

(*In Mad Love and War* 55)

INTRODUCTION

1. For a sampling of theorizing about and reliance upon the rhetoric of borders, see Anzaldúa; Appadurai; Behar; Bhabha; Braidotti; Calderón; Canclini; Chambers; Clifford; Featherstone; Gilroy; Grewal and Kaplan; Hall; Hicks; Caren Kaplan; Kirby; Higonnet; Moore; Peréz-Torres; Radhakrishnan; Robertson; Spivak; Thongchai; Visweswaran; Yaeger, *Geography*.

2. See also the widely used first and second editions of Robyn Warhol and Diane Price Herndl's *Feminisms*.

3. I resist in particular the conventional practice of identifying different feminisms according to such categories as reformist feminism, radical feminism, socialist feminism, Third World feminism, Black feminism, lesbian feminism, etc. The theory and political practice of feminists who are associated with such categories are frequently so overlapping or contradictory as to render the categories largely useless or misleading for analytic purposes. I find it useful to work with a definition of feminism based on two shared principles: (1) the oppression of women and (2) commitment to social change. The analysis of the origins and nature of oppression differs widely; so does the theory on the nature of and strategies for change. For discussions of the politics of location as a basis for feminist theory, see especially Rich, "Notes"; Caren Kaplan, *Questions* 143–87; Probyn; Mani; Grewal and Kaplan 1–36; Chandra Mohanty, "Feminist Encounters"; Smith and Katz; Clifford, "Notes"; and Dhareshwar.

4. Elsewhere Spivak expresses concern about the tendency to use race relations in the United States as a template for understanding race/ethnicity in global terms. "Don't forget the Third World at large," she says for example, "where you won't be able to dissolve everything into Black against White, as there is also Black against Black, Brown against Brown, and so on" (*Post-Colonial Critic* 65). In my view, the reduction of race relations in the United States to "Black against White" is also seriously misleading. For feminist discussions of multiculturalism in global context, see also Gunew and Yeatman; Grewal and Kaplan.

5. I speak here mainly about the academy in the United States, with an awareness that institutions of higher education in other countries differ significantly to varying degrees. I am also aware that the American academy is an institution in transition as we cross the millennial divide: with the future of tenure uncertain; the increase in non-tenure-track instruction accelerating; the primary location of research on campuses under erosion (foundations and businesses are rapidly growing sites); the phenomenon of "distance" and cyberspatial education on the rise, threatening to replace residence learning on campuses and in classrooms.

6. Although frequently credited to the West alone, these advances were not exclusively produced in the West. Papermaking (necessary for book production) was invented in China, for example. A form of movable type and printing was also developed very early in China, while the Arabs were important navigational pioneers, predating European exploration of the fifteenth and sixteenth centuries (see Lach esp. 81–85). My thanks to Edward Friedman for introducing me to these and other sources that undermine conventional eurocentric accounts of the rise of the West and stress the importance of exchange between Europe, Asia, and the Arab world.

7. My special debt to narrative studies is evident in the fact that nearly every chapter grew out of a paper presented at one of the annual Narrative Conferences sponsored by the Society for the Study of Narrative Literature.

8. Some have been published before and appear here in revised or updated forms (chapters 1, 2, 4, 7, 8, 9); others have been reserved for this volume (3, 5, 6, and new sections of 7). Virginia Woolf wrote somewhere that books continue each other. So do articles, I have found. A clever reader could no doubt locate the loose ends in each that led to full exploration in the next. For the curious, the order of composition for the chapters is as follows: 7, 9, 2, 8, 1, 5, 4, 3, and 6. Among the threads that could benefit from their own essay is the issue of identity, performativity, and narrative, especially (but not exclusively) in relation to queer theory. Discussions of performativity in chapters 1 and 3 gesture in this direction.

9. See Bhabha, "Commitment to Theory" (*Location* 19–39); Spivak, *Post-Colonial Critic* esp. 73, 138–39; Frankenberg and Mani, who adapt the term from Lawrence Grossberg and Norma Alarcón; Alarcón, "Theoretical Subjects"; Visweswaran, *Fictions* esp. 11, 13–14, 139–40. Spivak's strategy of using one theoretical/political discourse to interrupt another is evident throughout her work. See for example "Feminism and Critical Theory," "French Feminism," and "A Literary Representation of the Subaltern," in *In Other Worlds*. "Marxism and feminism must become persistent interruptions of each other," she writes (249). Adapting Clifford's notion of ethnographic conjuncturalism, Visweswaran's *Fictions of Feminist Ethnography* engages in "staging a series of encounters with individual interlocutors" (13).

10. See also Sneja Gunew and Anna Yeatman's qualified use of the term *beyond* in their introduction to *Feminism and the Politics of Difference*; Teresa de Lauretis in "Queer Theory" and Eve Kosofsky Sedgwick in *Epistemology of the Closet*, both of whom express a similar notion of "beyond" that incorporates "gay" and "lesbian" but goes beyond those terms in the notion of queer identity.

11. See especially Friedman, *Penelope's Web*; *Joyce: The Return of the Repressed*; "Lyric Subversion"; "The New Modernist Studies"; "Spatialization, Narrative Theory"; "Woolf's Pedagogical Scenes"; "Hysteria"; and "Weavings."

CHAPTER 1

A slightly revised and updated version of "'Beyond' Gynocriticism and Gynesis: The Geographics of Identity and the Future of Feminist Criticism," which appeared in *Tulsa Studies in Women's Literature* in 1996. I am grateful to Joseph Boone for asking me to address these issues for his Modern Language Association panel in 1994 and to Dawn Keetley, whose dissertation sparked my thoughts connecting geography and current theorizations of subjectivity. My thanks also go for their questions and criticism to Holly Laird, the English Department Draft Group at the University of Wisconsin–Madison, and to stimulating audiences at the University of Maryland at College Park, the Institute for Research on Women at Rutgers University, City University of New York Graduate Center, the Erasmus Consortium on Women's Studies at the University of Utrecht, and the UW–Madison Institute for Research in the Humanities.

1. See Showalter, "Women's Time." *Gynocriticism* and *gynesis* are both neologisms. Showalter first used gynocriticism in 1979 in "Toward a Feminist Poetics" to mean the literary history of women's writing, but the widely used term quickly expanded to include all methodologies of reading women's writing (not just literary historical ones). Showalter's use of gynesis to describe feminist poststructuralist readings of the feminine is an adaptation of Alice Jardine's neologism, which first appeared in 1982 in her "Gynesis." By

gynesis, Jardine does not mean a type of feminist critical practice, but rather the centrality of gender (specifically, the feminine) in poststructuralism's critique of humanism through the "reconceptualization of that which has been the master narratives' own 'non-knowledge,' what has eluded them, what has engulfed them" (25). Jardine defines gynesis as "the putting into discourse of 'woman' as that *process* diagnosed in France as intrinsic to the condition of modernity; indeed, the valorization of the feminine, woman, and her obligatory, that is, historical connotations, as somehow intrinsic to new and necessary modes of thinking, writing, speaking" (*Gynesis* 25). Showalter's 1984 binary description of feminist criticism as gynocriticism vs. gynesis replaces her earlier binary of gynocriticism vs. feminist critique of male writers, a form of feminist critical practice especially prevalent among feminists working on earlier periods in English literature ("Feminist Poetics").

2. For a sampling of feminist critics who combine gynocriticism and gynesis, see Carole Boyce Davies; Castillo; DuPlessis, *Pink Guitar*; Friedman, *Penelope's Web*; Henderson; Homans, *Bearing the Word*; Nancy K. Miller, *Subject to Change*; Valerie Smith; Spillers, "The Permanent Obliquity"; Spivak, *In Other Worlds*; and Yaeger, *Honey-Mad Women*.

3. I am adapting the epistemological opposition underlying Paul de Man's *Blindness and Insight*.

4. For other geographical formulations of the politics of identity, see especially Keith and Pile, who note and problematize the widespread use of spatial rhetoric in the social sciences (esp. 1–40, 67–83). Yaeger's *Geography of Identity*, Kirby's *Indifferent Boundaries*, and Jones et al.'s *Thresholds in Feminist Geography* all appeared after the article version of this chapter went to press. Yaeger calls for a rethinking of history, narrative, and identity in multiply spatialized forms that disrupt the "territorial imaginary" of traditional binaries like center/periphery (38), decode the "ghostly effects" of "spatial cryptography" (7), and "reterritorialize" the "social terrain" in politically progressive ways (17). Kirby uses an interdisciplinary methodology informed by poststructuralist and psychoanalytic theory to "view the subject through the lens of space" and to "bring together and understand the connections between the psychic and the social, the personal and the political" (ix). Jones, Nast, and Roberts have drawn together a wide spectrum of feminist essays under the theme of relational readings of space-as-location in reference to feminist geography. See also Geraldine Pratt's critique of geographical rhetoric in feminist theory.

5. Other new rhetorics of identity include those based on performativity, especially important for queer theory (e.g., masquerade, ventriloquism, drag, etc.), and those based on technology (e.g., cyborgian subjectivity, Foucauldian technologies). See for example Butler, *Gender Trouble*; Haraway, "A Manifesto"; de Lauretis, *Technologies*.

6. For quoted terms, see Appadurai, "Global Ethnoscapes"; Mary Louise Pratt, *Imperial Eyes*; Richard White; and Anzaldúa, *Borderlands*. For a sampling of geographical allegorizations, see Norma Alarcón; Benhabib; Bhabha, *Location, Nation* esp. 1–7 and 291–322; Boone, "Vacation Cruises"; Braidotti; Clifford, "Traveling Cultures," *Routes*; Clifford and Dhareshwar; Carol Boyce Davies; Donaldson; Ferguson and Gupta esp. 6–23; Grewal and Caren Kaplan esp. 137–53, 231–54; Gunew and Yeatman; Hall, "Old and New"; Hekman; Hewitt; Hicks; Higonnet; Higonnet and Templeton; hooks, *Feminist Theory*; Hutcheon, Special Issue of *PMLA*; JanMohamed and Lloyd; Jones, Nast, and Roberts; Caren Kaplan, "Deterritorializations," *Questions*; Keetley; Keith and Pile; Kirby; Koshy, "Geography"; Lawrence; Layoun; Lowe, *Critical Terrains*, "Heterogeneity"; Miyoshi; Peréz-Torres; Phelan; Geraldine Pratt; Ray; Soja; Yaeger, *Geography*; and Young. See also the journal *Diaspora*.

7. See chapter 3 in this volume; Moore; Keith and Pile, who write that "identity emerges through difference. . . . Difference becomes *located* difference within a relational field. . . . There is no identity outside of its context" (27–28); and, conversely, the discussion by anthropologist Michael Taussig in *Mimesis and Alterity* of sameness, imitation, and mimesis as a central component of identity in cross-ethnic encounters, an aspect rendered largely invisible by the discourse of difference and alterity.

8. Susan Koshy, for example, warns against metaphoric appropriations of historical realities of diaspora: "Migrancy and exile need to be spoken of not just as metaphors of a nomadic sensibility but as a specific historical and cultural location" ("Other Skies" ix). See also Keith and Pile's insistence that the relationship between metaphoric and material spatiality be noted and interrogated (1–41, esp. 23).

9. I echo Clifford Geertz's resonant term in *The Interpretation of Culture*. See also the interview with Michel Foucault conducted by geographers who chide him for his lack of attention to geography as a discipline given that his discussions of power and situated knowledge rely so heavily upon spatial rhetoric; at first defensively insisting that geographers do their own archaeology of the discipline, Foucault acknowledges by the end that a spatial rhetoric is especially suited to his interest in the relation between knowledge and the dispersal of power and that geography's rise in relation to military conquest requires special scrutiny ("Questions of Geography," in Foucault's *Power/Knowledge*). My thanks to Kärin Wigen for alerting me to this interview. Yaeger also discusses Foucault's spatial tropes (*Geography* 7–9).

10. To my knowledge, Frances Beal was the first to use the term "double jeopardy" in her 1970 essay "Double Jeopardy: To Be Black and Female," published in Robin Morgan's *Sisterhood Is Powerful*. By the late 1970s, black women like Audre Lorde, Alice Walker, Barbara Smith, and the Combahee River Collective forged the discourse of multiple oppression, a concept developed further by many other feminists in the 1980s. See Lorde, *Sister Outsider*; Walker, *In Search*; Barbara Smith; Hull, Scott, and Smith et al.; Combahee River Collective; Norma Alarcón; Albrecht and Brewer; Anzaldúa, *Making Face*; Chai; Dill; hooks, *Feminist Theory*, *Talking Back*; Hurtado; Deborah K. King; Lugones; Lugones and Spelman; Chandra Talpade Mohanty, "Cartographies of Struggle" and "Under Western Eyes"; Moraga and Anzaldúa; Rich, "Disloyal to Civilization"; and Romero and Arguelles.

11. See Carlston for a discussion of socially constructed (e.g., race, class, sexuality, gender) and chosen identities (e.g., radical, student, writer) in Lorde's mythopoetic autobiography. She argues that Lorde's plural identities left her feeling alienated within each group, a form of fluidity that anticipates Linda Alcoff's concept of positionality.

12. See for example Alcoff; Anzaldúa, *Borderlands*; Benhabib; Bourne; Cole; de Lauretis, *Technologies*, "Eccentric Subjects," and *Feminist Studies* 1–19; Donaldson; Fellows and Razack; Frankenberg and Mani; Linda Gordon, "On 'Difference'"; Gunew and Yeatman; Haraway, "Situated Knowledges"; Harding; Harstock; Hekman; Henderson; Hewitt; Hurtado; Kirby; Martin and Mohanty; Mani; Chandra Mohanty; S. P. Mohanty; Phelan; Radhakrishnan; Rich, "Notes"; Smiley; Sedgwick, *Epistemology*; and Spivak, *In Other Worlds*.

13. Rachel Blau DuPlessis's well-known term "(ambiguously) non-hegemonic," coined in "For the Etruscans" (1979), represents an early feminist formulation of contradictory subject positions. See also Bulkin, Smith, and Pratt's *Yours in Struggle* and Martin and Mohanty's essay on Pratt's contribution ("Feminist Politics"); June Jordan, "Report from the Bahamas," an essay often taught in feminist classrooms for its exploration of the contradictory interplay of race, class, and gender; Bourne; Donaldson; Frye, "On Being

White" and "White Woman Feminist"; Hurtado; Molina; Pheterson; Spivak, *In Other Worlds*; Radhakrishnan; and Ray.

14. For other discussions of Larsen, see for example Wall, 85–138; McDowell, 78–100.

15. I develop this concept more fully in chapter 2 of this volume. See also my "Relational Epistemology"; Boelhower; Fellows and Razack; Hurtado; Jones, Nast, and Roberts; June Jordan; Chandra Mohanty; Molina; Radhakrishnan; and Patricia J. Williams, esp. 98–132.

16. See Behar's "Story of Ruth," "Desire and Deception," and *Vulnerable Observer*.

17. In literary studies, situational identity has not, to my knowledge, been theorized as such, although critics (especially in postcolonial studies) might well note the shifts in identity at different locations. Anthropologist Arjun Appadurai puts the global phenomenon of increasing movement of individuals through different cultural spaces at the center of his analysis of "global ethnoscapes." In social and political theory, the term "situated knowledge" is common; see especially Haraway; Hekman (accompanied in *Signs* by extensive commentary and response); Smiley; Norma Alarcón.

18. For extended discussion of hybridity, see chapter 3 in this volume. Postcolonial and recent American immigrant and/or ethnic narratives are replete with the rhetoric of hybridity and hyphenated identity. See for example Erdrich; Mukherjee; Tan; Rushdie; Silko; and Jen. For overviews of the concept of hybridity in social theory and cultural studies, see for example Papastergiadis; Young; Pieterse; and Werbner and Modood.

19. See also Rushdie's *The Satanic Verses*, frequently cited for its thematization and performance of hybridity, as in, for example, Keith and Pile, 22–40; and Bhabha, *Location* 212–35.

20. See for example Paula Gunn Allen; Braxton; Braxton and McLaughlin; Carby; Christian, *Black Feminist Criticism*, *Black Women Novelists*; Frances Smith Foster; Ling; Rebolledo; Sánchez; Springfield; Zimmerman, *Safe Sea*.

21. See for example Judith Butler's *Gender Trouble* (1990), one of the most influential texts linking subjectivity and performativity. Butler's radical challenge to the concept of the "feminine" or "woman" can be regarded as the ultimate disruption of western discourses of identity and thus as an inheritor (of sorts) of the project of gynesis. However, as an important precursor to queer theory (a highly diverse discourse in which Butler's work is just one current), *Gender Trouble* looks ahead to queer theorists' various contributions to the new geography of identity.

22. In *Bodies That Matter* (1993), Butler insists that her theory of performative subjectivity is materialist, taking into full account that "bodies matter" and distancing herself from notions of identity as the result of intentional selection, a kind of costume-for-the-day. In my view, intentionality (based in the rhetoric of dramatic performance) and discursive determinism (based in Foucault's notion of policing discourses and Althusser's concept of hailing ideologies) remain as an unresolved contradiction in both books. Butler retains her notion of identity/subjectivity as an effect of discourse; consequently, concepts of material conditions on the one hand and the agency of the subject on the other are largely incompatible with her approach, whatever her claims to the contrary. For a more materialist use of the rhetoric of performativity, see Sedgwick, "Queer Performativity" and *Epistemology of the Closet*, another influential text in queer theory; de Lauretis, Special Issue.

23. Narrative studies examine many other issues, including reader response, which would also be fruitful for my purposes, especially given the multiple, shifting, and complexly constituted epistemological locations of different readers. The new geography of identity is relevant as well to lyric and dramatic modes of discourse, but poetry and drama are enough different from narrative fiction to require separate discussion.

24. Feminist and other criticisms of these writers (especially Rhys and Joyce) have already begun to consider the implications of the multiple constituents of identity. See for example Emery; Gregg; Doyle; and Dekoven. For Rhys's autobiographical account of her multilayered identity, see her *Smile Please*.

25. For discussion of horizontal and vertical dimensions of narrative, see my "Spatialization"; Jameson's *The Political Unconscious* and DuPlessis's *Writing beyond the Ending* have been influential in promoting the reading of cultural narratives in cultural studies and feminist criticism. See also Carby; Doyle; Dekoven; Boone; and Spillers, "Permanent Obliquity."

26. I cite from the 1986 Hans Walter Gabler edition, and following Joycean convention, quotations are identified by episode and line. For discussions of race, nation, and Irish colonial subjects in Joyce, see especially Doyle and Cheng.

27. I am indebted to DuPlessis, who termed what I here advocate as "locational criticism" (personal communication on draft version). Other responses to earlier drafts that have been particularly important for this section include those from Paul Boyer, Marianne Dekoven, Jane Marcus, Nancy K. Miller, Alicia Ostriker, Sangeeta Ray, Martha Nell Smith, and Mary Helen Washington—most (if not all) of whom argue eloquently for the continuing importance of feminist analysis (however modified) as distinct from other forms of cultural critique.

28. Conversation with author, 23 March 1995, based on Yung-Hsing Wu's dissertation-in-process, "Reading Beyond" (Indiana University) on the problematics of *beyond* in feminist discourse; see also the discussion of *beyond* as interstitial back-and-forthness in Bhabha, *Location* 1–18, and the introduction to this volume.

29. See Caughie's related argument about cultural studies' displacement of women's studies and Hawkesworth's defense of the category of gender.

30. Conversation with author, 24 March 1995, in response to an earlier version of this essay.

31. Nancy K. Miller, letter to author, 4 December 1995.

32. For this point, I am particularly indebted to the lively discussion following a presentation of this essay at the Rutgers Institute for Research on Women, especially the comments of Richard Miller, Rick Schroeder, and Ruth Gilmore. For discussion and critique of the "politics of location" in feminist theory, see for example Frankenberg and Mani; Probyn; Caren Kaplan, *Questions* 143–88; and the introduction to this volume.

33. See Woolf, "Sketch" esp. 68–69; H.D., *Asphodel* esp. 107–17, 151–66; Friedman, *Penelope's Web* 183–90.

CHAPTER 2

Reprinted, with a few updated references and occasional rephrasings, from *Signs* 21 (Autumn 1995); earlier versions were delivered at the Carolyn G. Heilbrun conference, New York, October 1992; the International Conference on Narrative, Troy, New York, 1993; the Modern Language Association convention, Toronto, December 1993; and the Women's Studies Research Center at University of Wisconsin–Madison. For their challenges and encouragement, I am indebted to these audiences, to the many who read earlier drafts (especially Joseph Boone, Edward Friedman, Linda Gordon, Amy Ling, Nellie McKay, and the Draft Group of the UW–Madison English department), and to my toughest critics, the anonymous readers for *Signs*.

1. See especially Robert Gooding-Williams's invaluable collection, *Reading Rodney King/ Reading Urban Uprising* for information about and different interpretations of the

Los Angeles events, some of which attest to the continued relevance of the white/black binary, others of which place the events within larger socioeconomic contexts, and still others of which reflect upon the multiracial aspect of the events.

2. Racist ideologies often assume that "race" is a property only of the racial other. For analysis of the construction of whiteness as a racial identity, see for example Frye; Frankenberg; Minnie Bruce Pratt; Nielson; Domínguez; and duCille's critique of "a would-be oppositional feminist criticism whose practitioners continue to see whiteness as so natural, normative, and unproblematic that racial identity is a property only of the nonwhite" (607).

3. For explicit critiques of the white/black binary, see especially Cho; Omi and Winant, "Los Angeles 'Race Riot'"; Oliver; Lowe, "Heterogeneity"; and Spillers, "Notes." For analysis of the rise of multiracialism in the context of census data collection and affirmative action in the United States, see Wright. For an anthropological perspective on increasing mobility, the "global ethnoscape," and identity, see Appadurai, "Global Ethnoscapes."

4. Throughout, I refer to race and ethnicity as related but not identical categories, both of which reflect the propensity of human beings to organize themselves into groups defined in opposition to others. I assume both *race* and *ethnicity* to be cultural constructs, with *race* usually connoting biological and *ethnicity* suggesting cultural difference, although this distinction repeatedly breaks down in actual usage (see, for example, Michaels and Rensberger, who report on the multimillion dollar genome project aimed at analyzing DNA samples from four hundred "ethnic" groups worldwide). For an evolving tradition of overviews of social science treatments of these terms, see Stocking, *Race, Culture, and Evolution*; Fortney; Peterson, Novak, and Gleason; Stepan; Omni and Wallant, *Racial Formation*; Banton; and Richard Thompson. For analysis of racial discourse, see Higginbotham; Fields; Goldberg; Gates, *"Race"*; Dikötter; and Robb. For a sampling of those who regard "race" as a false, dangerous construct, see Gates, introduction to *"Race"*; Appiah, "Uncompleted Argument"; Appiah and Gates, editors' introduction; Higginbotham; and Radhakrishnan. For those who advocate continued use of racial categories because of their ideological force and material consequences, see, for example, Houston Baker, "Caliban's Triple Play," and Cornel West, "Marxist Theory." For examples of the conflation of race and ethnicity, see Sollors and Boelhower; for examples of insistence on their distinction, see Wald; Omi and Winant, *Racial Formation*.

5. I here adapt Barbara Christian's title, "The Race for Theory," to suggest that similar power dynamics are at work in discussions of race in the 1990s as in those she critiqued in the academy's "race for theory" in the 1980s. See also note 14.

6. For some accounts of such stalled discussions, see Frye, "On Being White"; Anzaldúa, "Bridge" and *Making Face* xix–xxi; Hurtado; Fellows and Razack; Pheterson; Wyatt; and Ellsworth. Conferences of the National Women's Studies Association have included many partially fruitful but also some often nonproductive discussions. See, for example, Sandoval's report on the 1981 NWSA conference ("Feminism"); Albrecht and Brewer's *Bridges of Power* about the 1988 NWSA conference focused on coalitional politics; and the accounts of the walkout of women of color from the 1990 NWSA conference and the consequent near-demise of NWSA in Longnecker; Musil; NWSA Women of Color Caucus; Osborne; Ruby and Douglas; Sales; and Schweickart. For more hopeful accounts in the classroom, see Romero; Thompson and Disch.

7. For the white/color binary as the basis for alliance among women of color, see, for example, Moraga and Anzaldúa; Anzaldúa, "Bridge" and *Making Face*; Sandoval, "Feminism"; Longnecker; Musil; NWSA Women of Color Caucus; Osborne; Ruby and Douglas; Sales; and Schweickart. For discussion of the difficulties of alliance among different groups, see especially Sandoval, "Feminism"; Chai; Harris and Odoña; Uttal; Lorde, "I

Am Your Sister"; and Anzaldúa, "En rapport." For alliance building among women of color that includes white women, see Molina.

8. See Lyotard, esp. 10–11, 16. While agonistic narrative may well be universal, narrative is not exclusively agonistic; see, for example, Paula Gunn Allen, "Kochinnenako." For other discussions of cultural narratives, see Jameson, *Political Unconscious*; DuPlessis, *Writing*; and Heilbrun, *Writing*.

9. See chapter 1 in this volume; Yaeger, *Geography*; Kirby; Keith and Pile; Jones, Nast, and Roberts; Peréz-Torres; Carole Boyce Davies; Braidotti, *Nomadic Subjects*; Hicks; Caren Kaplan, *Questions*; and Lowe, "Heterogeneity."

10. In "Situated Knowledges," Haraway considers only gender (see Norma Alarcón, Hekman), but for other articulations of locational politics and epistemology that include other constituents of subjectivity, see especially Haraway, "Manifesto"; DuPlessis, "For the Etruscans"; Dill; Harstock; Rich; Minnie Bruce Pratt; Martin and Mohanty; Spivak; Alcoff; Deborah King; Hurtado; de Lauretis, *Technologies*; Chandra Talpade Mohanty; Kondo; Phelan; Frankenberg and Mani; Mani; Grewal and Kaplan; Caren Kaplan, *Questions*; Russo; Sandoval, "U.S. Third World Feminism"; Smiley; Harding; Laslett; duCille; Fellows and Razack; Kirby esp. 11–37; and my "Relational Epistemology." See also chapter 1 in this volume.

11. Mary Daly's notorious response to a question about race at the 1979 Simone de Beauvoir conference—words to the effect that race did not interest her—epitomizes these scripts of denial. Daly's appropriation of Indian, Chinese, and African women's experience to a gender analysis isolated from an analysis of race, class, and colonialism in *Gyn/Ecology* (1978) led to the question. See Lorde's critique in "An Open Letter to Mary Daly."(*Sister Outsider* 66–71).

12. For discussion of the rhetoric of feminist confession, see Susan Bernstein. Confessional scripts focus mainly on race in the United States, not, for example, on anti-Semitism or heterosexism. For feminist discussions of Christian ethnocentrism and Jewish identity, see for example, Bulkin, Pratt, and Smith; Pheterson; Beck; and Bourne.

13. See, for example, Adrienne Rich's examination of her two "mothers," white and black in *Of Woman Born*, 253–55, and her subsequent attempts to construct a global feminist theory based in her lesbian/feminism in "Disloyal to Civilization" (1979).

14. See, for example, Jane Gallop's assertion that black women now occupy the position of authority for her that she once gave to Jacques Lacan and other French theorists (Gallop, Hirsch, and Miller 363–64). See also Valerie Smith, duCille, Elizabeth Abel, Jean Wyatt, and Margaret Homans ("'Women of Color' Writers") who variously critique the white feminist tendency to place women of color in the position of ultimate authority and authenticity as a fetishized object of desire or as a form of embodiment for theory; Biddy Martin and Chandra Mohanty's view that the "assignment of fixed positions—the educator/critic (woman of color) and the guilty and silent listener (white woman)" prevents a "working through [of] the complex historical relations between and among structures of domination and oppression" ("Feminist Politics" 199); and Sara Suleri's criticism of women of color who use "strategies designed to induce a racial discomfort" and accord an "iconic status" for themselves and postcolonial feminism in relation to white women ("Woman Skin Deep" 92, 764, 759).

15. One structured format for promoting antiracism used at some women's studies conferences and programs involves women of color speaking about racism to white women, who must remain silent for a predetermined amount of time, after which they may speak, but only about their own racism.

16. I am borrowing Houston Baker's metaphor of soundings in *Modernism and the Harlem Renaissance* for the different racial narratives that underlie African American modernity.

17. For discussions of European racialism, which included not only identification of major racial groups but also the division of Europeans into many different races, see esp. Stocking, *Race*; Poliakov; Stepan; and Banton. See Kamm on the current status of the Roma (Gypsies) in Europe.

18. For further discussion in the context of various theoritical approaches to cultural syncretism and hybridity, see chapter 3 in this volume.

19. Fellows and Razack report on this phenomenon in the roundtable discussions they led among a group of women in which, "with respect of one another, every participant was simultaneously a member of a subordinate as well as a dominant group" (1051).

20. See Johnetta Cole; and Linda Gordon, "On 'Difference,'" for discussions of the importance of feminist identification of commonality among women as well as of differences. See also Barbara Crossette's report on this issue at the 1994 United Nations conference on population in Cairo, and chapter 3 in this volume.

21. See the debate in *Contention* involving Ruth Bloch, Barbara Laslett, and Sarah Harding. Bloch critiques what she sees as feminist theory's exclusive emphasis on models of domination, exploitation, and power, which she believes omit aspects of gender that cannot be explained entirely within a victim paradigm. While criticizing parts of Bloch's call for a "culturalist feminist theory," Laslett argues for the need to understand feminist pleasure in terms that exceed models of domination.

22. Anzaldúa's vision of healing here refers specifically to the syncretism of Anglo, Mexican, and Indian (Aztec) within herself, not to alliances among different groups of women. In *Borderlands*, however, she suggests the possibility of broader alliance through her dedications of poems to Judy Grahn, Vita Sackville-West, and Irena Klepfisz. In "Bridge" she also acknowledges the role of "love and friendship" and ritual behaviors such as breaking bread together as a "good basis" for alliance work, as long as it does not render differences of power invisible (229–30).

23. See chapter 1 in this volume for distinctions among types of relationality (termed *contradictory*, *relational*, *situational*, and *hybridic*) developed after I wrote the *Signs* version of this chapter; for an even earlier formulation, see my "Relational Epistemology." Throughout his essays (now mostly collected in *Diasporic Mediations*), R. Radhakrishnan uses the terms *relational* and *relationality* in similar ways. See also Chandra Talpade Mohanty's somewhat different use of *relationality* ("Cartographies" 12–13) and the introduction to *Thresholds in Feminist Geography*, in which Jones, Nast, and Roberts stress the importance of spatial relationality for feminist analysis. For examples of integrated and/or interactive analysis of multiple oppressions, see especially Alice Walker; Barbara Smith; Moraga and Anzaldúa; Dill; Lorde, *Sister Outsider*; Chai; Deborah King; hooks, *Talking Back*; Chandra Talpade Mohanty; Anzaldúa; Sandoval; and Higginbotham. For rhetoric of standpoint, location, and positionality, see references in note 10. For object relations theory, see, for example, Chodorow; Gardiner, "On Female Identity"; and Jessica Benjamin. For a sampling of the vast literature on subjectivity influenced by poststructuralism and postcolonial studies, see Belsey; Bhabha; Braidotti; de Lauretis; Spivak; Nancy K. Miller; Paul Smith; Valerie Smith; Hicks; Caren Kaplan, *Questions*; Lowe; Appiah and Gates; Peréz-Torres; Carol Boyce Davies; Radhakrishnan; Spivak; and Kirby.

24. I distinguish here *fundamentalist* identity politics from other kinds of identity politics, particularly what I might call a syncretist identity politics based in a notion of identity

as culturally constructed, historically specific, and open to change and interweaving with other identities. As I have written elsewhere, I do not believe that feminists and other marginalized groups can afford to give up the concept of identity and political organizing based on various group identities in favor of poststructuralist notions of identity as sheer play and performance (see chapter 6 in this volume).

25. Since I published this essay, these divisions have continued to widen, evident in the passage of Proposition 209 in California in the 1996 election, eliminating affirmative action in the state, as well as congressional attacks on benefits to all immigrants, legal or illegal.

26. The multicultural mosaic appears quite frequently in ethnic studies as a replacement for the assimilationist image of the "melting pot" without sufficient attention to its potential reinforcement of fundamentalist identity politics. See Peterson, Novak, and Gleason; and Chametzky. The term *multicultural* is highly problematic, without consistent meanings in its many usages and easily open to co-optation into celebrations of pluralist diversity that obscure underlying power relations. In its North American context, *multicultural* most often means nonwhite racial groups considered together, but it also sometimes refers to cultural diversity of all kinds (including white and western); to a group that is itself multicultural (e.g., African Americans or Asian Americans); and even to individuals of mixed heritage (e.g., Louise Erdrich or Leslie Marmon Silko). See Jameson, *Postmodernism*; Peréz-Torres; Miyoshi; Gutmann; Romero and Arguelles; and Gordon and Newfield.

27. For discussions of minority filmmakers and the entertainment industry, see, for example, Fregoso; Parkerson; and Dash. For discussion of the increasingly globalized economy of mass media, see Jameson, *Postmodernism*; and Miyoshi.

28. See for example Fiske; Gray; and D'Acci.

29. These examples have been taken mostly from the *New York Times*, *Wisconsin State Journal*, and *Washington Post National Weekly Edition* between July of 1992 and 1994.

30. If accurate, this Louis Harris survey, called "Taking America's Pulse," may reflect the success of scripts of accusation resulting in white self-censorship of continued stereotypical thinking, as well as the permission victimization often brings to think stereotypically of all others. Two other polls had similar results.

31. See, for example, Sollors, *Invention*, ix–xx; and West, "A Genealogy of Modern Racism." The belief that racism and ethnocentrism are European and Euro-American inventions widely underwrites cultural narratives of accusation.

32. See for example Louis Dumont's classic structuralist study of caste, *Homo Hierarchicus* (1966); Kolenda esp. 23–36; Gould; and Robb's more recent collection, *The Concept of Race in South Asia*, in which Robb notes nonwestern concepts of race and racism in India before the British occupation. The impact of western forms of racial thinking on indigenous Indian concepts of difference is much debated. Whatever its influence, the occupational stratification embodied in the caste system is hereditary, traditionally justified in terms of inborn nature, a form of biological determinism central to various forms of racialism. My thanks to Edward Friedman and Sivagami Subbaraman for directing my attention to the forms of colorism in China and India.

33. For critique of primordialist views of ethnic conflict, see Richard Thompson. For discussions of othering applicable globally (even if not discussed as such), see, for example, Appiah, "Conversation"; Radhakrishnan, *Diasporic Mediations* esp. 203–14; and Gates, *"Race."*

34. For some of Jordan's other films, see *A Neil Jordon Reader*. Nair, educated in sociology at Delhi University and documentary film at Harvard University, is known for her award-winning documentaries like *India Cabaret* (1985) and *Salaam Bombay!* (1989).

See Nair and Taraporevala; Appudurai, "Global Ethnoscapes"; and Gwendolyn Audrey Foster's discussion of Nair in relation to nomadic subjectivity and race in her *Women Filmmakers* (111–27), which appeared after the publication of my article.

35. For a critical reading of *Mississippi Masala*, see bell hooks and Anuradha Dingwaney, who retain the white/other binary in their condemnation of the film as antinationalist and colonialist and as "another shallow comment on interracial, inter-ethnic, transnational 'lust'" (41). Hooks also objects to the racial politics of *The Crying Game*, which she interprets as an appropriative film that commodifies race while denying its significance, "cannibalizes" the other, and perpetuates "white cultural imperialism" ("Seduction and Betrayal" 53–62). While hooks and Dingwaney are usefully alert to the political limitations of popular film, their readings of the filmic texts are often one-dimensional, ignoring important iconographic and narrative nuances and demonstrating the Procrustean dangers of interpreting texts entirely through the lens of culture as a system of (white/western) domination. My thanks to Meryl Schwartz for sending me their article.

36. Although hooks and Dingwaney complain that the film's seeming realism obscures its stereotypical mockery of Indian culture, I think they miss the self-mocking but also celebratory humor characteristic of many "ethnic" films produced by members of the ethnic group they portray, films such as *The Wedding Banquet, Joy Luck Club, Dim Sum, The Great Wall, Brighton Beach Memoirs, Stardust Memories, Moonstruck, Secrets and Lies, Family Thing, My Beautiful Launderette*, and *Soul Food*. See also *The Bird Cage* in reference to gay culture in the United States. Such humor has often been a central survival strategy.

37. Morrison made this point at a lecture at the University of Wisconsin–Madison in October 1990; see also her *Playing in the Dark*, 47.

38. Repressed within the cultural unconscious of the film, as well as in June Jordan's "Report from the Bahamas," is the history of nineteenth-century English racist designations of the Irish as "white monkeys," a "simian race" closely linked to Africa. See Elsie Michie; and Cheng.

39. Despite its historical association with the former colonialists, cricket has become a passionately nationalist sport in South Asia and the British West Indies and is often the site of relational politics. When India, Pakistan, and Sri Lanka jointly hosted the 1993 World Cup in cricket, for instance, the president of the Bombay Cricket Association, who is also a leader of the militant Hindu party, threatened to refuse to allow the Pakistanis to play in Bombay. Yet when India played England in Bombay, Muslim and Hindi fans joined in support of the Indian cricket team (Wagstyl). See Gikandi, *Maps* 9–13; Appadurai, *Modernity*.

40. My thanks to Linda Rugg for this insight. At another level, Dil's donning of Jody's clothes prefigures her refusal of the position of victim, for in this garb she ties up Fergus, takes his gun, and shoots Jude. (In using female pronouns for Dil, I follow the screenplay.)

41. My thanks to Morris Beja for pointing this out; see also Beja, *Film* 126. I am indebted as well to James Phelan and Jacques Lezra for suggestions on the multilayered interpretations of this fable.

42. The multiple resonances of the film certainly support other readings of Jude, as well as the other androgynous names in the film, Dil and Jody. As an echo of Jody, the name Jude name undermines absolute gender difference as do its associations with the biblical figures of Judith, who decapitated Holifernes, and Judas, who betrayed Jesus. Eric Rothstein suggested to me that Dil's name may be a shortened form of "daffodil," slang since about 1945 for an effeminate youth, that Maguire, the ruthless IRA commander, may invoke the nineteenth-century secret society called the Molly Maguires, known for their transvestite disguises; and that Jude's masculinist behavior could be read as a critique of

rather than a reflection of patriarchy. Helen Cooper also noted to me that Jude's power can be read as a revision of feminine passivity and her death as yet another transformation from victimizer to victim.

43. My thanks to Rebecca Saunders for pointing out to me the importance of these religious allusions. Jordan's use of African British homosexual figures as symbolic occasions for the *Bildung* of a white, heterosexual man undermines the film's relational narrative, an element that Sharon Capel finds all too common in the film industry. "Unrealistic and degrading images of black people" often serve, she writes, as "mule" to a "message" directed at a "specific audience: a white one." "What relevance," she asks, "did interracial relations have to the story line other than expediency? And would the film have worked with an all-white cast?" Within relational terms, however, interracial connections are central to the story; and Dil and Jody are not one-dimensional figures; both have nuanced subjectivities.

44. My thanks to Jacques Lezra for the insight about fluidity in *The Crying Game* and its relation to the work of Derrida and Irigaray; also to Hortense Spillers for her warning to me about the politics of deconstruction.

45. My thanks to Amy Ling for this observation.

CHAPTER 3

Based on papers delivered at the Conference on Theorizing Differences among Women: Cross-Disciplinary and Cross-National Approaches at Michigan State University in February 1997, and the Conference on Contact and Power: Transgressions in the Borderlands of Intercultural and Interdisciplinary Encounter at the University of Wisconsin–Madison in March 1997. I am greatly indebted to the stimulating challenges and discussion at both conferences, particularly to Ruth Behar, my co-speaker at Michigan State, and to Neil L. Whitehead and Richard Flores, my conference co-coordinators in Madison.

1. I am adapting Mary Louise Pratt's resonant term "contact zones," which she defines as "social spaces where disparate cultures meet, clash, and grapple with each other, often in highly asymmetrical relations of domination and subordination—like colonialism, slavery, or their aftermaths as they are lived out across the globe today" (*Imperial Eyes* 4).

2. Continuities and discontinuities between first and second wave feminism on the issue of difference exist, but are beyond the scope of this essay.

3. I am indebted to Aili Tripp for this point in her account to me of attending a conference on African feminism in Africa, where the American stress on differences among women met with considerable resistance from some African feminists whose experience with severe ethnic strife led them to stress what they had in common as women rather than what ethnic differences might divide them. To cite another example, differences among women was not the primary focus of the 1995 United Nations conference on women in Beijing, whose achievements included forging an international definition of "human rights" for women; see discussions of the conference in *Signs* 21 (Autumn 1997); 181–226.

4. Distinctions between second wave and third wave feminism are fluid, reflecting different political agendas and generational tensions. Intensifying terminological contestation is the overlapping time frame of the second and third waves, unlike the significant gap of some forty years between first and second wave feminism in Britain and the United States. For a range of views, see Siegel and collections edited by Heywood and Drake; Looser and Kaplan; Findler; and Rebecca Walker.

5. Widely read in the United States, the following (in roughly chronological order) were particularly influential in the formation of gender difference discourse during the late

1960s and 1970s: the rediscovered and transplanted Virginia Woolf and Simone de Beauvoir; Kate Millett; Shulamith Firestone; Germaine Greer; Ti-Grace Atkinson; Juliet Mitchell and Sheila Rowbotham (transplanted from Britain); Radical Lesbians; Sherry Ortner; Gayle Rubin; Dorothy Dinnerstein; Adrienne Rich; Nancy Chodorow; Mary Daly; Carol Gilligan; Elaine Showalter; and Sandra Gilbert and Susan Gubar. Some incorporated other differences like class or sexuality, but their emphasis was on gender, not differences among women. *Women's Ways of Knowing*, edited by Mary Field Belenky et al. (1986), is a later, often cited addition to this genealogy.

6. With the exception of Hélène Cixous's "The Laugh of the Medusa" (1974), which appeared in English translation in *Signs* in 1975, most French feminism was not available to Anglo-American feminism until the publication of Elaine Marks and Isabel de Courtivron's *New French Feminisms* in 1980. Translations of Kristeva, Irigaray, Cixous, and Wittig followed, supplementing the translations of poststructuralist theory in general that proliferated and increasingly became standard academic fare in many disciplines.

7. This gender binary is foundational for poststructuralists such as Derrida, Lacan, Barthes, Kristeva, Irigaray, and Cixous; less so for Althusser, Foucault, and Lyotard (among others). For a sampling of influential American feminist theorists who have adapted poststructuralism in the production of a feminist difference discourse in the 1980s, see the work of Chris Weedon, Toril Moi, Catherine Belsey, Alice Jardine, Naomi Schor, Nancy K. Miller, Margaret Homans, Linda Nicholson, Teresa de Lauretis, Jane Gallop, Diana Fuss, and Kaja Silverman.

8. For influential feminist attacks on androgyny, see Showalter, *Literature* 263–97; Daly, "Qualitative Leap" and *Gyn/Ecology*; and Raymond. For feminist debate, see the special issue on androgyny of *Women's Studies* 2 (Fall 1974). For the widespread use of the concept in feminist social science research (esp. psychology), see for example Alexandra Kaplan; Kaplan and Bean. Nancy Topping Bazin (author of *Virginia Woolf and the Androgynous Vision*, 1973) and I directly experienced the effects of the shift away from the discourse of androgyny. Before we could complete the lengthy process of editing a two-volume collection on androgyny and feminism, the term had basically lost its legitimacy in feminist discourse; we reluctantly abandoned the project. For a mapping of feminist use and resistance to androgyny in the 1960s and 1970s, see my "Androgyny."

9. The concept of androgyny exists as well in some French feminist thought, particularly in Cixous's concept of "vatic bisexuality" ("Laugh"), and in the insistence that the feminine is not an exclusive attribute of women, however privileged women's access to the feminine.

10. Such early analyses include essays in Robin Morgan's *Sisterhood Is Powerful* (1970) by Frances Beal, Eleanor Holmes Norton, the Black Women's Liberation Group, and Enriqueta Longauex y Vasquez, as well as those on race, class, lesbianism, age, prostitution, women in China, etc.; essays in Vivian Gornick and Barbara Moran's *Woman in Sexist Society* (1971) by Catherine Stimpson and Sidney Abbott and Barbara Love; Alice Walker's "In Search of Our Mothers' Gardens" (1974) and "One Child of One's Own" (1979); Barbara Smith's "Toward a Black Feminist Criticism" (1977); and the Combahee River Collective (1977). Novels, poetry, and autobiographies frequently taught in early second wave feminist courses also incorporated such perspectives (e.g., texts by Harriet Jacobs, Radclyffe Hall, Zora Neale Hurston, Toni Morrison, Alice Walker, Maxine Hong Kingston, Audre Lorde, and Paula Gunn Allen). Marxist and socialist feminism in general stressed class differences among women, as well as those produced by imperialism.

11. For a sampling of the vast literature theorizing differences among women published in the 1980s and 1990s, especially those based on racial or ethnic categories, see Norma

Alarcón, "Theoretical Sugjects(s)"; Albrecht and Brewer; Paula Gunn Allen; Anzaldúa; Bourne; Chai; Cole; Collins; Dill; duCille; Frankenberg and Mani; Gallin and Ferguson; Gordon, "'Difference'"; Gunew and Yeatman; Hewitt; Higgonbotham; hooks; Hull, Scott, and Smith; Hurtado; Deborah King; Lorde; Lugones; Lugones and Spelman; Mani, "Multiple Mediations"; Martin and Mohanty; Moraga and Anzaldúa; Chandra Talpade Mohanty; Molina, "Fragmentations"; Shane Phelan; Rich, "Notes"; Saldívar-Hull; Sandoval; Spivak; Zimmerman; and Zinn and Dill.

12. Cosby examines what she sees as a fundamental circularity underlying this privileging of difference, but does not offer much in the way of moving beyond what troubles her. For other thoughtful metacritical essays on the prevalence of difference discourse in feminist theory, see Gallin and Ferguson; Gordon, "On 'Difference'"; Kessler-Harris; Gunew; and Hewitt.

13. See for example Johnnetta Cole's "Commonalities and Differences"; Gloria Joseph and Jill Lewis's *Common Differences*, in which they argue that "coalitions depend, however, on the *recognition of differences* in the territory that Black women and White women of different classes and of different sexual preferences occupy as they enter the struggle against exploitation and oppression" (3). I hesitate to make this examination of differences a universal prerequisite to coalition because in certain situations, such preliminary attention to differences can retard filiations based on common interests.

14. Lugones attacks in particular Judith Butler and Donna Haraway, claiming that their advocacy of heterogeneity fragments rather than fosters an understanding of the "enmeshing of race, gender, culture, class and other differences" ("Purity" 475). See also Lugones and Spelman.

15. Adaptation of Taussig's work should incorporate critique of the unexamined role gender plays in his analysis of mimesis. He opens his book, for example, by invoking without any problematization the instance of a birthing woman as representative of the "objectness of the object," of "the true real," observed by two men (himself as ethnographer and the native shaman) as wielders of mimesis and representation. Thus he reproduces the production of alterity from a chain of interlocking binaries (woman/man, nature/culture, the real/representation) that he sets out to critique.

16. This emphasis on sex/gender/sexuality difference does not preclude attention to other axes of difference. See for example Teresa de Lauretis's introduction to the inaugural event in the formation of queer theory—the special issue of *Differences* on Queer Theory (1991), in which she thoroughly integrates questions of race and ethnicity in a locational analysis of subjectivity and politics. Although *Gender Trouble* examines only the sex/gender/sexuality nexus, Butler's *Bodies That Matter* (1993) includes consideration of race, and her introduction to Butler and Scott, *Feminists Theorize the Political* (1992) insists upon consideration of multiple positionality.

17. See especially Butler, *Gender Trouble* x, 1–34, 43–56, 142–49; Irigaray, "Power of Discourse" 68–85; Bhabha, "Of Mimicry and Man" and "Signs Taken for Wonders" (*Location* 85–92, 102–22). For another use of the performative in queer theory, see Sedgwick's "Queer Performativity." Sedgwick's formulation of queer theory and sexuality as an axis of difference in *Epistemology of the Closet* (esp. 1–90) enacts the dialogic of difference and sameness by advocating a negotiation between a "minoritizing" discourse about homosexuality (emphasizing the difference between heterosexual and gay/lesbian sexualities, advocating rights for a marginalized and despised minority) and a "universalizing" discourse (stressing the constructedness of all sexualities, opening up to all a spectrum of transgressively queer subjectivities).

18. Personal communication in response to a draft of this chapter, 8 August 1997. My thanks for his astute comments (hereafter cited in text) and report on Smith's performance onstage, which I have not myself seen. The video of *Fires in the Mirror* cuts sharply from scene to scene, with no transition visible in costume or setting changes.

19. See Modleski for an overview and analysis of the controversy over caricature in the reception of Smith's work. Space limitations prevent me from addressing the different locations in which Smith performs, the various receptions of her plays, or the revisions Smith's texts undergo—all issues that Modleski addresses. To her point about minstrelsy, I would add that Smith transgresses theatrical conventions that allow men to play women (e.g., classical and Renaissance drama, drag) and whites to play blacks in "blackface" or other races (e.g., *The Mikado*, *Madame Butterfly*, and *Miss Saigon*) but consider theatrically unconvincing for women to play men, blacks and other racial minorities to play whites.

20. Pearce also points out that Smith goes beyond Brecht's famous "alienation effect" because she does more than demonstrate the social and economic construction of the self but also shows it to be "multiple and malleable" as well as performative.

21. In the text versions of both plays, Smith lineates the words of the monologists like poems, which in part marks performative pauses, gaps, and speech rhythms and in part reminds readers of her intervention as writer. Smith deletes some of what her interviewees say, but she insists that all the words were actually spoken to her.

22. My thanks to Ismail Abdalla for introducing me to the Arabic concept of *tahjien*, which, he says, has both positive and negative connotations. He explains, for example, that in the Sudan, regional, religious, and ethnic differences between north and south produce both an embrace of and resistance to cultural hybridity. Hereafter the Spanish *mestizaje* and *mestizo* will not be italicized since they have increasingly been absorbed into the English language.

23. Although I prefer the term *syncretism* myself, with its roots in comparative religious and cultural studies and for its less racially charged history, I have found that many people remain indifferent to or uncertain about syncretism but have immediate recognition of and response to discussing hybridity. I sense that within Mexican, Latin American, Puerto Rican, and generally Hispanic circles, the word *mestizo*, with its racial overdeterminations, invokes a parallel response for similar reasons. For critical discussion of the overdetermination of various terminology, see Young; and Jonathan Friedman, "Global System."

24. The *OED* cites the Latin root *hibrida*, meaning the offspring of a wild boar and a tame sow. Earliest usage of the term in English dates to the 1600s, including a 1630 one by Ben Jonson linking hybridity to racial issues: "She's a wild Irish bairn, sir, and a hybride" (*OED* 1354).

25. More comparative work on the history of interracial, interethnic, and interreligious rape, sexuality, cohabitation, and/or marriage needs to be done because of considerable variation regionally, geopolitically, historically, and by racial/ethnic/religious group.

26. While examining the entwined history of hybridity and racialism, Young refuses a simple binary of white/other by insisting upon the heterogeneity of western attitudes and practices. The English in the nineteenth century, for example, defended themselves proudly as a hybrid, mongrel race, an amalgamation of Celts, Saxons, and others; this refusal of attachment to racial purity developed alongside racist ideology against blacks, Celts, Jews, Asians, and others, as well as during the rise on continental Europe of Ayran ideology (Young 1–28). See also Werbner's historical overview of hybridity's relationship to colonialism (Werbner and Modood 1–28); Jonathan Friedman, "Global System."

27. Users of the term hybridity tend to shift among at least two, if not all three, of these meanings. However, I would loosely affiliate some key theorists of cultural mixing with the following: Rushdie, Young, and Shohat with hybridity as fusion; Gilroy, Thongchai, Nandy, Hannerz, Mary Louise Pratt, Clifford, Appadurai, Lowe, Hall, Gikandi, and Trihn with hybridity as intermixture; and Rosaldo, Canclini, Bhabha, Werbner, Clifford, Strathern, Ferguson and Gupta, Pieterse, and Whitehead with culture as inherently syncretist. For a spectrum of views, see Werbner and Modood. For overviews of debate, see Werbner, Papastergiadis, and Pieterse.

28. See esp. Bakhtin, *Dialogic Imagination* 375–429; adaptations of his views by Young, esp. 20–24; and Werbner and Modood, esp. 4–6.

29. Like sounds, the human body across the globe appears in multiple focuses and shadings of difference. As I discuss in chapter 6, concepts of race function like phonemes, singling out certain physiological and/or cultural differences as meaning-bearing distinctions. Thus while colors of skin cover a countless number of tones, the phonemes of skin color that reflect cultural constructions of race are relatively few; currently, in the West, these phonemic colors are white, black, brown, red, and yellow, signifying arbitrarily five distinct biological races.

30. Werbner locates the origin of the paradox in the transition from modernity (which she associates with fixed and bounded epistemological systems that hybridity disrupts) to postmodernity (for which disruption and hybridity are routine) (1–28). This too narrowly locates hybridity in the "modern" (whatever that means) in my view. I think the paradox she usefully identifies is present in the concept itself, as well as its current deployments, perhaps because of its origins in notions of mixing species. For others who see cultural hybridity as routine, see note 27; for those who see it as transgressive and/or liberatory, see also Papastergiadis; Trihn, "Other"; Chambers; and Rushdie.

31. See also Alexander's *Fault Lines*. For others who conceptualize hybridity in spatial terms, see Rushdie; Appadurai; Chambers; Clifford; Braidotti; Carol Boyce Davies; Pérez-Torres; Trihn. For those who associate hybridity particularly with (post)modernity, see also Canclini; Werbner; Hannerz; Rushdie; Mukherjee; Thongchai; Visweswaran, esp. 114–42; and most of the contributors to Werbner and Modood's *Debating Cultural Hybridity*.

32. The notion of the cultural hybrid as more resilient, creative, and able to adjust to and benefit from changes parallels the arguments that Virginia Woolf and Sandra Bem (see Kaplan and Bean, 48–62) make about androgynous men and women. Many of the arguments I have been making about cultural hybridity are applicable to gender hybridity, a topic complex enough to deserve its own extended discussion.

33. For definitions of transculturation, see Mary Louise Pratt, *Imperial Eyes* (6); for transfiguration, see Gilroy, *Black Atlantic*, 37, where he cites Seyla Benhabib's discussion of the term in *Critique, Norm, and Utopia*; for the concept of negotiation, see Bhabha, "The Commitment to Theory" (*Location* 19–39).

34. See Judy Purdom's "Mapping Difference," which focuses centrally on Bhabha's notions of hybridity, as a revisionist blending of Derridian concepts of *différence* and *différance*. But where she objects to a lack of consistency in Bhabha's work on hybridity, I argue that these shifting meanings represent a strength and reflect a healthy resistance to circumscribing the concept to one out of many possible forms.

35. See for example Shohat; Grewal and Kaplan, *Scattered Hegemonies* 7–8; Jonathan Friedman, "Global System"; Spivak, *Outside* 255; Ray, "Rethinking Migrancy"; and Koshy. Coming under particular attack are the theorizations of hybridity by Bhabha, Hall, Gilroy, and Rushdie.

36. For other influential Chicano aesthetic works that have achieved "theoretical status" in border studies, see, for example, Guillermo Gómez-Peña's *The New World Border* and his performance art in general, which combines hybridity, performativity, play, and "'world'-travelling." For discussions of Latin American, Mexican, and Chicano/a border writing, see Canclini; Medina; Saldívar-Hull; Hicks; Calderón and Saldívar; Saldívar; Rebolledo; and Sandoval.

37. For some substantial discussion of *Borderlands*, see for example Grewal, "Autobiographic Subjects"; Saldívar-Hull; Norma Alarcón, "Theoretical Subject(s)"; Chang; Medina; Quintana; and Torres. Brief discussion or passing reference to the text is far more common, as in Rebolledo and Saldívar.

38. Saldívar-Hull, Saldívar, Medina, Rebolledo, Quintana, and Grewal all comment on the text's multilingual, multigeneric, postmodern or experimental form. Grewal identifies *Borderlands* with a "postmodern" deconstruction of "modernist" subjectivity that she finds particularly characteristic of feminists of color ("Autobiographic Subjects"). The slippage between the terms *modernism* and *modernity* ignores the development of montage, collage, generic hybridity, and decentered subjectivities as hallmarks of modernist experimentalism. Anzaldúa's text certainly reflects her standpoint as a Chicana, but as a feminist-hybridic quest text, it also has a lot in common with modernist works like H.D.'s *Trilogy*. The exclusivity of difference discourse in Grewal's essay obscures the formalist hybridity of the text, a suppression of complexity against which Grewal and Kaplan's admirable collection, *Scattered Hegemonies* works.

39. See chapter 9 in this volume for discussion of the twentieth-century women's long poem, the "new" genre within which I would place *Borderlands*, along with such hybrid texts as Silko's *Storyteller* and Cha's *DICTEE*.

40. I am indebted to Rubén Medina for helping me to refine my argument on this point by his willingness to share in manuscript his thoughtful critique of *Borderlands*, "Gloria Anzaldúa: The Politics and Poetics of *Mestizaje*." Among other things, he argues that the personal focus of the text and the Chicano appropriation of Mexican history elide the variation of conditions affecting Chincano/as (particularly those caught up in material border economies), the difference between Mexican and Chicano/a societies, and the actual condition of Indians in Mexico today. His critique reminds me of that leveled by lesbians and women of color against heterosexual and white feminists who relied on the slogan "the personal is political": not everyone's "personal" is the same. There is a danger in the use of autobiography for the production of theory. One person's set of conditions, even when tied to a communal history, is not necessarily generalizable.

41. Part one ends with section 7, entitled *La consciencia de la mestiza*: Towards a New Consciousness," the last subsection of which is called "el retorno"; Part two ends with section VI, *El Retorno*, four poems (one in Spanish, then English) about mestiza consciousness. Sections 2–6 of part one and sections 2–5 of part two are roughly parallel in thematic emphasis, covering the historical oppression of Chicanos and Indians; the meanings of gender and sexuality within patriarchal Anglo, Chicano, Mexican, and Aztec systems; and the forging of an oppositional poetics inspired by reconstituted female/maternal deities buried in the palimpsests of history, psyche, and desire.

42. Daniel Cooper Alarcón cites Anzaldúa favorably for her critique of Chicano romanticizations of Mexican and Aztec cultures and for her acknowledgment of intracultural differences, but he suggests that she participates in some of the mythmaking about indigenous Mesoamerican Indianness that he believes characterizes the heuristic reconstruction of a precontact past in much contemporary Chicano/a writing (see esp. 141). Since the notes to part one of *Borderlands* provide a source map of Anzaldúa's reading, an intellec-

tual genealogy of the meanings of Mexicanness as developed in twentieth-century Mexican and Chicano/a constructions of national and ethnic identities could usefully be developed.

43. Anzaldúa's mythopoetic narrative of the evolution of the Serpent Goddess into the split forms of Aztec and Christian religion may or may not have empirical basis. Within the text, it functions much like the "new mythos" of a once reviled and newly recovered female divinity in texts like Lorde's *Zami*; Judy Grahn's *Queen of Wands*; and H.D.'s *Trilogy*, *Helen in Egypt*, and *Hermetic Definition*. Medina is correct, I believe, in noting that *Borderlands* makes little effort to connect the material effects of border culture present in the text with the spiritual transformations upon which the metaphoric and psychological dimensions of mestiza focus. Grahn and H.D. in *Trilogy* use different strategies, perhaps more successful ones, to clarify the link between the material and the spiritual.

44. In a personal communication, Sonita Sarker provocatively asks why it is that a woman of color like Anzaldúa is allowed to "have no country" in an imagined sisterhood of feminists and lesbians, while the Englishwoman she so clearly echoes in this passage, Virginia Woolf, is challenged in making a similar assertion in *Three Guineas*: "as a woman, I have no country. As a woman I want no country. As a woman my country is the whole world" (109). Adrienne Rich uses this quotation as her exemplary negative text as the basis for her critique of feminist obliterations of differences among women ("Notes"). See also Chang's uncritical discussion of Anzaldúa's passage (255) and my discussion of Woolf's passage in chapter 6 in this volume.

45. Perhaps highlighting an urgency to reach even non-Spanish-speaking readers, this poem (unlike most of the text) contains notes translating the Spanish words: "*gabacha*—a Chicano term for a white woman; *rajetas*—literally, 'split,' that is, having betrayed your word; *burra*—donkey; *buey*—oxen; *sin fronteras*—without borders" (195). The two poems that follow (the last of which appears in both Spanish and English) focus on the religious syncretism of her muse and the cultural syncretism of *la Raza*, which, founded deeply in the Indian, "in a few years or centuries" will "rise up, tongue intact/carrying the best of all the cultures" (203).

CHAPTER 4

A substantially revised version of a paper written for the Symposium on Virginia Woolf International, Clemson University, June 1996, and the article that appeared in Virginia Woolf International, a special issue of the *South Carolina Review* (1996). I am grateful to Wayne Chapman, who edited the special issue, and to Dale Bauer and Christine Froula for their cogent suggestions.

1. Mary Daly's *Gyn/Ecology* is the most notorious example of such decontextualized internationalization of feminism. Trihn Min-ha's *Woman—Native—Other* is not usually challenged for its Third World bricolagic methodology, but I think that for all the value of its theorizing, it should be.

2. See especially Sedgwick, *Epistemology*, 27–35, for her discussion of what she calls "axiom 2": "The study of sexuality is not coextensive with the study of gender; correspondingly, antihomophobic inquiry is not coextensive with feminist inquiry" (27). There has been considerable discussion, especially among queer theorists, about Sedgwick's designation of sexuality and gender as distinct axes because of the problematics of distinguishing between (chromosomal) sex and gender in the sex/gender system. See for example Butler, *Bodies That Matter*, and Biddy Martin, "Extraordinary Homosexuals." Nonetheless, Sedgwick's seminal formulation has been widely influential in establishing sexuality

in cultural studies as something more than a subcategory of gender issues or homosexual/lesbian issues.

3. It appears inevitable that space beyond the Earth will increasingly be subject to political construction as well; but my main focus is on space that is inhabited and/or controlled by human societies. The solar system and "outer space" play significant roles in the human imaginary and geopolitics on earth.

4. Some theorists distinguish between space and place, with "space" signifying the preexisting entity that becomes a culturally constructed "place" with specific meanings. However, I question the distinction, just as I would for "time," because I think that any way in which we think about space is always a form of cultural construction. Something clearly preexists human thinking about it, but I don't think we have access to it outside of various culturally constructed ways of thinking about it. See chapter 5 and note 14 in this volume. For a feminist critique of masculinism in the discipline of geography, see Rose.

5. Although he does not theorize it directly, this is, I believe, the gist of Tariq Modood's somewhat veiled critique of Paul Gilroy in "'Difference,' Cultural Racism and Anti-Racism," where he objects to the progressive use of racial categories like "black" in Britain that render invisible the ethnic differences between people of Caribbean, Pakistani, and Indian descent. In defining herself so thoroughly as a "woman of color" in opposition to all white/anglo women, María Lugones elides the geopolitical axis of her identity, rooted in her Argentinean background. Because geopolitical borders figure so centrally in the work of Gloria Anzaldúa, the racial axis does not subsume the geopolitical one in *Borderlands/La Frontera*. See the discussion of their work in chapter 3 of this volume and Saldívar-Hull's theorization of geopolitical borders and feminism.

6. See this chapter's epigraph, from Said's "The Politics of Knowledge," 28.

7. He defends his focus on British, French, and American imperialism by saying that other European imperial projects (e.g., the Russian, Spanish, Portuguese) and the Ottoman Empire lack the "unique coherence and a special cultural centrality" of the former (*Culture and Imperialism* xxii). He does not even mention twentieth-century Japanese imperialism, nor the existence of other nonwestern empires (e.g., those of China, Mongols, Mughal India, Dahomey, Zulu, Songhai, Aztec, Inca, etc.). From a global perspective, Said's meta-narrative of "culture and imperialism" is quite eurocentric, reinscribing the very centrality of the West to which he objects. Where *Orientalism* examined only European dominance in the Middle East, *Culture and Imperialism* examines (British, French, and American) imperialism globally in relation to forms of resistance: "These two factors—a general world-wide pattern of imperial culture, and a historical experience of resistance against empire—inform this book in ways that make it not just a sequel to *Orientalism* but an attempt to do something else" (xii). See Gikandi, *Maps*, for an analysis of the construction of "Englishness" through engagement with colonial others, one that avoids the tendency to binarist reductionism evident in Said's work.

8. Robertson adapts the term "glocalization" widespread in Japanese business studies where it means micromarketing on a global scale (28) to a more broadly conceived cultural concept. See also Featherstone, Lash, and Robertson; Anthony King; and Hall, "Local and the Global."

9. Spivak distinguishes her notion of transnational analysis from both comparativist analysis and advocacy of global multiculturalism. She focuses instead on "transaction in an international frame" and suggests that "we must both anthropologize the West, and study the various cultural systems of Africa, Asia, Asia-Pacific, and the Americas as if peopled by historical agents" ("Scattered Speculations" 262). In their introduction to *Feminism and the Politics of Difference*, Sneja Gunew and Anna Yeatman propose a related methodology

for resisting the binary of global and local, one they call "thinking in terms of interested universalisms," by which they mean the universal as it is particularized and embedded in power relations (xiv).

10. Debate about the instability and constructedness of the category "home" is widespread. For a sampling of discussions (esp. feminist ones), see Martin and Mohanty; Anzaldúa, *Borderlands*; Grewal, *Home and Harem*; Minnie Bruce Pratt; George Robertson; Sarup; Trinh, "Other"; Lawrence; Kirby; Broe and Ingram; Caren Kaplan, *Questions* esp. 161–66; Braidotti, *Nomadic Subjects*; Alexander, *Shock*; Carol Boyce Davies esp. 113–29; Bammer; Thomas Foster; Chambers; and Radhakrishnan, *Diasporic Mediations*. I make no attempt here to map this debate, but instead use quotation marks around "home" to indicate its lack of fixed meaning.

11. See especially Ruth Behar's introduction to Behar and Gordon, *Women Writing Culture* (3–6) for an account of the anguish and anger caused by Clifford and Marcus's failure to include any women anthropologists in *Writing Culture*, an exclusion that the coeditors justify with the highly inaccurate statement that feminist anthropology "has not produced either unconventional forms of writing or a developed reflection on ethnographic textuality as such" (21). Behar does not mention Clifford's incomplete analysis of the Tyler photo, but feminist critique of his discussion is widespread in conversation. Clifford's "Notes on Travel and Theory" and the volume of *Inscriptions* in which it appears in 1989 attempt to make up for these exclusions by featuring the importance of feminist theory for cultural theory. My thanks to anthropologists Kirin Narayan and Maria Lepowsky for discussions of these issues.

12. Trained in the discipline of comparative literature, Spivak distinguishes what she calls "transnational Culture Studies" from "comparativist work" because of the latter's association with eurocentrism ("Scattered Speculations"). See also Said's attack on the discipline of comparative literature in *Culture and Imperialism* 43–61. In *Home and Harem*, Grewal argues "for a transnational mode of analysis rather than a comparative one, since the comparative approach does not include within it a notion of the geopolitical forces that are the condition of possibility for comparative analysis" (17). "Much comparative focus on distant cultures ends up," she writes in citing the journal *Public Culture*'s inaugural statement, "first, 'exceptionalizing the West through its absence on the discursive stage,' and, second, homogenizing the 'Third World'" (18). She does, however, allude positively to some "comparative work" that either deconstructs colonial discourses "by bringing them home" or identifies locational specificities, power flows, and asymmetries (18–19). See also Bhabha's call for a "critical comparativism" in *Location* 6.

13. Held in conjunction with the annual conference of the International Virginia Woolf Society, the symposium on Virginia Woolf International examined the reception of Woolf in many parts of the world, as well as the inscriptions of the international in her work. See Chapman's special issue of *South Carolina Review* devoted to the symposium.

14. See especially Woolf, *The Common Reader* and *Three Guineas*; and my "Virginia Woolf's Pedagogical Scenes."

15. Rich is quoting from chapter 3 of *Three Guineas* (108–9), where Woolf's epistolary writing persona refuses to send a guinea to join a society devoted to peace, outlining instead the Society of Outsiders to which she would have the daughters of educated men belong, a Society requiring "indifference" to patriotism and a refusal of national identity. In prior essays, Rich quoted approvingly from related passages in *Three Guineas*, ones in which Woolf warned against joining the processions of educated men (*On Lies* 131–34, 212–13, 278, 303). See also Caren Kaplan's related critique of Woolf's "global feminism,"

to which she contrasts transnational feminism (*Questions* 161–62). For a discussion of Gloria Anzaldúa's adaptation of Woolf's passage and Sonita Sarker's critique of Rich in this context, see chapter 3, 100 and note 44.

16. See Bradbury and McFarlane, "The Name and Nature of Modernism," and Bradbury, "The Cities of Modernism," in *Modernism* (19–56, 96–104). See also Perloff's overview of modernist studies, which includes internationalism as a key definitional component ("Modernist Studies" esp. 158).

17. For discussions of the role of such disciplines as classics and anthropology in the formation of constructs like "the West" and "Europe," see especially Bernal and Trouillot.

18. See for example Torgovnik's *Gone Primitive*, especially the discussion of Bloomsbury's Roger Fry in "Making Primitive Objects High Art," 75–140. Torgovnik argues that Fry, like many western artists, greatly admired African sculpture and masks, but could not bring himself to call such "primitive" expression "art" until it was brought into a European context. Trouillot makes a parallel case in reference to post-Renaissance travel writing and the development of western anthropology as a discipline.

19. An important exception to this pattern was Woolf's weeklong trip to France with Vita Sackville-West at the height of their affair in 1928. Her brother George Duckworth died while Woolf was on holiday in Ireland in 1934. Tracking Woolf's travels as represented in Quentin Bell's biography, I believe that Woolf's most frequent foreign destination was Italy, which she visited at the very least in 1904, 1908, 1909, 1928, and 1935. Bell also notes in a section on the 1930s that the Woolfs took "an annual excursion abroad" (2:189). But he writes that Woolf "was never at home outside her own country" (1:154). Whatever the case, Woolf does not appear to have had the zest or restlessness for travel or foreign residence that modernists like Stein, Joyce, Conrad, Pound, H.D., Lawrence, Forster, Rhys, and Mina Loy had, for all of whom leaving home was a precondition and/or inspiration for writing. My thanks to Jean Moorcraft Wilson for pushing me to refine this brief foray into Woolf's travels.

20. *The Voyage Out*, *Flush*, and to a lesser extent *Orlando* are the novels set substantially outside Britain. Woolf's essays include some on American and Russian writers, for example, but in relation to essayists like Pound, Eliot, and even H.D., Woolf's focus is largely on British texts.

21. See especially *The Dream of a Common Language*; "Disloyal to Civilization" (*On Lies* 275–310); and "Compulsory Heterosexuality" (*Blood* 23–75).

22. In their canonical collection *Modernism*, Bradbury and McFarlane's glossary of brief biographies includes one hundred entries, with only four slots designated for women: Woolf, Stein, Dorothy Richardson, and Edith Södergran. Entries for the first three all contain dismissive evaluations, unlike the more descriptive entries for male modernists.

23. See for example Mary Layoun, Lydia Liu, Nalini Natarajan, and Norma Alarcón in Grewal and Kaplan's *Scattered Hegemonies*.

24. See for example Dekoven 85–138; Lawrence 154–206; Tratner 79–96; Cummings; Doyle 139–73; and Friedman, "Spatialization, Narrative Theory."

25. Among Woolf critics, June Cummings in "*The Voyage Out* and *Between the Acts*: Readings of Empire" is an exception. I agree with her that Woolf, much like Forster, both critiqued and participated in British orientalism. While I concur with Kathy Phillips in *Virginia Woolf against Empire* that Woolf mounted a pervasive and powerful attack on the British Empire throughout her work, I think she too quickly dismisses the significance of what she refers to as Woolf's "unpleasant prejudice," "annoying" references to non-Europeans, and racial "insensitivity" (xxxiv; xxxv) and does not see ways in which Woolf's work participates in the ideological formations she critiques.

26. Cummings developed her paper at the Sixth Annual Virginia Woolf Conference around this removal, arguing that her choice of Skye was influenced by her reading of Samuel Johnson's *Journey to the Hebrides* ("Lily Briscoe's Journey").

27. The prefix "Mc" is characteristically Irish, in contrast to the Scottish "Mac," which appears in the name of the Hebrideans Macalister and son, who take the boat to the lighthouse in the final section of the novel. See Cummings's discussion of the Macalisters' primitivist function ("Lily Briscoe's Journey"). According to Trevor-Roper, much of western Scotland was settled by migrations of Irish northeastward, which may explain why the typically Irish prefix would be attached to a name in northwestern Scotland. The name McNab may also carry undertones of Shelley's Queen Mab, the queen of the fairies in his politically radical poem, *Queen Mab* (1813), a favorite among Britain's working-class activists in the nineteenth-century.

28. See 130–31, which mentions her drinking twice, along with her fondness for music hall songs and gossip. Unlike modernists such as Joyce, Lawrence, Rhys, Forster, and Stein, Woolf seldom attempts extended representations of the interior life of working-class people or those from other countries. Rezia in *Mrs. Dalloway* is an important exception. Isa in *Between the Acts* is less clearly an exception because the only allusion to her Irishness is her passing reference to being "niece of the two old ladies at Wimbledon who were so proud, being O'Neils, of their descent from the Kings of Ireland" (16). However, Isa's identification with the woman gang-raped by the military Whitehall guard whom she reads about in the newspaper (20), along with her inner emotional and romantic citations of poetry, may resonate with Irish victimization and English cultural narratives about the Irish as an irrational, intuitive, emotional, and verbally gifted "race." For discussions of English racialism and the Irish, see for example Doyle; Cheng; and Michie.

29. Woolf attempts to do what S. P. Mohanty argues is essential in bridging the gap between "us" and "them": imagine the agency of the other.

30. Rachel's journey upriver in *The Voyage Out*, where she becomes engaged and catches the tropical fever, is of course an important exception. Clearly rescripting Conrad's *Heart of Darkness*, Woolf uses the South American "natives" upriver as a primitivist backdrop against which she projects the "primitive" passions of her protagonists, as Dekoven, Lawrence, and Lisa Williams point out. However, there is a puzzling break in Woolf's use of the primitivist plot where she records not the ethnographic gaze of the western travelers looking at the natives in their village, but rather the gaze of the native women piercing the English as alien other. In briefly describing the intercultural encounter, Woolf reiterates the native gaze no less than ten times (284–85). These women remain inarticulate, their subjectivity unimagined, but their stares reverse the conventional plot of imperial specularity. Generalized references to "savages," without particular geographical and cultural locations, do appear with some regularity in Woolf's work.

31. A parallel statement could be made about *The Voyage Out*, which begins with the sea voyage as a trip away from home. But with a few important exceptions (e.g., the scenes upriver and Dr. Rodriguez, "with his unintelligent, hairy face" [338]), what Rachel finds in the English colony of Santa Marina is another version of home.

32. For accounts of the role of media (especially newspaper and photography), see Lambert and Badsey; Green. For discussion of Florence Nightingale and the Crimean War, see for example Barker, who states that she was known as an "eminently practical woman . . . undeterred by hypocrisy and male bluster" (212, 212–23). For discussion of Nightingale in relation to Caroline Stephen, Julia Stephen, and Woolf, see Marcus, *Virginia Woolf* 45, 80–81. See also Woolf's reference to Nightingale in *A Room*: "thanks, curiously enough, to two wars, the Crimean which let Florence Nightingale out of her drawing-room,

and the European War which opened the doors to the average woman some sixty years later, these evils [lack of money and intellectual freedom] are in the way to be bettered" (112).

33. Tennyson's son claimed that this phrase was the origin point for the poem (Tennyson, *Selected Poems* 367). See also Tucker, who quotes from the editorial in describing the Light Brigade as "hurried to their doom by some inextricable error," and the British soldier as "not paralyzed by feeling that he is the victim of some hideous blunder" (27). Tennyson first published the poem in the *Examiner* on 9 December 1854, and then a year later omitted the controversial phrase, only to reinstate it in a version he called the "soldier's version" sent to the Crimea, where it was very popular (Marshall 135). The poem underwent many changes in various publications. For nineteenth-and twentieth-century accounts of the "blunder," see Paget, 68–79; Gibbs, 212–24; and Barker, 160–73.

34. See, for example, Kincaid who assumes the irony of the poem to be self-evident (219–20), and Morton Luce, who calls the poem a "glowing tribute to military glory, for which, both the tribute and the glory, a whole nation may well be thankful" (266). Tennyson's alterations in published versions intensify the ambiguity. In addition to omitting "Some one had blunder'd," he altered the final lines of the poem (quoted in text), which some see as significantly ironic, to blander versions (Kincaid 219–20).

35. The narrator also repeats some of these lines and echoes others on 31, 32, and 36.

36. My reading of the Crimean War in *To the Lighthouse* was written before I saw Phillips's parallel discussion in *Virginia Woolf against Empire* (113–15), in which she reads the passage as satire that unravels through absurd juxtapositions the link between Tennyson's fatuous patriotism and patriarchal domesticity, militarism, and empire (113–15). Our emphases differ in her use of the passage to defend her view of Woolf's critique of empire and my use of the passage to theorize the place of the geopolitical in Woolf's domestic scenes.

37. See for example, Irigaray, "The Power of Discourse."

38. Tennyson as the very public poet laureate of Britain also had a very direct place within Woolf's intimate family history. For a time, Tennyson lived on the Isle of Wight, where Woolf's maternal great-aunt, the photographer Julia Margaret Pattle Cameron, often photographed the poet and his family, leading in some quarters to rumors of an affair with Tennyson. Woolf's play *Freshwater: A Comedy* (written 1923, 1935) satirizes the Victorian circle on Wight, centrally working into the domestic scenes a spoof of the British Empire in India, as Phillips discusses (116–20). Tennyson met Cameron at Little Holland House at the pre-Raphaelite salon of her sister, Sarah Pattle Prinseps, where Woolf's mother, Julia Jackson, often served as model before her marriage. As one of Woolf's many direct family links to the British Empire, three of the Pattle sisters were married to Anglo-Indians, including Woolf's maternal grandmother; their mother was also "foreign," from France. See Bell, 1:15–18; Drabble, 970–71.

39. I am indebted to Tratner (50) for bringing to my attention the presence of India in this well-known passage.

40. I am borrowing here from Jameson's *The Political Unconscious*; Derrida's *"Fors"*; and Abraham and Torok's concept of cryptonomy.

41. See Marcus's discussion in *Virginia Woolf* of the importance of Caroline Emelia Stephen to Woolf (esp. 85) and of Caroline and Leslie's father, James Stephen, as rationalizer of the British Empire (80). See also Bell's account of Woolf's legacies and 1904 residence in Cambridge (vol. 2:39, 1:90–91).

42. As I discovered after writing this analysis, Phillips also discusses this passage (xxxviii). She reads it as exposure of Woolf's conscious guilt and critique of empire,

whereas I see little evidence of either in the passage. In my view, the five hundred pounds a year remains an uninterrogated allusion to the economics of empire in Woolf's text.

43. For a pathbreaking reading of Woolf in relation to Walker and Buchi Emecheta, see Tuzyline Jita Allan's *Womanist and Feminist Aesthetics*. At the 1996 Virginia Woolf Conference, several panels presented comparativist readings of Woolf in relation to African American and nonwestern writers, featuring papers by Lisa Williams, Tuzyline Allan, Chella Courington, Ellen Argyros, Susan Howard, Jennifer Margulis, Sydney Gail Recht, Ji-Moon Suh, Beth Rigel Daugherty, and June Cummings. Such work represents a vitally important part of internationalizing the reading of Woolf.

44. See chapter 6 of *Their Eyes Were Watching God*, Hurston's fictional presentation of folklore she collected from the South in the late 1920s and early 1930s and published in *Mule Bone* (cowritten with Langston Hughes in 1930, published 1991), *Jonah's Gourd Vine* (1934), and *Mules and Men* (1935). In all of these the porch functions metonymically as the site of African American performativity. I am aware of no evidence suggesting that Hurston knew of *A Room of One's Own*.

45. Juxtaposition of Hurston and Woolf, who most likely did not know of each other's work on poetics produces the haphazard parallel of "porches" as originary points for creativity: Woolf's writing career beginning at her Aunt Caroline's Cambridge home, The Porch; and Hurston's, on the porch in her hometown, the all-black Eatonville, Florida. See Carla Kaplan's *The Erotics of Talk*, in which she argues against the conventional feminist readings about Janie's movement from silence to voice by asserting that Janie always had the power of speech (99–122). Although cogent, Kaplan's reading underestimates the careful wordplay between silence, suppressed language, and explosive speech in the vital "porch talk" chapter (chap. 6) of the novel, as I argue in "The New Modernist Studies."

46. Ramphele did in fact complete her autobiography, which appeared in South Africa in 1996, but is apparently not available through American bookstores.

CHAPTER 5

Based on papers delivered at the Narrative Conference in Columbus, Ohio, April 1996; the University of Wisconsin–Madison Institute for Research in the Humanities, September 1996; and the UW–Madison English Department, October 1996. Special thanks to anthropologist Neil Whitehead, who first introduced me to relevant readings in anthropology, and to Kamala Visweswaran, Kirin Narayan, Maria Lepowsky, and the various audiences whose challenging questions helped greatly in the revision process.

1. In "Ethnographic Allegory," Clifford holds up Shostak's book as a positive example of experimental or postmodern ethnography in which the ethnographer dismantles the subject/object binary of classical ethnographic writing to highlight the anthropological project as a form of *écriture*. But curiously, in the introduction to the seminal collection, *Writing Culture*, in which his own essay appears, Clifford and Marcus justify the absence of women anthropologists from the contributor's list by stating that women have not written experimental ethnographies. For feminist critique of this exclusion, see particularly Behar and Gordon's collection, *Women Writing Culture*.

2. While *Nisa* reflects the collaborative production of joint agencies, Shostak for the most part ignores the larger political and economic forces that permeate contemporary !Kung existence. Participating to some degree in anthropology's earlier tendency to "capture" a vanishing culture before it is lost, Shostak's focus on Nisa's personal history within family and community ignores for the most part the oppressive intercultural encounters

between the !Kung and surrounding peoples. For a report on the political status of the !Kung, see Daley.

3. See for example Allen, "Kochinnenako"; Anderson, "Reading 'Revenge'"; and Becker. I am indebted to Thongchai Winichakul and Ellen Rafferty for references about South and Southeast Asian narrative practices. Whatever cultural differences might exist, we should guard against too easily assuming essentialist or homogenized narrative traditions for "East" or "West," "First World" or "Third World." Teleological linearity is not the exclusive property of western narrative; nor is all western narrative linear. Shostak, for example, stresses that Nisa's stories, like !Kung stories in general, have a strong linear flavor, with a clear sense of beginning, middle, and end (*Nisa* 40).

4. See Barthes, "Introduction" 295; *Pleasure* 10, 44–45, 47; and *S/Z* 62–63, 187–88, 209–10. For variations on and critiques of Barthes's assertions, see for example, Kristeva, *Revolution* esp. 19–106 and *Powers of Horror* esp. 165; Brooks, *Reading* esp. 90–112; de Lauretis, *Alice Doesn't* esp. 103–57; and Friedman, "Lyric Subversion." Barthes's structuralist approach to narrative owes a great deal to Vladimir Propp's *The Morphology of the Folktale*, which (as Kirin Narayan reminded me) identifies the initiating "function" of folktale narrative to be the act of leaving home: first, when a family member leaves (function I); then, when the hero leaves (function XI) (26, 39).

5. By "post-oedipal," I do not mean what comes developmentally after the Oedipus complex; I refer instead to the psychoanalytically informed theories of narrative that adapt or critique the oedipal model of narrative but do not move beyond its borders. For overviews of theories of desire and narrative, see Clayton, *Pleasures* 61–90, and Martin, *Recent Theories* esp. 40–41, 120–22. Brooks's *Reading for the Plot, Body Work*, and *Psychoanalysis and Storytelling* represent a range of engagements with desire and narrative. For preoedipal and/or homoerotic theories of narrative, see Hirsch; DuPlessis, *Writing*; Friedman, "Lyric Subversion"; Abel, "Narrative"; and Boone, "Vacation Cruises." For theories of narrative as a policing of desire, see for example, Kristeva; D. A. Miller, *Novel*; and Bersani. For the desire to detect and detective fiction, see Todorov; Brooks, *Psychoanalysis* 61–72, *Reading* 23–32, 269–80. For associations of narrative and sexual intercourse, see especially Brooks, *Reading* esp. 48, 61; Scholes; D. A. Miller, *Narrative* ix–xv; and feminist critiques of this linkage in de Lauretis, *Alice Doesn't* 107–9, Winnett; Mulvey; and Boone; "Modernist Maneuvering."

6. As anthropologists increasingly turned a metacritical eye on their own discipline in the past twenty years, many have borrowed heavily from literary studies and poststructuralist theory as they interrogate the significance of ethnography as a form or even distinct genre of writing. See especially Clifford and Marcus; Clifford, *Predicament*; Behar and Gordon; Behar, *Vulnerable Observer*; Visweswaran; and Manganaro. Literary critics have long turned to anthropology for insight, particularly the "armchair" comparativism of James Frazer and Jessie Weston; and the structuralist theory of Claude Lévi-Strauss, Marcel Mauss, and Victor Turner. I am drawing on more recent anthropological theory, especially postmodern, feminist, and indigenous forms of it.

7. A synthesis of psychoanalytic and anthropological approaches is possible, but beyond the scope of this essay. See Waud Kracke's adaptation of Freudian transference for discussion of intercultural encounters between ethnographers and the subjects of such study. Another approach might develop the central importance of self/other encounters in infancy in much object relations psychoanalysis, especially that rooted in the work of D. W. Winnicott. The infant/(m)other encounters that initiate the process of individuation through desire for merging and separation could be regarded as an emotional/psychic foun-

dation for intercultural encounters beyond the family in other borderlands where differences meet.

8. Clifford Geertz defines culture somewhat more narrowly and statically than I do as "an ordered system of meanings and symbols, in terms of which social interaction takes place" (*Interpretation of Culture* 144). See Rosaldo's urging for a more "processual" rather than static concept of culture in which "change rather than structure becomes a society's enduring state" (*Culture and Truth* 91–108, esp. 103); and Gerd Baumann's statement that " 'Culture' is not a real thing, but an abstract . . . a heuristic means towards explaining how people understand and act upon the world" (211). For a critique of the concept of "culture" in anthropology, see Abu-Lughod, "Writing" ("Culture is the essential tool for making other. As a professional discourse that elaborates on the meaning of culture in order to account for, explain, and understand cultural difference, anthropology also helps construct, produce, and maintain it" [143]). For anthropological theory that has been particularly influential in my formation of a provisional notion of "culture" and "intercultural," see Fox's *Recapturing Anthropology*; Behar and Gordon's *Women Writing Culture*; Clifford and Marcus's *Writing Culture*; Ferguson and Gupta's Special Issue of *Cultural Anthropology* on Space, Identity, and the Politics of Difference; Clifford's Special Issue of *Inscriptions* on Traveling Theories, Traveling Theorists; and Visweswaran's *Fictions of Feminist Ethnography*.

9. In making this distinction, I am indebted to Thongchai Winichakul's *Siam Mapped*; see chapter 6 in this volume for further discussion of Thongchai's seminal work.

10. I say *partially* based, because the uniqueness of individual identity can never be fully articulated solely in relationship to categories of social stratification and the multiple group affiliations they engender.

11. Personal communication, 11 October 1995.

12. Though brief, important exceptions to this privileging of time in narrative theory include Michel de Certeau, whose aphoristic chapter "Spatial Stories" (115–30) in *The Practice of Everyday Life* argues that stories are "spatial trajectories" (115) that mark and transgress boundaries or establish frontiers as spaces of interaction (126); Edward Said, who argues in *Culture and Imperialism* against the emphasis on time in narrative theory and advocates discussion of space and location (84). For parallel discussion of the need for spatiality to complement temporality as a category in the social sciences, see Ferguson and Gupta; Clifford, "Spatial Practices," in *Routes* 52–91; Soja; Featherstone and Lash, "Globalization"; Robertson; Friedland and Boden; Keith and Pile; Jones, Nast, and Roberts; Harvey; and Rose. For an overview of space/time debates in cultural theory, see Caren Kaplan, *Questions* 143–87.

13. Ricoeur has produced the most extended study of the temporal dimension of narrative. See *Time and Narrative* and "Narrative Time," in which he critiques structuralist approaches to narrative for the way their model-building, paradigm-making theory eliminates the temporal element. However, the spatialization of structuralist theory has nothing to do with the locational space through which characters move in the plot; rather, what Ricoeur objects to is the synchronic activity of theory. The spatialization I advocate in "Spatialization" and "Spatialization, Narrative Theory" examines reading practices of narrative, not the locational spaces within the narrative. The issue of temporal sequence remains critical for much narrative theory, with much less attention being paid to spatiality or "setting." See for example Wallace Martin, esp. 122–29; Chatman, esp. 45–145; Morson. For a critique of the binary of description (including setting) and narration as canonical in narrative studies, see Ronen. Her article in *Narrative* provoked a fascinating E-mail exchange on the Narrative List in December 1997, one that confirms the prevailing association of setting or description with background as an element somehow outside of or in

back of narration. Monika Fludernik, for example, observes that "characters (agents) require a setting (description), whereas narrative (plot) is configured mostly in terms of actions (and chronology)" (1 December 1997). Marie-Laure Ryan responds: "About the relations of description to Eco's ghost chapters, I'd say that (to the extent that the description is reasonably free from narration) it is one of inversion. Descriptions are textualized, yet they can be skipped by the reader without serious damage for the understanding of the plot (this is not to say that they are altogether deprived of function, of course; they may contribute to thematic development or 'l'effet de reel,' as Barthes calls it)" (4 December 1997).

14. Differing from Lefebvre, de Certeau distinguishes between place (*lieu*) and space (*espace*), associating place with ordered stability and space with the effect of movement (*Practice* 117). For other discussions of space as constitutive of identity, see for example, Gupta and Ferguson; Grewal and Kaplan; Yaeger; Keith and Pile; Kirby; Jones, Nast, and Roberts; Rose; Sennett; Higonnet and Templeton; and Friedland and Bogen. De Lauretis also integrates spatial analysis into her feminist/psychoanalytic consideration of narrative in *Alice Doesn't*, where she argues that the oedipal subject of all narrative penetrates spaces figured as feminine (see esp. 12–36).

15. For discussions of detective narrative as definitive for narrative in general or for the production of psychoanalytic narrative, see especially Todorov; Brooks, *Reading* esp. 23–29, 90–112; Lacan; Eco and Sebeok; and Muller and Richardson, ix. For discussion of the Oedipus narrative as the "specimen story" of psychoanalysis, see for example Felman, "Beyond Oedipus."

16. The study of travel writing is rapidly expanding in both literary studies and anthropology. For discussions of the interrelationship of travel writing and ethnography, see for example, Mary Louise Pratt; Grewal, *Home and Harem*; Caren Kaplan; Lawrence; Robertson et al.; Sharpe; Clifford and Marcus; Clifford, *Predicament* and *Routes*; Spurr; Trinh, *Woman*; Behar and Gordon; and *Studies in Travel Writing* (Spring 1997).

17. *Tell My Horse*, based on her travels and fieldwork in Jamaica and Haiti, oscillates between narratives of connection based on shared African-based cultural identification and narratives of self/other encounter based on her status as a citizen of the United States, which had an occupying army in Haiti at the time, a policy that Hurston supported. Hurston's fiction of the period, *Jonah's Gourd Vine* and *Their Eyes Were Watching God*, relies heavily on ethnographic narrative, just as her ethnographies repeatedly adapt fictional strategies—a reciprocal exchange that anticipates postmodern ethnography. See Hernández.

18. Trouillot's attack on "Third-World-ism" implicitly challenges Said's work, which tends to erase the heterogeneity of both "East" and "West," his disclaimers of such homogenization to the contrary. In "Representing the Colonized," Said critiques the "fetishization and relentless celebration of 'difference' and 'otherness'" in the West and argues that anthropology, even in its indigenous forms, remains "intimately tied to imperialism" (213–14); colonizer and colonized remain largely fixed and unproblematic categories in Said's theorization.

19. For an overview of current spatialized rhetorics of identity, see Kaplan, *Questions* 143–87; Kirby; and chapter 1 in this volume.

20. See chapters 1 and 3 in this volume.

21. For some cogent readings of orientalist desire in Forster's novel in the context of postcolonial studies, see for example, Sharpe, 113–36; Suleri, *Rhetoric* 131–48; Lowe, *Immigrant Acts* 102–35; and Bakshi. For a queer reading of Adela as autobiographical representation, see Piggford.

22. In the trial scene, the association of the caves with Jainism, as distinct from Buddhism, is emphasized (223). The relation of the Marabar Caves to Jainism, one of India's oldest religions, has been noted often in the criticism of the novel. See for example, Parry; Sahni, 99–138; Ganguly, 141–68; and Pintchman. But its powerful resonance for the transformation of Mrs. Moore into a woman beyond caring and ethical intervention did not really become clear for me until I read Gita Mehta's partially satiric novel, *A River Sutra* (1993), about a wealthy merchant who embraces the ascetic life of a Jainist pilgrim, "free from doubt," "delusion," and "extremes" (41). I do not mean to suggest, however, that the Marabar Caves in the novel or the Barabar Caves upon which they are based should be reduced to a single meaning or religion. In both, the caves are sites of palimpsestic syncretism and spaces that invite the projection of conflicting human desires.

23. Although some contemporary antiwestern, nationalist movements promote traditional confinements for women (e.g., in Iran and Afghanistan), a number of other nationalist movements have directly linked modernity, the freeing of women from "tradition," and national liberation. See, for example, Mernissi on Morocco in the 1940s; Bâ on Senegal in the 1950s and early 1960s. However, western justifications for imperialism often included the "civilizing" function of eliminating such "barbaric" practices as sati and purdah. Consequently, feminism within a (post)colonial setting often negotiates between rejection of the imperial binary of civilized/barbaric and the desire for change. For discussions of the complicated role of gender in nationalist and anticolonialist movements, see for example, Parker, Russo, Sommer, and Yaeger; *Nationalisms*; Grewal and Kaplan; Mani, "Multiple Mediations"; and Radhakrishnan, *Diasporic Mediations*, 119–32.

24. See Furbank's biography for accounts of Forster's travels in Egypt and India. For Forster's own experience of Indianization and resistance to it, see the collection of his letters and journals from India in *The Hill of Devi*.

25. For discussion of the psychic effects of colonialism on the colonizers, see especially Gikandi, *Maps*; and Nandy.

26. For related critiques and observations of *Nisa*, see Gupta and Ferguson; M. L. Pratt, "Fieldwork"; Gordon, as reported in Behar, "Writing." My thanks to Kirin Narayan, Ruth Behar, Maria Lepowsky, and Kamala Visweswaran for helping me contextualize Shostak's work within the field of anthropological debate.

27. As Kamala Visweswaran pointed out in a personal communication, such disciplinary mixing has produced considerable backlash and retreat: in anthropology, against the postmodern turn, advocating a return to science; in literary studies, against cultural studies, promoting the restitution of aesthetic formalism.

CHAPTER 6

An expanded version of a paper delivered at the International Conference on Narrative, Gainesville, Florida, April 1997. I owe special thanks to Nellie McKay for helping me to appreciate *Daughters of the Dust* and urging me to write about it; and to Edward Friedman for constant illuminations about things Chinese and Asian. My copanelists, Marilyn Brownstein and Sabina Sawhney, also examined the issues of postcolonial hybridity in ways that influenced my own.

1. Richard Sennett writes: "Ethnicity is a sense of identity established by awareness of difference, and this awareness of difference comes in turn through a history of displacement; the peasant moves, and in the alien land becomes Polish" (198). See also Stuart Hall's "New Ethnicities" for discussion of how an identity like "blackness" is historically and locationally produced; Clifford's "Spatial Practices" and "Diasporas" in *Routes* 52–91, 244–78.

2. Homi Bhabha briefly uses the term *fort/da* in a related way in "The Commitment to Theory," when he discusses "the importance of the space of writing, and the problematic of address, at the very heart of the liberal tradition: It is this to-and-fro, this *fort/da* of the symbolic processes of political negotiation, that constitutes a politics of address" (*Location* 24–25). See also 1, 183.

3. As a feminist object relations theorist, Jessica Benjamin uses a revamped, de-oedipalized narrative of the mother/child interaction to posit a notion of intersubjectivity in which both individuals in an encounter have subjectivity and agency. Although gender difference is important for her model, Benjamin does not deal with other formations of difference and largely ignores issues of power and historical specificity.

4. See chapter 3 of this volume for a review of the debate about the politics of hybridity.

5. Dash began work on the film in 1985, started shooting in 1986, went on the festival circuit in 1991, and finally saw the film released in movie theaters in 1992. For an account of the making and reception of the film, see *Daughters of the Dust: The Making of an African American Woman's Film*, a volume that includes the filmscript, Dash's excerpts from her diary, a dialogue between Dash and bell hooks, and commentary by Toni Cade Bambara and Greg Tate. Gwendolyn Audrey Foster's substantive discussion of the film in *Women Filmmakers* (47–71) emphasizes the film's cinematic and narrative Afrocentrism and departure from Hollywood conventions.

6. In "New Ethnicities" Hall makes a related point about the representation of black heterogeneity in some recent black films in Britain. He greets with "relief" the passing of the fiction that seemed at one time a political necessity, the cinematic representation of "either that all black people are good or indeed that all black people are *the same*" (444). He acknowledges the difficulty of conceiving a politics that "works with and through difference" among blacks at the same time that it builds "forms of solidarity and identification which make common struggle and resistance possible" (444). But he clearly privileges the emphasis on heterogeneity, routes instead of roots.

7. In her dialogue with bell hooks about her intended audience, Dash says that she did not mean to direct the film solely to African Americans or black women, but she did envision a kind of layering of audiences: "I wanted black women first, the black community second, white women third. That's who I was trying to privilege with this film. And everyone else after that" (40).

8. I have made a parallel argument about Louise Erdrich's *Tracks*, which initially invites a reading privileging Nanapush as embodiment of cultural roots and discrediting Pauline as westernized buffoon ("Identity Politics"). The underlying syncretism of both Nanapush and Pauline undermines interpretations based in fundamentalist identity politics.

9. See Bhabha, *Location* esp. 33–39, 85–92, 102–22, and discussion in chapter 4 of this volume.

10. For a definition of what I mean by fundamentalist identity politics, see chapter 2, note 24, in this volume. As I argue about Jen herself, I believe in a significant distinction between absolutist or essentialist identity politics and an identity politics based on a fluid understanding of how identity develops and changes.

11. *Mona* is a sequel to Jen's first novel, *Typical American*, which tells the story of Chang Yifeng's immigration to the United States, adoption of the name Ralph Chang, developing success in the fast food business, and marriage to Helen. Ralph and Helen Chang are Mona's parents; Aunt Theresa, a central character in the first novel, appears only briefly, but significantly, in *Mona*.

12. Jen does not problematize sexuality as an axis of identity and works thoroughly within a heterosexual frame in the novel, in contrast to films like *The Wedding Banquet* (Ang Lee) or *My Beautiful Launderette* (Hanif Kureshi), which deal centrally with multiple

forms of sexuality as they intersect with ethnicity, race, national origin, class, and gender issues. *Mona* examines sexism quite substantially, but does not play with gender blending in the same way that it does with cultural hybridity.

13. In one of the novel's many intertextual "in jokes," Jen echoes Twain when Barbara tosses the keys to her house to Alfred: "He catches it [key ring], of course—this being reflexive in men, not to let things get by them" (152). His catch echoes an episode in chapter 11 of *Huckleberry Finn*, where Huck tries to pass himself off as a girl needing help but fails to deceive the woman to whom he appeals. She constructs a number of tests for him, the last of which is throwing keys at him and detecting how he catches them as a boy in pants would instead of a girl in skirts.

14. Japanese citizenship now passes through the mother as well as the father, but geographical location of birth does not confer citizenship, just as it does not in Germany.

15. Chip Kidd designed a different cover for the paperback edition, one that features the same cut of Asian eyes, this time surrounded by a grid of many American flags. The repetition of the flags, inspired perhaps by Andy Warhol's gridded American cultural icons like Campbell Soup cans or Marilyn Monroe denaturalizes "American" through mimicry and repetition. This cover calls into question, as the novel does, what it means to be "American," but it does not capture the novel's play with hybridity as the first cover did. What role Gish Jen might have had in the design or approval of either cover is not evident; typically, determinations of cover design are linked directly to market forces, not the wishes of the author.

16. There are interesting parallels between Mona's thoughts on skin color and body hair and early articulations of racial difference in Chinese writings as discussed in Frank Dikötter's *The Discourse of Race in Modern China* (1–17). Arab traders had sold black slaves in China as early as the Tang Dynasty. Considering everyone not Chinese to be barbarian, many early Chinese accounts associate white skin color with elite Chinese; dark or black skin with Africans and Chinese peasants; excessive body hair, blue eyes and a devilish, "ashen" whiteness with Europeans.

17. See for example Chirot and Reid on links between Chinese and Jews.

CHAPTER 7

Reprint of "Post/Poststructuralist Feminist Criticism: The Politics of Recuperation and Negotiation," which originally appeared in *New Literary History* (1991), and was based on a paper delivered at the Modern Language Association Convention, 1989. I am indebted to Celeste Schenck and Lisa Ruddick for asking me to write the paper and to Linda Gordon, Elaine Marks, Rachel Blau DuPlessis, and Judith Walzer Leavitt for encouragement and criticism.

1. For others who frame the decade in similar ways, see for example, Harari; Eisenstein and Jardine; Kauffman; and Cohen. See especially Cohen's introduction, which argues in ways parallel to this essay (written before I saw his analysis) that theory is undergoing massive revision in relation to current political and historical forces.

2. For a feminist-psychoanalytic discussion of this generational tension as a displaced form of mother/daughter dynamics, see Evelyn Fox Keller and Moglen.

3. Woolf's impassioned plea in *Three Guineas* that women and men of good will remain "outside" the procession of the powerful has been widely influential in American feminism, particularly radical feminism. As important as her argument is as a critique of patriarchy in family and state, however, I think *Three Guineas* should also be read within the context of its historical moment and society: namely, the rise of fascism and the imminence

of war, which were the immediate issues Woolf addressed; and the overwhelming absence of higher education for women of any class in Britain, a significant difference from the American system. Woolf's warning against co-optation is as compelling today as it was in 1938, but women's studies in the academy would not exist in the United States if feminist educators had believed that they could do significant political work only "outside the system." As a writer, Woolf thoroughly immersed herself in the masculine tradition of letters that she subjected to a dialogic transformation akin to the contradictory position I have described for academic feminists in the United States.

4. See especially Kristeva, "From One Identity to an Other," in her *Desire in Language* 124–47 and *Revolution* esp. 13–20.

5. For further discussion of Barthes, "The Death of the Author," as well as Michel Foucault's related "What Is an Author?" see Cheryl Walker and my "Weavings."

6. For the notion of certain critical terms as taboo, I am indebted to the title of Lisa Ruddick's proposed paper for the MLA session she and Celeste Schenck organized: " 'Self,' 'Spirit,' and Other Taboo Words." This sense of the taboo was somewhat humorously and mysteriously present in the fate of my original title for this essay for the same MLA session. The MLA program listed the title as "The Politics of Agency and Subjectivity . . . ," while my notes clearly read "The Politics of Agency and Identity. . . ." Schenck would never have changed my title without permission. Did she mis-hear when I phoned it in? Did I mis-speak? Did a poststructuralist computer balk at the tainted word *identity*?

7. French feminism is itself not monolithic, a point made forcefully in Elaine Marks and Isabelle de Courtivron's *New French Feminisms*; nor is American feminism. Important differences exist among the commonly linked trio of Kristeva, Cixous, and Irigaray. But the even greater difference between these psychoanalytic and deconstructive feminisms and the existentialist/materialist feminisms of Simone de Beauvoir and Monique Wittig are too often forgotten. This erasure in turn has confused the "American" and "French" feminist split because it also represses the enormous influence that de Beauvoir's existential formulations of Otherness and authenticity had on American feminists during the late 1960s and 1970s. Like the rereadings of Woolf, the rediscovery of *The Second Sex* (1949) was vital to the development of American feminist theory, particularly "radical feminism" and Marxist or socialist feminism.

8. Smith's brief exempla of "humanist" feminism includes phrases from Elaine Showalter (a 1969 essay) and Judith Kegan Gardiner, ones that hardly do justice to the complexity and evolution of their critical work. They are the same phrases he quoted in an earlier essay, "H.D.'s Identity," in which he uses feminist readings of H.D. as the occasion for a critique of "American" feminist "humanism." Without identification in the text, he also quotes as a negative example a phrase from my *Psyche Reborn*: "In short the goal of much of this early kind of ('American') feminist writing on literature seems sometimes to be the discovery of 'woman' as some sort of 'changeless essence [shining] through all the erasure of external change' " (136), a goal he also imputes to me in "H.D.'s Identity," in which he also quotes the phrase. What is not clear in either *Discerning the Subject* or "H.D.'s Identity"—unless a curious reader looks up my original discussion—is how radically Smith distorts what I was saying to serve his critique of "American" feminist "humanism." I was not discussing either "woman" or some sort of feminist "goal." I was interpreting "the Lady," H.D.'s dream-image of a goddess figure, in her epic poem *Trilogy*; my actual sentence reads: "In the palimpsest of history the Lady's changeless essence shines through all the erasures of external change" (*Psyche Reborn* 109), which is a reference to H.D.'s use of the palimpsest and her belief in a divine (female) presence that resides in centuries of

cultural artifacts of Mary and maternal deities (109). The surrounding pages make clear that my reference to "changeless essence" was not an essentialist argument about "woman" or a goal of my own, but a reading of a central image in H.D.'s poem, one that I used to discuss her structuralist and palimpsestic view of historical change and continuity within the context of Freud and Lévi-Strauss. My words were wrenched out of context to demonstrate the "depressingly familiar . . . humanist values" that Smith connects with a belief in "essence," "experience," and unmediated "communication." The charge he makes against me and other feminist critics of H.D. he also makes against what he regards as H.D.'s regressive tendencies in his essay "H.D.'s Flaws." Smith's antihumanist agenda in this essay ironically makes it difficult for him to read the dynamics of H.D.'s agency and subjectivity in her texts, but his chapter on H.D. in his *Pound Revised*, which interprets H.D. in the context of Pound, is excellent (110–33).

9. I want to distinguish here between the deadening expectation of complete agreement in "sisterhood," which I think most feminist critics never had or gave up early on, and the assumption of a common "project" under a broadly defined umbrella of feminisms. The sense of betrayal, I think, has come out of a belief that some poststructuralist critics have felt more closely identified with Derrida, Lacan, and other male masters than they have with non-poststructuralist feminists.

10. When I used the term "politically correct" in December of 1989, I of course had no idea that it was to be appropriated with lightning swiftness by those lashing back at the de-formations and re-formations of the canonical tradition of "western culture" that has taken place in the academy in the past two decades. The attack on the advocates of diversity has curiously borrowed the discourse of the left that decades ago invented the term "politically correct" as a form of self-criticism to address the tendency toward orthodoxy, sectarianism, and fundamentalist thinking within its own ranks. A term used by the left as a means of reminding its various members of the importance of open-ended inquiry has now become a term widely used in the mass media to condemn the entire project of the diverse progressive forces in the academy. Perhaps the term has become so tainted by its recent appropriation that I should not use it. But I have found as yet no substitute term useful for the fundamentalist current I want to critique in some forms of post/poststructuralist theory.

11. In their advocacy of poststructuralism for feminism, Toril Moi, Chris Weedon, and Rita Felski present sharp critiques of what they variously call "American," "liberal," or "humanist" feminism with what I see as inadequate knowledge of the history of feminist literary theory and practice in the United States. See also Jardine, *Gynesis*. A number of other recent books on poststructuralism and feminism frame the debates in terms of "humanism" and "poststructuralism" with varying degrees of dismissive and respectful rhetoric on "humanism"; see for example, Kauffman; Nicholson; Fuss; and Weed.

12. In the first chapter, "'Woman's Era': Rethinking Black Feminist Theory," Carby invokes a number of the poststructuralist insignia (e.g., "essentialist," "humanistic," "experience," "a very simple one-to-one correspondence between fiction and reality," etc.) in her critique of earlier black feminist criticism and comes close to the dismissive rhetoric of some other poststructuralist critics, but her discussion of black women intellectuals, like her title, presumes their subjectivity and agency.

13. For a sampling of other feminist critics who present their work as a self-conscious negotiation, see for example, Sedgwick, *Between Men*; Bauer; Trinh; and Chessman. In *Gynesis*, Jardine presents her project as a negotiation between "American" and "French" theories of the feminine and subjectivity, but her "American" perspective is, I believe, swallowed up by the "French."

14. I discuss the Americanization of "intertextuality" at length in "Weavings." See also Gates's *Signifying Monkey* for an analysis of intertextual practice that presumes the conscious agency of the "author."

CHAPTER 8

Reprinted with occasional updating from *Feminism Beside Itself*, edited by Diane Elam and Robyn Wiegman, 1995. My thanks to the editors for inviting me to write this essay and to Diane Elam and Judith Walzer Leavitt for their criticisms and encouragement.

1. See for example discussions of Hegel's formulation of the double meaning of *history* in Orr, 12; Bahti, 7–8. For stress on history writing as a narrative act, see for example Hall, "Local and the Global" esp. 38; Spivak, *Outside* (282, quoted in epigraph) and *Post-Colonial Critic*, where she insists that Derrida and Lyotard are not "waging war on narratives, but they're realising that the impulse to narrate is not necessarily a solution to the problems of the world" (19).

2. For critiques of "presentism," see for example Butterfield; and Stocking, esp. 1–12. Others, like LaCapra (*History* 43–44) and Orr (15–16), see the teleological nature of history writing as inevitable.

3. Although few currently practicing historians operate out of a fully positivist framework, metahistorians continue to identify positivist historiography as worthy of critique. LaCapra claims that G. R. Elton's modified positivist assumptions in *The Practice of History* (1967) still embody a consensus among many practicing historians (*History* 136). See also Bahti; Hayden White; Harlan; Orr; LaCapra, *History* esp. 15–44, 135–42, "Intellectual History," and *Soundings* esp. 182–210; and the advocacy of a historiography of pragmatics, based on a consensus-based theory of historical truth, in Appleby, Hunt, and Jacob.

4. I capitalize the Real of history throughout as an adaptation of Fredric Jameson's reconfiguration of the Lacanian Real. Like Jameson and LaCapra, I object to the "fashionable conclusion that because history is a text, the 'referent' does not exist" (Jameson, *Political Unconscious* 35). Like Jameson, I believe that the Real of history "is *not* a text, not a narrative, master or otherwise, but that, as an absent cause, it is inaccessible to us except in textual form, and that our approach to it and to the Real itself necessarily passes through its prior textualization [and] its narrativization" (35). See also LaCapra, *History* 38 and "Intellectual History"; Kramer esp. 122–28; Harlan; Hayden White; and Orr.

5. See Bahti; Orr; Spivak, "Literary Representation"; Hayden White, "Question"; and LaCapra's related discussion of the "documentary model" of history (which is aware of or denies the existence of rhetoric as part of the practice of history), White's model of the "figural origins of historical knowledge," and White's own "dialogic" model in which the historian engages in a "dialogue with the dead who are reconstituted through their 'textualized' remainders" (*History* 18, 21, 34, 36). For overviews of White's and LaCapra's influential work, see Kramer; Jacoby.

6. See for example Coyner's "Women's Studies as an Academic Discipline," in Bowles and Klein's *Theories of Women's Studies*, a collection that contains the contradictory epistemologies that underlie women's studies as a field.

7. For developments in this kind of feminist epistemology, see for example, standpoint theory developed especially in feminist philosophy (e.g., Harstock, Haraway, Hekman); and theories of locational or positional knowledge in writers such as Rich, Alcoff, Allen, Caren Kaplan, Braidotti, Martin and Mohanty, Deborah King, and Smiley. Although the

notion of the constructedness of all human discourse, including history, is often associated with poststructuralist theory, subjectivist epistemologies have been a part of women's studies since its origins in the late 1960s.

8. For other discussion of these epistemological issues in feminism, see Smiley; Nicolson's *Feminism/Postmodernism*, esp. essays by Flax, DiStefano, Harding, Benhabib, Harstock, and Bordo.

9. See the Special Issue of *Democratic Culture* on Sommers's *Who Stole Feminism?* edited by John Wilson, esp. Wilson's account of the right-wing promotion of the book.

10. The title may also echo the titles of widely disseminated feminist texts like Audre Lorde's *Sister Outsider* and Robin Morgan's *Sisterhood Is Powerful* and *Sisterhood Is Global*. For another attack on women's studies from a self-identified feminist standpoint, see Lehrman.

11. See Barthes, "The Reality Effect" and "The Discourse of History," esp. 140.

12. See also James Scott's *Domination*, which argues that members of hegemonic and nonhegemonic groups are continually engaged in interpretive storytelling in the form of public or hidden transcripts. A peasant, for example, might produce an acquiescent transcript in the presence of a landlord and a rebellious transcript for other peasants.

13. In *Feminists Theorize the Political*, Butler and Joan Scott misleadingly appropriate for poststructuralism the initial challenge to the category of "woman" (or "women") as an erasure of differences based on race, class, sexuality, religion, national origin.

14. See also Swindells, who warns against reading texts such as *The Diaries of Hannah Cullwick* as the unmediated, authentic expression of a workingclass woman. Cullwick, a scrubwoman in Victorian England, wrote the diaries at the command of her master, who was sexually aroused by her descriptions of drudgery.

15. For a sampling of poststructuralist feminist texts influential in the 1980s, see Marks and de Courtivron; Gallop; Jardine; Belsey; Weedon; Moi.

16. See Teresa de Lauretis's insistence in *The Technologies of Gender* on the necessity, however utopian, of seeking the "subject of feminism." But where Butler means by the phrase the advocacy for women based on a common gender-identity, de Lauretis uses the phrase to indicate what she calls the "elsewhere" or "space-off" of a differently constituted feminist subjectivity. Like Kamuf and Butler, de Lauretis returns centrally to Foucault, but her reliance on Foucauldian concepts of discursive practice is tempered by an insistence that feminists must recognize the limitations of his critiques of identity and experience.

17. See also Swindells; Judith Stacey's call for poststructuralist historiography; and Gluck and Patai's brief acknowledgment in their introduction of the importance of "contemporary literary theory" for an analysis of linguistic mediations in oral history. At the 1993 Berkshire Conference for Women's Historians, poststructuralist theory was noticeably a more significant presence than at the prior Berkshire conferences.

18. See Hayden White's "The Discourse of History" and his discussion of the general hostility of (post)structuralism to historical narrative in "The Question of Narrative." See also Walter Benjamin's critique of conventional narrative historicism and advocacy of a messianic, revolutionary "historical materialism" that juxtaposes constellations of time (*Illuminations* 253–64).

19. See for example, Kristeva, *Revolution* esp. 58–59, 88, 92 and "Women's Time"; Cixous, "Laugh" esp. 250.

20. See for example Bersani, who argues that narrative is inherently authoritarian, allied to the state through its connection to mimesis (esp. 3–16, 51–88, 189–316); Clayton's critique of Bersani, 71–82; de Lauretis's *Alice Doesn't* (103–58), in which she finds narrative inseparable from an oedipal configuration of desire in which subjectivity is constituted

as masculine (a position she moves beyond in *Technologies of Gender*, in which she specifies "the modes of consciousness of a feminist subjectivity and its inscription" [xi]). Peter Brooks, who values narrative as an important mode of knowing in *Reading for the Plot*, is a notable exception among poststructuralist theorists. A number of feminist critics find in women's writing a resistance to oedipal narrative and a location of female subjectivity in pre-oedipal narrative patterns. See for example DuPlessis, *Writing*; Homans, *Bearing*; Hirsch, *Mother/Daughter Plot*; Sprengnether; and Abel, "Narrative." For extended discussion, see Friedman, "Craving Stories" and "Lyric Subversion."

21. See also de Man, *Blindness and Insight* esp. 142–66, 187–228 and *Allegories of Reading* in which he argues against the referential and for the figural function of narrative. See also Caserio's discussion of de Man; Foucault's analysis of the relation between allegory and story in *The Order of Things*. For a variety of poststructuralist interrogations of history and historiography, see Attridge, Bennington, and Young.

22. The other essays in Gluck and Patai's *Women's Words* also urge that the problems they reflect upon not lead to the abandonment of oral history methodologies. See also Shostak, whose article on the production of *Nisa*, the personal narrative of a !Kung woman, on the one hand problematizes her own extensive mediation and on the other hand testifies to the urgency of (re)telling narratives of people whose way of life is under erasure ("What the Wind").

23. I realize I risk here homogenizing the complex and different discourses of poststructuralism, but I do so strategically to emphasize what these various theories share in their common focus on constructivist discourse and their insistence on problematization, however much they might differ in other regards.

24. For others who make variations on this point in relation to specific groups of women, see for example Wall, esp. 10; Radhakrishnan, *Diasporic* 62–79; de Lauretis, "Feminist Studies"; Wolfe and Penelope, 1–24; McDowell; Mohanty's concept of "Third World women" as an "imagined community" in "Cartographies"; and Sedgwick's notion of the "minoritizing" discourse about gays and lesbians that must complement the universalizing discourse of queer theory (see esp. *Epistemology* 86–90). See also Cohen esp. vii–xx.

25. See for example Paul Smith's chapter on feminism, in which he credits poststructuralist feminism with bringing poststructuralist theory in general back to historical and political questions but dismisses what he calls humanist feminism out of hand (*Discerning the Subject* 133–52). See chapter 7, note 8 in this volume for extended discussion.

26. Similarly, as an implicit dismissal of literary history, Butler explains that "the sudden intrusion, the unanticipated agency, of a female 'object' who inexplicably returns the [male] glance, reverses the [male] gaze, and contests the place and authority of the masculine position . . . couldn't quite hold my attention" (*Gender Trouble* ix).

27. Also cited in Gayle Greene, "Looking at History" (11–12), which defends the urgency of feminist histories of feminism.

28. It is beyond the scope of this essay to explore what I believe is an (not *the*) underlying cause of much conflict among academic feminists—namely, the generational issue. See for example Helena Michie; Evelyn Fox Keller and Moglen; Minor and Longino; Siegel; Rebecca Walker; Findler; Looser and Kaplan; and Heywood and Drake. An effort to historicize the positions and perspectives of each generation could foster the multiplicity of generational voices rather than the silencing of one by another.

29. For extended discussion, see chapter 9.

30. See also Molly Hite's discussion of the dual functions of narrative and its necessity for feminism (esp. 127).

31. Pomata's interesting historiographic essay favors "particular" or local histories over any kind of generalizing histories and spatial/topical histories over chronological narratives.

32. See Peter Brooks, *Reading* esp. 37–61; Clayton, *Pleasures* esp. 3–31, 61–89; Hutcheon, *Politics* esp. 62–92.

33. I discuss this at length in "Forbidden Fruits."

34. See Bahti's discussion of the will-to-power inherent in the "historicism in man," that is, the desire within man to make and write history (5–6).

35. Scott's approach to agency is based in the early work of Foucault, who by the late 1970s and early 1980s reintroduced concepts of the self and agency that his earlier work had discredited.

36. See my "Weavings" for discussion of this (post)colonial dynamic.

37. See esp. Kelly, "Did Women Have a Renaissance?" and "The Social Relation of the Sexes" for influential examples.

38. However much Showalter can be criticized for her privileging of gynocriticism over gynesis in "Women's Time, Women's Space," "Feminist Criticism in the Wilderness," or *The New Feminist Criticism*, it should be noted that she acknowledges the importance of poststructuralist feminist theory and criticism more thoroughly and respectfully than many feminist poststructuralists acknowledge the work of non-poststructuralist feminist critics.

39. See also Spivak's "Three Women's Texts" in which she shows how western feminist emphasis on narratives of individual female awakening obscures the colonial politics of novels such as *Jane Eyre*.

40. I am adapting Radhakrishnan's argument against the attempt by any single discourse of class, gender, nationality, sexuality (etc.) to subsume the others under its own hegemony.

CHAPTER 9

A condensed version of "Craving Stories: Narrative and Lyric in Contemporary Theory and Women's Long Poems," which appeared in *Feminist Measures: Soundings in Poetry and Theory*, edited by Lynn Keller and Cristanne Miller (1994). This essay is dedicated to feminist scientist and mentor Ruth Bleier, who died while I was writing it in 1992.

1. See also Maxine Hong Kingston's *The Woman Warrior*; Louise Erdrich's *Tracks*; Amy Tan's *The Joy Luck Club* ("Oh, what good stories! Spilling out all over the place!" [11]) and *The Kitchen God's Wife*; Silko's *Ceremony*; Morrison's *Beloved*; and Kim Chernin's *In My Mother's House* ("Very softly, whispering, I say to her, 'Mama, tell me a story.' . . . And yes, with all the skill available to me as a writer, I will take down her tales and tell her story" [17]).

2. Perloff's use of the timeless lyric to characterize modernism ignores the enormous importance of narrative—however altered from nineteenth-century conventions—for modernism, including many modernist long poems.

3. Literary histories of the twentieth-century long poem deal almost exclusively with male poets. See for example, James E. Miller; Michael Bernstein; Rosenthal and Gall; Dickie; Gardner; and Baker. For important exceptions, see Keller; and Kamboureli.

4. Their long poems include H.D.'s *Trilogy* (1944–46), *By Avon River* (1949), *Helen in Egypt* (1952–55, 1961), *Sagesse* (1957, 1972), *Vale Ave* (1957, 1982), *Winter Love* (1959, 1972), and *Hermetic Definition* (1960, 1972); Gertrude Stein's *Tender Buttons* (1911–12, 1914), *Lifting Belly* (1915–17, 1953), *Patriarchal Poetry* (1927, 1953), and *Stanzas in Meditation* (1932, 1956); Mina Loy's *Anglo-Mongrels and the Rose* (1923–25), never

published in toto until 1982 in *The Last Lunar Baedeker*; and Gwendolyn Brooks, *A Street in Brownsville* (1945), *The Anniad* (1949), and *In the Mecca* (1968). (Where two dates are given, the first refers to composition, the second to publication; the delayed publication dates for H.D., Loy, and Stein may reflect writers' and readers' anxiety about the coupling of women and the long poem). Edna St. Vincent Millay's *Fatal Interview* (1931), a sequence of fifty-two sonnets organized seasonally, can also be read as a long poem.

5. In *Mythologies*, Barthes does not directly connect myth with narrative, but his demystifications of mass culture in the book analyze the operations of what are now termed cultural narratives. Moreover, the opposition he sets up between myth and poetry as well as his selection of the term myth (which etymologically means *story* in Greek) for ideology suggest that the binary that underlies the volume is the one that appears elsewhere in Barthes's work: narrative vs. lyric. See also his 1967 essay "The Discourse of History" (esp. 136, 140).

6. Kristeva's alliance with poetic and against novelistic modalities represents an interesting departure from M. M. Bakhtin's formulation of the narrative/lyric opposition in *The Dialogic Imagination*, where he argues that novelistic discourse, in contrast to poetry, has a "fundamentally dialogic relationship to heteroglossia" (the heteroglossic being his version of transgressive discourse) (399).

7. Bedient argues that Kristeva's privileging of poetry, poetic practice, and the semiotic ignores the way poetry is also associated *with* (not just against) culture and meaning. But he does not deal with the opposition between narrative and poetic.

8. See especially Bersani, 3–16, 51–88, 189–316; Clayton's critique of Bersani and defense of narrative in "Narrative and Theories of Desire"; de Lauretis, *Alice Doesn't* 103–58. In *Technologies of Gender*, de Lauretis moves beyond the position of *Alice Doesn't* to "specify the modes of consciousness of a feminist subjectivity and its inscription" (xi). For location of female subjectivity in the pre-oedipal, see for example DuPlessis, *Writing*; Homans, *Bearing*; Hirsch, *The Mother/Daughter Plot*; Sprengnether; and Abel, "Narrative."

9. I have discussed at length the gender inflection of epic tradition and its impact on twentieth-century long poems in "Gender and Genre Anxiety" and "When a 'Long' Poem Is a 'Big' Poem."

10. A few critics attempt to avoid weighting lyric in relation to narrative by stressing the play of both modes in the long poem. Keller, for example, refers to "the triadic base of lyric, epic, and prose elements" in the modern long poem ("Twentieth-Century Long Poem" 535). Kamboureli sees the long poem as a heterogeneous mix of lyric, epic, and documentary characterized by "generic restlessness": "The long poem as I read it finds its energy in its incorporation of various genres and its simultaneous resistance to generic labels" (xiii–xiv).

11. Definitions of "long poem" vary considerably. I use the term to cover a variety of forms that includes reflexively identified epics and long poems, lyric sequences of substantial length and scope, volumes of discrete poems whose coherence and/or progression are somehow marked by the poet as a whole, and texts that can be read innovatively at the borders of the genre (such as Silko's *Storyteller*; Anzaldúa's *Borderlands/La Frontera*; Shange's *For Colored Girls . . .*); and Warland's *Proper Deafinitions*. For discussion of definition, see Keller; Riddel's Special Issue of *Genre* on the long poem; Li; Kamboureli; and my "When a 'Long' Poem."

12. A more tenuous narrative function is implicit in a meditative, philosophical/literary discourse that is particularly common in avant-garde long poems by such poets as Susan Howe, Bernadette Mayer, Beverley Dahlen, Kathleen Fraser, and Rachel Blau DuPlessis.

Such poems implicitly contain a narrative of dialogic play with the traditional philosophic and linguistic discourses from which women have been excluded. DuPlessis, *Pink Guitar* 110–39 on Howe and Dahlen; my "When a 'Long' Poem," on Warland; Keller, *Forms*, on DuPlessis and Howe.

13. The Greek root for *history* is *historia*, which means learning or knowing by inquiry; for *myth*, *mythos*, which means story.

14. See for example Allen Ginsberg, *Howl*; John Berryman, *Homage to Mistress Bradstreet*; Robert Lowell, *History*; and Charles Olson, *The Maximus Poems*.

15. Such representations are not confined to western traditions; they are present in Confucian culture, for example. They are not, however, universal. Some American Indian cultures, such as the Laguna Pueblo people to which Silko belongs, exhibit a less gynophobic theology.

16. In the longer version of this chapter, "Craving Stories," I review some different types of historical and mythic narratives, with reference to long poems by Ruth Whitman, Susan Howe, Karen Brodine, Denise Levertov, Bernadette Mayer, Daphne Marlatt and Betsy Warland, Diane Glancy, Anne Sexton, Anne Cameron, Lucille Clifton, Toi Derricotte, Rita Dove, Pat Parker, Diane Wakowski, Charlotte Mandel, Judy Grahn, Gloria Anzaldúa, Louise Erdrich, Carolyn Grassi, Rena Rosenwasser, and Ntozake Shange.

17. I owe thanks to Meryl Schwartz, whose seminar paper on *Keeper of Accounts* as a coherent volume first directed my attention to Klepfisz. Another long poem ideal for this discussion is Theresa Hak Kyung Cha's *DICTEE*.

18. Klepfisz's inscription of Judaism in this poem differs markedly from that of writers such as Kim Chernin, E. M. Broner, and I. B. Singer. In cultural and religious terms, Klepfisz does not portray the rich communal life and heritage of many Jews; nor does she connect with the specifically religious (especially mystical or Chassidic) aspects of Judaism. Nonetheless, her poem contains powerful intertextual resonances with biblical narratives.

Abel, Elizabeth. "Black Writing, White Reading: Race and the Politics of Feminist Interpretation." *Critical Inquiry* 19 (Spring 1993): 470–98.

———. "Narrative Structure(s) and Female Development: The Case of *Mrs. Dalloway.*" *The Voyage In: Fictions of Female Development.* Ed. Elizabeth Abel, Marianne Hirsch, and Elizabeth Langland. Hanover, NH: U of New England P, 1983. 161–85.

———. *Virginia Woolf and the Fictions of Psychoanalysis.* Chicago: U Chicago P, 1989.

———, ed. *Writing and Sexual Difference.* Special Issue of *Critical Inquiry* 8.2 (Winter 1981).

Abel, Elizabeth, Barbara Christian, Helen Moglen, eds. *Female Subjects in Black and White: Race, Psychoanalysis, Feminism.* Berkeley: U of California P, 1997.

Abraham, Nicolas, and Maria Torok. *The Wolf Man's Magic Word.* Trans. Nicholas Rand. Minneapolis: U of Minnesota P, 1986.

Abu-Lughod, Lila. "Is There a Feminist Ethnography?" *Women and Performance* 9.1 (1990): 1–24.

———. "Writing against Culture." Fox 137–62.

Alarcón, Daniel Cooper. *The Aztec Palimpsest: Mexico in the Modern Imagination.* Tucson: U of Arizona P, 1997.

Alarcón, Norma. "The Theoretical Subject(s) of *This Bridge Called My Back* and Anglo-American Feminism." Anzaldúa, *Making Face* 356–69.

Albrecht, Lisa, and Rose M. Brewer, eds. *Bridges of Power: Women's Multicultural Alliances.* Philadelphia: New Society Publishers, 1990.

Alcoff, Linda. "Cultural Feminism versus Poststructuralism: The Identity Crisis in Feminist Theory." *Signs* 13 (Spring 1988): 405–36.

Alexander, Meena. *Fault Lines: A Memoir.* New York: Feminist Press, 1993.

———. *The Shock of Arrival: Reflections on Postcolonial Experience.* Boston: South End Press, 1996.

Allan, Tuzyline Juta. *Womanist and Feminist Aesthetics: A Comparative Review.* Columbus: Ohio State UP, 1993.

Allen, Paula Gunn. "Kochinnenako in Academe: Three Approaches to Interpreting a Keres Indian Tale." Allen, *Sacred Hoop* 222–44.

———. *The Sacred Hoop: Recovering the Feminine in American Indian Traditions.* Boston: Beacon Press, 1986.

———, ed. *Spider Woman's Granddaughters: Traditional Tales and Contemporary Writing by Native American Women.* New York: Fawcett, 1989.

Amirthanayagam, Indran. "Rogue Elephants, Deadly Tigers." *New York Times* (19 May 1993).

Anderson, Benedict R. *Imagined Communities: Reflections on the Origin and Spread of Nationalism.* New York: Verso Books, 1983.

———. "Reading 'Revenge' by Prmaoedya Ananta Toer (1978–1982)." *Writing on the Tongue.* Ed. A. L. Becker. Ann Arbor: Michigan Papers on South and Southeast Asia, 1989. 13–64.

Anzaldúa, Gloria. *Borderlands/La Frontera: The New Mestiza.* San Francisco: Spinsters/Aunt Lute, 1987.

———. "Bridge, Drawbridge, Sandbar or Island: Lesbians of Color Hacienda Alianzas." Albrecht and Brewer 216–31.

———. "En rapport, In Opposition: Cobrando cuentas a las nuestras." Anzaldúa, *Making Face* 142–50.

———, ed. *Making Face/ Making Soul—Haciendo Caras: Creative and Critical Perspectives by Women of Color.* San Francisco: Aunt Lute, 1990.

Appadurai, Arjun. "Disjuncture and Difference in the Global Cultural Economy." *Public Culture* 2.2 (1990): 1–24. Rpt. Appadurai, *Modernity* 27–47.

———. "Global Ethnoscapes: Notes and Queries for a Transnational Anthropology." Fox 191–210. Rpt. Appadurai, *Modernity* 48–65.

———. *Modernity at Large: Cultural Dimensions of Globalization.* Minneapolis: U of Minnesota P, 1996.

Appiah, Anthony. "The Conservation of 'Race.'" *Black American Literary Forum* 23 (Spring 1989): 37–60.

———. "The Uncompleted Argument: Du

Bois and the Illusion of Race." Gates, *"Race"* 21–37.

Appiah, Kwame Anthony, and Henry Louis Gates, Jr. "Editors' Introduction: Multiplying Identities." Appiah and Gates 625–29.

———, eds. Special Issue on Identities. *Critical Inquiry* 18 (Summer 1992).

Appleby, Joyce, Lynn Hunt, and Margaret Jacob. *Telling the Truth about History.* New York: Norton, 1994.

Asian Women United of California, eds. *Making Waves: An Anthology of Writings by and about Asian American Women.* Boston: Beacon Press, 1989.

Attridge, Derek, Geoff Bennington, and Robert Young, eds. *Post-structuralism and the Question of History.* Cambridge: Cambridge UP, 1987.

Bâ, Mariama. *So Long a Letter.* Trans. Modupé Bodé-Thomas. London: Heinemann, 1981.

Bahti, Timothy. *Allegories of History: Literary Historiography after Hegel.* Baltimore: Johns Hopkins UP, 1992.

Baker, Houston, Jr. "Caliban's Triple Play." Gates, *"Race"* 381–95.

———. *Modernism and the Harlem Renaissance.* Chicago: U of Chicago P, 1987.

Baker, Peter. *Obdurate Brilliance: Exteriority and the Modern Long Poem.* Gainesville: U of Florida P, 1991.

Bakhtin, M. M. *The Dialogic Imagination.* Ed. Michael Holquist. Trans. Caryl Emerson and Michael Holquist. Austin: U of Texas P, 1981.

Bakshi, Parminder. "The Politics of Desire: E. M. Forster's Encounters with India." Davies and Wood 23–64.

Bambara, Toni Cade. Preface. Dash, *Daughters of the Dust: The Making of an African American Woman's Film* xi–xvi.

Bammer, Angelika, ed. *Displacements: Cultural Identities in Question.* Bloomington: Indiana UP, 1994.

Banton, Michael P. *Racial Theories.* Cambridge: Cambridge UP, 1987.

Barker, A. J. *The Vainglorious War, 1854–1856.* London: Weidenfeld and Nicolson, 1970.

Barrett, Michèle. "Ideology and the Cultural Production of Gender." *Feminist Criticism and Social Change: Sex, Class and Race in Literature and Culture.* Ed. Judith Newton and Deborah Rosenfelt. London: Methuen, 1985. 65–85.

Barthes, Roland. "The Death of the Author." *Rustle of Language* 49–55.

———. "The Discourse of History." 1967. *Rustle of Language* 127–40.

———. "Introduction to the Structural Analysis of Narratives." *A Barthes Reader.* Ed. Susan Sontag. New York: Hill and Wang, 1982. 251–95.

———. *Mythologies.* 1957. Trans. Annette Lavers. New York: Hill and Wang, 1972.

———. *The Pleasure of the Text.* Trans. Richard Miller. New York: Hill and Wang, 1973.

———. "The Reality Effect." 1968. *Rustle of Language* 141–48.

———. *The Rustle of Language.* Trans. Richard Howard. New York: Hill and Wang, 1986.

———. *S/Z.* Trans. Richard Miller. New York: Hill and Wang, 1974.

———. *Writing Degree Zero.* 1953. Trans. Annette Lavers and Colin Smith. New York: Hill and Wang, 1967.

Bauer, Dale. *Feminist Dialogics: A Theory of Failed Community.* Albany: State UP of New York, 1988.

Baumann, Gerd. "Dominant and Demotic Discourses of Culture: Their Relevance to Multi-Ethnic Alliances." Werbner and Modood 209–25.

Bazin, Nancy Topping. *Virginia Woolf and the Androgynous Vision.* New Brunswick, NJ: Rutgers UP, 1973.

Beauvoir, Simone de. *The Second Sex.* 1949. Trans. H. M. Parshley. New York: Bantam, 1961.

Beck, Evelyn Torton, ed. *Nice Jewish Girls: A Lesbian Anthology.* Watertown, MA: Persephone Press, 1982.

Becker, A. L. "Text-Building, Epistemology, and Aesthetics in Javanese Shadow Theatre." *The Imagination of Reality.* Ed. A. L. Becker and Aran Yengoyan. Norwood, CT: Ablex Publishing, 1979. 211–43.

Bedient, Calvin. "Kristeva and Poetry as Shattered Signification." *Critical Inquiry* 16 (Summer 1990): 807–29.

Behar, Ruth. "Desire and Deception in Feminist Border-Crossings." Paper presented at the Conference on Theorizing Differences among Women: Cross-Disciplinary and Cross-National Approaches. Michigan State University. East Lansing, MI. February 1997.

———. "The Story of Ruth, the Anthropologist." *People of the Book: Thirty Scholars*

Reflect on Their Jewish Identity. Ed. Jeffrey Rubin-Dorsky and Shelley Fisher Fishkin. Madison: U of Wisconsin P, 1996. 261–79.

———. *The Vulnerable Observer: Anthropology That Breaks Your Heart.* Boston: Beacon Press, 1996.

———. "Writing in My Father's Name: A Diary of *Translated Woman*'s First Year." Behar and Gordon 65–82.

Behar, Ruth, and Deborah A. Gordon, eds. *Women Writing Culture.* Berkeley: U of California P, 1995.

Beja, Morris. *Film and Literature.* New York: Longman, 1979.

Belenky, Mary Field, Blythe McVicker Clinchy, Nancy Rule Goldberger, and Jill Mattuck Tarule. *Women's Ways of Knowing: The Development of Self, Voice, and Mind.* New York: Basic Books, 1986.

Bell, Quentin. *Virginia Woolf: A Biography.* Vols. 1 and 2. New York: Harcourt Brace Jovanovich, 1972.

Belsey, Catherine. *Critical Practice.* London: Methuen, 1980.

Bem, Sandra. "The Measurement of Psychological Androgyny." *Journal of Consulting and Clinical Psychology* 42.2 (1974): 155–62.

———. "Probing the Promise of Androgyny." 1975. Kaplan and Bean 48–62.

Benhabib, Seyla. *Situating the Self: Gender, Community and Postmodernism in Contemporary Ethics.* London: Routledge, 1992.

Benjamin, Jessica. *The Bonds of Love: Psychoanalysis, Feminism, and the Problem of Domination.* New York: Pantheon, 1988.

Benjamin, Walter. "Theses on the Philosophy of History." 1950. *Illuminations: Essays and Reflections.* Ed. Hannah Arendt. New York: Schocken Books, 1968. 253–64.

Benstock, Shari, ed. *Feminist Issues in Literary Scholarship.* Bloomington: Indiana UP, 1987.

Bernal, Martin. *Black Athena: The Asiatic Roots of Classical Greece.* New Brunswick: Rutgers UP, 1987.

Bernstein, Michael. *The Tale of the Tribe: Ezra Pound and the Modern Verse Epic.* Princeton: Princeton University Press, 1980.

Bernstein, Susan. "Confessing Feminist Theory: What's 'I' Got to Do with It?" *Hypatia* 7 (Spring 1992): 120–47.

Berryman, John. *Homage to Mistress Bradstreet.* New York: Farrar, Straus, and Cudahy, 1956.

Bersani, Leo. *A Future for Astyanax: Character and Desire in Literature.* New York: Columbia UP, 1984.

Bhabha, Homi K. "DissemiNation: time, narrative, and the margins of the modern nation." Bhabha, *Nation* 291–322.

———. "Introduction: narrating the nation." Bhabha, *Nation* 1–7.

———. *The Location of Culture.* London: Routledge, 1994.

———. "The Other Question..." *Screen* 24 (November/December 1983): 18–36.

———, ed. *Nation and Narration.* London: Routledge, 1990.

Binder, David, with Barbara Crossette. "As Ethnic Wars Multiply, U.S. Strives for a Policy." *New York Times* (7 February 1993).

Bloch, Ruth H. "A Culturalist Critique of Trends in Feminist Theory." *Contention* 2 (Spring 1993): 79–106.

Boelhower, William. *Through a Glass Darkly: Ethnic Semiosis in American Literature.* Oxford: Oxford UP, 1987.

Bonner, Raymond. "A Once-Peaceful Village Shows the Roots of Rwanda's Violence." *New York Times* (11 July 1994).

Boone, Joseph A. "Modernist Maneuverings in the Marriage Plot: Breaking Ideologies of Gender and Genre in James' *The Golden Bowl.*" *PMLA* 101 (May 1986): 374–88.

———. "Vacation Cruises; or, The Homoerotics of Orientalism." *PMLA* 110 (January 1995): 89–107.

Borland, Katherine. "'That's Not What I Said': Interpretive Conflict in Oral Narrative Research." Gluck and Patai 63–76.

Bourne, Jenny. "Homelands of the Mind: Jewish Feminism and Identity Politics." *Race and Class* 29 (1987): 1–24.

Bowles, Gloria, and Renata Duelli Klein, eds. *Theories of Women's Studies.* London: Routledge and Kegan Paul, 1983.

Bradbury, Malcolm, and James McFarlane, eds. *Modernism, 1890–1930.* New York: Penguin, 1976.

Braidotti, Rosi. "Embodiment, Sexual Difference, and the Nomadic Subject." *Hypatia* 8 (Winter 1993): 1–13.

———. *Nomadic Subjects: Embodiment and Sexual Difference in Contemporary Feminist Theory.* New York: Columbia UP, 1994.

Braxton, Joanne. *Black Women Writing Autobi-*

ography: A Tradition within a Tradition. Philadelphia: Temple UP, 1989.

Braxton, Joanne M., and Andrée Nicola McLaughlin, eds. Wild Women in the Whirlwind: Afra-American Culture and the Contemporary Literary Renaissance. New Brunswick, NJ: Rutgers UP, 1990.

Broe, Mary Lynn, and Angela Ingram, eds. Women's Writing in Exile. Chapel Hill: U of North Carolina P, 1989.

Brooks, Gwendolyn. The Anniad. 1949. Brooks, Blacks 97–112.

———. Blacks. Chicago: Third World Press, 1987.

———. "In the Mecca." 1968. Brooks, Blacks 401–34.

———. A Street in Bronzesville. 1945. Brooks, Blacks 14–41.

Brooks, Peter. Body Work: Objects of Desire in Modern Narrative. Cambridge: Harvard UP, 1993.

———. Psychoanalysis and Storytelling. Oxford: Basil Blackwell, 1994.

———. Reading for the Plot: Design and Intention in Narrative. New York: Vintage, 1984.

Bulkin, Elly, Minnie Bruce Pratt, and Barbara Smith. Yours in Struggle: Three Feminist Perspectives on Anti-Semitism and Racism. Brooklyn, NY: Long Haul Press, 1984.

Butler, Judith. Bodies That Matter: On the Discursive Limits of "Sex." London: Routledge, 1993.

———. Gender Trouble: Feminism and the Subversion of Identity. London: Routledge, 1990.

Butler, Judith, and Joan W. Scott, eds. Feminists Theorize the Political. London: Routledge, 1992.

Butterfield, Herbert. The Whig Interpretation of History. 1959. New York: Norton, 1965.

Calderón, Héctor, and José David Saldívar, eds. Criticism in the Borderlands: Studies in Chicano Literature, Culture, and Ideology. Durham, NC: Duke UP, 1991.

Canclini, Néstor García. Hybrid Cultures: Strategies for Entering and Leaving Modernity. Trans. Christopher L. Chiappari and Silvia L. López. Minneapolis: U of Minnesota P, 1995.

Capel, Sharon. Letter to New York Times (7 March 1993).

Carby, Hazel V. Reconstructing Womanhood: The Emergence of the Afro-American Woman Novelist. Oxford: Oxford UP, 1987.

Carlston, Erin G. "Zami and the Politics of Plural Identity." Sexual Practice, Textual Theory: Lesbian Cultural Criticism. Ed. Susan J. Wolfe and Julia Penelope. Oxford: Basil Blackwell, 1993. 226–36.

Caserio, Robert L. " 'A Pathos of Uncertain Agency': Paul de Man and Narrative." Journal of Narrative Technique 20 (Spring 1990): 195–209.

———. Plot, Story, and the Novel. Princeton: Princeton UP, 1979.

Castillo, Debra A. Talking Back: Toward a Latin American Feminist Literary Criticism. Ithaca, NY: Cornell UP, 1992.

Caughie, Pamela. "Passing as Pedagogy: Feminism in(to) Cultural Studies." English Studies/Cultural Studies: Institutionalizing Dissent. Ed. Isaiah Smithson and Nancy Ruff. Urbana: U of Illinois P, 1994): 76–93.

Cha, Theresa Hak Kung. DICTEE. New York: Tanam, 1982.

Chai, Alice Yun. "Toward a Holistic Paradigm for Asian American Women's Studies: A Synthesis of Feminist Scholarship and Women of Color's Feminist Politics." Women's Studies International Forum 8.1 (1985): 59–66.

Chambers, Iain. Migrancy, Culture, Identity. London: Routledge, 1994.

Chametzky, Jules. "Beyond Melting Pots, Cultural Pluralism, Ethnicity—or, Déjà Vu All Over Again." Melus 16 (Winter 1989–90): 3–17.

Chang, Elaine K. "A Not-So-New Spelling of My Name: Notes toward (and against) a Politics of Equivocation." Displacements: Cultural Identities in Question. Ed. Angelika Bammer. Bloomington: Indiana UP, 1994. 251–66.

Chapman, Wayne, ed. Special Issue on Virginia Woolf International. South Carolina Review 29.1 (Fall 1996).

Chatman, Seymour. Story and Discourse: Narrative Structure in Fiction and Film. Ithaca: Cornell UP, 1978.

Cheng, Vincent J. Joyce, Race, and Empire. Cambridge: Cambridge UP, 1995.

Chernin, Kim. In My Mother's House: A Daughter's Story. New York: Harper and Row, 1983.

Chessman, Harriet Scott. The Public Is Invited to Dance: Representation, the Body, and Dialogue in Gertrude Stein. Stanford, CA: Stanford UP, 1989.

Chirot, Daniel, and Anthony Reid, eds. *Essential Outsiders: Chinese and Jews in the Modern Transformation of Southeast Asia and Central Europe*. Seattle: U of Washington P, 1997.

Cho, Sumi K. "Korean Americans vs. African Americans: Conflict and Construction." Gooding-Williams 196–211.

Chodorow, Nancy. *The Reproduction of Mothering: Psychoanalysis and the Sociology of Gender*. Berkeley: U of California P, 1978.

Christian, Barbara. *Black Feminist Criticism: Perspectives on Black Women Writers*. New York: Pergammon Press, 1985.

————. *Black Women Novelists: The Development of a Tradition, 1892–1976*. Westport, CT: Greenwood Press, 1980.

————. "The Race for Theory." 1987. *Gender and Theory: Dialogues on Feminist Criticism*. Ed. Linda Kauffman. Oxford: Basil Blackwell, 1989. 225–37.

Cixous, Hélène. "The Laugh of the Medusa." 1975. Marks and de Courtivron 254–64.

Clayton, Jay. "The Narrative Turn in Recent Minority Fiction." *American Literary History* 2.3 (Fall 1990): 375–93.

————. "Narrative and Theories of Desire." *Critical Inquiry* 16 (1989): 33–53.

————. *The Pleasures of Babel: Contemporary American Literature and Theory*. Oxford: Oxford UP, 1993.

Clifford, James. "Diasporas." *Routes* 244–77.

————. "Notes on Travel and Theory." *Inscriptions* 5 (1989): 177–88.

————. "On Ethnographic Allegory." Clifford and Marcus 98–121.

————. *The Predicament of Culture: Twentieth-Century Ethnography, Literature, and Art*. Cambridge: Harvard UP, 1988.

————. *Routes: Travel and Translation in the Late Twentieth Century*. Cambridge: Harvard UP, 1997.

————. "Spatial Practices: Fieldwork, Travel, and the Disciplining of Anthropology." *Routes* 52–91.

————. "Traveling Cultures." *Cultural Studies*. Ed. Lawrence Grossberg, Cary Nelson, and Paula Treichler. London: Routledge, 1992. 96–116. Rpt. *Routes* 17–47.

Clifford, James, and Vivek Dhareshwar, eds. Special Issue on Traveling Theories, Traveling Theorists. *Inscriptions* 5 (1989).

Clifford, James, and George Marcus, eds. *Writing Culture: The Poetics and Politics of Ethnography*. Berkeley: U of California P, 1986.

Clifton, Lucille. "Last Note to My Girls." *An Ordinary Woman*. New York: Random House, 1977. 29.

Cohen, Ralph, ed. *The Future of Literary Theory*. London: Routledge, 1989.

Cole, Johnnetta B., "Commonalities and Differences." *All American Women: Lines that Divide, Ties that Bind*. Ed. Johnnetta B. Cole. New York: Free Press, 1986. 1–30.

Collins, Patricia Hill. *Black Feminist Thought: Knowledge, Consciousness, and the Politics of Empowerment*. New York: Routledge, 1991.

Combahee River Collective. "A Black Feminist Statement." 1977. Hull, Scott, and Smith 13–22.

Coyner, Sandra. "Women's Studies as an Academic Discipline: Why and How to Do It." Bowles and Klein 46–71.

Crosby, Christina. "Dealing with Differences." Butler and Scott 130–34.

Crossette, Barbara. "Women's Advocates Flocking to Cairo, Eager for Gains." *New York Times* (2 September 1994).

Cruikshank, Margaret, ed. *Lesbian Studies, Present and Future*. Old Westbury, NY: Feminist Press, 1982.

Cuddy-Kean, Melba, and Kay Li. "Passage to China: East and West and Woolf." *South Carolina Review* 29.1 (Fall 1996): 132–49.

Cummings, June. "Lily Briscoe's Journey to the Western Islands of Scotland: Kunstlerroman, Colonial Travelogue, or Intertextual Appreciation." Paper delivered at the Sixth Annual Virginia Woolf Conference. Clemson, SC., June 1996.

————. "*The Voyage Out* and *Between the Acts*: Readings of Empire." *Virginia Woolf Texts and Contexts*. Ed. Beth R. Daugherty and Eileen Barrett. White Plains, NY: Pace UP, 1996. 204–90.

D'Acci, Julie. *Defining Women: The Case of Cagney and Lacy*. Durham: Duke UP, 1994.

Daly, Suzanne. "Botswana Pressuring Bushmen to Leave Reserve." *New York Times* (14 July 1996).

————. "Endangered Bushmen Find Hope." *New York Times* (18 January 1996); A4.

Daly, Mary. *Gyn/Ecology: The Metaethics of Radical Feminism*. Boston: Beacon Press, 1978.

————. "The Qualitative Leap beyond Patriarchal Religion." *Quest* 1.4 (Spring 1975): 21–28.

Daly, Mary. Response. Session on Developing Feminist Theory at *The Second Sex—Thirty Years Later: A Commemorative Conference on Feminist Theory.* New York City, 28 September 1979.

Dash, Julie. *Daughters of the Dust,* film written and directed by Julie Dash. 1992.

———. *Daughters of the Dust: The Making of an African American Woman's Film.* New York: New Press, 1992.

Davies, Carole Boyce. *Black Women, Writing and Identity: Migrations of the Subject.* London: Routledge, 1994.

Davies, Tony, and Nigel Wood, eds. *A Passage to India.* Philadelphia: Open University Press, 1994.

de Certeau, Michel. *The Practice of Everyday Life.* 1974. Trans. Steven Rendell. Berkeley: U of California P, 1984.

DeFrees, Madeline. *Imaginary Ancestors.* Seattle: Broken Moon Press, 1990.

Dekoven, Marianne. *Rich and Strange: Gender, History, Modernism.* Princeton: Princeton UP, 1991.

de Lauretis, Teresa. *Alice Doesn't: Feminism, Semiotics, Cinema.* Bloomington: Indiana UP, 1984.

———. "Eccentric Subjects: Feminist Theory and Historical Consciousness." *Feminist Studies* 16 (Spring 1990): 115–50.

———. "Feminist Studies/Critical Studies: Issues, Terms, and Contexts." *Feminist Studies* 1–19.

———. *Technologies of Gender: Essays on Theory, Film, and Fiction.* Bloomington: Indiana UP, 1987.

———, ed. *Feminist Studies/Critical Studies.* Bloomington: Indiana UP, 1986.

———, ed. Special Issue on Queer Theory: Lesbian and Gay Sexualities. *Differences* 3 (Summer 1991).

DeLombard, Jeannine. "Buffalo Gals." *New York Times Book Review* (24 October 1993); 24.

de Man, Paul. *Allegories of Reading: Figural Language in Rousseau, Nietzsche, Rilke, and Proust.* New Haven: Yale UP, 1979.

———. *Blindness and Insight: Essays in the Rhetoric of Contemporary Criticism.* 1971. Rev. ed. Minneapolis: U of Minnesota P, 1983.

———. "Reading and History." *The Resistance to Theory.* Minneapolis: U of Minnesota P, 1986. 54–72.

Dembo, L. S. *Conceptions of Reality in Modern American Poetry.* Berkeley: U of California P, 1966.

Derrida, Jacques. "*Fors.*" Abraham and Torok xi–xlviii.

———. "Ulysses Gramophone: Hear Say Yes in Joyce." *Acts of Literature.* Ed. Derek Attridge. London: Routledge, 1992. 253–309.

Dhareshwar, Vivek. "Marxism, Location Politics, and the Possibility of Critique." *Public Culture* 6.1 (1993): 41–54.

Dickie, Margaret. *On the Modernist Long Poem.* Iowa City: U of Iowa P, 1986.

Dikötter, Frank. *The Discourse of Race in Modern China.* Stanford: Stanford UP, 1992.

Dill, Bonnie Thornton. "Race, Class, and Gender: Prospects for an All-Inclusive Sisterhood." *Feminist Studies* 9 (Spring 1983): 129–50.

Domínguez, Virginia R. *White by Definition: Social Classification in Creole Louisiana.* New Brunswick, NJ: Rutgers UP, 1996.

Donaldson, Laura E. *Decolonizing Feminisms: Race, Gender, and Empire-Building.* Chapel Hill: U of North Carolina P, 1992.

Doyle, Laura. *Bordering on the Body: The Racial Matrix of Modern Fiction and Culture.* New York: Oxford UP, 1994.

Drabble, Margaret, ed. *The Oxford Companion to English Literature.* 5th ed. Oxford: Oxford UP, 1985.

duCille, Ann. "The Occult of True Black Womanhood: Critical Demeanor and Black Feminist Studies." *Signs* 19 (Spring 1994): 591–629.

Dumont, Louis. *Homo Hierarchicus: An Essay on the Caste System.* 1966. Trans. Mark Sainsbury. Chicago: U of Chicago P, 1970.

DuPlessis, Rachel Blau. 1979. "For the Etruscans." Showalter, *New Feminist Criticism* 271–91.

———. *The Pink Guitar: Writing as Feminist Practice.* London: Routledge, 1990.

———. *Writing beyond the Ending: Narrative Strategies of Twentieth-Century Women Writers.* Bloomington: Indiana UP, 1985.

Eco, Umberto, and Thomas A. Sebeok, eds. *The Sign of Three: Dupin, Homes, Peirce.* Bloomington: Indiana UP, 1983.

Eisenstein, Hester, and Alice Jardine, eds. *The Future of Difference.* New Brunswick, NJ: Rutgers UP, 1980.

Eisenstein, Sergei. "Principles of Film Form." *Close Up* 8.3 (September 1931): 167–81.

Elam, Diane, and Robyn Wiegman, eds. *Feminism Beside Itself*. London: Routledge, 1995.

Eliot, T. S. "Tradition and the Individual Talent." 1919. *Selected Prose*. Ed. Frank Kermode. New York: Harcourt Brace Jovanovich, 1975. 37–44.

Ellsworth, Elizabeth. "Why Doesn't This Feel Empowering? Working through the Repressive Myths of Critical Pedagogy." *Harvard Educational Review* 59.3 (August 1989): 297–324.

Elton, G. R. *The Practice of History*. New York: Crowell, 1967.

Erdrich, Louise. *Tracks*. New York: Henry Holt, 1988.

Fanon, Frantz. *Black Skin, White Masks: The Experiences of a Black Man in a White World*. 1952. Trans. Charles Lam Markmann. New York: Grove Press, 1967.

Featherstone, Mike, Scott Lash, and Roland Robertson, eds. *Global Modernities*. London: Sage, 1995.

Fellows, Mary Louise, and Sherene Razack. "Seeking Relations: Law and Feminism Roundtables." *Signs* 19 (Summer 1994): 1048–83.

Felman, Shoshana. "Beyond Oedipus: The Specimen Story of Psychoanalysis." *Lacan and the Adventure of Insight*. Cambridge: Harvard UP, 1987. 98–159.

Felman, Shoshana, and Dori Laub. *Testimony: Crises of Witnessing in Literature, Psychoanalysis, and History*. London: Routledge, 1992.

Felski, Rita. *Feminist Aesthetics: Feminist Literature and Social Change*. Cambridge: Harvard UP, 1989.

Ferguson, James, and Akhil Gupta, eds. Special Issue on Space, Identity, and the Politics of Difference. *Cultural Anthropology* 7 (February 1992).

Fields, Barbara. "Ideology and Race in American History." *Region, Race, and Reconstruction*. Ed. J. Morgan Kinsser and James M. McPherson. New York: Oxford UP, 1982. 143–77.

Findler, Barbara, ed. *Listen Up: Voices from the Next Feminist Generation*. Seattle: Seal Press, 1995.

Fiske, John. *Television Culture*. London: Methuen, 1987.

Forster, E. M. *Aspects of the Novel*. New York: Harcourt Brace Jovanovich, 1927.

———. *The Hill of Devi*. New York: Harcourt Brace Jovanovich, 1953.

———. *A Passage to India*. 1924. New York: Harcourt Brace Jovanovich, 1952.

Fortney, Nancy D. "The Anthropological Concept of Race." *Journal of Black Studies* 8 (September 1977): 35–54.

Foster, Frances Smith. *Written by Herself: Literary Production of African American Women, 1746–1892*. Bloomington: Indiana UP, 1993.

Foster, Gwendolyn Audrey. *Women Filmmakers of the African and Asian Diaspora: Decolonizing the Gaze, Locating Subjectivity*. Carbondale: Southern Illinois UP, 1997.

Foster, R. Thomas. "Homelessness at Home: Oppositional Practices and Modern Women's Writing." Diss. U of Wisconsin–Madison, 1990.

Foucault, Michel. *The Archaeology of Knowldge*. 1969. Trans. A. M. Sheridan Smith. New York: Pantheon, 1972.

———. *The Order of Things: An Archaeology of the Human Sciences*. 1966. New York: Vintage, 1970.

———. *Power/Knowledge: Selected Interviews and Other Writings, 1972–1977*. Ed. and trans. Colin Gordon. New York: Pantheon, 1980. 63–77.

Fox, Richard G., ed. *Recapturing Anthropology: Working in the Present*. Sante Fe, NM: School of American Research Press, 1991.

Frankenberg, Ruth. *White Women, Race Matters: The Social Construction of Whiteness*. Minneapolis: U of Minnesota P, 1993.

Frankenberg, Ruth and Lata Mani. "Crosscurrents, Crosstalk: Race, 'Postcoloniality' and the Politics of Location." *Cultural Studies* 7.1 (May 1993): 292–310.

Fregoso, Rosa Linda. *The Bronze Screen: Chicana and Chicano Film Culture*. Minneapolis: U of Minnesota P, 1993.

Freud, Sigmund. *Beyond the Pleasure Principle*. 1920. Trans. James Strachey. New York: Norton, 1961.

Friedan, Betty. *The Second Stage*. New York: Summit Books, 1981.

Friedland, Roger, and Deirdre Boden, eds. *Now-Here: Space, Time and Modernity*. Berkeley: U of California P, 1994.

Friedman, Edward. "The Rise of China and the Asianization of the World." *State and Sovereignty in the World Economy*. Ed. David Smith, Dorothy Solinger, and Steven Topik. London: Routledge, forthcoming.

Friedman, Jonathan. "Global Crises, the Struggle for Cultural Identity, and Intellectual Porkbarrelling." Werbner and Modood 70–89.

———. "Global System, Globalization and the Parameters of Modernity." Featherstone, Lash, and Robertson, 69–90.

Friedman, Susan Stanford. "Androgyny: An Overview of Feminist Definition and Debate." Unpublished essay.

———. "Craving Stories: Narrative and Lyric in Contemporary Theory and Women's Long Poems." *Feminist Measures: Soundings in Poetry and Theory*. Ed. Lynn Keller and Cristanne Miller. Ann Arbor: U of Michigan P, 1994. 15–42.

———. "Forbidden Fruits of Knowledge: The Psychodynamics of the Education of Women and Women in Education." *Annual of Psychoanalysis* 15 (1987): 353–74.

———. "Gender and Genre Anxiety: Elizabeth Barrett Browning and H.D. as Epic Poets." *Tulsa Studies in Women's Literature* 5 (Fall 1986): 203–31.

———. "Hysteria, Dreams, and Modernity: A Reading of the Origins of Psychoanalysis in Freud's Early Corpus." *Rereading the New: A Backward Glance at Modernism*. Ed. Kevin J. H. Dettmar. Ann Arbor: U of Michigan P, 1992. 41–72.

———. "Identity Politics, Syncretism, Catholicism, and Anishinabe Religion in Louise Erdrich's *Tracks*." *Religion and Literature* 26 (Spring 1994): 107–33.

———. "Lyric Subversion of Narrative in Women's Writing: Virginia Woolf and the Tyranny of Plot." *Reading Narrative: Form, Ethics, Ideology*. Ed. James Phelan. Columbus: Ohio State UP, 1989. 162–85.

———. "The New Modernist Studies: A Polemical Call." Paper delivered at the Conference on American Modernism. Montréal, June 1995.

———. *Penelope's Web: Gender, Modernity, H.D.'s Fiction*. Cambridge: Cambridge UP, 1990.

———. *Psyche Reborn: The Emergence of H.D.* Bloomington: Indiana UP, 1981.

———. "Relational Epistemology and the Question of Anglo-American Feminist Criticism." *Tulsa Studies in Women's Literature* 12 (Fall 1993): 247–62.

———. "Spatialization, Narrative Theory, and Virginia Woolf's *The Voyage Out*." *Ambiguous Discourse: Feminist Narratology and British Women Writers*. Ed. Kathy Mezei. Chapel Hill: U of North Carolina P, 1996. 109–36.

———. "Spatialization: A Strategy for Reading Narrative." *Narrative* 1 (January 1993): 12–23.

———. "Virginia Woolf's Pedagogical Scenes of Reading: *The Voyage Out*, *The Common Reader*, and Her 'Common Readers.'" *Modern Fiction Studies* 38 (Spring 1992): 101–25.

———. "Weavings: Intertextuality and the (Re)Birth of the Author." *Influence and Intertextuality in Literary History*. Ed. Jay Clayton and Eric Rothstein. Madison: U of Wisconsin P, 1991. 146–80.

———. "When a 'Long' Poem Is a 'Big' Poem: Self-Authorizing Strategies in Women's Twentieth-Century 'Long Poems.'" *Lit* 2 (1990): 9–25.

———. "Women's Autobiographical Selves: Theory and Practice." *The Private Self: Theory and Practice in Women's Autobiography*. Ed. Shari Benstock. Chapel Hill: U of North Carolina P, 1988. 38–62.

Frye, Marilyn. "On Being White: Thinking toward a Feminist Understanding of Race and Race Supremacy." 1981. *The Politics of Reality: Essays in Feminist Theory*. Trumansburg, NY: Crossing Press, 1983. 110–27.

———. "White Woman Feminist." *Willful Virgin: Essays in Feminism*. Trumansburg, NY: Crossing Press, 1992. 147–69.

Furbank, P. N. *E. M. Forster: A Life*. 2 vols. London: Secker and Warburg, 1977–78.

Fuss, Diana. *Essentially Speaking: Feminism, Nature and Difference*. New York: Routledge, 1989.

Gallin, Rita S., and Anne Ferguson. "The Plurality of Feminism: Rethinking 'Difference.'" *The Women and International Development Annual*. Vol. 3. Boulder, CO: Westview Press, 1993. 1–16.

Gallop, Jane. *The Daughter's Seduction: Feminism and Psychoanalysis*. Ithaca: Cornell UP, 1982.

Gallop, Jane, Marianne Hirsch, and Nancy K. Miller. "Criticizing Feminist Criticism." *Conflicts in Feminism*. Ed. Marianne Hirsch and Evelyn Fox Keller. New York: Routledge, 1990. 349–69.

Ganguly, Adwaita P. *India: Mystic, Complex, and Real*. Dehli: Motilal Banarsidass, 1990.

Gardiner, Judith Kegan. "On Female Identity

and Writing by Women." *Critical Inquiry* 8 (Winter 1981): 347–61.

Gardner, Thomas. *Discovering Ourselves in Whitman: The Contemporary American Long Poem*. Urbana: U of Illinois P, 1989.

Gaskell, Elizabeth. *North and South*. 1854–55. Oxford: Oxford UP, 1982.

Gates, Henry Louis, Jr. Introduction. *"Race"* 1–20.

———. "A Liberalism of Heart and Spine." *New York Times* (27 March 1994).

———. *The Signifying Monkey: A Theory of African-American Literary Criticism*. New York: Oxford UP, 1988.

———. ed. *"Race," Writing, and Difference*. Chicago: U of Chicago P, 1986.

Geertz, Clifford. *The Interpretation of Cultures*. New York: Basic Books, 1973.

———. *Local Knowledge: Further Essays in Interpretive Anthropology*. New York: Basic Books, 1983.

Gibbs, Peter. *Crimean Blunder: The Story of War with Russia a Hundred Years Ago*. New York: Holt, Rinehart and Winston, 1960.

Gikandi, Simon. *Maps of Englishness: Writing Identity in the Culture of Colonialism*. New York: Columbia UP, 1997.

———. *Writing in Limbo: Modernism and Caribbean Literature*. Ithaca: Cornell UP, 1992.

Gilbert, Sandra M., and Susan Gubar. *The Madwoman in the Attic: The Woman Writer and the Nineteenth-Century Literary Imagination*. New Haven: Yale UP, 1979.

Gilroy, Paul. *The Black Atlantic: Modernity and Double Consciousness*. Cambridge: Harvard UP, 1993.

Ginsberg, Allen. *Howl, and Other Poems*. San Francisco: City Lights Books, 1956.

Glancy, Diane. *Claiming Breath*. Lincoln: U of Nebraska P, 1992.

———. *Lone Dog's Winter Count*. Albuquerque: West End Press, 1991.

Gluck, Sherna Berger. "Advocacy Oral History: Palestinian Women in Resistance." Gluck and Patai 205–20.

Gluck, Sherna Berger, and Daphne Patai, eds. *Women's Words: The Practice of Oral History*. London: Routledge, 1991.

Goldberg, David Theo, ed. *Anatomy of Racism*. Minneapolis: U of Minnesota P, 1990.

Gómez-Peña, Guillermo. *The New World Border: Prophecies, Poems, and Loqeras for the End of the Century*. San Francisco: City Lights Books, 1996.

Gooding-Williams, Robert, ed. *Reading Rodney King/Reading Urban Uprising*. London: Routledge, 1993.

Gordon, Avery F., and Christopher Newfield, eds. *Mapping Multiculturalism*. Minneapolis: U of Minnesota P, 1996.

Gordon, Linda. "On 'Difference.'" *Genders* 10 (Spring 1991): 91–111.

———. "Reponse to Scott." *Signs* 15 (Summer 1990): 852–53.

———. Review of *Gender and the Politics of History*, by Joan Wallach Scott. *Signs* 15 (Summer 1990): 853–58.

Gornick, Vivian, and Barbara K. Moran, eds. *Woman in Sexist Society: Studies in Power and Powerlessness*. New York: Basic Books, 1971.

Gould, Harold A. *The Hindu Caste System: The Sacralization of a Social Order*. Delhi: Chanakya Publications, 1987.

Grahn, Judy. *Common Woman Poems*. 1969. *The Work of a Common Woman*. Trumansburg, NY: Crossing Press, 1978. 59–74.

———. *The Queen of Wands*. Trumansburg, NY: Crossing Press, 1982.

Gray, Herman. "The Endless Slide of Difference: Critical Television Studies, Television and the Question of Race." *Critical Studies in Mass Communication* 10 (June 1993): 190–97.

———. "Television, Black Americans, and the American Dream." *Critical Studies in Mass Communication* 6 (December 1989): 376–86.

Green, Jennifer M. "Stories in an Exhibition: Narrative and Nineteenth-Century Photographic Documentary." *Journal of Narrative Technique* 20 (Spring 1990): 147–66.

Greene, Gayle. "Looking at History." Greene and Kahn 4–30.

Greene, Gayle, and Coppélia Kahn, eds. *Changing Subjects: The Making of Feminist Literary Criticism*. London: Routledge, 1993.

Grewal, Inderpal. "Autobiographic Subjects and Diasporic Locations: *Meatless Days* and *Borderlands*." Grewal and Kaplan 231–54.

———. *Home and Harem: Nation, Gender, Empire, and the Cultures of Travel*. Durham: Duke UP, 1996.

Grewal, Inderpal, and Caren Kaplan, eds. *Scattered Hegemonies: Postmodernity and Transnational Feminist Practices*. Minneapolis: U of Minnesota P, 1994.

Gross, Jane. "Body and Victim Trampled, a Riot

Victim Fights On." *New York Times* (22 October 1993).

Gunew, Sneja. "Feminism and the Politics of Irreducible Differences: Multiculturalism/Ethnicity/Race." Gunew and Yeatman 1–19.

Gunew, Sneja, and Anna Yeatman, eds. *The Politics of Difference*. Boulder, CO: Westview Press, 1993.

Gupta, Akhil, and James Ferguson. "Beyond 'Culture': Space, Identity, and the Politics of Difference." Ferguson and Gupta 6–23.

Guttman, Amy, ed. *Multiculturalism: Examining the Politics of Recognition*. Princeton: Princeton UP, 1994.

Hadas, Pamela White. *Beside Herself: Pocahontas to Patty Hearst*. New York: Knopf, 1983.

Hale, Sondra. "Feminist Method, Process, and Self-Criticism: Interviewing Sudanese Women." Gluck and Patai 121–36.

Haley, Alex. *Roots*. New York: Dell, 1976.

Hall, Stuart. "Cultural Identity and Difference." *Colonial Discourse and Post-Colonial Theory: A Reader*. Ed. Patrick Williams and Laura Christian. New York: Columbia UP, 1994. 392–403.

———. "Ethnicity: Identity and Difference." *Radical America* 23.4 (1989): 9–20.

———. "The Local and the Global: Globalization and Ethnicity." Anthony King 19–40.

———. "New Ethnicities." *Stuart Hall: Critical Dialogues in Cultural Studies*. Ed. David Morley and Kuan-Hsing Chen. London: Routledge, 1996. 441–49.

———. "Old and New Identities, Old and New Ethnicities." Anthony King 41–69.

Hannerz, Ulf. *Cultural Complexity: Studies in the Social Organization of Meaning*. New York: Columbia UP, 1992.

———. "Scenarios for Peripheral Cultures." Anthony King 107–28.

———. "The World in Creolisation." *Africa* 57.4 (1987): 546–59.

Harari, Josué V. *Textual Strategies: Perspectives in Post-Structuralist Criticism*. Ithaca: Cornell UP, 1979.

Haraway, Donna. "A Manifesto for Cyborgs: Science, Technology, and Socialist Feminism of the 1980s." *Feminism/Postmodernism*. Ed. Linda J. Nicholson. London: Routledge, 1990. 190–234.

———. "Situated Knowledges: The Science Question in Feminism and the Privilege of Partial Perspective." *Feminist Studies* 14 (Fall 1988): 575–99.

Harding, Sarah. "Culture as an Object of Knowledge." *Contention* 2 (Spring 1993): 121–26.

Harjo, Joy. *In Mad Love and War*. Middletown, CT: Wesleyan UP, 1990.

Harlan, David. "Intellectual History and the Return of Literature." *American Historical Review* 94 (June 1989): 581–609.

Harris, Virginia R., and Trinity A. Ordoña. "Developing Unity among Women of Color: Crossing the Barriers of Internalized Racism and Cross-Racial Hostility." Anzaldúa, *Making Face* 304–16.

Harstock, Nancy C. M. "The Feminist Standpoint: Developing the Ground for a Specifically Feminist Historical Materialism." *Discovering Reality: Feminist Perspectives on Epistemology, Metaphysics, Methodology, and Philosophy of Science*. Ed. Sandra Harding and Merrill B. Hintikka. Boston: D. Reidel, 1983. 283–310.

Harvey, David. *The Condition of Postmodernity*. Oxford: Basil Blackwell, 1990.

Hawkesworth, Mary. "Confounding Gender." *Signs* 22.3 (1997): 649–85.

H.D. [Hilda Doolittle] *Asphodel*. Ed. Robert Spoo. Durham, NC: Duke UP, 1992.

———. *Bid Me to Live (A Madrigal)*. New York: Grove Press, 1960.

———. *By Avon River*. New York: Macmillan, 1949.

———. *Helen in Egypt*. 1961. New York: New Directions, 1974.

———. *Hermetic Definition*. New York: New Directions, 1972.

———. *Hermetic Definition*. H.D., *Hermetic Definition* 1–56.

———. *Sagesse*. H.D., *Hermetic Definition* 57–84.

———. "Thorn Thicket." 1960. Unpublished memoir. Beinecke Rare Book and Manuscript Library, Yale University.

———. *Trilogy*. 1944–46. New York: New Directions, 1973.

———. *Vale Ave. New Directions: An International Anthology of Poetry and Prose* 44 (1982). 18–166.

———. *Winter Love*. H.D., *Hermetic Definition* 85–117.

Heilbrun, Carolyn G. *Toward a Recognition of Androgyny*. New York: Harper and Row, 1973.

———. *Writing a Woman's Life*. New York: Norton, 1988.

Hekman, Susan. "Truth and Method: Feminist

Standpoint Theory Revisited." *Signs* 22.2 (Winter 1997): 341–65.

Henderson, Mae Gwendolyn. "Speaking in Tongues: Dialogics, Dialectics, and the Black Woman Writer's Literary Tradition." Wall 16–37.

Hernández, Graciela. "Multiple Subjectivities and Strategic Positionality: Zora Neale Hurston's Experimental Ethnographies." Behar and Gordon 148–64.

Herz, Judith Scherer. *"A Passage to India": Nation and Narration.* New York: Twayne, 1993.

Hewitt, Nancy A. "Compounding Difference." *Feminist Studies* 18.2 (Summer 1992): 313–26.

Heywood, Leslie, and Jennifer Drake, eds. *Third Wave Agenda: Being Feminist/Doing Feminism.* Minneapolis: U of Minnesota P, 1997.

Hicks, D. Emily. *Border Writing: The Multidimensional Text.* Minneapolis: U of Minnesota P, 1991.

Higginbotham, Evelyn Brooks. "African-American Women's History and the Metalanguage of Race." *Signs* 17 (Winter 1992): 251–74.

Higonnet, Margaret R., ed. *Borderwork: Feminist Engagements with Comparative Literature.* Ithaca: Cornell UP, 1994.

Higonnet, Margaret R., and Joan Templeton, eds. *Reconfigured Spheres: Feminist Explorations of Literary Space.* Amherst: U of Massachusetts P, 1994.

Hirsch, Marianne. *The Mother/Daughter Plot: Narrative, Psychoanalysis, Feminism.* Bloomington: Indiana UP, 1989.

Hite, Molly. "'Except thou ravish me': penetrations into the life of the (feminine) mind." Greene and Kahn 121–28.

Holmes, Steven A. "Study Finds Minorities Resent One Another Almost as Much as They Do Whites." *New York Times* (3 March 1994).

Homans, Margaret. *Bearing the Word: Language and Female Experience in Nineteenth-Century Women's Writing.* Chicago: U of Chicago P, 1986.

————. "'Women of Color' Writers and Feminist Theory." *New Literary History* 25 (Winter 1994): 73–94.

hooks, bell. "Feminism: A Transformational Politic." *Talking Back* 19–27.

————. *Feminist Theory: From Margin to Center.* Boston: South End Press, 1984.

————. "Seduction and Betrayal: *The Crying Game* Meets *The Bodyguard*." *Outlaw Culture: Resisting Representations.* London: Routledge, 1994. 53–62.

————. *Talking Back.* Philadelphia: South End Press, 1989.

————. *Yearning: Race, Gender, and Cultural Politics.* Boston: South End Press, 1990.

hooks, bell, and Anuradha Dingwaney. "Mississippi Masala." *Z Magazine* 5 (July/August 1992): 41–43.

Hull, Gloria T., Patricia Bell Scott, and Barbara Smith, eds. *All the Women Are White, All the Men Are Black, But Some of Us Are Brave.* Old Westbury, NY: Feminist Press, 1982.

Hurston, Zora Neale. "Characteristics of Negro Expression." 1934. *The Gender of Modernism: A Critical Anthology.* Ed. Bonnie Kime Scott. Bloomington: Indiana UP, 1990. 175–87.

————. *Jonah's Gourd Vine.* Philadelphia: J. B. Lippincott, 1934.

————. *Mules and Men.* 1935. Bloomington: Indiana UP, 1978.

————. *Tell My Horse: Voodoo and Life in Haiti and Jamaica.* 1938. New York: Harper and Row, 1990.

————. *Their Eyes Were Watching God.* 1937. Urbana: U of Illinois P, 1978.

Hurston, Zora Neale, and Langston Hughes. *Mule Bone: A Comedy of Negro Life.* Ed. George Houston Bass and Henry Louis Gates, Jr. New York: Harper, 1991.

Hurtado, Aída. "Relating to Privilege: Seduction and Rejection in the Subordination of White Women and Women of Color." *Signs* 14.4 (1989): 833–55.

Hutcheon, Linda. *The Politics of Postmodernism.* London: Routledge, 1990.

————, ed. Special Issue on Colonialism and the Postcolonial Condition. *PMLA* 110 (January 1995).

Hutnyk, John. "Adorno at Womad: South Asian Crossovers and the Limits of Hybridity-Talk." Werbner and Modood 106–38.

Irigaray, Luce. "The Power of Discourse and the Subordination of the Feminine" 1975. *This Sex Which Is Not One.* Trans. Catherine Porter. Ithaca: Cornell UP, 1985. 68–86.

Jacobs, Harriet A. *Incidents in the Life of a Slave Girl.* 1861. New York: Harcourt Brace Jovanovich, 1973.

Jacoby, Russell. "A New Intellectual History?" *American Historical Review* 97 (April 1992): 405–39.

Jameson, Fredric. *The Political Unconscious:*

Narrative as a Socially Symbolic Act. Ithaca: Cornell UP, 1981.

———. *Postmodernism, or, The Cultural Logic of Late Capitalism.* Durham: Duke UP, 1991.

JanMohamed, Abdul, and David Lloyd, eds. *The Nature and Context of Minority Discourse.* Oxford: Oxford UP, 1990.

Jardine, Alice. "Gynesis." *Diacritics* 12 (Summer 1982): 54–65.

———. *Gynesis: Configurations of Woman and Modernity.* Ithaca: Cornell UP, 1985.

Jen, Gish. *Mona in the Promised Land.* New York: Knopf, 1996.

———. *Typical American.* New York: Penguin, 1991.

Jones, John Paul III, Heidi J. Nast, and Susan M. Roberts, eds. *Thresholds in Feminist Geography: Difference, Methodology, Representation.* Lanham, MD: Rowman and Littlefield, 1997.

Jordan, June. "Report from the Bahamas." *On Call: Political Essays.* Boston: South End Press, 1985. 39–54.

Jordan, Neil. *The Crying Game. A Neil Jordan Reader.* New York: Vintage, 1993. 177–267.

———. *The Crying Game*, film written and directed by Jordan. 1992.

Joseph, Gloria I., and Jill Lewis. *Common Differences: Conflicts in Black and White Feminist Perspectives.* New York: Anchor, 1981.

Joyce, James. *Ulysses.* Ed. Hans Walter Gabler et al. New York: Random House, 1986.

Kamboureli, Smaro. *On the Edge of Genre: The Contemporary Canadian Long Poem.* Toronto: U of Toronto P, 1991.

Kamm, Henry. "In New Eastern Europe, An Old Anti-Gypsy Bias." *New York Times* (17 November 1993).

Kamuf, Peggy. "Replacing Feminist Criticism." *Diacritics* 12 (Summer 1982): 42–47.

Kaplan, Alexandra G. *Psychological Androgyny.* New York: Human Sciences Press, 1979.

Kaplan, Alexandra G., and Joan P. Bean, eds. *Beyond Sex-Role Stereotypes: Readings toward a Psychology of Androgyny.* Boston: Little, Brown, 1976.

Kaplan, Caren. "Deterritorializations: The Rewriting of Home and Exile in Western Feminist Discourse." JanMohamed and Lloyd 357–68.

———. "The Politics of Location as Transnational Feminist Practice." Grewal and Kaplan 137–53.

———. *Questions of Travel: Postmodern Discourses of Displacement.* Durham, NC: Duke UP, 1996.

Kaplan, Carla. *The Erotics of Talk: Women's Writing and Feminist Paradigms.* Oxford: Oxford UP, 1996.

Kauffman, Linda S. "The long goodbye: against the personal testimony or, an infant grifter grows up." Greene and Kahn 129–46.

———, ed. *Gender and Theory: Dialogues in Feminist Criticism.* Oxford: Basil Blackwell, 1989.

Kavanagh, Thomas M., ed. *The Limits of Theory.* Stanford, CA: Stanford UP, 1989.

Keetley, Dawn. "Contested Terrains of Feminine Subjectivity: Conflicts over Self and Space in Nineteenth-Century American Women's Autobiography." Diss. U of Wisconsin–Madison, 1994.

Keith, Michael, and Steve Pile, eds. *Place and the Politics of Identity.* London: Routledge, 1993.

Keller, Evelyn Fox, and Helene Moglen. "Competition and Feminism: Conflicts for Academic Women." *Signs* 12 (1987): 493–511.

Keller, Lynn. *Forms of Expansion: Recent Long Poems by Women.* Chicago: U of Chicago P, 1997.

———. "Poems Containing History: Some Problems of Definition of the Long Poem." Paper delivered at the Modern Language Association Convention, December 1988.

———. "The Twentieth-Century Long Poem." *Columbia History of American Poetry.* Ed. Jay Parini. New York: Columbia UP, 1993. 534–63.

Kelly, Joan. "Did Women Have a Renaissance?" 1977. *Women, History, and Theory: Essays of Joan Kelly.* Chicago: U of Chicago P, 1984. 19–50.

———. "The Social Relations of the Sexes: Methodological Implications of Women's History." *Signs* 1 (Summer 1976): 809–23.

Kenner, Hugh. "The Making of the Modernist Canon." *Chicago Review* 34.2 (Spring 1984): 49–61.

Kessler-Harris, Alice. "The View from Women's Studies." *Signs* 17.4 (1992): 794–804.

Kim, Elaine H. "Home Is Where the *Han* Is: A Korean-American Perspective on the Los Angeles Upheavals." Gooding-Williams 215–35.

Kincaid, James R. *Tennyson's Major Poems: The Comic and Ironic Patterns*. New Haven: Yale UP, 1975.

King, Anthony D., ed. *Culture, Globalization, and the World-System*. 2d ed. Minneapolis: U of Minnesota P, 1997.

King, Deborah K. "Multiple Jeopardy, Multiple Consciousness: The Context of Black Feminist Ideology." *Signs* 14 (Autumn 1988): 42–72.

Kingston, Maxine Hong. *The Woman Warrior: Memoirs of a Girlhood among Ghosts*. New York: Vintage, 1976.

Kirby, Kathleen M. *Indifferent Boundaries: Spatial Concepts of Human Subjectivity*. New York: Guilford Press, 1996.

Klepfisz, Irena. *Keeper of Accounts*. Watertown, MA: Persephone Press, 1982.

Kogawa, Joy. *Obasan*. Boston: David R. Godine, 1981.

Kolenda, Pauline. *Caste in Contemporary India: Beyond Organic Solidarity*. Amsterdam: Benjamin/Cummings, 1978.

Kolodny, Annette. "Dancing between Left and Right: Feminism and the Academic Minefield in the 1980s." *Feminist Studies* 14 (Fall 1988): 433–66.

Kondo, Doreen. "Women of Color and the Cultural Politics of Identity." Romero and Arguelles 57–70.

Koshy, Susan. "The Geography of Female Subjectivity: Ethnicity, Gender, and Diaspora in Mukherjee's Fiction." *Diaspora* 3 (1994): 69–84.

———. " 'Under Other Skies': Writing, Gender, Nation, and Diaspora." Diss. U California at Los Angeles, 1992.

Kracke, Waud. "Encounter with Other Cultures: Psychological and Epistemological Aspects." *Ethos* 15.1 (1987): 58–81.

Kramer, Lloyd S. "Literature, Criticism, and Historical Imagination: The Literary Challenge of Hayden White and Dominick LaCapra." *The New Critical History*. Ed. Lynn Hunt. Berkeley: U of California P, 1989. 97–128.

Kristeva Julia. *About Chinese Women*. Trans. Anita Barrows. London: Marion Boyars. 1977.

———. *Desire in Language: A Semiotic Approach to Literature and Art*. Ed. Leon S. Roudiez. Trans. Thomas Gora, Alice Jardine, and Leon S. Roudiez. New York: Columbia UP, 1980.

———. *Powers of Horror: An Essay in Abjection*. Trans. Leon Roudiez. New York: Columbia UP, 1982.

———. *Revolution in Poetic Language*. 1974. Trans. Margaret Waller. New York: Columbia UP, 1984.

———. "Women's Time." Translated by Alice Jardine and Harry Blake. *Signs* 7 (1981): 13–35.

Kuhn, Thomas. *The Structure of Scientific Revolutions*. 2d ed. Chicago: U of Chicago P, 1970.

Kureshi, Hanif. *The Buddha of Suburbia*. London: Penguin, 1990.

Lacan, Jacques. "Seminar on 'The Purloined Letter.'" Muller and Richardson 28–54.

Lach, David. *Asia in the Making of Europe*. Vol 1. Chicago: U of Chicago P, 1965.

LaCapra, Dominick. *History and Criticism*. Ithaca: Cornell UP, 1985.

———. "Intellectual History and Its Ways." *American History Review* 97 (April 1992): 425–39.

———. *Soundings in Critical Theory*. Ithaca: Cornell UP, 1989.

———, ed. *The Bounds of Race: Perspectives on Hegemony and Resistance*. Ithaca: Cornell UP, 1991.

Lambert, Andrew, and Stephen Badsey. *The War Correspondents: The Crimean War*. Dover, NH: Alan Sutton, 1994.

Lanser, Susan Sniader. "Compared to What? Global Feminism, Comparativism, and the Master's Tools." Higonnet 280–300.

Larsen, Nella. *Quicksand*. 1928. New Brunswick: Rutgers UP, 1986.

Laslett, Barbara. "Gender Analysis and Social Theory: Building on Ruth Bloch's Proposals." *Contention* 2 (Spring 1993): 107–20.

Lawrence, Karen. *Penelope Voyages: Women and Travel in the British Literary Tradition*. Ithaca: Cornell UP, 1994.

Layoun, Mary. "Telling Spaces: Palestinian Women and the Engendering of National Narratives." Parker et al. 407–423.

Lefebvre, Henri. *The Production of Space*. Trans. Donald Nicholson-Smith. Oxford: Basil Blackwell, 1991.

LeGuin, Ursula K. "It Was a Dark and Stormy Night; or, Why Are We Huddling around the Campfire?" *On Narrative*. Ed. W. J. T. Mitchell. Chicago: U of Chicago P, 1981. 187–96.

Lehrman, Karen. "Off Course." *Mother Jones* (September/October 1993): 45–51, 65–68.

Lerner, Gerda. *The Majority Finds Its Past: Placing Women in History.* Oxford: Oxford UP, 1979.

Li, Victor P. H. "The Vanity of Length: The Long Poem as Problem in Pound's *Cantos* and Williams' *Paterson.*" *Genre* 14 (Spring 1986): 3–20.

Ling, Amy. *Between Worlds: Women Writers of Chinese Ancestry.* New York: Pergammon Press, 1990.

Livesay, Dorothy. *The Documentaries.* Toronto: Ryerson Press, 1968.

———. "The Documentary Poem: A Canadian Genre." *A Family Romance: Critical Essays.* Ed. Eli Mandel. Winnipeg: Turnstone Press, 1987. 267–81.

Longnecker, Marlene. "Marlene Longnecker Responds." *off our backs* 20 (October 1990): 24.

Looser, Devoney, and E. Ann Kaplan, eds. *Generations: Academic Feminists in Dialogue.* Minneapolis: U of Minnesota P, 1997.

Lorde, Audre. "Age, Race, Class, and Sex: Women Redefining Difference." Lorde, *Sister Outsider* 114–23.

———. "I Am Your Sister: Black Women Organizing across Sexualities." Anzaldúa, *Making Face* 321–25.

———. Interview with Pratibha Parmar and Jackie Kay. *Charting the Journey: Writings by Black and Third World Women.* Ed. Shabman Grewal, Jackie Kay, Liliane Landor, Gail Lewis, and Pratibha Parmar. London: Sheba Feminist Publications, 1988.

———. *Sister Outsider: Essays and Speeches.* Trumansburg, NY: Crossing Press, 1984.

———. *Zami: A New Spelling of My Name, Biomythography.* Trumansburg, NY: Crossing Press, 1982.

Lowe, Lisa. *Critical Terrains: French and British Orientalisms.* Ithaca: Cornell UP, 1991.

———. "Heterogeneity, Hybridity, Multiplicity: Marking Asian American Differences." *Diaspora* 1 (Spring 1991): 24–44.

Lowell, Robert. *History.* New York: Farrar, Straus, and Giroux, 1973.

Loy, Mina. *Anglo-Mongrel and the Rose. The Last Lunar Baedecker.* Ed. Roger L. Conover. Highlands, NC: Jargon Society, 1982. 109–76.

Luce, Morton. *A Handbook to the Works of Alfred Lord Tennyson.* New York: Burt Franklin, 1970.

Lugones, María C. "Hablando cara a cara/Speaking Face to Face: An Exploration of Ethno-

centric Racism." Anzaldúa, *Making Face* 46–54.

———. "On the Logic of Pluralist Feminism." *Feminist Ethics.* Ed. Claudia Card. Lawrence: UP of Kansas, 1991. 35–44.

———. "Playfulness, 'World'-Travelling, and Loving Perception." Anzaldúa, *Making Face* 390–402.

———. "Purity, Impurity, and Separation." *Signs* 19.2 (Winter 1994): 458–78.

Lugones, María C., and Elizabeth V. Spelman. "Have We Got a Theory for You! Feminist Theory, Cultural Imperialism and the Demand for 'The Woman's Voice.'" *Women's Studies International Forum* 6.6 (1983): 573–81.

Lyotard, Jean-François. 1979. *The Postmodern Condition: A Report on Knowledge.* Trans. Geoff Bennington and Brian Massumi. Minneapolis: U of Minnesota P, 1984.

Manganaro, Marc, ed. *Modernist Anthropology: From Fieldwork to Text.* Princeton: Princeton UP, 1990.

Mani, Lata. "Multiple Mediations: Feminist Scholarship in the Age of Multinational Reception." Clifford and Dhareshwar 1–24.

Marcus, Jane. "Britannia Rules *The Waves.*" *Decolonizing Tradition: New Views of Twentieth-Century "British" Literary Canons.* Ed. Karen R. Lawrence. Urbana: U of Illinois P, 1992. 136–64.

———. *Virginia Woolf and the Languages of Patriarchy.* Bloomington: Indiana UP, 1987.

Marks, Elaine, and Isabel de Courtivron, eds. *New French Feminisms: An Anthology.* Amherst: U of Massachusetts P, 1979.

Marshall, George O., Jr. *A Tennyson Handbook.* New York: Twayne, 1963.

Marshall, Paule. *Daughters.* New York: Penguin, 1992.

Martin, Biddy. "Extraordinary Homosexuals and the Fear of Being Ordinary." *Differences* 6.2/3 (1994): 100–126.

Martin, Biddy, and Chandra Talpade Mohanty. "Feminist Politics: What's Home Got to Do with It?" de Lauretis, *Feminist Studies* 191–212.

Martin, Douglas. "Korean Store Owners Join Forces, Seeking Ties, Opportunity and Clout." *New York Times* (22 March 1993).

Martin, Wallace. *Recent Theories of Narrative.* Ithaca: Cornell UP, 1986.

McDowell, Deborah. "Reading Family Matters." Wall 75–97.

Medina, Rubén. "Gloria Anzaldúa: The Politics and Poetics of *Mestizaje*." *Critica: A Journal of Critical Essays*, forthcoming.

Mehta, Gita. *A River Sutra*. New York: Vintage, 1993.

Mernissi, Fatima. *Dreams of Trespass: Tales of a Harem Girlhood*. London: Addison-Wesley, 1994.

Michaels, Walter Benn. "Race into Culture: A Critical Genealogy of Cultural Identity." *Critical Inquiry* 18 (Summer 1992): 655–85.

Michie, Elsie. "Race, Empire, and the Brontës." *Novel* 25 (Winter 1992): 125–40.

Michie, Helena. "Mother, Sister, Other: The 'Other' Woman in Feminist Theory." *Literature and Psychology* 32 (1986): 1–10.

Millay, Edna St. Vincent. *Fatal Interview*. 1931. *Collected Sonnets of Edna St. Vincent Millay*. Rev. ed. New York: Harper and Row, 1988.

Miller, D. A. *Narrative and Its Discontents: Problems of Closure in the Traditional Novel*. Princeton: Princeton UP, 1981.

———. *The Novel and the Police*. Berkeley: U of California P, 1988.

Miller, James E. *The American Quest for a Supreme Fiction: Whitman's Legacy in the Personal Epic*. Chicago: U of Chicago P, 1979.

Miller, Nancy K. *Subject to Change: Reading Feminist Writing*. New York: Columbia UP, 1988.

Miner, Valerie, and Helen E. Longino, eds. *Competition: A Feminist Taboo?* New York: Feminist Press, 1987.

Miyoshi, Masao. "A Borderless World? From Colonialism to Transnationalism and the Decline of the Nation-State." *Critical Inquiry* 19 (Summer 1993): 726–51.

Modleski, Tania. "Doing Justice to the Subjects: Mimetic Art in a Multicultural Society: The Work of Anna Deavere Smith." Abel et al. 57–76.

Modood, Tariq. " 'Difference,' Cultural Racism, and Anti-Racism." Werbner and Modood 154–72.

Mohanty, Chandra Talpade. "Cartographies of Struggle: Third World Women and the Politics of Feminism." Mohanty, Russo, and Torres, *Third World Women* 1–49.

———. "Feminist Encounters: Locating the Politics of Experience." *copyright* 1 (Fall 1987): 30–44.

———. "On Race and Voice: Challenges for Liberal Education for the 1990s." *Cultural Critique* 14 (Winter 1989–90): 170–208.

———. "Under Western Eyes: Feminist Scholarship and Colonial Discourses." Mohanty, Russo, and Torres, *Third World Women* 51–80.

Mohanty, Chandra Talpade, Ann Russo, Lourdes Torres, eds. *Third World Women and the Politics of Feminism*. Bloomington: Indiana UP, 1991.

Mohanty, S. P. " 'Us' and 'Them': On the Philosophical Bases of Political Criticism." *Yale Journal of Criticism* 2.2 (1989): 1–31.

Moi, Toril. *Sexual/Textual Politics: Feminist Literary Theory*. London: Methuen, 1985.

Molina, Papusa. "Fragmentations: Meditations on Separatism." *Signs* 19.2 (Winter 1994): 449–57.

———. "Recognizing, Accepting and Celebrating Our Differences." Anzaldúa, *Making Face* 326–35.

Montefiore, Jan. *Feminism and Poetry: Language, Experience, Identity in Women's Writing*. London: Pandora, 1987.

Moore, Henrietta L. *A Passion for Difference: Essays in Anthropology and Gender*. Bloomington: Indiana UP, 1994.

Moraga, Cherríe, and Gloria Anzaldúa, eds. *This Bridge Called My Back: Writings by Radical Women of Color*. Watertown, MA: Persephone Press, 1981.

Morgan, Robin, ed. *Sisterhood Is Global: The International Women's Movement Anthology*. New York: Anchor, 1984.

———. *Sisterhood Is Powerful: An Anthology of Writings from the Women's Liberation Movement*. New York: Vintage, 1970.

Morrison, Toni. *Beloved*. New York: Knopf, 1987.

———. "Memory, Creation, and Writing." *Thought* 59 (December 1984): 385–90.

———. *Playing in the Dark: Whiteness and the Literary Imagination*. Cambridge: Harvard UP, 1992.

———. "Unspeakable Things Unspoken: The Afro-American Presence in American Literature." *Michigan Quarterly Review* 28 (Winter 1989): 1–34.

Morson, Gary Saul. *Narrative and Freedom: The Shadow of Time*. New Haven: Yale UP, 1994.

Mukherjee, Bharati. *Jasmine*. New York: Fawcett, 1989.

Mukherjee, Bharati. *The Tiger's Daughter*. New York: Fawcett, 1971.

Muller, John P., and William J. Richardson, eds. *The Purloined Poe: Lacan, Derrida, and Psychoanalytic Reading*. Baltimore: Johns Hopkins UP, 1988.

Mulvey, Laura. "Visual Pleasure and Narrative Cinema." *Screen* 16 (Autumn 1975): 8–18.

Musil, Caryn McTighe. " 'Rivers, Swamps, and Vanishing Ponds.' " *NWSAction* 3 (Winter 1990): 2–4, 22.

Nair, Mira. *Mississippi Masala*, film written by Sooni Taraporevala and directed by Mira Nair. Mirabai Films, 1991.

Nair, Mira, and Sooni Taraporevala. *Salaam Bombay!* New York: Penguin Books, 1989.

Nandy, Ashis. *The Intimate Enemy: Loss and Recovery of Self under Colonialism*. Oxford: Oxford UP, 1983.

Narayan, Kirin. "How Native Is a 'Native' Anthropologist?" *American Anthropologist* 95.3 (September 1993): 671–86.

Nicholson, Linda J., ed. *Feminism/Postmodernism*. London: Routledge, 1990.

Nielsen, Aldon Lynn. *Reading Race: White American Poets and the Racial Discourse in the Twentieth Century*. Athens: U of Georgia P, 1988.

Nelson, Cary, and Lawrence Grossberg, eds. *Marxism and the Interpretation of Culture*. Urbana: U of Illinois P, 1988.

NWSA Women of Color Caucus. "Institutionalized Racism and the National Women's Studies Association." *Sojourner: The Women's Forum* (August 1990): 8–9.

Oliver, Melvin L., James H. Johnson, Jr., and Walter C. Farrell, Jr. "Anatomy of a Rebellion: A Political-Economic Analysis." Gooding-Williams 117–41.

Olson, Charles. *The Maximus Poems*. Ed. George F. Butterick. Berkeley: U of California P, 1983.

Omi, Michael, and Howard Winant. "The Los Angeles 'Race Riot' and Contemporary U.S. Politics." Gooding-Williams 97–116.

———. *Racial Formation in the United States: From the 1960s to the 1980s*. London: Routledge, 1986.

Orr, Linda. "The Revenge of Literature: A History of History." *New Literary History* 18 (Autumn 1986): 1–22.

Ortner, Sherry. "Is Female to Male as Nature Is to Culture?" *Woman, Culture and Society*. Ed. Michelle Rosaldo and Louise Lamphere. Stanford, CA: Stanford UP, 1974. 67–87.

Osborne, Nancy Seale. "Caryn McTighe Musil Resigns after Six Years as Director." NWSAction 3 (Winter 1990): 1–2.

Ostriker, Alicia Suskin. *Stealing the Language: The Emergence of Women's Poetry in America*. Boston: Beacon Press, 1986.

Ozanne, Julian. "Old Clan Rivalries Fuel Bloodshed in Somalia." *Financial Times of London* (8–9 August 1992).

Paget, General Lord George. *The Light Cavalry Brigade of the Crimea: Extracts from Letters and Journal*. 1881. London: EP Publishing, 1975.

Papastergiadis, Nikos. "Restless Hybrids." *Third Text* 32 (Autumn 1995): 9–18.

Parker, Andrew, Mary Russo, Doris Sommer, and Patricia Yaeger, eds. *Nationalisms and Sexualities*. London: Routledge, 1992.

Parkerson, Michelle. "Did You Say the Mirror Talks?" Albrecht and Brewer 108–17.

Parry, Benita. "Passage to More Than India." *Perspectives on E. M. Forster's "A Passage to India."* Ed. V. A. Shahane. New York: Barnes and Noble, 1968. 151–66.

Patai, Daphne. "Is Ethical Research Possible?" Gluck and Patai 137–53.

Peréz-Torres, Rafael. "Nomads and Migrants: Negotiating a Multicultural Modernism." *Cultural Critique* 26 (Winter 1993–94): 161–89.

Perloff, Marjorie. "From Image to Action: The Return of Story in Postmodern Poetry." *The Dance of Intellect: Studies in the Poetry of the Pound Tradition*. Cambridge: Cambridge UP, 1985. 155–71.

———. "Modernist Studies." *Redrawing the Boundaries: The Transformation of English and American Literary Studies*. Ed. Stephen Greenblatt and Giles Gunn. New York: Modern Language Association Publications, 1992. 154–78.

Personal Narratives Group. *Interpreting Women's Lives: Feminist Theory and Personal Narratives*. Bloomington: Indiana UP, 1989.

Peterson, William, Michael Novak, and Philip Gleason. *Concepts of Ethnicity*. Cambridge: Harvard UP, 1980.

Phelan, James. *Reading People, Reading Plots: Character, Progression, and the Interpretation of Narrative*. Chicago: U of Chicago P, 1989.

Phelan, Shane. "(Be)Coming Out: Lesbian Identity and Politics." *Signs* 18.4 (Summer 1993): 765–90.

Pheterson, Gail. "Alliances between Women: Overcoming Internalized Oppression and Internalized Domination." Albrecht and Brewer 34–48.

Phillips, Kathy. J. *Virginia Woolf against Empire*. Knoxville: U of Tennessee P, 1994.

Pieterse, Jan Nederveen. "Globalization as Hybridization." Featherstone, Lash, and Robertson 45–68.

Piggford, George. "'The Queer, Cautious Girl': Adela Quested and Gender Performance in Forster's *A Passage to India*." Paper delivered at Conference on Gender Politics and Twentieth-Century Multicultural Texts. Duquesne University, Pittsburgh, PA, November 1993.

Pintchman, Tracy. "Snakes in the Cave: Religion and the Echo in E. M. Forster's *A Passage to India*." *Soundings* 75.1 (Spring 1992): 61–78.

Poliakov, Leon. *The Ayran Myth: A History of Racist and Nationalist Ideas in Europe*. Trans. Edmund Howard. New York: Basic Books, 1971.

Polumbo-Liu, David. "Los Angeles, Asians, and Perverse Ventriloquisms: On the Functions of Asian America in the Recent American Imaginary." *Public Culture* 6.2 (1994): 365–81.

Pomata, Gianna. "History, Particular and Universal: On Reading Some Recent Women's History Textbooks." *Feminist Studies* 19.1 (Spring 1993): 7–50.

Pratt, Geraldine. "Traveling Metaphors in Feminist Theory." Manuscript, 1993.

Pratt, Mary Louise. "Arts of the Contact Zone." *Profession 91*. New York: Modern Language Association, 1991. 33–40.

———. "Fieldwork in Common Places." Clifford and Marcus 27–50.

———. *Imperial Eyes: Travel Writing and Transculturation*. London: Routledge, 1992.

Pratt, Minnie Bruce. "Identity: Skin Blood Heart." Bulkin, Pratt, and Smith 9–64.

Probyn, Elspeth. "Travels in the Postmodern: Making Sense of the Local." Nicholson 176–89.

Propp, Vladimir. *The Morphology of the Folk-Tale*. 1928. Trans. Laurence Scott. 2d ed. Austin: U of Texas P, 1969.

Pryse, Marjorie, and Hortense J. Spillers, eds. *Conjuring: Black Women, Fiction, and Literary Tradition*. Bloomington: Indiana UP, 1985.

Purdom, Judy. "Mapping Difference." *Third Text* 32 (Autumn 1995): 19–32.

Quintana, Alvina E. *Home Girls: Chicana Literary Voices*. Philadelphia, PA: Temple UP, 1996.

Radhakrishnan, R. *Diasporic Mediations: Between Home and Location*. Minneapolis: U of Minnesota P, 1996.

———. "Ethnicity in an Age of Diaspora." *Transition* 54 (November 1991): 104–15.

———. "Feminist Historiography and Post-structuralist Thought." *The Difference Within: Feminism and Critical Theory*. Ed. Elizabeth Meese and Alice Parker. Philadelphia: John Benjamins, 1989. 189–205.

———. "Post-Structuralist Politics: Toward a Theory of Coalition." *Jameson/Postmodernism/Critique/*. Ed. Douglas Kellner. Washington, DC: Maisonneuve Press, 1989. 276–90.

Radical Lesbians. "Woman-Identified Woman." 1970. *The American Sisterhood: Writings of the Feminist Movement from Colonial Times to the Present*. Ed. Wendy Martin. New York: Harper and Row, 1972. 333–38.

Ray, Sangeeta. "Gender and the Discourse of Nationalism in Anita Desai's *Clear Light of Day*." *Genders* 20 (1994): 96–119.

———. "Rethinking Migrancy: Nationalism, Ethnicity, and Identity in *Jasmine* and *The Buddha of Suburbia*." Paper delivered at the Modern Language Association Conference, 1992.

Raymond, Janice. "The Illusion of Androgyny." *Quest* 1.4 (Spring 1975): 20-40.

Rebolledo, Tey Diana. *Woman Singing in the Snow: A Cultural Analysis of Chicana Literature*. Tuscon: Arizona UP, 1995.

Reeves, Jimmie L., and Richard Campbell. *Cracked Coverage: Television News, the Anti-Cocaine Crusade, and the Reagan Legacy*. Durham: Duke UP, 1994.

Rensberger, Boyce. "The Melting Pot under a Microscope." *Washington Post National Weekly Edition* (15–21 March 1993): 38.

Rhys, Jean. *Smile Please: An Unfinished Autobiography*. Berkeley, CA: Creative Arts Books, 1979.

———. *Wide Sargasso Sea*. 1966. New York: Norton, 1982.

Rich, Adrienne. *An Atlas of the Difficult World, Poems 1988–1991*. New York: Norton, 1991. 3–28.

Rich, Adrienne. *Blood, Bread and Poetry: Selected Prose, 1979–1985*. New York: Norton, 1986.

———. "Cartographies of Silence." *Dream* 16–20.

———. "Disloyal to Civilization: Feminism, Racism, Gynophobia." 1978. *On Lies* 275–310.

———. *The Dream of a Common Language, Poems, 1974–1977*. New York: Norton, 1978.

———. "Notes toward a Politics of Location." 1984. *Blood* 210–32.

———. *Of Woman Born: Motherhood as Experience and Institution*. New York: Norton, 1976.

———. *On Lies, Secrets, and Silence: Selected Prose, 1966–1978*. New York: Norton, 1979.

———. *Sources*. 1982. *Your Native Land, Your Life*. New York: Norton, 1986. 3–17.

———. *Twenty-One Love Poems*. 1976. *Dream* 25–38.

———. "When We Dead Awaken: Writing as Re-Vision." 1971. *On Lies* 35–50.

Ricoeur, Paul. "Narrative Time." *On Narrative*. Ed. W. J. T. Mitchell. Chicago: U of Chicago P, 1981. 165–86.

———. *Time and Narrative*. 2 vols. Chicago: U of Chicago Press, 1983–85.

Riddel, Joseph N., ed. Special Issue on the Long Poem in the Twentieth Century. *Genre* 11 (Winter 1978).

Robb, Peter, ed. *The Concept of Race in South Asia*. Delhi: Oxford UP, 1995.

Robertson, George, Melinda Mas, Lisa Tickner, Jon Bird, Barry Curtis and Tom Putnam, eds. *Travellers' Tales: Narratives of Home and Displacement*. London: Routledge, 1994.

Robertson, Roland. "Glocalization: Time-Space and Homogeneity-Heterogeneity." Featherstone, Lash, and Robertson 25–44.

———. "Social Theory, Cultural Relativity and the Problem of Globality." Anthony King 69–90.

Rodriguez, Richard. "Changing Faces." Transcript of MacNeil/Lehrer Newshour. Show no. 4756, 13–14. 16 September 1993.

Romero, Gloria J. " 'Nose raje, chicanita': Some Thoughts on Race, Class, and Gender in the Classroom." *Aztlan* 20 (Spring/Fall 1991): 203–18.

Romero, Gloria J., and Lourdes Arguelles, eds. Special Issue on Culture and Conflict in the Academy: Testimonies from a War Zone. *California Sociologist* (Winter/Summer 1991).

Ronen, Ruth. "Description, Narrative and Representation." *Narrative* 5.3 (October 1997): 274–86.

Rosaldo, Renato. *Culture and Truth: The Remaking of Social Analysis*. Boston: Beacon Press, 1993.

———. Foreword. *Hybrid Cultures*. Canclini xi–xvii.

Rose, Gillian. *Feminism and Geography: The Limits of Geographical Knowledge*. Minneapolis: U of Minnesota P, 1993.

Rosenthal, M. L., and Sally M. Gall. *The Modern Poetic Sequence: The Genuis of Modern Poetry*. New York: Oxford UP, 1983.

Rowbotham, Sheila. *Women's Consciousness, Man's World*. Baltimore: Penguin, 1973.

Rubin, Gayle. "The Traffic in Women: Notes on the 'Political Economy' of Sex." *Toward an Anthropology of Women*. Ed. Rayna R. Reiter. New York: Monthly Review Press, 1975. 157–210.

Ruby, Jennie, and Carol Anne Douglas. "NWSA: Troubles Surface at Conference." *off our backs* 20 (August/September 1990): 1, 10–16.

Rushdie, Salman. "In Good Faith." *Imaginary Homelands: Essays and Criticism, 1981–1991*. London: Granta, 1991. 393–414.

———. *Midnight's Children: A Novel*. New York: Knopf, 1981.

———. *The Satanic Verses*. London: Viking, 1988.

Russo, Ann. " 'We Cannot Live without Our Lives': White Women, Antiracism, and Feminism." Mohanty, Russo, and Torres, *Third World Women* 288–96.

Sahni, Chaman L. *Forster's "A Passage to India": The Religious Dimension*. New Delhi: Arnold-Heinemann, 1981.

Said, Edward W. *Culture and Imperialism*. New York: Viking, 1993.

———. *Orientalism*. New York: Vintage, 1978.

———. "The Politics of Knowledge." *Raritan* 11.1 (Summer 1991): 17–31.

———. "Representing the Colonized: Anthropology's Interlocutors." *Critical Inquiry* 15.2 (1989): 205–25.

———. "Traveling Theory." *The World, the Text, and the Critic*. Cambridge: Harvard UP, 1983. 226–48.

Saldívar, José David. *The Dialectics of Our America: Genealogy, Cultural Critique, and*

Writing History. Durham, NC: Duke UP, 1991.

Saldívar-Hull, Sonia. "Feminism in the Border: From Gender Politics to Geopolitics." *Criticism in the Borderlands: Studies in Chicano Literature, Culture, and Ideology*. Ed. Héctor Calderón and José David Saldívar. Durham, NC: Duke UP, 1991. 203–20.

Sales, Ruby. "Letter from Ruby Sales." *off our backs* 20 (August/September 1990): 25.

Sánchez, Marta Ester. *Contemporary Chicana Poetry: A Critical Approach to an Emerging Literature*. Berkeley: U of California P, 1985.

Sandoval, Chela. "Feminism and Racism: A Report on the 1981 National Women's Studies Association Conference." Anzaldúa, *Making Face* 55–74.

———. "U.S. Third World Feminism: The Theory and Method of Oppositional Consciousness in the Postmodern World." *Genders* no. 10 (Spring 1991): 1–24.

Sarup, Madan. "Home and Identity." George Robertson et al. 93–105.

Schechner, Richard. *Performance Theory*. Rev. ed. London: Routledge, 1997.

Scholes, Robert. *Fabulation and Metafiction*. Urbana: U of Illinois P, 1979.

Schumacher, Michael. "A Marriage of Minds: Louise Erdrich and Michael Dorris." *Writer's Digest* (June 1991): 28–59.

Schweikart, Patsy. "Reflections on NWSA 190." *NWSAction* 3 (Fall 1990): 3–4, 9–10.

Scott, James C. *Domination and the Arts of Resistance: Hidden Transcripts*. New Haven: Yale UP, 1990.

———. "History According to Winners and Losers." *History and Peasant Consciousness in Southeast Asia*. Ed. Andrew Tarton and Shigenharu Tanabe. Osaka: National Museum of Ethnology, 1984. 161–210.

Scott, Joan Wallach. *Gender and the Politics of History*. New York: Columbia UP, 1988.

———. "Response to Gordon." *Signs* 15 (Summer 1990): 859–60.

———. Review of *Heroes of Their Own Lives*, by Linda Gordon. *Signs* 15 (Summer 1990): 848–51.

Sedgwick, Eve Kosofsky. *Between Men: English Literature and Male Homosocial Desire*. New York: Columbia UP, 1985.

———. *Epistemology of the Closet*. Berkeley: U of California P, 1990.

———. "Queer Performativity: Henry James's *The Art of the Novel*." *GLQ* 1 (1993): 1–16.

Sennett, Richard. "The Rhetoric of Ethnic Identity." *The Ends of Rhetoric: History, Theory, Practice*. Ed. John Bender and David E. Wellberg. Stanford, CA: Stanford UP, 1990. 191–231.

Sharpe, Jenny. *Allegories of Empire: The Figure of Woman in the Colonial Text*. Minneapolis: U of Minnesota P, 1993.

Shohat, Ella. "Notes on the 'Post-Colonial.'" *Social Text* 31/32 (1992): 99–113.

Shostak, Marjorie. *Nisa: The Life and Words of a !Kung Woman*. 1981. New York: Vintage, 1983.

———. "'What the Wind Won't Take Away': The Genesis of *Nisa: The Life and Words of a !Kung Woman*." Personal Narratives Group 228–40.

Showalter, Elaine. *A Literature of Their Own: British Women Novelists from Brontë to Lessing*. Princeton: Princeton UP, 1977.

———. "Feminist Criticism in the Wilderness." 1981. Showalter, *New Feminist Criticism* 243–70.

———. "Toward a Feminist Poetics." 1979. *New Feminist Criticism* 25–43.

———. "Women's Time, Women's Space: Writing the History of Feminist Criticism." 1984. Benstock 30–44.

———, ed. *The New Feminist Criticism: Essays on Women, Literature, and Theory*. New York: Pantheon, 1985.

Siegel, Deborah L. "The Legacy of the Personal: Generating Theory in Feminism's Third Wave." *Hypatia* 12.3 (Summer 1997): 46–75.

Silko, Leslie Marmon. *Ceremony*. New York: Viking, 1977.

———. "A Conversation with Leslie Marmon Silko." *Sun Tracks: An American Indian Literary Magazine* 3 (1976): 26–32.

———. *Storyteller*. New York: Little, Brown, 1981.

Smiley, Marion. "Feminist Theory and the Question of Identity." *Women and Politics* 13.2 (1993): 91–122.

Smith, Anna Deavere. *Fires in the Mirror: Crown Heights, Brooklyn and Other Identities*. New York: Doubleday, 1994.

———. *Twilight: Los Angeles, 1992*. New York: Doubleday, 1994.

Smith, Barbara. "Toward a Black Feminist Criticism." 1977. Showalter, *New Feminist Criticism* 168–85.

Smith, Neil, and Cindi Katz. "Grounding Metaphor: Towards a Spatialized Politics." Keith and Pile 67–83.

Smith, Paul. *Discerning the Subject*. Minneapolis: U of Minnesota P, 1988.

———. "H.D.'s Flaws." *Iowa Review* 16 (Fall 1986): 77–86.

———. "H.D.'s Identity." *Women's Studies* 10 (1984): 321–38.

———. *Pound Revised*. London: Croom Helm, 1983.

Smith, Valerie. "Black Feminist Theory and the Representation of the 'Other.'" Wall 38–57.

Soja, Edward. "History: geography: modernity." *The Cultural Studies Reader*. Ed. Simon During. London: Routledge, 1993. 135–50.

———. *Postmodern Geographies: The Reassertion of Space in Critical Social Theory*. London: Verso, 1989.

Sollors, Werner. *Beyond Ethnicity: Consent and Descent in American Culture*. New York: Oxford UP, 1986.

———, ed. *The Invention of Ethnicity*. Oxford: Oxford UP, 1989.

Sommers, Christina Hoff. "Sister Soldiers." *New Republic* (5 October 1992): 29–33.

———. *Who Stole Feminism? How Women Have Betrayed Women*. New York: Simon and Schuster, 1994.

Spillers, Hortense. "Notes on an Alternative Model—Neither/Nor." *The Difference Within: Feminism and Critical Theory*. Ed. Elizabeth Meese and Alice Parker. Philadelphia: John Benjamins, 1989. 165–87.

———. "'The Permanent Obliquity of an In(ph)allibly Straight': In the Time of the Daughters and the Fathers." Wall 127–49.

Spivak, Gayatri Chakravorty. "Can the Subaltern Speak?" Nelson and Grossberg 271–313.

———. "French Feminism in an International Frame." *In Other Worlds* 134–53.

———. *In Other Worlds: Essays in Cultural Politics*. New York: Methuen, 1987.

———. "A Literary Representation of the Subaltern: A Woman's Text from the Third World." *In Other Worlds* 241–68.

———. *Outside in the Teaching Machine*. London: Routledge, 1993.

———. *The Post-Colonial Critic: Interviews, Strategies, Dialogue*. Ed. Sarah Harasym. London: Routledge, 1990.

———. "Scattered Speculations on the Question of Culture Studies." Spivak, *Outside* 255–84.

———. "Three Women's Texts and a Critique of Imperialism." *Feminisms: An Anthology of Literary Theory and Criticism*. Warhol and Herndl 798–814.

Sprengnether, Madelon. *The Spectral Mother: Freud, Feminism, and Psychoanalysis*. Ithaca: Cornell UP, 1990.

Springfield, Consuelo Lopez. *Daughters of Caliban: Caribbean Women in the Twentieth Century*. Bloomington: Indiana UP, 1997.

Spurr, David. *The Rhetoric of Empire: Colonial Discourse in Journalism, Travel Writing, and Imperial Administration*. Durham, NC: Duke UP, 1993.

Stacey, Judith. "Can There Be a Feminist Ethnography?" Gluck and Patai 111–20.

Steel, Melissa. "New Colors: Mixed Race Families Still Find a Mixed Reception." *Tolerance* 4 (Spring 1995): 44–49.

Stein, Gertrude. "Lifting Belly." *Yale Gertrude Stein* 4–54.

———. *Patriarchal Poetry*. *Yale Gertrude Stein* 106–46.

———. *Stanzas in Meditation*. *Yale Gertrude Stein* 316–464.

———. *Tender Buttons*. *The Selected Writings of Gertrude Stein*. Ed. Carl Van Vetchen. New York: Vintage, 1962. 459–510.

———. *The Yale Gertrude Stein*. Ed. Richard Kostelanetz. New Haven, CT: Yale UP, 1980.

Stepan, Nancy. *The Idea of Race in Science: Great Britain, 1800–1960*. New York: Archon Books, 1982.

Stocking, George W., Jr. "On the Limits of 'Presentism' and 'Historicism' in the Historiography of the Behavioral Sciences." *Race, Culture, and Evolution: Essays in the History of Anthropology*. 1968. Rev. ed. Chicago: U of Chicago P, 1982. 1–12.

Strathern, Marilyn. "An Awkward Relationship: The Case of Feminism and Anthropology." *Signs* 12 (1987): 276–92.

———. "Cutting the Network." *Journal of the Royal Anthropological Institute* 2.3 (1996): 517–35.

Suleri, Sara. "Woman Skin Deep: Feminism and the Postcolonial Condition." *Critical Inquiry* 18 (Summer 1992): 756–69.

———. *The Rhetoric of British India*. Chicago: U of Chicago P, 1992.

Swindells, Julia. "Liberating the Subject? Autobiography and 'Women's History': A Reading of *The Diaries of Hannah Cullwick*." Personnel Narratives Group 228–40.

Sykes, Charles J. *The Hollow Men: Politics and Corruption in Higher Education*. Washinton, DC: Regnery Gateway, 1990.

Tan, Amy. *The Joy Luck Club*. New York: Ivy Books, 1989.

Taussig, Michael. *Mimesis and Alterity: A Particular History of the Senses*. London: Routledge, 1993.

Tennyson, Alfred Lord. "The Charge of the Light Brigade." 1854. *Selected Poems*. Ed. Aidan Day. London: Penguin, 1991. 289–90.

Thompson, Becky, and Estelle Disch. "Feminist, Anti-Racist, Anti-Oppression Teaching: Two White Women's Experience." *Radical Teacher* no. 41 (Spring 1992): 4–10.

Thompson, Richard H. *Theories of Ethnicity: A Critical Appraisal*. Westport, CT: Greenwood Press, 1989.

Thongchai Winichakul. *Siam Mapped*. Honnolulu: U of Hawaii P, 1994.

Todorov, Tzvetan. *The Poetics of Prose*. Trans. Richard Howard. Ithaca: Cornell UP, 1977.

Torgovnik, Maria. *Gone Primitive: Savage Intellects, Modern Lives*. Chicago: U of Chicago P, 1990.

Torres, Lourdes. "The Construction of Self in U.S. Latina Autobiographies." Mohanty, Russo, and Torres 271–87.

Tratner, Michael. *Modernism and Mass Politics: Joyce, Woolf, Eliot, Yeats*. Stanford, CA: Stanford UP, 1995.

Trevor-Roper, Hugh. "The Highland Tradition of Scotland." *The Invention of Tradition*. Ed. Eric Hobsbawm and Terence Ranger. Cambridge: Cambridge UP, 1983. 15–42.

Trinh, Minh-ha T. "Other than myself/my other self." George Robertson et al. 9–28.

———. *Woman—Native—Other: Writing Postcoloniality and Feminism*. Bloomington: Indiana UP, 1989.

Trouillot, Michel-Rolph. "Anthropology and the Savage Slot: The Poetics and Politics of Otherness." Fox 17–44.

Tucker, Herbert F. *Tennyson and the Doom of Romanticism*. Cambridge: Harvard UP, 1988.

Twain, Mark. *The Adventures of Huckleberry Finn*. New York: Signet, 1983.

Uttal, Lynet. 1990. "Nods That Silence." Anzaldúa, *Making Face* 317–20.

van der Veer, Peter. "'The Enigma of Arrival': Hybridity and Authenticity in the Global Space." Werbner and Modood 90–105.

Visweswaran, Kamala. *Fictions of Feminist Ethnography*. Minneapolis: U of Minnesota, 1994.

Wagstyl, Stefan. "Inter-religious Forgiveness Is Just Not Cricket." *Financial Times of London* (22 February 1993).

Wald, Alan. "Theorizing Cultural Difference: A Critique of the Ethnicity School.'" *Melus* 14 (Summer 1987): 21–33.

Walker, Alice. "Everyday Use." 1973. *"Everyday Use."* Ed. Barbara T. Christian. New Brunswick, NJ: Rutgers UP, 1994. 23–38.

———. "In Seach of Our Mothers' Gardens." 1974. *In Search* 231–43.

———. *In Search of Our Mothers' Gardens: Womanist Prose*. New York: Harcourt Brace Jovanovich, 1983.

———. "One Child of One's Own." 1979. *In Search* 361–83.

Walker, Cheryl. "Feminist Literary Criticism and the Author." *Critical Inquiry* 16 (Spring 1990): 551–71.

Walker, Rebecca, ed. *To Be Real: Telling the Truth and Changing the Face of Feminism*. New York: Anchor Books, 1995.

Wall, Cheryl A., ed. *Changing Our Own Words: Essays on Criticism, Theory, and Writing by Black Women*. New Brunswick, NJ: Rutgers UP, 1989.

Warhol, Robyn, and Diane Price Herndl, eds. *Feminisms: An Anthology of Literary Theory and Criticism*. New Brunswick, NJ: Rutgers UP, 1991.

Weed, Elizabeth, ed., *Coming to Terms: Feminism, Theory, Politics*. New York: Routledge, 1989.

Weedon, Chris. *Feminist Practice and Poststructuralist Theory*. Oxford: Basil Blackwell, 1987.

Werbner, Pnina. "Introduction: The Dialectics of Cultural Hybridity." Werbner and Modood 1–28.

Werbner, Pnina, and Tariq Modood, eds. *Debating Cultural Hybridity: Multi-Cultural Identities and the Politics of Anti-Racism*. London: ZED Books, 1997.

West, Cornel. "A Genealogy of Modern Racism." *Prophesy Deliverance! An Afro-American Revolutionary Christianity*. Philadelphia: Westminster Press, 1982. 47–68.

———. "Marxist Theory and the Specificity of Afro-American Oppression." Nelson and Grossberg 17–34.

White, Hayden. *The Content of the Form: Nar-*

rative Discourse and Historical Representa-tion. Baltimore: Johns Hopkins UP, 1990.

————. *Metahistory: The Historical Imagination of Nineteenth-Century Europe.* Baltimore: Johns Hopkins UP, 1974.

————. "The Question of Narrative in Contemporary Historical Theory." *History and Theory* 23 (1984): 1–33.

White, Richard. *The Middle Ground: Indians, Empires, and Republics in the Great Lakes Region.* Cambridge: Cambridge UP, 1991.

Whitehead, Neil L. "Monstrosity and Marvel: Symbolic Convergences and Mimetic Elaboration in Trans-Cultural Representation: An Anthropological Reading of Ralegh's *Discoveries.*" *Studies in Travel Writing* 1 (Spring 1997): 72–95.

Williams, Lisa. *"Playing in the Dark* and *The Voyage Out*: Reading Woolf with Morrison's Criticism." Paper delivered at the Sixth Annual Virginia Woolf Conference. Clemson, SC, June 1996.

Williams, Patricia J. "The Obliging Shell." *The Alchemy of Race and Rights: Diary of a Law Professor.* Cambridge: Harvard UP, 1989. 98–132.

Wilson, John, ed. Special Issue on *Who Stole Feminism? Democratic Culture* 3.2 (Fall 1994).

Winnett, Susan. "Coming Unstrung: Women, Men, Narrative, and Principles of Pleasure." *PMLA* 105 (1990): 505–18.

Wolfe, Susan J., and Julia Penelope, eds. *Sexual Practice/Textual Theory: Lesbian Cultural Criticism.* Oxford: Basil Blackwell, 1993.

Women's Studies. Special Issue on Androgyny. 2.2 (Fall 1974).

Woolf, Virginia. *Between the Acts.* New York: Harcourt, Brace, 1941.

————. *The Common Reader.* 1925. New York: Harcourt Brace Jovanovich, 1953.

————. *Flush.* 1933. New York: Harcourt Brace and Co., 1961.

————. *Freshwater: A Comedy.* Ed. Lucio P. Ruotolo. New York: Harcourt Brace Jovanovich, 1976.

————. "Modern Fiction." 1919. *The Common Reader* 150–58.

————. "Mr. Bennett and Mrs. Brown." 1924. *The Captain's Death Bed and Other Essays.* New York: Harcourt Brace Jovanovich, 1950. 94–119.

————. "The Narrow Bridge of Art." *Granite and Rainbow: Essays.* New York: Harcourt Brace Jovanovich, 1958. 11–23.

————. *A Room of One's Own.* 1929. New York: Harcourt Brace Jovanovich, 1957.

————. "A Sketch of the Past." *Moments of Being.* Ed. Jeanne Schulkind. 2d ed. New York: Harcourt Brace Jovanovich, 1985. 61–160.

————. *To the Lighthouse.* 1927. New York: Harcourt Brace Jovanovich, 1981.

————. *Three Guineas.* 1938. New York: Harcourt, Brace, and World, 1963.

————. *The Voyage Out.* 1915. New York: Harcourt Brace Jovanovich, 1948.

Wright, Lawrence. "One Drop of Blood." *New Yorker* (25 July 1994): 46–55.

Wyatt, Jean. "Hazards of Idealization in Cross-Cultural Feminist Dialogues: Abel, Cisneros, Gallop, McDowell, and Moraga." *Journal for the Psychoanalysis of Culture and Society* 1.2 (Fall 1996): 95–111.

Yaeger, Patricia. *Honey-Mad Women: Emancipatory Strategies in Women's Writing.* New York: Columbia UP, 1988.

————, ed. *The Geography of Identity.* Ann Arbor: U of Michigan P, 1996.

Young, Robert J. C. *Colonial Desire: Hybridity in Theory, Culture and Race.* London: Routledge, 1995.

Zimmerman, Bonnie. *The Safe Sea of Women: Lesbian Fiction, 1969–1989.* Boston: Beacon Press, 1990.

————. "What Has Never Been: An Overview of Lesbian Feminist Criticism." Showalter, *New Feminist Criticism* 200–224.

Zinn, Maxine Baca, and Bonnie Thornton Dill. "Theorizing Difference from Multiracial Feminism." *Feminist Studies* 22.2 (Summer 1996): 321–31.

About the Author

SUSAN STANFORD FRIEDMAN is Virginia Woolf Professor of English and
Women's Studies and Senior Fellow at the Institute for Research in the
Humanities at the University of Wisconsin, Madison.